Catch That Rockabilly Fever

Catch That Rockabilly Fever

Personal Stories of Life on the Road and in the Studio

SHEREE HOMER
Foreword by Ken Burke

McFarland & Company, Inc., Publishers
Jefferson, North Carolina, and London

LIBRARY OF CONGRESS CATALOGUING-IN-PUBLICATION DATA

Homer, Sheree, 1978–
  Catch that rockabilly fever : personal stories of life on the road and in the studio / Sheree Homer ; foreword by Ken Burke.
    p.   cm.
  Includes bibliographical references and index.

  ISBN 978-0-7864-3841-9
  softcover : 50# alkaline paper ∞

  1. Rockabilly musicians—United States—Biography.
  I. Title.
  ML394.H66   2010
  781.66092'2—dc22   2009037615
  [B]

British Library cataloguing data are available

©2010 Sheree Homer. All rights reserved

No part of this book may be reproduced or transmitted in any form or by any means, electronic or mechanical, including photocopying or recording, or by any information storage and retrieval system, without permission in writing from the publisher.

On the cover: Elvis Presley, 1950s, with guitar player Scotty Moore and bass player Bill Black (Photofest); record ©2010 Shutterstock

Manufactured in the United States of America

McFarland & Company, Inc., Publishers
  Box 611, Jefferson, North Carolina 28640
  www.mcfarlandpub.com

For my mom, Carole,
the original rockin' mama

Acknowledgments

Without God, this project would not have been possible. It's all thanks to him for introducing me to the wonderfully talented, generous, and kind folks that I have met in the short time I have embraced the rockabilly community and for giving me the opportunity to tell their stories. I battled breast cancer in 2004 and due to the numerous prayers I received, I am healthy today. My hope in writing this book is for rockabilly and its unsung heroes to finally receive the respect and recognition that has been deserved for over fifty years.

Thanks to my mom who introduced me to rock and roll and for being the best mom anyone could ever hope for. Your love and support has meant everything to me. I will always remember and cherish the times we spent together attending rockabilly festivals and shows.

Thanks, too, to my brother Gary who helped my mom and me through several rough patches. We wouldn't have survived without you. You came to our rescue when we needed you the most.

Phil Doran, Marc Mencher, and the Oneida Casino staff in Green Bay, Wisconsin — you assembled the greatest gathering of rockabilly and rock and roll artists in the history of music. Those festivals were the highlight of our lives. We will never forget the wonderful times we had and the kind people we met.

Ken Burke, author of *Country Music Changed My Life* and *The Blue Moon Boys*— you encouraged me to write this book. Even though you were busy with your own writings, you always found time to share ideas and edit my profiles. Words cannot express how thankful I am for that. I respect you as a fellow writer, rockabilly fan, and most of all as a friend. I wish you all the luck and success that a person could ever achieve.

Steve Bonner — you certainly saved the day by providing me with rare and otherwise difficult to obtain photos of many of the singers included in my book. Without you, this book would never have seen the light of day. I appreciate your willingness to help me in my time of need.

Many thanks to all the singers, musicians, and notables for providing my book with rare photos and invaluable insight into your lives and careers. Your music has meant so much to me. It changed my life. I am honored to know all of you and to be able to call many of you my friends. Extra special thanks to Art Adams, Bo Berglind and *American Music Magazine*, Sonny Burgess, Larry Donn, Narvel Felts, Glen Glenn, James Kirkland, Laura Lee Perkins, Ronnie Smith, Hayden Thompson, and Stanley Walker.

I owe my gratitude to those individuals who helped me with contact information and resources or supported my magazine, *Rockabilly Revue*: Bruce Berenson and XM Radio, Michael Bloom Media Relations, Bob Bowen, Marc Bristol and *Blue Suede News*, Bobby Brom, Ruth Canard, Ed Carroll, Alan Clark, J.D. Cooper, Jr., Bobby Crafford, Kim Curtis, John DeBord, Bennie Dingo and Rock-It-Radio, Imperial Anglares Dominique, Dianne Duran, Steve Ford, Dave Gilbaugh, Ronnie Haig, Ken Haskins, Roland Janes, Howard Kasten, Ken King, James Kitts, Cathie Knoploch, Steve Lester, Bobby Lollar, Lisa Lucka, Ken Lyons, Glenn Lee Martin, Tony Mattiaccio, Mark Mattos Photography, Marc Mencher, Lacy Mitchell, Dave Moore, Craig Morrison, Roger Moser, Jr., Rita Posselt, Don Rieck, Mel Spinella, Adriaan Sturm, Bennie Sturman, Bob Timmers and the Rockabilly Hall of Fame, Johnny Vallis, J.M. Van Eaton, Wanda VanZant, David Vienna, Del Villarreal, Nol Voorst, Maggie Warwick, Mark Weber, Ronnie Weiser, Richard Weize and Bear Family Records, Martin Willis, and Dennis Winton.

I wanted to give special thanks to my favorite English teachers: Walter Graffin, Don Kummings, Patrick Mcguire, Lynn Schmidt, and Geraldine Stallman. Without their inspiration and guidance, I would not be a writer today.

Last but certainly not least, thanks to all the rockabilly singers and musicians who are still rockin' today, both contemporary and legendary, the fans, the festival and club promoters, the disk jockeys, the writers, and anyone else who helps keep the rockabilly flame alive.

Contents

Acknowledgments vii
Foreword by Ken Burke 1
Introduction 5

ONE • SUN LEGENDS

Sonny Burgess	11
Ray Smith	18
Hayden Thompson	22
Dickey Lee	27
Ed Bruce	31
Carl Mann	36
Johnny Powers	42
Jack Earls	47

TWO • LOUISIANA HAYRIDE STARS

Wanda Jackson	52
Bob Luman	57
Maddox Brothers and Rose	64
Elvis Presley	70

THREE • ARKANSAS ROCKABILLIES

Larry Donn	78
Pat Cupp	82
Bobby Lee Trammell	86
Ronnie Hawkins	91

FOUR • TEXAS ROCKABILLIES

Buddy Holly and the Crickets	95
Sonny West	102

Gene Summers	107
Lew Williams	109
Huelyn Duvall	115

Five • California Rockabillies

Ricky Nelson	120
The Collins Kids	129
Glen Glenn	134

Six • Rockabilly Pioneers

The Rock and Roll Trio	142
Narvel Felts	148
Art Adams	153
Laura Lee Perkins	157
Big Al Downing	162
Charlie Gracie	168

Seven • Rockabilly Revivalists

Martí Brom	174
Go Cat Go	178
Josie Kreuzer	182
The Dave and Deke Combo	187
High Noon	193
Tex Rubinowitz	199

Eight • Today's Sensations

Kim Lenz	205
The Casey Sisters	209
Carl Sonny Leyland	213
Eddie Clendening	215
Ruby Ann	220
Sue Moreno	222
Dawn Shipley	224
Buddy and Suzy Dughi	227
Cari Lee Merritt	230
Cole	235

Chapter Notes 239
Bibliography 247
Index 251

Foreword
by Ken Burke

With the title of her first book, my friend and colleague Sheree Homer has asked that you readers "Catch That Rockabilly Fever." She didn't have to ask me. I've been joyously afflicted with this rambunctious rhythm since I was six years old. My older sister's collection of 45 rpm singles turned me onto Elvis Presley, the Everly Brothers, Wanda Jackson, Brenda Lee, Johnny Horton, and Ricky Nelson.

As a teenager, I became completely obsessed with the greatest piano pumper of them all, Jerry Lee Lewis. From that point on, I dug deep into any record store bin I came across, purchasing every Sun International cut-out and Charly Records' import I could find, hoping to find more of that ever seductive sound from Sun Records in Memphis, Tennessee.

In the years before the internet, I thought some crazed English audiophiles and I were the only ones who knew about this wild, liberating music. I was wrong, of course. Rockabilly music was slowly clawing its way back to prominence, despite surprising apathy on behalf of the music business. At its best, the raw musical form known as rockabilly music is rebellious, quirky, sex-crazed, moody, and intensely cathartic. Yet this effervescent hybrid of high-throttle hillbilly and hip-grinding R&B is America's most misunderstood and least appreciated commercial genre.

Mention it to a major label exec or mainstream radio programmer, and they will run from the room screaming in terror. Classic rock fans from the equally stylized '70s and '80s confuse rockabillies with the often sad oldies acts that play Native American casinos and custom car shows. Country music lovers, who should have a natural affinity for the rebel yell persona of the genre, are completely embarrassed by the greasy-haired aggression and implied back seat sexuality. Further, big name critics and respected historians alike downplay its role, preferring to bestow their eloquence on trends and performers not possible without rockabilly's emergence.

On the latter point, I ask that you consider the following:

Without Link Wray's fuzz-tone electric guitar riffs on the bolero tempo instrumental "Rumble" (a recording so rife with greasy, switchblade wielding attitude that—fearing rock-inspired juvenile delinquency—it was banned in some Eastern cities), the whole genre of heavy metal might not exist.

If Buddy Holly hadn't melded pop music with his Tex-Mex sounds, or if Gene Vincent hadn't added his erotic R&B tinged vocals to the Blue Caps' crazed bop, or if Carl Perkins hadn't combined John Lee Hooker licks with bluegrass tempos, a whole fleet of mid-'60s British Invasion acts might never have formed. Moreover, none of the above would even be remotely imaginable without the efforts of Elvis Presley, who inspired them all to make music that provoked chills and screams from the teenaged populace. In the process he created, some say stumbled upon, a musical form that provided the basic musical vocabulary for garage rock, punk, hard rock, folk rock, surf, and many other sub-genres.

Many historians make bold attempts to trace the roots of rockabilly to the days of Bob Wills and his Texas Playboys. No less an authority than Carl Perkins, whose work at Sun Records defines rockabilly as completely as Elvis Presley's did, proclaimed that country singer Hank Williams started it all for him. Yet, despite the efforts of European reissue labels hoping to make it so, rockabilly is not country boogie, western swing, or honky-tonk music.

Old-line country performers a la Faron Young and Little Jimmy Dickens have cut some convincing rockabilly numbers as have such R&B cats as Chuck Berry and Big Al Downing. And, in the pre-rock era, Arthur "Hardrock" Gunter, piano-pounding Moon Mullican, and Johnnie and Jack all retrofitted blues or R&B for their country releases. However, it wasn't until mid–1954 that Elvis Presley, Scotty Moore, and Bill Black captured lightning in a bottle as they clowned their way into creating rockabilly with incendiary renditions of "That's All Right" and "Blue Moon of Kentucky."

Presley, Moore, and Black opened the floodgates for a plethora of young acts hoping to stir the pot with even more vigor. One of the reasons rockabilly sounds so good today is that the original artists weren't merely coping Elvis Presley in an attempt to get girls—although clearly that happened too—they were all taking a palpable societal risk. By mixing black and white music they deliberately provoked the wrath of stuffed-shirt authority figures every time they opened their mouths to sing. Lyrically, the works may seem tame today, but the dangerous intentions in the style and passion of the music are unmistakable.

Strictly speaking, any combo that features more than two guitars and a standup bass isn't traditional rockabilly. However, Presley was not a purist. The music he created grew by adding instruments, voices, and approaches during his RCA years. Subsequently, his followers, hoping to emulate his success, did likewise. As the newly crowned King of Rock 'n' Roll's astounding commercial success reached epic proportions—he is still the best selling single artist of all-time—the Mississippi-born icon no longer felt compelled to rely on stripped down, three-chord rockabilly and the genre began to disappear from mainstream radio playlists by the time he entered the Army in 1958. Subsequently, the form became laughable in the eyes of some. In one scene at the beginning of the 1961 film *Don't Knock the Twist*, a sideburn-wearing rockabilly is told that he is no longer hip enough to sell to bookers and that the kids were looking for something new, specifically the Twist. From that point on, with some notable exceptions, rockabilly went underground.

The term rockabilly, invented by one of the glib reviewers at *Billboard*, was seldom used during the music's heyday. Indeed, many of the genre's pioneers never even heard the word and felt that they were playing rock and roll, cat music, or western bop. Some performers even felt that writers were smugly trying to brand them as hillbillies, which infuriated them. "Rockabilly" as a descriptive phrase grew in England and Europe during the 1960s. Britain's working class Teddy Boys, or greasers, the unsung heroes of American music, kept the phrase alive as a spirited act of rhythmic rebellion, as in "Rockabilly rules, OK mate?"

During the early 1970s, the ever pedantic European transplant Ronny Weiser created a new American label based on the developing style and spread the word through Greg Shaw at *Bomp Magazine*. Suddenly, the phrase rockabilly became a brand name that fans of the original big beat could rally round. True, this stripped-down, hot pants rhythm seldom reared its greasy head in the musical mainstream, but year by year it has become more popular the world over.

Modern rockabilly fans are completely different from any other music lovers. Knowledgeable and discerning, they often regard a previously unreleased demo from a regional rockabilly star with the same reverence that a folkie would a bootleg from Bob Dylan. Further, rediscovered regional performers, who never enjoyed anything resembling a hit record during the hallowed 1950s, are often revered with the same intensity usually reserved for bop cats who once topped charts.

Rockabilly is now something of a cult industry. Men and women who cut solid rockin' records during the 1950s are rediscovered and adored by select fans all over the world because they once had the youthful nerve to defy authority and rock it out. Backing them are younger acts that are just as courageous and rebellious as rockabilly's original pioneers. Giving their respective hearts to a financially limiting genre, these determined hot-blooded newcomers continually set the stage for future rockabilly uprisings that I am expecting to occur hourly.

After writing two books, contributing to two dozen others, and penning hundreds of reviews and articles, I'm proud to say that the rockabilly fever I caught way back when still burns fiercely within me. As a collector and fan, I'm also pleased to note that during her immersion into this remarkable subculture, Sheree Homer has done her best to document the life and times of this pulsating swivel-hipped music by interviewing its big stars, regional favorites, survivors, and revivalists. In the process, she hopes to spread the only virus guaranteed to make you shake your blues away, the rockabilly fever. To which I must add if this is a sickness, I don't ever want to get well.

    Keep rockin'.

Ken Burke is a contributing editor of Blue Suede News.

Introduction

Rockabilly music is a precursor to rock and roll and the grandfather of punk. It has influenced countless acts since its creation in the 1950s. The Beatles, Tom Petty, Bob Dylan, John Fogerty, the Rolling Stones, Bruce Springsteen, Aerosmith, and Robert Plant and Jimmy Page formerly of Led Zeppelin are all fans and have recorded their own versions of rockabilly anthems.

What is rockabilly? Everyone has his own definition, but my definition of it is a hybrid of rhythm and blues with its twelve-bar blues progression, traditional country with its simplistic lyrics and chord changes, and gospel with its intensity and raw emotion. Traditional rockabilly is sung in a rebellious manner with a standup bass and two guitars, acoustic and electric. However, instrumentation may vary since I consider Sonny Burgess and Jerry Lee Lewis to be rockabilly musicians. Sonny has a trumpet and a piano in his band, and Jerry Lee has a piano beyond the standard rockabilly instrumentation. The vocals are usually characterized by hiccups. To explain rockabilly, look no further than Elvis Presley's "Baby, Let's Play House," which was recorded in 1955 for the Sun record' label in Memphis, Tennessee. Elvis and his band the Blue Moon Boys are in their element. Their self-esteem shines through, and gone are the nerves and the anxiety over what to play and how to play it. They know they are achieving the sound they were desperately searching for.

Elvis had it all: talent, good looks, and the ability to cause a sensation. He came on the scene at the right time. The teenagers were ready for someone new and exciting and someone who would be different from what their parents were listening to. His impact left a mark on the world that will never be replicated. He was very important to rockabilly. Without him, I am not sure if there would have been a surge of artists doing that same sort of music. I know that several stopped singing country music once Elvis made an appearance, including Eddie Cochran, Buddy Holly, and Glen Glenn.

Rockabilly music was short lived. It didn't appear on the charts for very long, only from 1954 to 1958. Many of the artists who are highly revered today didn't have a charted song back in its heyday. Rockabilly faded out in America after 1958. The music scene had changed with the formation of teen idols such as Fabian, Frankie Avalon, Bobby Rydell, and Paul Anka. Rockabilly was brought back to the forefront by British fans who rediscovered the acts. Through his *Rollin' Rock* magazine and record label releases, Ronnie Weiser introduced a new generation of rockabilly rebels to the music of Gene Vincent, Charlie Feathers, Bob Luman, Pat Cupp, Johnny Carroll, and Ray Campi. In the early 1980s, rockabilly singers began playing festivals overseas to fervent audiences. The rockabilly revival hit stateside in 1982 when the Stray Cats scored a top ten single with "Rock This Town." Within ten to fifteen years, new bands emerged and festivals, such as Viva Las Vegas and the Rockabilly Rebel Weekend in Indianapolis, Indiana, sprang to life. Today, the Rockin' '50s fests in Green Bay, Wisconsin, bring in legions of fans representing twenty-six countries.

It's important to discover artists like Elvis Presley, Carl Perkins, Ricky Nelson, Eddie Cochran, Gene Vincent, and Buddy Holly since they are the backbone of rockabilly. However, it's also crucial that people don't forget about the lesser-known acts who should have been superstars but weren't for one reason or another. People like Sonny Burgess, Glen Glenn, Gene Summers, Larry Donn, the Collins Kids, Bob Luman, Lew Williams, and all the rest.

Rockabilly music is my passion. It fuels my soul. I don't know how I existed before embracing it. I cannot imagine life without listening to the music and attending shows. Unfortunately, it took me awhile to get to that stage because I wasn't fully aware of rockabilly until 2001. Rockabilly music is fairly new to me, but rock and roll is not. My mom, who was lucky enough to be a teenager in the 1950s, introduced me to many of the artists I love today through her impressive 45 rpm record collection. Elvis Presley was the love of her life, so she joined his fan club. There she bought her first mementos, two tubes of Elvis Presley lipstick. She had scrapbooks with his photos and articles about him. By the time I was born in 1978 she had seen him four times in concert and had amassed a vast collection of memorabilia.

Even before I was born, she was turning the hi-fi up loud and clear, so I could hear her singles by Elvis Presley, Jerry Lee Lewis, Fats Domino, Chuck Berry, and Little Richard. My mom was always playing Elvis' music. In fact, she was going to name me Elvis if I had been a boy. Instead, I was named after Marilyn Monroe's character in the movie *Bus Stop*. When I was three years old, I wore Elvis T-shirts and butterfly cowboy boots while dancing to my favorite song at the time, "Shake, Rattle, and Roll/Flip, Flop, and Fly" from the *This Is Elvis* soundtrack. He is my favorite singer. Elvis epitomized cool and inspired legions of fans through his music, fashion sense, and humanitarianism. In 2003, my mom and I traveled to Memphis and were treated to an Elvis tour by our good friend Wanda VanZant, Charlie Feathers' daughter. Any site that was Elvis-related we sought out. I recorded at Sun Studio at that same time with Carl Perkins' son Stan, Carl's original drummer, W.S. Holland, Sun pianist Jerry Lee "Smoochy" Smith, and Joe Fick of the Dempseys. One of the songs I recorded was one Elvis made famous, "Mystery Train." I also performed at the Overton Park Shell, the same venue in which Elvis gave one of his first performances. Even though I have met many wonderful musicians in the short time I have loved rockabilly, I'll always regret that I wasn't born sooner to have known Elvis personally.

As I got a little older, I remember with fondness my first cousin Jennifer coming to visit. I always looked forward to these occasions since I knew she liked vintage items, and she would play my mom's records. A few of her favorites included Wanda Jackson, Brenda Lee, and Buddy Holly, so I quickly became acquainted with their music, thanks to her visits.

When I attended school, I was ashamed to admit that I liked Elvis Presley's music. I was already overlooked by my peers, and I felt I would further insolate myself. I didn't follow my mom's advice when she suggested that I showcase my talent during show and tell by dancing to the tunes of Elvis Presley's "Shake, Rattle, and Roll/Flip, Flop, and Fly" or Jerry Lee Lewis' "Whole Lotta Shakin' Goin' On." In the process, I discovered that it didn't matter if I liked Elvis since no one would care. Liking Elvis was part of who I am, and if they didn't like it then they wouldn't like me. After all, it's more important to be happy with yourself since you can't please everyone anyway. After that realization, I showcased my love for Elvis. I think by that time I was a senior in high school.

In 1996, after an ill-fated move to Michigan and upon our return to Kenosha, Wisconsin, I helped my mom reorganize her 45 rpm records. I was seventeen at the time and the reorganization guided me in discovering rockabilly. It took us several days to renumber and rewrite all the names and titles. Throughout the process, my mom suggested I listen to different artists since she figured if I liked Elvis I may like them too. One of those artists was Ricky Nelson. She handed me "Believe What You Say" backed with "My Bucket's Got a Hole in It." Once I set the needle on the vinyl and heard the two sides, I was hooked. Today, Ricky Nelson remains my second favorite singer. Ricky's shy and quiet persona appealed to me as soon as I watched my very first episode of the *Adventures of Ozzie and Harriet*. In October 2007, I had the privilege of singing "Just a Little Too Much" and "Believe What You Say" on stage with Ricky's original bassist James Kirkland. A lot of people have said that Ricky wasn't rockabilly, but "Believe What You Say," "Waitin' in School," "My Babe," and many of his other late '50s recordings are as rockin' as rockabilly can get. He was underrated and underappreciated. Thanks to his music I discovered Johnny and Dorsey Burnette, Carl Perkins, Eddie Cochran, and Gene Vincent.

Rockabilly music became a mainstay after I purchased a three-CD box set of Sun recording artists entitled *The Sun Records Collection*. I bought it mostly because I recognized the songs by Elvis Presley, Carl Perkins, and Jerry Lee Lewis. As I was tuning into each individual track, I stumbled upon "Red Headed Woman" by Sonny Burgess and the Pacers. I couldn't believe what I was hearing. I had never heard a song so wild and rockin' in my life. It blew me away with its raw intensity and wild abandon. I wondered if these guys could play any faster. I played it over and over.

A few weeks later, my mom and I were in the car listening to disk jockey Dick Biondi's program on Chicago's 104.3 FM when he played one of his rare 45s. The song that piqued our curiosity was "See You Soon Baboon" by Dale Hawkins. It was different from anything we had ever heard before. The Tarzan yell that he inserted into the beginning and ending of the song really stood out. It was a catchy tune, similar lyrically to Bill Haley's "See You Later Alligator." My mom immediately fell in love with it and requested that I find out where to buy that song. I found a copy of the CD *Oh! Suzy Q: The Best of Dale Hawkins* on eBay, and my mom snatched it up. Within a few months, we were on our way to New Orleans to attend the Ponderosa Stomp. The two-day musical spectacular featured rockabilly acts Dale Hawkins (our main reason for attending), Joe Clay, Rocky Burnette with the Rock and Roll Trio's guitarist Paul Burlison, Elvis Presley's original guitarist Scotty Moore and original drummer D.J. Fontana, and Ricky Nelson's original guitarist James Burton.

That was 2002, and I was set to graduate from the University of Wisconsin–Parkside with no clue about my career path. However, my eyes were open to my destiny when I watched those legendary performers onstage. After the concert was over, I returned with new insight and hope for the future as I knew what I would do with my writing degree. I would start my own rockabilly magazine and give recognition to the talented artists I had just witnessed firsthand. Dale Hawkins was the first person I interviewed, and *Rockabilly Revue's* premier issue hit the streets in September 2002.

That was a banner year because we attended our first rockabilly festival, the Ponderosa Stomp, I started my own rockabilly magazine, and we attended the best festival in the world, the Green Bay (Wisconsin) Rockin' '50s Fest. There my mom and I saw Sonny Burgess, Billy Lee Riley, the Collins Kids, Dale Hawkins, Jack Scott, the Crickets, the Comets, Big Al Downing, etc. Several gave me interviews at the time, which was prior to the magazine's launching, and I will always be grateful that they were so nice to me, a newcomer. It was such a treat to be able to sit and talk freely with the Crickets because I grew up listening to their records with Buddy Holly. My mom couldn't believe her luck. She never thought she would get the opportunity to meet the singers or bands that appeared on the records she owned in her collection.

Unfortunately, only eight issues of *Rockabilly Revue* were produced when I had to go on hiatus because I was stricken with breast cancer. The doctors caught it early enough, and I have been cancer free since I was diagnosed in 2004.

A few years later, my good friend Ken Burke planted the idea in my head that perhaps I should write a rockabilly book. I had accumulated several dozen interviews with various rockabilly musicians in the hopes they would be featured in an upcoming issue of my magazine. A book would give me the perfect opportunity to use those interviews and give credit to the forgotten foot soldiers of rock and roll. I felt it was important to showcase these artists and tell their histories before it was too late. Once they pass on, their stories will be lost forever. A book preserves their histories for generations to come.

I didn't want any tabloid fodder or swearing in my book as it needed to be appropriate for all ages. Concentration on the music was key, not their personal lives. It was not necessary to talk about their vices but instead how the music was created and its influence. It is vital to keep this music alive for generations to come. The profiles are not merely biographies but first-hand personal accounts by the musicians. I conducted numerous interviews, read various magazine articles and books, and researched websites. The Rockabilly Hall of Fame and the Rockin' Country Style online discography were especially helpful.

For further reading, other rockabilly books include *Go Cat Go! Rockabilly Music and Its Makers* by Craig Morrison, *We Wanna Boogie: An Illustrated History of the American Rockabilly Movement* by Randy McNutt, *Good Rockin' Tonight: Sun Records and the Birth of Rock 'n' Roll* by Colin Escott and Martin Hawkins, and *Rockabilly Legends: They Called It Rockabilly Long Before It Was Called Rock 'n' Roll* by Jerry Naylor and Steve Halliday. They are the most popular publications on the subject. Of course, there are autobiographies and biographies available on some of the artists as well, including Buddy Holly, Elvis Presley, Ricky Nelson, Carl Perkins, Jerry Lee Lewis, and Eddie Cochran.

Thanks to rockabilly music, I get an idea of how times were in the 1950s. Hearing stories from the musicians gives me a key to the past. If I could time-travel, I would want to go back to Sun Studio in Memphis and spend time watching the musicians record. They didn't know it at the time, but they were making history, and their music continues to stand the test of time. Rockabilly music and its artists have been a major influence. Elvis Presley jumpstarted the rockabilly revolution and several artists credit him with their career.

I want everyone to get a chance to experience rockabilly firsthand. Buy the music, read about the artists, and most importantly, go to the shows. Without their fans, the musicians can't continue. They need your support. Here's hoping that everyone catches that rockabilly fever!

ONE

Sun Legends

Sonny Burgess

Sonny Burgess claimed, "Everybody in the world wanted to record for that little old label. It didn't last but ten years, but it was magic."[1] From 1954 to 1959, every singer within a few hundred miles made the trek to audition at Sun with a hopeful heart that they would get signed. Sonny Burgess and his band The Pacers were one of those acts who made the trip to Memphis. On July 5, 1954, Elvis Presley walked into Sun Studio in Memphis, Tennessee, and made history. His recording of "That's All Right" b/w "Blue Moon of Kentucky" inspired legions of musicians to either step in front of a microphone or pick up a musical instrument. Sun was a rockabilly breeding ground for hot new artists. In 1956, Burgess and the Pacers recorded "We Wanna Boogie" b/w "Red Headed Woman."

Albert Burgess was born on May 28, 1929, in Anderson, Arkansas. At an early age, Burgess received his nickname Sonny from his family. His family were farmers who raised a little of everything, including peanuts, watermelon, and cotton. Burgess hated picking cotton because his back would hurt, and his fingers would bleed: "Anything's better than picking cotton." There were two other boys and three girls in the family. Burgess would be the only one to choose a musical career, but his parents didn't mind. He tuned into WDIA, a rhythm and blues station, out of Memphis and the *Grand Ole Opry*.

When Burgess was fourteen years old, he began playing the guitar. He had two uncles who played fiddle and harmonica, and Burgess would play guitar with them at country dances. The trio would play square dances and whatever country songs were popular at the time. One of Burgess' early performances was on a Hedacol Medicine Show in Arkansas. In 1949, Burgess' first band The Drifting Cowboys backed future country superstar, Freddie Hart, then known as Freddie Seagrest. As a guitarist, Burgess was naturally influenced by guitarists of the day, including Elvis Presley's guitarist Scotty Moore, Les Paul, Chet Atkins, and Merle Travis. In regard to singers, Presley was his main influence. He was also inspired by Big Joe Turner, Jimmy Reed, Ernest Tubb, Bob Wills and His Texas Playboys, and Dean Martin.

Drafted into the United States Army in 1951, Burgess was sent to Fort Chaffee in Fort Smith, Arkansas, to take aptitude tests, which led to training at the Counter Intelligence School in Baltimore, Maryland. As it turned out, Burgess' IQ was 186. The rest of his unit was deployed to Korea, and eighty percent lost their lives. Burgess was neither interested in world affairs nor being a counter intelligence agent, so the Army made him an MP and sent him to Germany. While stationed in Germany, he had a band, which was comprised of cooks from Texas. They were one of only eight bands from Europe who appeared on the Frankfort edition of the *Grand Ole Opry*. One of the songs that was a mainstay in their act was "Little Red Wagon."

Burgess recollected, "[During my enlistment] I got to play music and baseball. It was great, but I didn't like it well enough to stay." After his tour of duty was completed in 1953, Burgess played guitar behind Paul Whaley, a Hank Thompson sound alike. The band known then as the Rocky Road Ramblers had a regular job at Bob King's, a honky tonk in Swifton, Arkansas. However, when Whaley moved back to California, someone had to take over as lead singer. Since no one else wanted to sing, Burgess filled in. However, for the first hour, he sang with his back to the crowd because he was too nervous and scared to face them. The first song he ever sang was "Little Red Wagon," but he also sang a lot of Hank Williams' tunes. Burgess deeply admired the legendary singer songwriter, proclaiming "he was just ahead of his time."

Burgess had first seen Elvis Presley at Porky's, the subject of two teen exploitation comedy films, in Newport, Arkansas. In 1955, Burgess and his band the Moonlighters opened two different shows for Presley and his band the Blue Moon Boys. The next time Presley came to town, he and his band played the Silver Moon, a high class gambling joint that imported some of the top touring names in show business, with Bud Deckelman and Wanda Jackson. Burgess conveyed, "We booked him into the Moon and did well."

The other show in which they opened for Presley occurred at Bob King's, taking place just two weeks prior to Presley signing with RCA Victor. Johnny Cash was also on the bill that night. Presley watched Burgess' portion of the show, and he was so impressed that he offered two members of the band a job with him. Burgess remembered, "I had Punky Caldwell, who weighed four hundred pounds, but played saxophone and clarinet, Kern [Kennedy], Johnny Ray [Hubbard], and Russ [Smith] on those shows. We had an excellent band back then. Elvis offered [Punky and Kern both] a job that night. That would have made his band. He wanted a bigger band." Neither Caldwell nor Kennedy accepted his offer because they didn't want to travel. As the Moonlighters were closing the show, Presley came back onstage, started out singing, and the next thing you know both bands are onstage for an hour long jam session. Burgess added, "Elvis was the best there ever was. No one could electrify the crowd like he could."

Inspired by Presley and the Blue Moon Boys, Burgess and his friend Joe

With his first band, the Rocky Road Ramblers, Sonny Burgess was originally the lead guitarist and not the singer (courtesy Sonny Burgess).

Lewis renamed their band The Pacers after the Pacer airplane in late 1955. The group then consisted of Burgess on lead guitar and vocals, Hubbard on bass, Smith on drums, and Kennedy on piano. Sun owner, Sam Phillips, suggested a couple of members be added to fill out the lineup after their first audition. Rounding out the band were Joe Lewis, who was still in high school, playing rhythm guitar and high school music teacher Jack Nance, who switched from playing drums to playing trumpet.

According to Burgess, "the group's live act was incomparable. The Pacers were better than anybody, even with Elvis" in regard to live performances. They could play for four hours and never play the same song twice unless it was requested. At the time, they were playing four to five nights a week. Bob Neal booked shows for them, and they worked on all of the Sun package shows. Roy Orbison's The Teen Kings played the Silver Moon, and the bug dance was introduced to Burgess. The bug dance was where one band member picked an imaginary bug off the floor and threw it on one of the other guys. That guy would then jump around trying to catch the bug. When he finally did, he'd throw it onto another member of the band. Smith and Kennedy kept the beat going while Burgess, Hubbard, Nance, and Lewis participated in the dance.

Their antics would get pretty wild and sometimes an injury would incur. Once at a show in Michigan, Burgess pulled a leg muscle: "I had these white bucks [with] rubber soles on them. I was onstage there, and man I was going to do the splits. I pulled a leg muscle and thought I wasn't going to be able to finish the show." They used to jump off the stage: "At the end of our show, we'd do 'Goin' Home' [otherwise known as 'Ain't Gonna Do It'] and a bunch of different songs and jump off the stage out into the audience." The shows that were held at auditoriums, they would jump off at least three foot stages: "We had fifty foot guitar cords made."

Burgess recollected, "We were in excellent shape back then. We didn't think we'd get hurt. One time, we did a show in Little Rock, Arkansas, with Maddox Brothers and Rose, Ray Price, and Marty Robbins. We opened the show for them, but we never thought about checking things out. We jumped off that stage at the Robinson Auditorium and jumped into the orchestra pit. We fell about four more feet [so seven feet total]. Aww, man I thought we never were going to hit the bottom." Johnny Ray Hubbard hit the bottom, and the tailpiece and bridge on his bass broke. They had to take the stairs to get back onstage. The following night when they played the Ellis Auditorium in Memphis, they closed the show instead of opening it.

On May 2, 1956, Burgess and his six piece band headed back to Sun. Sam Phillips did the engineering, and they cut the 45 rpm single "We Wanna Boogie" b/w "Red Headed Woman." Burgess revealed, "Red Headed Woman" was written about his wife. A Flivver, which is mentioned in "We Wanna Boogie," was a Model T Ford, and the pounding lyric referred to pounding on tables at the clubs in time with the music. "We Wanna Boogie" and "Red Headed

Woman" stand among the rawest recordings released during the first flowering of rock and roll. The lyrics were almost unintelligible, and the accompaniment teetered on the edge of atonality, giving the record an atmosphere of total abandon.[2]

As it turned out, "Red Headed Woman" was a big hit in the Boston area. Burgess found out forty years later through Jack Nance. To this day, Burgess doesn't have a clue why the song hit in that particular area and not nationwide: "I don't have the least idea why." The single reportedly sold over ninety thousand copies.[3]

In 1957, Sun released "Ain't Got a Thing" b/w "Restless" and "My Bucket's Got a Hole in It" b/w "Sweet Misery." Jack Clement engineered these sessions and all those that followed for Burgess. Clement wrote the lyrics to "Ain't Got a Thing" while Burgess composed the music. "My Bucket's Got a Hole in It" was promoted by Dewey Phillips on his radio program *Red, Hot, and Blue*, which aired on WHBQ-AM in Memphis. Burgess added, "I thought we did a pretty good job on it." As far as how Phillips reacted to the song, Burgess replied, "he got all excited about everything. He was a crazy dude." Burgess and the Pacers also appeared on Phillips' television program on Channel 13 four different times. *Wink Martindale's Dance Party* also showcased their talent a few times. Steve Stevens, who had a show similar to *American Bandstand* in Little Rock, had the Pacers as his first musical guest.

"My Bucket's Got a Hole in It" was also recorded by Ricky Nelson. In 1958, Nelson had a number twelve hit with it on the Billboard charts. Burgess never held any animosity toward Nelson for recording the song: "I like Ricky Nelson, so I like his version. He was a real good artist." Years later, Nelson commented to *Now Dig This* editor Trevor Cajiao that he modeled his version after Burgess.'

The two instrumentals "Itchy" and "Thunderbird" were written because Clement had become frustrated with the material that was recorded. They were originally composed without harmonica, but Clement thought it would be a good idea to add Billy Lee Riley to the mix. Burgess commented: "I liked it [the addition of Riley]. It turned out good." Burgess mentioned, "the best piano player that ever played at Sun, Charlie Rich" was also featured on the songs. By this time, J.C. Caughron had joined the band on guitar, and Bobby Crafford was now playing drums. The Pacers had become a four piece band since Russ Smith quit working with Jerry Lee Lewis, and Jack Nance and Joe Lewis went to work with fellow Arkansas rocker Conway Twitty.

The last single released by Sun under Phillips International was "Sadie's Back in Town" b/w "A Kiss Goodnite." Sun only released five singles. Burgess said that if Sun had released six singles then they would have had to release an album. The Pacers recorded plenty of material for an album, but an album was never discussed. Burgess figures that they cut one hundred and fifty songs at Sun, but most of them were erased and taped over to save money: "I'm surprised as much stuff got saved as it did." Burgess thought that "Goin' Home" should have been released as a single: "I thought that was really good." However, it went undiscovered until 1980.

Thanks to Charly, Bear Family, and Rounder Records, Burgess' unreleased material appeared first on compilations then on full length solo CDs. Burgess very seldom listens to his old records, but he has recently added songs to his repertoire that he hasn't sung in years such as "The Prisoner's Song" and "Find My Baby for Me." Coincidentally, Burgess' favorite that he recorded is "Restless." Unfortunately, he is no longer able to whistle, so "Restless" has been cut from his set list.

Even though, there have been accusations that Burgess drank while recording, he pointed out that "there never was a drink in the house." They came there to record and acted professionally.

Another myth that he put to rest was the one in which Billy Lee Riley destroyed equipment at Sun. Riley had overheard Sam Phillips on the phone pulling distribution on his "Red Hot" and replacing it with Jerry Lee Lewis' "Great Balls of Fire." As the story went, Riley got drunk, threatened Phillips, and poured liquor on the mixing board and master tapes. Burgess commented, "Sam wouldn't stand there and let him ruin all that equipment when Sam didn't have any money to start with. He might have kicked over a table or two or something like that [but] as far as destroying someone's recording equipment, no." He would have been arrested and thrown in jail if that had been the case.

Burgess quit the Pacers in 1960 and joined Nance and Lewis in Twitty's touring band. He first played guitar then switched to electric bass for Twitty's Twitty Birds. Incidentally, Nance co-wrote Twitty's biggest rock and roll hit "It's Only Make Believe." In 1962, Jim Aldridge joined the Pacers to play saxophone, and in 1963 Fred Douglas replaced Johnny Ray Hubbard on bass. Today, Charles Watson II plays fiddle and appears live with the band.

Burgess decided to get a full time job as a traveling salesman in 1972. He worked for St. Louis Trimming, which sold lace and trim for ladies' clothing: "When I first started, I didn't know anything about the sewing business. Talk about dumb, I'd have to show them samples and let them tell me what they wanted." After a couple of years he knew enough to suggest things that they needed. He worked with St. Louis Trimming for twenty-five years.

In the 1980s, Burgess coached baseball for the American Legion. During that time, he discovered he had diabetes. Before Burgess became a singer, he wanted to be a professional baseball player. In fact, he signed with the Orlando Senators, the farm team of the Washington Senators. He went to Orlando and stayed for a year. Starting out as a shortstop and ending up as a third baseman, he discovered he couldn't hit the curve ball, which was necessary to play third base. Disheartened, "I loved baseball," he went home and picked up music again. His two sons, Payton and John, both went to college on baseball scholarships.

In 1984, Burgess made his first trip of many to England as part of the rockabilly revival. Two years later, the Smithsonian Institute helped to coordinate the formation of the Sun Rhythm Section, which included Burgess, Marcus Van Story, J.M. Van Eaton, D.J. Fontana, Paul Burlison, Stan Kesler, and Jerry Lee "Smoochy" Smith. They recorded for the now defunct Rounder Records' subsidiary, Flying Fish. They toured the world on behalf of the State Department, bringing rockabilly music to such exotic locales as Kuwait and North Africa. They disbanded in 1998 as members started to get ill and pass away.

Hightone Records teamed The Blasters' guitarist Dave Alvin with Burgess for the critically acclaimed 1992 release, *Tennessee Border*. Burgess also worked with Bruce Springsteen and the E Street Band and recorded one of Springsteen's songs, "Tiger Rose," for his self-titled album on Rounder Records. Alvin is one of his favorite singers along with Jerry Lee Lewis, Bob Seger, Marty Robbins, Ray Price, Roy Orbison, and Elvis Presley, who is number one on his list.

Burgess performed on *Late Night with Conan O'Brien*, in 1996, with contemporary rockabilly songstress Rosie Flores. The 1998 documentary, *The Mississippi: River of Song* featured Burgess prominently. In 2001, Burgess was a part of the documentary, *Good Rockin' Tonight: the Legacy of Sun Records*. On July 5, 2004, he and the Pacers helped celebrate the fiftieth anniversary of "That's All Right" at a Sun Studio block party, which was broadcasted worldwide. Also in 2004, Burgess' "Itchy" was featured in the John Waters' movie *A Dirty Shame*, starring Chris Isaak.

KASU 91.9 FM at Arkansas State University in Jonesboro, Arkansas gave Burgess his own radio show in 2006. "We Wanna Boogie" airs every Sunday night from 5–7 P.M. CST and is available at http://www.wewannaboogie.org for those who do not live in the listening area. He plays a wide variety of music, mostly rockabilly and country and interviews guest musicians, such as Narvel Felts, Billy Lee Riley, and Larry Donn.

Inducted into the Arkansas Entertainers Hall of Fame in 2007, Burgess frequently records and does shows with the Pacers. However, since 2004, festival promoters have asked Swiss band Mars Attacks to back the singer when he tours solo. Burgess is especially thankful to the European fans for keeping rockabilly music alive: "Without them, we wouldn't still be playing. Nobody would care." In Europe, Burgess and the Pacers were voted one of the Top 50 rock and roll acts of all-time. Overseas, Burgess is expected to sing his Sun sides. Like many European rockabilly revivalists, Mars Attacks have studied the songs, so it is easier if they play them, plus they have a trumpet player just like the Pacers did in the '50s.

The five singles that Burgess released at Sun remain part of his rockabilly legacy. Even though, he never cared too much for those records, they have stood the test of time. Burgess stated, "Sometimes people don't go on record as well as they do live. To me, Elvis' live performances were better than he ever got on record. When we were live, we were like a three ring circus. You can't see that on record. All you can hear is the music."

Ray Smith

Sun Records in Memphis proved vital to the career of Rockin' Ray Smith. After signing with the label in 1958, they released five singles by Smith that are still highly regarded today. However, Smith scored his biggest commercial hit, "Rockin' Little Angel" for Sam Phillips' brother Jud on the Atlanta based Judd label. During the 1970s, Smith was rediscovered by European fanatics and enjoyed a short comeback before he abruptly ended it all. Carl Perkins commented on his friend's legacy: "Well, to say something about Ray Smith, you're talking about a man who had as much to do with the foundation of rockabilly music as anybody I knew."[4]

Born October 31, 1934, in Melber, Kentucky, Raymond Eugene Smith grew up with six brothers and one sister. Smith's father made a living as both a sharecropper and a sheet metal worker. His mother died when he was young. At age twelve, he moved in with one of his sisters after his father bought his own farm and remarried.

Smith began singing publicly in the second grade, where he sang Tex Ritter songs to his classmates. His early favorites included Eddy Arnold, Ernest Tubb, and Gene Autry. At the end of the eighth grade, he quit school, so he could work full-time to support his sister's family. In 1952, after dismissal due to goofing off on his job at a shoe factory, he enlisted in the Air Force and served as a medic. Around the same time, he married his childhood sweetheart, Lillie. He was eighteen, and she sixteen.

During basic training, a sergeant ordered him to enter a talent contest. Smith recollected, "One day while I was taking a shower, this sergeant walked into our barracks and asked if anyone was going to sing in the contest. I came out of the shower in my baggy shorts and clogs, and he asked me if I could sing. I answered no. So he ordered me to sing." Smith sang Hank Williams' "Lovesick Blues," and "the officer said 'Smith, you sing tomorrow night!'" The next night he again sang "Lovesick Blues." "The whole place went wild, and I got first prize. That's when I decided that music was my cup of tea."[5] He was officially discharged from the Air Force in 1960.

In 1956, Smith formed his first band, The Rock 'n' Roll Boys with Raymond Jones on guitar, James Webb on bass, Dean Perkins on steel guitar, and Henry Stevens on drums. Shortly after, Jones quit and was replaced by Stanley Walker.

Walker first met Smith when his uncle convinced him to grab his guitar and attend a Smith show with him at a skating rink in Metropolis, Illinois. All the teenage girls were screaming, a fact that Walker was not used to: "I listened to country and gospel music back then."[6] Prior to playing with Smith, he worked with gospel singers Bucky and Dottie Rambo. "I knew he had something different, so I told my uncle, well, that man's not going to listen to me with the band he has. When the show was over, they were packing up, and my uncle

Ray Smith, left, and original guitarist Stanley Walker rockin' onstage to "Right Behind You Baby" (courtesy Steve Lester).

told Ray Smith, 'Would you listen to this kid play the guitar?' I used one of the boy's amps, and Ray listened to me." Impressed by Walker's rendition of Chet Atkins' "Blue Echo," Smith took the guitarist home with him, where they sat up and played all night. Walker remembered, "First he took me by a club where a band was playing. He had me sit in with that band." Then he took him in, to live with him and his family: "He gave me three dollars a night. He fed me, clothed me, and gave me a place to sleep. We were as close as brothers. He got me started in this business, and he was really generous to me."

Smith and The Rock and Roll Boys played all over the country. Radio and television appearances led to their very own television show *The Ray Smith Show*, which aired on WPSD-TV in Paducah, Kentucky. Smith met future manager Charlie Terrell because of the program, which aired for two and a half years. Even though Smith was not sure that he wanted a manager, Terrell was persistent. After two unsuccessful attempts, Terrell finally asked 'If I can get you a contract with a leading label, will you sign me as your manager?' Smith agreed, and three days later, Terrell presented him with his Sun contract, already signed by Sam Phillips.[7]

On May 9, 1958, Smith made his first recordings for Sun, which were produced and engineered by Jack Clement. Future country superstar Charlie Rich played piano and wrote all four songs recorded that day: "So Young," "Right Behind You Baby," "Break Up," and "Why Why Why." Smith showcased "So Young" on *American Bandstand*. "Break Up" was originally intended for a Smith release, but Sam Phillips believed the song was a perfect fit for Jerry Lee Lewis and stopped the release of Smith's version. Lewis' rendition hit #59 on the pop charts. Rich also recorded it at Sun and did the song as part of his concerts until his death.

For Smith's second session in September of 1958, producer/songwriter Bill Justis brought in "You Made a Hit." "Willing and Ready" and "Shake Around" were also cut at that particular session. A few months later, Smith recorded "Rockin' Bandit," a novelty tune that featured gunshot effects, identical to those used on the Olympics' hit "Western Movies." According to guitarist Walker, "Rockin' Bandit" was also showcased on *American Bandstand*. It peaked at #99 on the pop charts. On the flip side was Rich's "Sail Away," which featured Stanley Walker harmonizing with Smith. According to Smith, "We took five stacks of records; in fact it was Bill Justis' record of 'Raunchy,' and stood Stanley up there on those, so he could get even with me to sing in the mike."[8]

Walker played lead on all the cuts, and his sound is different from any other guitarist because he tuned his guitar to straight E rather than natural tuning. Walker stated, "Everything I learned, I had to learn my own way." He wanted to achieve his own sound, one that would give Smith an edge over his competition. Walker reflected on his performances: "On 'Willing and Ready,' I wanted to come up with something different on my intro. I managed to pull that off. 'You Made a Hit' was pretty good. I never will forget; we were recording 'So Young,' and Jack Clement took my fingers and placed them and showed me just exactly that right idea. I tried to come up with my own stuff, and I did on all the others, the intros and the turnarounds, I came up with all of that." Working with Smith on those recordings meant a lot to Walker: "Ray featured me quite a bit on those records. I was proud of that."

Jerry Lee Lewis and Smith became good friends while they were both at Sun. Noted record collector Tommie Wix remembered, "One day right in front of Ray, Jerry Lee's dad told him, 'Son you've got a good voice, but you'll never be as good as this guy.' And he pointed to Ray. Ray told me, 'I almost went through the floor. You do NOT tell Jerry Lee something like that."[9] Walker commented, "A lot of times we'd be sitting at Sun, doing a session or something, and Jerry Lee would come in, and we'd just jam. That just thrilled us to death because Ray and I just loved Jerry Lee Lewis."

During the late 1950s and early 1960s, Elvis Presley and Smith were also good friends. They played pool together as well as darts. Presley won at playing pool, but Smith always won playing darts. Wix further told *Original Cool*, "One of Ray's highlights of his life was when he walked into Elvis' house, and Elvis was playing one of Ray's records."[10] Presley was his musical influence along with Marty Robbins and Hank Williams.

Narvel Felts was another rockabilly artist who was close to Smith. They first met in the spring of 1957 when Felts played a drive-in theatre in Paducah. Felts recalled: "I got there, opened my trunk, and to my surprise I had forgotten to bring my PA system and guitar. We were just kind of going around in a panic when here pulls up this 1956 tan Cadillac Coupe DeVille. He drove up and introduced himself as Ray Smith. He had his PA and his guitar in his trunk, so I used his that night."[11]

About a year later, they became friends. "I played Paradise Club in Cairo, Illinois, on Sunday afternoon and night, and Ray would always come and just sit in the audience," recalled Felts. "I would always get him up to sing. He was a wild performer." When he would sing a fast number, it would usually be one of Presley's. "What really sticks out in my mind is when he would sing a slow song, you could just shut your eyes and think it's Dean Martin on stage singing 'Return to Me.'" Smith was spot on with his impersonations and always added comedy to his act. According to Wix's interview with *Original Cool*, "Even in the middle of a mostly country set, you could see that Ray was just too wild of a showman to go very long onstage without rockin' up a storm! He could imitate just about any other singer. He could do anything with his voice."[12] Walker added, "I think Ray was one of the greatest entertainers I ever saw in my life."

Smith was displeased with his success and promotion at Sun, so he moved to Judd Records, which was owned by Phillips' brother Jud. Recording with Nashville's "A Team" studio musicians, Bill Justis produced his biggest commercial single, "Rockin' Little Angel." According to Adriaan Sturm, "It entered Billboard's Hot 100 on January 10, 1960 and peaked at number twenty-two. The single was a number one hit in several U.S. cities and became a major hit in almost every country in Western Europe and the Far East."[13] This success led to months on the road, including gigs in Canada and working the Golden Nugget Casino and Freemont Hotel in Las Vegas with Wayne Newton.

When the hit streak didn't continue, Smith returned to familiar territory. In 1961, he recorded for the last time at Sun. Two singles were released: "Travelin' Salesman" b/w "I Won't Miss You" and "Candy Doll" b/w "Hey Boss Man." After his tenure at Sun, he recorded for several different labels, including Vee Jay, Boot, Corona, and Mercury. "Turn on the Moonlight," which was written by country legend Sonny James, "Rockin' Robin," and "Did We Have a Party" were highlights during this period.

Conway Twitty first pioneered the club circuit for American artists in Canada. He then recommended fellow rockabilly artists Narvel Felts and Ronnie Hawkins. In 1959, it was Felts who suggested Smith, who made it his home seven years later.

On the road for months at a time, Smith and Walker always got homesick. After thirteen years of constant traveling, Walker called it quits.

In 1972, the record label Cinnamon signed Smith and released four singles, including "It Wasn't Easy," which was a Top 10 country single in Canada. Cinnamon had him re-record "Rockin' Little Angel," with a steel guitar, but it was not released as a single. Around the same time, Cinnamon signed Narvel Felts, who also recorded the song: "It was Ray's track that I put my voice on." "Rockin' Little Angel" became Felts' first nationally charted country song, #71 in *Cash Box*.

Noted record collectors John and Tommie Wix brought Smith back into the spotlight with a fan club and new recordings. It was the first time in his career that he played his own piano, thanks to Tommie's persuasion. He had been taught a few tricks by Charlie Rich and Jerry Lee Lewis. "Break Up" b/w "Room Full of Roses" was the first single released on Wix Records. Due to its popularity, an album *I'm Gonna Rock Some More* was recorded and released in early 1979. Newfound interest prompted a European tour, including shows with fellow rockabilly Sleepy LaBeef.

Fame didn't bring happiness to Smith. The world was still reeling from the loss of Elvis Presley when on November 29, 1979, news spread quickly that Smith had died from a self-inflicted gunshot wound at his home in Burlington, Ontario, Canada. Walker knew something had been bothering Smith: "He called me two or three months before he died, and I knew he was in some kind of trouble. I just didn't know what." It's been thought that he had a hard time coping with the idea that he may be getting a divorce. Walker was surprised by the news of his friend's early demise because he was a religious person: "He'd read the Bible. He knew it well. Sometimes when he couldn't sleep, he'd sit up and read the Bible or play Hank Williams' music."

Smith never realized his impact on rockabilly by seeing the legions of fans who attend the festivals today. However, he knew that music was his dream come true, as he told *New Kommotion*: "You have to feel it. I've loved music all my life, and I'll continue to play and sing till I die! It's not work! Just good old Rock and Roll!!"[14]

Hayden Thompson

Glen Glenn, Eddie Cochran, and Buddy Holly all began their careers signing country music before switching to rockabilly. Sun artist Hayden Thompson was no exception: "Most everybody was singing country music until Elvis came along then everybody jumped on the rock and roll bandwagon."[15] Thompson joined the Sun Records' roster in 1956 with his signature tune, "Love My

Baby." Within a few years, he left Memphis and his rockabilly roots behind—concentrating on country music, his family, and a day job. In 1984, he reemerged on the rockabilly scene and is still going strong.

Hayden Thompson was born on March 5, 1938, in Booneville, Mississippi. His parents both had musical talent as Thompson explained, "My mom played a little harmonica, and my dad could play the guitar a little bit. Back in the country [where I was born], it seemed like everybody played just a little bit. I can remember as a little boy we used to go to somebody's house, get out the fiddle, and have dances. Everybody would play and sing. I was just a little bitty fella standing over in the corner watching all of this take place." At a young age, Thompson received a guitar as a gift from his parents. They were always very supportive of his musical endeavors: "They were the greatest fans in the world, absolutely behind me all the way."

At ten years of age, Thompson made his first radio show appearance, guest starring on his preacher's thirty minute radio program, where he sang "Where Could I Go But to the Lord?" Soon country and blues had an impact on his life as well. Thompson took particular interest in country acts Eddy Arnold, Webb Pierce, Ray Price, Lefty Frizzell, and Hank Snow and tuned into WLAC out of Nashville to hear blues' greats John Lee Hooker and Muddy Waters.

Two years prior to his high school graduation, Thompson fronted his own band the Southern Melody Boys, which was comprised of much older strictly country musicians. They played local radio stations and dances on Saturday nights, including the *Dixieland Jamboree* stage show which was held at the Von Theatre in Booneville, Mississippi. Rockabilly musicians Eddie Bond, Johnny and Dorsey Burnette, Elvis Presley, and Johnny Cash all made appearances. In fact, Von Records, which was operated by the same manager as the stage show, released Thompson's first record "I Feel the Blues Coming On" b/w "Act Like You Love Me" in late 1954. Once Elvis Presley arrived on the scene, Thompson incorporated Presley's "That's All Right" and "Blue Moon of Kentucky" into his act. Unfor-

Hayden Thompson resembling his fellow Mississippian Elvis Presley (courtesy Hayden Thompson).

tunately, his band didn't appreciate Presley's talent and often questioned Thompson's reasons for singing those particular tunes: "They just said there's a guy that'll never last. He'll just be a fly by night. Why are you singing his stuff? [However], I recognized straight away that this was something new and different and was music I wanted to play."[16] In May 1955, Thompson made his only appearance on the *Louisiana Hayride* where he sang Marty Robbins' "Call Me Up (and I'll Come Calling on You)" and Presley's "Baby, Let's Play House." Presley and another Sun alum Carl Perkins had made such an impression on teenaged Thompson that he knew that was the direction his musical career was going to take. Thompson acknowledged, "I've often said that I should have quit school maybe in my sophomore year and went to Nashville. I had made up my mind by that time that I wanted to make my living in the music business."[17]

Once Thompson embraced the new sounds of rockabilly it was time to find a band that more suited his needs, so he formed the Dixie Jazzlanders with Jimmy Hill on guitar, Bill Hurt on bass, and Bill Gunter on drums. They started out by playing the theatre circuit in and around Alabama, Arkansas, Mississippi, and Tennessee: "We traveled with the 1956 movie *Rock Around the Clock* for eight months. We'd do one show, they'd play the movie, and then we'd do another show." A four day stint at a theatre in West Memphis, Arkansas, led them to Sun Studio. Sun engineer Jack Clement read a five star review of the show in a Memphis, Tennessee, newspaper and decided to see the band for himself. He made the trip over the bridge and was so impressed with the performance that he commented to Thompson, "Why don't you stop by Sun? Let's talk awhile and see if we can come up with something." In the fall of 1956, Thompson and the Dixie Jazzlanders cut their first session of four songs, "Fairlane Rock," "Mama, Mama, Mama," "Blues, Blues, Blues," and "You Are My Sunshine." Incidentally, "Fairlane Rock" was written by Thompson, who owned a 1956 red and white Ford Fairlane at the time. Its guitar break taken by Jimmy Hill added a line of "Yankee Doodle Dandy" as part of a gimmick: "That's the way we did it on the road before we recorded it."

Shortly after their initial recording at Sun, some of the band members got married and returned to Mississippi. As it turned out, Thompson had a couple of months' worth of bookings left with them, so he paired up with fellow label mate Billy Lee Riley and the Little Green Men. On the road, they traveled in Thompson's red and white Fairlane which had a trailer of the same colors hitched behind to hold their stage clothes, PA system, and instruments. The trailer caught a lot of attention because each side of it was painted, in white letters, Hayden Thompson and the original Rock and Roll Revue while the back lit up with You Ain't Nothin' but a Hound Dog. Thompson commented, "It was quite a sight to see."

On October 1, 1956, Thompson recorded his signature tune, a cover of Little Junior Parker and his Blue Flames' "Love My Baby" with the Little Green Men — Roland Janes on guitar, Marvin Pepper on bass, and J.M. Van Eaton on drums. The version that was eventually released was recorded in December and augmented by the addition of Jerry Lee Lewis on piano. Thompson explained, "I never knew where 'Love My Baby' came from, but I did know that I liked it immediately. I thought it was a tremendous song for me."[18]

Unfortunately, the Sun subsidiary Phillips International didn't release "Love My Baby" b/w "One Broken Heart" until November 1957. Memphis disk jockey Dewey Phillips played "Love My Baby" several times and other stations around the country spun the platter as well. Thompson thought since it was released and receiving airplay that it could be a hit. Due to lack of promotion, the single didn't do as well as previously thought in the States. Thompson noted that other singles were released at the same time as his; including Bill Justis' instrumental hit "Raunchy": "Raunchy" really started getting some airplay and it looked like it was going to be a hit, so Sam [Phillips] took what money he had for promotion and put it all behind that one particular song. That was his policy if something took off then that's where he put his advertising money." Surprisingly many people in Europe thought that "Love My Baby" had been recorded by Elvis Presley under a pseudonym.

Although success didn't come his way, Thompson remained with Sun and recorded three more songs in 1957 — "Rockabilly Gal," "Don't You Worry," and "Congratulations to You, Joe." The latter two were again recorded with the Little Green Men and written by Thompson. They remained unreleased until the 1980s when England's Charly Records mistakenly issued them under Sid Watson's name. Contrary to publications, Roy Orbison didn't sing harmony on "Rockabilly Gal" instead it was Slim Rhodes' brother Dusty. Thompson worked with Slim Rhodes and his family band before moving to Chicago: "I worked with Slim a little bit in '57. He was a local guy that had a family band around Memphis. They were very popular and strictly country. Once rock and roll got hot, he used a number of different people as his part of the show. That's what I did for three or four months, I was his rock and roll singer. They just kind of took me under their wing and led me around. I learned a lot from these people."[19]

At Sun, Jack Clement engineered Thompson's sessions: "I learned that Jack was a perfectionist on what he wanted to hear, and he would keep you doing it until you got the sound he wanted. Probably one of the hardest things I ever cut was 'Love My Baby.' I couldn't even tell you how many times we actually tried to record that song before we got it the way we wanted it." Thompson is thankful that he had the chance to be part of Sun's legacy: "We were making history and didn't know it. We were just a bunch of young guys having a good time and taking one day at a time, not realizing that fifty years down the road that people would still want to hear this stuff, especially in Europe. If I had known, I would have taken pictures and made notes. It was quite an experience, and I'm glad I was part of it."

In mid–1958, Thompson made the decision to move to Chicago since he had the promise of a steady gig at the Tally Ho Club in Highwood, Illinois, for the next four years. There he played four to five nights a week besides working the club circuit in Milwaukee, Detroit, and Chicago. In the early 60s, Thompson did a session with Elvis Presley's bassist Bill Black after he formed the Bill Black Combo. Thompson recollected, "I actually auditioned for the lead singer for his group. I think Gene Simmons [of "Haunted House" fame] beat me out."[20] Throughout the 1960s, Thompson continued to record and perform country music on package shows with Merle Haggard, Willie Nelson, Waylon Jennings, and Buck Owens. Roy Acuff's suggestion to appear on the *Grand Ole Opry* led Thompson to Nashville and Kapp Records where in 1966 he recorded a very professional country album, *Here's Hayden Thompson*, with a top notch studio band and the Anita Kerr Singers. Nancy Sinatra's #1 smash "These Boots Were Made For Walkin'" was given the country treatment. Thompson recalled, "It was a good album. People still talk about it."

Thompson continued to perform until 1976 when he decided to become an airport limousine driver: "I just got tired of it all and hung up the guitar and called it quits, or so I thought."[21] He retired from driving at the end of 2003: "It was the kind of job where I always had a job to come back to if something came up in Europe where I needed a week or two weeks I could leave and come back to it."

His return to rockabilly didn't occur until 1984 even though he first received a call in 1981 to do a show in England: "They asked me to come over, and I really didn't know that all this was going on over there. By that time, they'd already started bringing over some people like Sleepy [LaBeef], Narvel [Felts], and others." He was unsure of what to expect and wondered why they would be interested in hiring someone like him who had never had a hit, so initially he declined their offer: "I wish I had gone in '81 to be honest with you." Afterward, he inquired about the shows to others who had already participated. The consensus was "if you get the chance to go you should because it's like turning back time, and they still like the old 50s sound."

The next time he got a call he didn't refuse: "My first show was with Carl Mann at the Rockhouse Festival in Holland. This was 1984. I hadn't really worked in six or seven years, especially in front of a crowd of three thousand people. I walked out on the stage, and you'd have thought it was 1957 all over again. They just rolled out the red carpet for us. While I was over there I also played in Sweden and England and did eight or nine shows total. I actually cut a record while I was over there, first time I had recorded in awhile. Dave Travis produced it. He's been a dear friend to all of us. It was quite an experience." The recordings were issued on both the Charly label as *Booneville Mississippi Flash* and on Sunjay as *The Rockin' Country Man*.

Thompson was back in the limelight. Next, producer John Hughes gave him a call asking him to record "Are You Lonesome Tonight?" for his 1985 movie *Ferris Bueller's Day Off*. Thompson remembered, "I went to California to cut 'Are You Lonesome Tonight?' Originally, they wanted to use Elvis' version but couldn't get the rights to use it, so they brought me out and put the same identical music to it, and I cut it. There was supposed to be a scene where Ferris [Matthew Broderick] goes into a nightclub with his two friends. He was going to walk over and play the jukebox and pantomime the song. I went through about six months thinking that boy I've got a song coming out here in a movie. We cut it very close to Presley's version."[22] Two weeks prior to its release, he was notified that the scene had been cut: "It was very disappointing."

Also in 1985, Thompson saw Robert Plant of Led Zeppelin at a concert in Chicago: "I was able to get backstage, and I have never been treated with so much respect in my life. He's a big fan of Sun Records and not ashamed to tell you either."

In 1990, Thompson recorded a mostly country album, *The Time Is Now*. Unfortunately, it didn't receive much press or airplay here in America. Recordings and constant touring followed. He has traveled to Europe thirty-two times accompanied always by his wife Georgia, playing shows in Germany, France, Spain, Norway, and Finland. He has played all the major festivals—Americana and the Rockabilly Rave in England, the Ponderosa Stomp in New Orleans, and the Rockin' 50s Fest in Green Bay, Wisconsin. Thompson doesn't have a regular backing band, so he is usually paired with a young rockabilly band: "I tell all these guys to play the Sun material as close as they can to the original, and I'll try and do the rest. I'll tell you sometimes it gets a little spooky how close we get to that original sound."[23] He has been busiest in recent years thanks in part to his critically acclaimed 2005 St. George Records release *Rockabilly Rhythm* and 2007's Bluelight Records country release *Hayden Thompson*. Regarding the Bluelight release, Thompson acknowledged, "I just love that album, very proud of it. It was a week I'll never forget."

He loves all the rockabilly artists: "We're all one big happy family. Something I enjoy so much is getting to meet people, like Dale Hawkins, that I respect. I've been singing "Susie Q" ever since it came out. I get a kick out of meeting these people." Performing is very rewarding for Thompson: "It means a lot to me to still be appreciated. I'm very grateful to all the publications for having kept my name alive over the years. I would love to have a hit record, but I'm smart enough to know the chances." WGN Radio disk jockeys Steve King and Johnnie Putman are faithful friends who continually showcase Thompson's music: "I wish we had more stations that could play our rockabilly music then we could work more here in the States." Even though he is working more now than he has in his entire career, he admitted, "I'd like to be doing a lot more."

Dickey Lee

Many talented youngsters came to 706 Union in the hopes that they would be signed by its owner Sam Phillips; unfortunately he couldn't deal with them all appropriately. Some auditioned and never received a recording contract, while others had their singles shelved and promotion set aside due to lack of funds and manpower. After all, it was basically a one man operation. Dickey Lee was one of the artists who recorded for Sun, but he didn't enjoy success until the early 1960s. His first release, "Patches," became a number one national pop hit and million seller, and he penned the standard country song "She Thinks I Still Care." The tune charted at #1 for three different artists in the country field: George Jones, Elvis Presley, and Anne Murray. Today, he continues to perform on rock and roll revival shows along with pop acts Bobby Vee, Brian Hyland, and the Shirelles as well as continuing to keep active as a songwriter, hoping to write another hit like "She Thinks I Still Care."

Royden Dickey Lee was born on September 21, 1936, in Memphis, Tennessee. As far as he knows, there were no other relatives who were musically inclined. He grew up on his family's farm, where their two major crops were cotton and corn. Lee recalled, "All I did was work on the farm, play sports mostly baseball and football, go to school, and play my guitar."[24] Lee was pitcher for the Whitehaven High School in Whitehaven, Tennessee, which is a suburb of Memphis, and won many championships. In fact, he once played against Tim McCarver, catcher for the St. Louis Cardinals, who won the 1964 World Series. Lee admitted, "I wanted to play professional baseball, but I wasn't as good as I thought I was. I hurt my arm in high school, and that kind of slowed me down a lot too."

Besides playing baseball, Lee started singing, playing the guitar, and songwriting. Lee remembered, "There was a guy at my high school that played at Friday assemblies. He would play these songs that he wrote, and I thought it was pretty cool. That's kind of what got me going, so I went out and bought a guitar at a pawn shop and started trying to write songs too." The first song he wrote but never recorded was "Anna Lee," which was about a lost love who died: "I think the only person that ever liked that song was my aunt."

He participated in local talent contests and even auditioned for the *Ted Mack Amateur Hour*, to no avail. Then in his junior year, he formed a country band of three pieces. They began playing some of the high school assemblies.

Dewey Phillips helped to launch Elvis Presley's career by being one of the first disk jockeys to play "That's All Right" b/w "Blue Moon of Kentucky." Phillips was also instrumental in aiding Lee's career: "He and Elvis kind of started out at the same time. He had everything to do with starting me out. I was the first kid that had a hit record out of Memphis after Elvis came along. Before I even had a recording deal, Dewey had a radio show called *Red, Hot, and Blue* on WHBQ. It was on nine o'clock to midnight five or six nights a week and all the kids were just crazy about him. I don't think there was a disk jockey that could even touch him, and I heard 'em all. I went up to his radio station one night, and I actually got to see him and got him to listen to a couple of songs I'd written. He said 'why don't you get a group together and come back and let me hear those again?' A year later, Elvis had come along and really influenced me [along with Jimmy Sacca and the Hilltoppers], and my group evolved into a little four piece rhythm section rock and roll band. We went back to Dewey and redid those songs. He liked them so much that he actually recorded them in the radio studio." The two songs they recorded were "Dream Boy" and "Stay True Baby." A friend of Phillips' released them as a single on his label, Tampa Records. The single became a smash hit in the Mid-South because Phillips played both sides frequently. Lee conveyed, "The combo played shows around Memphis and the Mid-South, including fraternity and sorority dances. At the time, Elvis had his song 'Teddy Bear' out, so our songs came out at the same time and went up the charts together. Elvis was #1 for about fourteen weeks on the Memphis charts, and I was #2. I never got to #1 because of Elvis."

Presley heard the single and was impressed by what he heard. He personally told Lee that he liked what he was doing, encouraged him to continue, and invited him out to Graceland. Lee went to Presley's home a few times. On one occasion Presley personally served him a vanilla milkshake from his ice cream bar.

In the fall of 1957, he entered Memphis State University on a boxing scholarship. Incidentally, he was a Golden Gloves' champion. In college, he formed the Collegiates, which included Eddie Weil on guitar and Allen Reynolds, who today produces Garth Brooks, on backup vocals.

In 1957, Phillips got Lee a deal with Sun Records: "I was so excited just to be there." Lee figures that Phillips talked Sam Phillips into putting him on the label: "Sam Phillips wasn't a big Dickey Lee fan. I wasn't his type of artist really. I read

Dickey Lee scored No. 1 hits as a singer and a songwriter in the early 1960s (courtesy Dickey Lee).

an article in *Billboard* years later that he said two of the guys that he did not do right by were Conway Twitty and me. Sam really had an eye for talent, but he needed more manpower. I don't think at that time he trusted a whole lot of people." Lee also recalled that Phillips told him, "You never found yourself until you left Sun. You were an imitator. You sounded too much like those darn teen idols out of Philadelphia." At Sun, he met engineer Jack Clement, with whom he remained friends: "Jack's such a crazy guy but loveable, a super talented person. He could do anything. He's had a little success at everything." Clement is one of his mentors and gave him invaluable advice when it came to songwriting: 'When you write a song, you try to write a song in the sense that anybody that hears it would say well I can write that.' Lee explained, "It's not as simple as it sounds though."

Lee had two official releases on Sun: "Good Lovin'" b/w "Memories Never Grow Old" and "Fool, Fool, Fool" b/w "Dreamy Nights." "Dreamy Nights" was a real doo wop song that Lee thought would be a big hit. Lee's reign on Sun was short lived: "I think there are a lot of people out there that aren't even aware that I was on Sun. My national popularity started after Sun." Fellow Sun acts Billy Lee Riley and Bill Justis added Lee as special vocalist on some of their shows at local colleges: "Everybody intermingled back then."

In 1961, engineer Clement was working at RCA and listening to songs for Chet Atkins when he stumbled upon "Patches." He sent it to both Lee and Reynolds, in the hopes that one of them would record it: "He kind of heard it for Allen, but Allen really didn't like that song that much. I just loved the song." He recorded it at a studio in Beaumont, Texas. Clement and Lee's manager at the time Bill Hall played it for Shelby Singleton and Smash Records' owner Charlie Fach. They picked it up, and the single rose to #6 on the charts. A year later, he scored again with "I Saw Linda Yesterday," a #14 hit also for Smash Records.

A year later, Lee graduated from Memphis State with a double major in both commercial art and English: "I loved the literature [especially] Greek mythology. I'm sure some of that stuff, including studying poetry, had something to do with my songwriting."

In 1963, Lee hit the jackpot when George Jones' recording of his "She Thinks I Still Care" shot to the top of the country charts. In fact, it was the Country Song of the Year. Lee recalled, "I wrote that song about a girl that I was in love with, but she wasn't in love with me. It was one of those heartbroken songs. I'm really thankful for her because that song made a lot of money for me. When I first wrote the song, Elvis was one of the guys I tried to pitch it to." Lee gave it to a member of the Memphis Mafia, who had promised to deliver it to Presley, but Presley never saw it. "She Thinks I Still Care" was one of Presley's favorite songs, and he vowed that someday he would record it. In 1977, he kept his promise and recorded it twice as both a strong ballad and an uptempo number. Lee disclosed, "Elvis was really nice to me. I was thrilled to death [that he recorded "She Thinks I Still Care"]. Presley had a #1 country hit with it in 1977. Anne Murray took it to the top of the country charts in 1974.

Even though "She Thinks I Still Care" is the song that is most often associated with Lee, he also wrote #1 songs for Reba McEntire ("You're the First Time I've Thought About Leaving"), George Strait ("Let's Fall to Pieces Together"), and John Schneider ("I've Been Around Enough to Know"). Brenda Lee, Waylon Jennings, Merle Haggard, Jerry Lee Lewis, and Marty Robbins have also recorded Lee's songs.

In 1971, Lee signed a ten year contract with RCA Victor and recorded several country hits, including "9,999,999 Tears" and "Never Ending Song of Love."

In the late 1980s, Lee began hitting the rock and roll revival circuit. The fans want to hear his country hits, so he always incorporates them. Lee revealed, "I love both rock and roll and country equally." He hasn't performed at many rockabilly shows or festivals but has appeared at car shows and been on the same bill as Jack Scott, Billy Lee Riley, and the Sun Rhythm Section. He performs a Sun medley of hits, including songs by Charlie Rich, Elvis Presley, Carl Perkins, Jerry Lee Lewis, and Roy Orbison: "It always goes over well."

Lee has received many accolades as both a singer and songwriter, including BMI awards and Million Performance awards. In 1995, he was inducted into the Nashville Songwriter's Hall of Fame. He loves all aspects of performing and continues to record, write songs, and tour. Lee acknowledged: "I've been blessed to get paid for what I love to do."

Ed Bruce

Similar to Dickey Lee, Ed Bruce enjoyed a brief stint on Sun Records before moving on to a very successful singing and songwriting career in country music. Since the rockabilly revival, Bruce hasn't played a show or festival. In fact, he was surprised to hear that anyone remembered his two singles on Sun: "I don't know how much interest there is. I guess I am surprised after all this time, but Sun was pretty special. It had its own unique sound."[25] His song "Mamas Don't Let Your Babies Grow Up to Be Cowboys" is in the top ten of the 100 Greatest Country Songs and is a two million certified BMI airplay award winner. Country fans may not be familiar with his rockabilly roots, but rockabilly fans will always hold a special place in his/her heart for "Rock Boppin' Baby" and "Sweet Woman."

William Edwin Bruce, Jr. was born on December 29, 1939, in Keiser, Arkansas. Although born in Arkansas, his parents moved with their only child to Memphis, Tennessee. Therefore, he considers himself a Tennessean. Bruce explained, "Arkansas' motto was the Land of Opportunity, but there wasn't much opportunity there in the late '30s for a young family, so he moved us to Memphis when I was less than a year old."

At four years old, he sang the song "Streets of Laredo," also known as the "Cowboy's Lament." In 1975, he recorded it for the United Artists' release, *Ed Bruce*, which also contained his hit "Mamas Don't Let Your Babies Grow Up to Be Cowboys." At ten years of age, Bruce purchased his first guitar with money he had saved from his paper route: "It wasn't much of a guitar. It would take a machine press to mash the strings down [because] the neck was so bowed on it. I worked at it, and my little ten year old fingers were bleeding because it was so hard to mash the strings down. The strings were probably so old on it, [and] I didn't know anything about changing strings. [In fact], Ben Franklin probably flew his kite with those things." Once his parents realized that their young son was serious about playing music, they went to a local music store and rented an entry level Martin guitar. Later on, Bruce graduated to a Gibson ES 175, which was the same guitar he took to Sun Studio.

When Bruce was in the eighth grade, he won third prize in the school talent contest by singing the theme song from the movie *High Noon*: "I saw that movie a dozen times to see Will Kane take out the bad guys and hear Tex Ritter sing 'High Noon.'"

At sixteen years of age, Bruce made a demo recording at Sun Studio. For fifteen dollars, anyone could record there: "I just went into Sun to put down the songs ["Rock Boppin' Baby" and "Eight Wheel Driver"], which were the first songs I recall writing at thirteen years old. This was at the time when that was a part of the income of Sun Records." He had his three piece band accompany him, Jack Mitchell on bass, David Morris on drums, and Roger Watson on lead guitar. Bruce remembered, "We started doing the demo, and the guy running the boards said 'hang on a minute,' and went down the hall to Mr. Sam's office and said 'come out here and hear this kid.' I like to think I have my own style. I don't hear anybody else in me. When Jack [Clement] went back to get Mr. Sam to hear me then immediately I think discussions started about my recording for the label. My first recording deal was with Sun Records." Since he was underage, his parents had to sign the contract, which was not the same day as the demo recording. His parents were skeptical at first of Bruce's musical ambitions: "My mother always wanted me to be a doctor." However, making a living as a physician was the last thing he would consider since that's all he ever heard.

Contrary to popular belief, Bruce was not recommended to Sun by Elvis Presley's guitarist Scotty Moore and bassist Bill Black: "I didn't even know Bill and Scotty then. They both later played some dates with me after Elvis had cut them loose. Bill and I remained friends until he died."

In early 1957, Bruce cut his first session at Sun. He revealed that egg carton fillers were used for deadening the sound while boxes of 45 rpm records were stacked up for sound baffling. Bruce added, "We recorded with two microphones, one for the band and one for the singer. There was no overdubbing then. If you didn't get it, you started over." Just prior to Bruce's high school graduation, Sun released "Rock Boppin' Baby" b/w "More Than Yesterday" under Edwin Bruce, his recording name at the time. Sun then issued his second single "Sweet Woman" b/w "Part of My Life" in June 1958. Two months later, Lorrie Collins of The Collins Kids provided her sultry vocals on the Columbia Records' release of "Rock Boppin' Baby." As far as the rest of his Sun material, many of Bruce's recordings remained on the shelf. It wasn't until 1986 when Bear Family Records released an LP, *Rock Boppin' Baby*, with the majority of his Sun material.

Bruce participated in a few of the Sun package shows. One he remembers in particular occurred in Mississippi with Carl McVoy, Carl Mann, Barbara Pittman, Billy Lee Riley, and Jerry Lee Lewis, who were also on the bill. He recalled Lewis' dynamic stage performance: "Nobody played piano like Jerry Lee."

While at Sun, Bruce learned an important lesson about songwriting, receive your credit when it is due. Bruce disclosed, "I learned something about the intricacies of songwriting, and that is to get your credit [at the time you write the song]. At that age, I had no concept of BMI or ASCAP or anything like that. I thought you wrote songs to make records. I used to hang down there [at Sun] a lot. Johnny Cash was one of my heroes. I was down there one day when Johnny was recording. Luther [Perkins, Cash's guitarist] was trying to get the lick down, and I was in the control room. Jack was running the recorder at the time. He stopped at some point and said 'Edwin we need a bridge or a chorus for this song.' I said okay. I had been listening to them do it, so I went out in the hall and a few minutes later I came back with [a bridge to "Guess Things Happen That Way"]. I was not given credit. I didn't know to ask for credit. I just thought wow man that's great; Johnny Cash has recorded a song that I wrote part of. It wasn't a completed song until I wrote the bridge. I don't know if Jack even remembers that. I'm not going to sue Jack Clement for anything, but it would be nice if he would acknowledge it."

About a year after his first release on Sun, Bruce performed with Moore and Black at the Rebel Club in Osceola, Arkansas: "Somebody called and wanted me to come over there and play Friday and Saturday nights. At the time, I didn't have a band together, so I called Bill Black. I said Bill, do you want to play some bass with me for a few weekends over in Arkansas? He said, 'yeah sure, you need another guitar player?' I said well yeah I'd probably use another one. He said, 'well man Scotty needs work, I'll call him for you.'" Black and Moore along with Johnny "Ace" Cannon on saxophone and Johnny Bernero on drums completed the band. Bruce added, "We played for so much against the door. We were getting ten bucks a man and all the pride we could swallow."

Many artists made the transition from rockabilly to country music once Elvis Presley made his appearance on the scene; however, this wasn't the case for Bruce: "Rockabilly, that term, was not even invented then. My first record came to be known as rockabilly. I didn't know what I was doing. It just felt good, and that's what I've always done. At that time, I sang all kinds of music. I did some Elvis songs." As a teenager, Chuck Berry and Johnny Cash were his favorites along with Carl Perkins, Jerry Lee Lewis, and Roy Orbison. Bruce added, "There was never a point where all of a sudden I opened a new door and said well I'm a country singer now. I sang country music when I was five years old. When I was in the tenth grade, I had a buddy named Phil Thomas. He and I double dated a lot, and when we'd drop our dates off we'd ride around and sing Hank Williams' songs. That was before I ever heard of Sun Records."

By 1962, Bruce made his pilgrimage to Nashville in hopes of becoming a well known songwriter. With the success of Tommy Roe's "Save Your Kisses," which was the B side of his #1 song "Sheila," and Charlie Louvin's "See the Big Man Cry," which was a #1 song in the country field, Bruce was on his way to making his mark.

Prior to Waylon Jennings and Willie Nelson's recording of "Mamas Don't Let Your Babies Grow Up to Be Cowboys," Bruce scored a top fifteen hit with his own version. According to Bruce, "I wrote the song regardless of the writers' credits. When I started 'Mamas' I was on the way to my house from a jingle session. I was probably about ten minutes from home when I just started singing. I was a little frustrated as I was making a good living [from singing jingles], but nobody really knew who Ed Bruce was. By the time I got to the house; I had the first of two verses and the chorus. When I finished the song [a few weeks later], it was discussed about whether I should do it to establish myself as an artist or whether to get it to Waylon [Jennings]. I felt so strongly that it would probably be a hit if Waylon did it." In 1975, Bruce recorded his version of the song, and then handed it over to Waylon, who recorded it in 1978: "I called Waylon, and I said hey why don't you cut 'Mamas?' He said 'hoss we did that already two weeks ago. Why don't you come in and listen to it?'" Both Jennings and producer Chips Moman had suggested the song for Jennings to record. Willie Nelson came in a few weeks later to overdub his vocals. In January 1978, "Mamas Don't Let Your Babies Grow Up to Be Cowboys" peaked at #1 on the Billboard Hot Country Singles charts: "I was tickled to death. I was just ecstatic." The chart topper was nominated for a Grammy for Song of the Year but lost out to "The Gambler" sung by Kenny Rogers and written by Don Schlitz.

In the late 1970s, the state of Tennessee brought Bruce in as a spokesman for a nationwide advertising campaign to promote tourism.

In 1981, James Garner called Bruce to co-star in his new television show, *Bret Maverick*. Bruce conveyed, "I had known Jim for several years. We met at a charity golf tournament. He's a big country music fan. He called my office to get me to come out and do a screen test with him. Stuart Margolin from *The Rockford Files* actually suggested me. Jim told me later they had read everyone in Hollywood, and he just wasn't satisfied." When Bruce went in to audition, they were only two weeks away from production. The cast's first day of filming

Ed Bruce enjoyed a short stint in rockabilly before achieving superstar status as a country songwriter (courtesy Ed Bruce).

was August 12, 1981: "I had a gig in Oregon on Saturday night, and we started shooting Monday morning. I've been called a quick study." The series lasted a year. Also in 1981, Bruce recorded a number one song with "You're the Best Break This Old Heart Ever Had."

His songwriting continued to reap rewards when his recordings of "After All" and "My First Taste of Texas" both became top five records. Crystal Gayle recorded his "Restless" while Tanya Tucker sang "The Man That Turned My Mama On" and "Texas (When I Die)," all were subsequent hits. In 2004, he and Ron Peterson, both born again Christians, co-wrote four songs for the CD, *Changed* and in 2007, they co-wrote two songs for the album, *Sing About Jesus*.

Even though Bruce is recognized as a cowboy by nature, he regards himself as a horseman: "A cowboy is somebody who literally makes his living working cows, and I don't do that. I've never owned a ranch. I've been riding horses since I was three years old." However, he has adopted the cowboy lifestyle: "That has been my lifestyle for awhile as far as the way I dress and [in regard to] my friends." He's also a fan of the old westerns: "They don't make enough westerns. The dearth of westerns hurts me."

Bruce can do it all from acting to singing to songwriting. Songwriting remains an integral part of Bruce's life: "I'll always be a songwriter. Some songs are better than others. I discard songs if I don't like them or don't think they're any good. I'm not one who thinks everything I write is a hit." He even provided his voice to several commercial jingles, including Kawasaki, McDonald's, United Airlines, John Deere, Toyota, as well as the Army/Navy/Marines "It's a Great Place to Start" ad campaign. Performances have also been a part of his busy schedule, touring overseas since 1980 with his wife Judith. Appearances at Wembley Stadium in England, Austria, Holland, and Switzerland round out his resume.

Carl Mann

In 1957, Carl Mann began his recording career with the regional label, Jaxon. Two years later, at the tender age of sixteen, Mann scored a #25 hit with "Mona Lisa," which earned him the title of the youngest Sun artist ever to sell a million records. Mann acknowledged, "The best feeling I ever had was when I heard 'Mona Lisa' on the radio."[26] His formula for reworking classic tunes didn't produce another top seller, and his popularity began to wane. However, throughout the 1960s and 1970s, he continued to record and tour. By the mid–1980s, he gave up secular music for the church. In 2006, thanks to numerous requests and his own desire to return to his rockabilly roots, Mann once again stepped onto a stage and wowed audiences with his signature tune "Mona Lisa."

Carl Mann was born on August 22, 1942, in Huntington, Tennessee. He was the third of five children, which included two sisters and two brothers.

Their father owned a timber business and a saw mill. Eventually, Mann partnered with his father and brothers. Then he ran the business after his dad couldn't anymore. Mann added, "I was involved in the business for thirty years."[27]

At seven years of age, he developed an interest in country music: "I got sick with the mumps or measles. My mother moved me into the front room by the heater. We had an old battery radio, and since my cot was right by it, all I could do for two weeks was listen to that radio. [One of the programs he listened to was the *Grand Ole Opry*.] That's when I first started taking an interest in music." Then two years later, he began singing in church. At ten years old, Mann learned how to play the guitar: "My mother had shown me three or four chords." The first song he learned how to play was "Wildwood Flower." At this time, he started venturing down to the amateur hour, which was held every Saturday morning on WDXI in Jackson, Tennessee. Mann recalled, "I did some old Webb Pierce songs like 'Slowly' and 'Even Tho,' and I did a Skeets McDonald song called 'Let Me Know.'"[28] It was held in a theater and broadcasted live. Kids from nine to sixteen years old participated in the little Opry. A year later, Mann formed his first band and received his own radio program. They played locally at schools, clubs, and community centers. Then he and his cousin took a bus trip to Nashville: "One of my grandmothers lived up there at the time, so we went and visited her. The *Grand Ole Opry* also had a [show called] *Friday Night Frolic*. We played in Studio C, not the Ryman Auditorium."

At thirteen, Mann saw Elvis Presley at the Overton Park Shell. His bassist, Robert Oatsvall, worked for Hart's Bakery in Memphis and invited Mann to attend the show with him: "I didn't know how I was going to manage that. [However,] there was a Pentecostal preacher holding a revival in Huntington, and he was from Memphis. I begged my mother to talk him into letting me ride back to Memphis with him. He took me right to my friend's house. We went to see Elvis. That was really a thrill for me to go down and see him right at the beginning. It was a big influence on me." Besides Presley, he also cited Lefty Frizzell, Hank Williams, Hank Snow, Carl Smith, Jerry Lee Lewis, and Carl Perkins as musical influences.

Even though Mann was already incorporating some uptempo songs into his repertoire, shortly after seeing Presley in concert, he switched from singing country to rockabilly: "As far as rockabilly, it was about the time that Elvis came out. I was doing country music at thirteen. Elvis came out, and we made the switch. I started doing a lot of his songs" [including "That's All Right," "Blue Moon of Kentucky," and "Baby, Let's Play House."] Then he did Jerry Lee Lewis tunes before developing his own style: "Eddie [Bush] and I developed this style through the way he played guitar and the harmonics he used. He had such a distinctive way of playing guitar. Eddie's picking added a lot to my records."

Although Mann switched styles, he kept his country band: "When I first started doing rockabilly, I had the same band. I just added a drummer [Tony

Moore.] We played that way for awhile and then when I did my first recording for the Jaxon label I met Eddie Bush at the studio [who was a member of the staff band on the *Louisiana Hayride*.] [Mann's only release on Jaxon, "Gonna Rock and Roll Tonight" b/w "Rockin' Love," was released under Carl Mann and the Kool Kats. Mann stated that "Gonna Rock and Roll Tonight" was "pure rockabilly."] Eddie was playing with Jimmie Martin, who owned the studio and had a band, the Jimmie Martin Combo. He suggested to Jimmie that they try to get me to join their band. I didn't want to split with my band, but a few weeks went by, and we corresponded back and forth. I then decided and they did too to split bands and form a new one. I just joined their band, and I took my bass player, Robert Oatsvall, with me."

When Mann was fourteen, he learned how to play the piano: "After I got with the Jimmie Martin Combo, I switched over from acoustic [guitar] to piano. I started learning because Jimmie said 'well we need somebody to play piano.' He took a magic marker and wrote the keys on the back part of the ivory. That's how I learned how to play. I started out playing a boogie rhythm like Jerry Lee Lewis." Incidentally, he played piano on his signature song, "Mona Lisa."

Mann and Bush remained with the Jimmie Martin Combo for a couple of years before parting ways to give their own sound a chance: "We split off, and we made some demos. We started shopping them around, and we went to Sun. A couple of times we went over there, and they said 'well send us a tape.' We

Carl Mann started his career with the Jimmie Martin Combo, from left, Jimmie Martin, Carl Mann, Eddie Bush, and Robert Oatsvall (courtesy Carl Mann).

sent them a tape, and we never heard back from them, so Eddie and I took a tape over there. We literally camped out on the doorstep. We got over there in the middle of the night, and we slept in the car out in front of the building. The next morning when they opened, we went in and talked to them. Jack Clement listened to the tape and said 'it sounds pretty good, but it needs a little more work. Work on it about two or three months and come back and see me.'"

They were playing at the Triple Club in Puryear, Tennessee, when they reworked "Mona Lisa" into an uptempo tune: "Eddie Bush and I worked it up together. Eddie had been playing in Hawaii before he got out of the service, and he came back through Jackson; that's how I met him. He had done that song [but in] Nat King Cole's style over there. He and I just started kicking it around one day. We hadn't really gotten it down to where we wanted it, but one night we were playing at the Triple Club. A lot of college kids would come across state line [from Kentucky] to that club. We started out doing 'Mona Lisa,' but I was doing it slow. The kids started hollering that they wanted something fast to dance to, so we just stopped and after about the first eight bars started on it fast. We had about eight or ten requests that night to do it, so we figured that was a pretty good indication that might be what we were looking for."

While waiting to hear from Sun, Carl Perkins' drummer W.S. Holland caught Mann's live show: "We started talking, and he talked like he might be able to help me get on the Sun label because he knew Sam and had been over there with Carl Perkins. He made a phone call, and then [later] we got set up for an audition. He went with us. [Holland played drums on 'Mona Lisa' and all subsequent recordings until March 1960.] 'Mona Lisa' was the audition recording. We did three takes on it, and then we did a backside, which was called 'Foolish Love.' While we were doing the song, Conway Twitty came in the studio. He came over and shook hands with me and said 'man I think you've got a hit record.' We left, and Jack said 'well I'll play it for Sam and see what he thinks.'"

At this point, Mann had not been offered a contract with Sun, and he was getting anxious. While playing a club date in Canada with Carl Perkins, W.S. Holland found out some news that would change Sam Phillips' mind about Mann: "After the show, Ronnie Hawkins [who had been playing at the club next door] and W.S. bumped into each other. Ronnie told W.S. that he had talked to his old buddy Conway Twitty that day. He told W.S. 'guess what Conway's next record is gonna be? You'll never guess; it's that old Nat King Cole song, 'Mona Lisa.' Conway went into Nashville and cut it as close to the style we had as he could. They told me he was gonna put it on an album. Later, he was gonna go ahead and do a single release on it, and that's what he did. [Actually, Twitty's version was released on an EP (extended play) 45 rpm record in February 1959 and received quite a bit of airplay after disk jockeys latched onto it.] W.S. heard that news, and he called me and Sam Phillips. Sam called and asked me 'how soon can you get down here and sign a contract?' That's how I got on Sun. If Conway hadn't cut it, I don't know that I would have gotten on Sun. I was aggravated at first, but then I thought it was a blessing in disguise. Jack told me later that he played my version for Sam, but he didn't think it was a hit and didn't really think it was that great." In April 1959, Phillips International released "Mona Lisa" b/w "Foolish One." It peaked at #25 on the Billboard charts.

To promote his new single, Mann did a Midwest and East Coast tour. He performed on several dance party shows, including *Wink Martindale's Dance Party* in Memphis. Between July 9 and July 26, General Artists Corporation set Mann out on a three week tour called the Summer Dance Party Tour with six other rock and roll acts: Jo Ann Campbell, Skip and Flip, The Tassels, the Addrissi Brothers, Dickey Doo and the Don'ts, and Jerry Keller. They performed at some of the same venues as Buddy Holly, the Big Bopper, and Ritchie Valens had on their ill fated Winter Dance Party Tour, including the Riverside Ballroom in Green Bay, Wisconsin: "It was kind of an eerie feeling to be in some of the dressing rooms of the places they had played."

"Mona Lisa" had been recorded at the old studio at 706 Union as would his next single "Rockin' Love" b/w "Pretend," which was released in September 1959. "Pretend" was another song from Nat King Cole's songbook: "After we did 'Mona Lisa,' and it was successful; I started pickin' some other Nat King Cole songs that I could do. That became my tag, taking old songs and redoing them." Unfortunately, that formula didn't work as well the second time around since "Pretend" rounded out at #57 on the Hot 100 charts.

Even though Mann's heart laid in country music, Phillips wanted him to incorporate a rhythm and blues side into his recordings: "Deep down I wanted to do country music. Every time I went to record, I'd do some country songs for Sam and he'd say 'naw that's too country,' but I slipped a few in there."[29] Mann added, "I always called Sam the searcher because he was always searchin' for something different and unique. Some of those recordings [we did] we hadn't even rehearsed."

By late 1959, Phillips began having his artists record at the new studio on 639 Madison: "The new studio was directly in back of the other one, across on Madison. I along with Charlie Rich did the first recordings in the new studio. It never did have the same effective sound that the old studio had. It just didn't have that same clean clear famous sound. I just never did like the sound as well. That old Sun Studio had a unique sound that I can't describe." Its wavy ceiling had an impact on the sound. Mann remembered, "Charlie [Rich] played on some of my recordings. He had written a song for me to do, 'I'm Comin' Home.' I always liked that song probably as good as any I ever recorded." His fourth single, "I'm Comin' Home" b/w "South of the Border," was released in May 1960. Mann found out Elvis Presley really liked "I'm Comin' Home": "We met briefly at the studio, and Elvis told me how much he enjoyed my singing.

A few songs he told me he really liked: 'Mona Lisa,' 'I'm Comin' Home,' and 'I Can't Forget You.' He told me he liked my style." In fact, "I'm Comin' Home" was the first song Presley recorded after his discharge from the Army, and it appeared on his 1961 LP *Something for Everybody*.

By July, W.S. Holland and Mann parted ways. After that, no longer did Holland appear on Mann's recordings, manage his career, or play drums for him at gigs. Their relationship fell apart because Holland demanded 50 percent of all earnings made by Mann, including royalties. Guitarist Eddie Bush was the only band member that remained with Mann. At the same time as Holland's departure, bass player Robert Oatsvall was replaced. J.M. Van Eaton, most well known for his rhythmic drumming on Jerry Lee Lewis' Sun recordings and a member of Billy Lee Riley's band the Little Green Men, stepped up to replace Holland on drums for Mann's next recording session, which produced several songs, including "Ubangi Stomp," "Don't Let the Stars Get in Your Eyes," and "Stop the World and Let Me Off."

"Mountain Dew" b/w "When I Grow Too Old to Dream" was the final single issued on Phillips International in 1962, seven singles in all. Unlike many other Sun artists, Mann was fortunate enough to have an album, *Like Mann*, released. In 1965, his contract ran out: "While I was in the Army, my contract ran out. I actually stopped recording about 1963. Carl Perkins then called me. His piano player had quit, and he wanted to know if I could go play piano with him at the Cimarron Ballroom in Tulsa, Oklahoma. I went and played that show with him. He had a couple more shows and then he was going to Vegas to play at the Golden Nugget, so he asked me if I wanted to do that. I said well I don't have anything booked yet. I would sing a few songs on the show. I wound up working with Carl for eight months. We finished our last gig in Las Vegas in October. He had a way of just captivating people around him." Perkins and Mann used to hang out down at the old Jaxon studio: "We did record some stuff together, but the tapes disappeared. I bought all the Jaxon tapes after Jimmie Martin died, from his widow. Some of those tapes that had my name on it had been taped over with country music from the radio." The songs that were salvageable appeared on the 1994 Stomper Time release *Gonna Rock 'n' Roll Tonight*.

After Mann's stint with Perkins, he returned home: "When I got back, I had a letter from Uncle Sam, and they had inducted me into the Army. I went into the service in February 1964." He spent two years in the Army, first in the military police and then in an infantry unit as a radio operator. He was transferred to Germany. His first night there he sat in and sang a couple of songs with a band at an enlistmen's club. That impromptu decision turned into regular weekend gigs and playing all over Germany at NCO clubs, Officer's Clubs, and German-American relation shows: "I really enjoyed that period of time in the Army. After I got with that band, I had a good time." They did one radio station recording for Armed Forces Radio, but it was never released.

After his discharge, Monument Records released "Down to My Last I Forgive You" b/w "Serenade of the Bells." In 1968, Mann got married and got out of the music business. After a few years, he came back: "This songwriter came to me and wanted me to go to Nashville and do a demo for him of some songs that he had written, so I agreed to do that. Then he and I started writing some together." Mann then signed with ABC Records in 1974. He had two releases on ABC then two on ABC-Dot, all country singles. He didn't tour to promote the singles, so they only briefly charted. His final release on ABC was a country take on the Platters' hit "Twilight Time." In 1978, he was one of the first artists to participate in the rockabilly revival over in Europe. He performed for the last time in 1984. Soon after, he performed only religious music at churches. Although in 1990, he did have a battle with throat cancer, enduring thirty-seven radiation treatments: "I couldn't sing for a long time."[30]

In 2001, Mann reunited with Eddie Bush's daughters on a talk radio program in Jackson: "We got together, and I found out that they hadn't heard from Eddie either." The last time Mann saw Bush was in 1989: "I knew something had happened." He thought it was strange because every year or two he received a visit or a letter from Bush. Mann explained, "His daughters and I got to searching. I made some phone calls, and they put an ad in the paper in a town in Arkansas that they knew Eddie's sister had lived. I called a friend of mine [Carl Belew's widow] in Oklahoma, and she confirmed that Eddie was dead. [Eddie had played with Carl Belew after he left Carl Mann.] She thought he had died in a nursing home over in Tulsa, but Eddie's brother-in-law had seen the ad in the paper and told them all about what had happened. Eddie was buried in Fort Gibson cemetery, a military cemetery outside of Tulsa. He was found on the street, and I believe they took him to the VA hospital, and he died there. I think he was still alive when they found him."

Many people had been requesting that Mann sing "Mona Lisa" at his shows, even though he was now singing entirely gospel tunes. Mann recollected, "I wrote some gospel lyrics to the tune of 'Mona Lisa,' a tune called 'Jesus Jesus,' [which is available on his gospel CD, *Carl Mann Legacy*.] One night while performing with a local rockabilly band, Mann decided to begin with "Jesus Jesus" and then segue into "Mona Lisa": "Just gradually I started back doing some more rock and roll, country, and rockabilly stuff." In 2006, rockabilly fans worldwide rejoiced when Mann reentered the scene after a long hiatus with a performance at the Hemsby Weekender in England. In regard to rockabilly festivals, fans enjoy hearing his Sun material: "That's what they want to hear, the old Sun stuff. That's what I do best."

Johnny Powers

"Long Blond Hair, Red Rose Lips" is Johnny Powers' signature song, and it has been covered by numerous rockabilly bands worldwide. He is highly revered for that classic rockabilly anthem, but he is also known for his one release on Sun Records, "With Your Love, With Your Kiss" b/w "Be Mine, All Mine." Powers was the last artist to record at the old studio on 706 Union before Sam Phillips moved his artists to Phillips International on 639 Madison. After recording for both Sun Records and Motown Records, Powers paved a successful career as a producer and music publisher. His singing career was revitalized in 1984 when he made his first trip to England. Since then, his popularity has not waned. Powers revealed, "I tour as much as I possibly can."[31]

John Leon Joseph Pavlik was born on May 25, 1938, in East Detroit, Michigan. Pavlik received his name Johnny Powers in 1955 when he recorded for the independent record label Fortune Records in Detroit: "I had recorded 'Your Love' and 'Honey, Let's Go (to a Rock and Roll Show).' [Co-owner] Devora Brown said I had to change my name. I said I never thought of that. I was eating a candy bar, and she said 'what are you eating?' I said a Powerhouse candy bar. She said 'your new recording name is Johnny Powers.'" Powers is the oldest of five children. His father was musically inclined: "My dad played banjo, and two of my uncles played accordions," another played guitar, while the other played trumpet. They had a polka band because they were of Polish descent and frequently played clubs and weddings.

At sixteen, Powers began singing, playing guitar, and songwriting: "Everybody said that I'd never be a singer. I drove everybody nuts. I couldn't sing, only trying to." He tuned into country singer Lonnie Barron, who had a radio program on WDOG in Marine City, Michigan: "I used to sit by the radio and try to play along and copy him on this old guitar I bought for $2.50 from a school mate, Tony Lawson."[32] Marvin Maynard, a guitar player originally from West Virginia, showed him a few chords. Around this time, Powers befriended Russ Williams, Jr., who played guitar in his brother's country band, Jimmy Williams and the Drifters. They played a regular gig at Bill's Barn in Utica, Michigan and had a radio program on WDOG every Saturday. Powers was soon added to the lineup on rhythm guitar. He also played on the band's recordings of "Rainbow Heart" b/w "Teardrops and Memories" and "Loveless Kisses" b/w "Dream on Little Heart." During Powers' year and a half stint with the group, he showcased his singing ability on songs such as Sonny James' "You're the Reason I'm in Love" and Webb Pierce's "Walkin' the Dog."

It was Williams who informed Powers about Elvis Presley: "Russ played me this record called 'Milkcow Blues Boogie,' and it just turned me on. I started following Elvis quite closely, and the more I listened to him, the more I got interested. I started putting that beat to the country songs I had been playing."[33] Carl Perkins' "Blue Suede Shoes" and "Honey Don't" also had a profound influence on the young singer.

In 1957, he heard Jack Scott for the first time, and he made the complete transition from singing country music to rockabilly: "Even though Jack Scott is a friend of mine, he influenced me because he had a hit record on ABC-Paramount called 'Baby, She's Gone.' I loved the song." Scott, along with Elvis Presley, Carl Perkins, and Lonnie Barron were cited as Powers' musical influences. Powers then paid $100 and recorded two songs for Fortune Records. The studio was very primitive with a dirt floor and a lamp stand used as anchorage for a microphone. His self penned "Honey, Let's Go (to a Rock and Roll Show)" and "Your Love" were released in August. Powers then began playing record hops with his band the Rockets, which included Russ Williams on guitar and Marvin Maynard on bass. By 1957, the Rockets would be renamed the Tom Cats, and Williams would be replaced by Stan Getz on guitar, who also played bass for Jack Scott. The Tom Cats honed their stage act by playing drive-ins: "At that time, everyone hung out at drive-in restaurants, and cars would cruise by slowly to see what was going on. We would just pull into the parking lot and start playing in the car. Next thing [you know,] the owner started building a stage for us."[34] Soon all the drive-ins had stages.

Next, Powers recorded for the Fox label, which produced his signature song "Long Blond Hair, Red Rose Lips" b/w "Rock Rock": "'Long Blond Hair' was really written as a B side. "Rock Rock" was originally the A side." It was popular locally and scored a #3 hit in Seattle, Washington. Due to the success of "Long Blond Hair," Powers opened a show for Jack Scott and Della Reese in Mount Clemens, Michigan. The audience screamed so loudly for Powers that he couldn't hear himself sing. Before vocalizing the second line of "Long Blond Hair," the fans jumped out of their seats and tugged at his hair and tore his clothes to shreds, including his white sports coat and purple pants: "They even took my shoelaces. The lights were in my eyes, and I didn't see anything at first, but when I turned around the band had split, and I hit the floor. I was told the show didn't go on cause they upset the whole theater."[35] Later that night, he and Frankie Lymon appeared at a record hop, hosted by Dick Drury of WBRB: "I looked a wreck."[36] Powers recalled, "Back then I never saw any money as far

Johnny Powers is the only artist ever to record for both Sun and Motown (courtesy Johnny Powers).

as being an artist. I was making more money playing a dance place called Bill's Barn in Utica on Saturday nights."

Powers returned to the studio in early 1958 to record "Mean Mistreater," "I'm Walkin,'" "Treat Me Right," "Be-Bop-A-Lula," "Someone's Gonna Hurt You," and "Oh So Far Away," at Basement Studios in Detroit. None of these songs were released at the time. Then he cut "Mama Rock," "Indeed I Do," and "Ooby Dooby Rock," which unfortunately has been lost, at Specialty Studios with Jack Scott's guitarist David Rowhillier. "Mama Rock" and "Indeed I Do" were leased out to Leedon Records in Australia, but released under the name Johnny "Scat" Brown. As Brown, Australia named Powers Artist of the Year. This recognition provided him with the opportunity to tour with the Everly Brothers and Buddy Holly. There was one stipulation though, that Powers would have to pay for his own trip, so he refused to go.

In 1959, six demos were cut at a recording studio in Utica, Michigan, including "Don't Go Away," "Waitin' For You," and Elvis Presley's "Trouble." While visiting relatives in Montgomery, Alabama, Powers' manager Tommy Moers played the demos for a disk jockey. Fans listening in liked the songs so much that Sam Phillips was contacted. Powers was on tour in Michigan at the time. Phillips called all over the area looking for him since he wanted Powers to be his next recording star. As soon as Powers arrived at Sun Studio, he was signed to a contract and immediately recorded his first sides, even though he was exhausted: "I'm pretty sure I was the last artist that recorded in the old studio." Jack Clement engineered the session, while the band included Charlie Rich on piano, Billy Lee Riley on bass, Martin Willis on saxophone, J.M. Van Eaton on drums, and Brad Suggs on lead guitar. There wasn't any rehearsal because it happened so fast. Powers was extremely nervous. "With Your Love, With Your Kiss" b/w "Be Mine, All Mine" was issued in September.

Powers returned to Michigan after the session, so it was difficult to promote the single properly. Even though he continued to send tapes of songs he had written, he never had another release on Sun. Powers continually received rejection letters from Scotty Moore, who worked for Sam Phillips at the time: "Johnny we're looking for some songs for you. This song you sent me just doesn't quite cut it. Keep trying. We want something a little stronger."

In 1960, a frustrated Powers concentrated his efforts toward Motown Records. He was the first white artist signed to the label, and he has been credited as being the only musician to ever record for both Sun and Motown. Unfortunately, Motown's way of recording wasn't something that Powers was used to, so he never had a release under his own name. He was a member of the Hornets along with Mike Valvano for a short time and appeared on the release "Give Me a Kiss" b/w "She's My Baby." Owner Barry Gordy wanted to shave their heads: "I didn't want to shave my head, so that's probably why that band never happened." Powers recalled, "'Barry Gordy used to tell me 'what do I have to do to get you started?' I said you're gonna have to let me go in there with my band, lay down the feel, and then you can recapture that with the Motown musicians. The biggest problem I had with Motown was that I wanted to bring my band in there, but the other part of it was they recorded the band tracks when I was not there. They would tell me for example to be there tomorrow at four o'clock for the recording session. Well when I would show up at four o'clock, they had already recorded the music the evening before and didn't have me there. It was a new style for me. I had to sing with the band tracks that were already cut, so the feel wasn't there. When I was with Motown [for five years], they constantly did that, which was kind of frustrating to me. It just didn't work."

For a short time, when he got married in 1961, Powers quit the music industry. He went to work for General Motors, spray painting truck bodies for the next three years. While still under contract with Motown, in 1965, he began concentrating on production: "I wasn't supposed to do that, but I did it anyway. I got involved with a recording studio with Stan Getz and Larry Lick, who owned the studio. Sound Incorporated offered studio time, pressing, and distribution. I brought my expertise in there, and we started having success. I started producing artists since I had had enough as far as an artist goes. I enjoyed being a producer."

Since the 1960s, Powers has had quite a bit of success with producing and music publishing. His current publishing company, Jet-Eye Music Inc., leases songs for use on CDs, which includes an association with England's Rollercoaster Records, in television shows, and movies. He owns the publishing for some of Big Al Downing's song catalog and the Rockin' Rebels' instrumental hit "Wild Weekend," which was featured in the Sci-fi movie *Mosquito*. Powers sang "Say It," which was also included in the movie. Thanks to Jet-Eye, Powers rejuvenated interest in both Link Wray and George Clinton: "I'm the guy that really launched Link Wray's career again in the States." "Long Blond Hair" showed up on the soundtrack to the Showtime movie *Reform School Girls*.

In 1984, Powers reemerged on the rockabilly scene with an appearance at a weekender in Birmingham, England: "They had been trying to get me there for about three or four years. Willie Jeffery from England finally convinced me to go. Ronnie Hawkins' manager really was the one that convinced me. Then I got the bug again. I should have done it when the Stray Cats came on the scene, but I didn't. I was having fun being a record producer and a music publisher. It was bringing me money, and I enjoyed working with new talent."

In 1997, he wrote a song "I Was There When It Happened," which was supposed to feature both Powers and his friend Carl Perkins sharing vocals: "Carl mentioned onstage, at a show we did together in Detroit, that everybody calls us rockabillies, but back then we called it rock and roll. I told Carl I say that every once in awhile onstage because it's true. We called it rock and roll; I never heard the term rockabilly until later on. I told Carl I'm going to write a song [about that.] He said 'sit down and write it, and we'll do it together.' I said that's a deal, but it took me awhile to write it. I was trying to write it and tour [at the same time.] I finished it, but he got sick, so then I had to rewrite it. I am proud of myself for writing that song. Carl never heard it." "I Was There When It Happened" was released on Powers' album of the same name in 2005.

Powers remains in high demand as an artist, but he wishes that promoters would allow him to bring his own band, which includes guitarist Chris Casello, formerly of the Starlight Drifters. Powers has had success with backing bands, including a gig in Japan in 2004: "It really blew me away. The band played every song I ever recorded note for note, and I thought I was pantomiming to my recorded band tracks. That never happened to me before." However, he feels he is not able to showcase his real showmanship with a band that just learned his songs a day prior to the show: "With my band, you'll see something you've never seen before. We put on one heck of a show."

Jack Earls

Jack Earls went to Sun Records after hearing Elvis Presley's recording of "That's All Right." Between 1955 and 1956, Earls recorded several songs, but Sam Phillips only released one single "Slow Down" b/w "A Fool for Lovin' You." By 1957, he called it quits to concentrate on raising his family: "I never thought the music would last, and nobody else did [either.] Maybe that's the reason I got out of it because I didn't think it was gonna do anything."[37] Today, his songs are quite popular, especially in Europe. Many bands have covered his Sun sides, most notably Brian Setzer, who recorded "Slow Down" for his 2005 release *Rockabilly Riot, Volume 1: A Tribute to Sun Records*. Earls remains in high demand for festivals, in fact, he has played the Hemsby Weekender in England more than any other rockabilly legend, a record breaking six times. 1999's Charly Records CD *Hey Slim, Let's Bop*, which includes all of Earls' recorded material for Sun, is only slightly less essential listening that Elvis Presley's Sun recordings.[38]

Jack Earls was born on August 23, 1932, in Woodbury, Tennessee. He was the youngest of four children. His two brothers and one sister all sang. His mother sang a lot of hymns: "She and her brothers sang in church all the time. I sang in the church choir." Earls remembered, "My mother taught me a lot of old songs, [including] 'Mother the Queen of My Heart.' At four years old, I sang on my mama's knee. I'd also get under the porch and sing because I was bashful. I used to sing 'Mule Skinner Blues.' People would come and listen to me." Dave Macon, who played banjo on the *Grand Ole Opry*, was one of those listeners. Earls' family had a battery powered radio, and he tuned into the *Grand Ole Opry* on Saturday nights. One of his favorite singers was Hank Williams: "I think he had a little rockabilly in him." Earls disclosed, "I could sing like anybody, including Ernest Tubb or Hank Williams, but my mother always told me 'now you sing like yourself. Don't be singin' like other people, you use your own voice.' I always loved to sing. She was a real good singer. I never saw my dad. He was wounded in the Army in World War I and was in the service when I was born. That was kind of hard on me. I used to have to fight [other kids] a lot on the count of that. My oldest brother, Richard, was like my dad." Earls cited his mother as his biggest musical influence, "if it hadn't been for my mother, I'd probably never be a singer." Ernest Tubb, Hank Williams, Marty Robbins, Grandpa Jones, Little Jimmy Dickens, and Roy Acuff also influenced his style.

At ten years old, Earls found his first guitar in an abandoned barn: "It took me almost all day to get the guitar. I had a hard time getting it out [because] it was in a corn crib. I wanted that guitar, and I got it. Some of the strings were missing, and the rest were out of tune, but I was walking up the highway, trying to make people think I could play the guitar. I tried to learn to play it. I couldn't, so I tore it all to pieces." Also during this time, Earls ran away from home and joined the circus for a short span: "They had the Jungle Man in a hole, and I was the Jungle Boy. I had fifty-seven baby alligators and one big artificial [one.] I was real dark complexioned back then, and I didn't wear any shoes. People would come by and look at me then they'd go look at the Jungle Man. My brothers told me not to leave with that circus. When the circus left, the Jungle Man and I were on that truck. We hitchhiked to my uncle's house in Chattanooga, [Tennessee.] My uncle sent me home." Matt Strickland and Paul "Smokey Links" Cook from the Hi-Q's, a rockabilly band from Detroit, Michigan, wrote about Earls in their song "Jungle Boy Jack," which was included on their 2005 release, *Hop and Bop*.

Jack Earls portrayed the Jungle Boy in a local circus before his recording career (courtesy Jack Earls).

In 1945, Earls and

his brother worked on a farm, and the owners' sons showed them how to play guitar: "Herb and I played rhythm guitar, and they played banjo and fiddle. We worked the farm from sun up to sun down and played music all night." They played mostly bluegrass music and Bill Monroe's songs. Four years later, Earls moved to Memphis and began working at Schnider's Bakery along with his oldest brother, where he met his future wife, Dorothy: "She'd come up there for milk and bread, wearing her short shorts." A year later, they eloped. She was fourteen, and he was seventeen. They started their family shortly after, which included six children. Twins Lisa and Lenny are both singers. Lenny has a blues band, the Union Avenue Band, which pays homage to his dad's legendary recordings. Incidentally, the Earls have enjoyed fifty-nine years of marital bliss.

In 1954, Earls teamed up with Bill Black's brother, Johnny: "I'd be sittin' out on my porch playing the guitar or singing. Johnny lived right close to me, on the next street. We got a little band together." In the summer of 1955, they paid ten dollars to record a demo at Sun Studio: "Elvis had just started recording there. In fact, Johnny Black and I used to play with Elvis at the Eagles' Nest [in Memphis.] We never thought we'd get on Sun. We just thought we'd make a demo, and we'd put it on the jukebox. I brought about five or six guitarists the first time, along with Johnny Black on bass and another guy who played the mandolin. Well, we did the demo of 'A Fool for Lovin' You,' and Sam told me 'I really like your voice, but you know we gotta get you a band. When you get that band, you come back to see me.'" The next time, Earls went back solo: "He wanted me to come back and sing by myself. I did, and he said I had a lot of tremolo to my voice."

Earls then added Warren Gregory on lead guitar and Danny Wahlquist on drums. The new lineup returned to Sun, and this time they recorded "Hey Jim" and "A Fool for Lovin' You." These songs were scheduled as his first release, but that soon changed when the next day Earls wrote "Slow Down" in his '54 Buick Roadmaster: "We went over to Sun and cut that one time [with Sam Phillips as engineer.] Sam came out [of the booth] jumping up and down. He loved 'Slow Down.' He had named our band [the Jimbos] after 'Hey Jim.' Sam told me 'I'd rather have one guy like you that writes his own songs than ten that don't because material is very hard to find.'" In fact, Earls wrote all of his own songs, although never writing them down on paper. In May 1956, Sun issued Earls' only release, "Slow Down" b/w "A Fool for Lovin' You." Warren Smith's "Rock 'n' Roll Ruby" b/w "I'd Rather Be Safe Than Sorry" was issued around the same time. Earls took Smith's single along with his own to local disk jockeys, such as Bob Neal and Dewey Phillips, in the hopes that they would give the records a spin. Smith and Earls drove around in high style, traveling the streets of Memphis in Smith's 1956 black Cadillac. Earls' single did extremely well both locally and regionally. "Slow Down" elicited interest from DJs as far away as Texas, who played the record on air.[39] Earls received royalties for fifty thousand copies; although he believes that it sold quite a bit more than that.

Between 1955 and 1956, the Jimbos recorded at least four sessions, which produced the unreleased tracks "They Can't Keep Me from You," "When I Dream," "If You Don't Mind," "Let's Bop," "Sign on the Dotted Line," "My Gal Mary Ann," "Crawdad Hole," "Hey Jim," and "Take Me to That Place." Even when he wasn't recording, Earls would hang out at the studio. He was present when Elvis Presley couldn't remember the lyrics to Little Junior Parker's "Mystery Train": "I rode home real quick on my Harley and got the record."

Earls was even featured as one of the headliners along with Eddie Bond, Warren Smith, Johnny Cash, Roy Orbison, and Carl Perkins on a Sun package show booked by Bob Neal and Stars Incorporated. Earls explained, "He wouldn't let my whole band come, just me and Johnny." He sang three songs: "Crawdad Hole," "A Fool for Lovin' You," and "Slow Down." He also performed on the *Louisiana Hayride* as well as the *Grand Ole Opry* when it came to Memphis where he sang "A Fool for Lovin' You" and "Crawdad Hole": "We got paid $75. That was union scale back then."

Also in 1956, the band began a six year stint at the Palms Club in Memphis: "Jack Clement used to come out there trying to get us to come back and record more. We just wouldn't do it." In January 1957, his contract at Sun expired. Soon after, "A guy came down from Cincinnati [from King Records] for an audition, but my guitar player Warren Gregory didn't show up. I could have gotten on Meteor Records too." Earls played weekends at the Palms, while during the week he held a day job as a delivery man for Colonial Bakery: "I wanted to take care of my family. I wasn't worried about my career." While he was delivering bread to Arkansas, he befriended B.B. King. They used to hang out at the Home of the Blues record shop on Beale Street in Memphis. Elvis Presley's bass player, Bill Black, sometimes came and sat in with the band at the Palms. However, since his brother Johnny also played bass, he played lead guitar. A blind saxophone/ piano player rounded out the band: "We had a heck of a band."

After their deal with the Palms ran out, Earls opened his own club, the Wagon Wheel, in Millington, Tennessee. Since it was located in the county, he kept it open until daylight. Elvis Presley's musicians Scotty Moore and Bill Black, Charlie Feathers, Ronnie Hawkins, and Gene Simmons [of "Haunted House" fame] all made guest appearances. Earls stated, "Charlie and I were like brothers. He'd ride on the back of my Harley. One time we were at the Cotton Club in West Memphis, [Arkansas.] As we were leaving, I was spinnin' the wheels getting away from the bouncers, spewing rocks on them."

In 1967, Earls moved his family to Detroit, Michigan. He went to work for American Motors as a truck driver. Throughout the 1970s, he continued to play weekend bookings and record. Olympic Records issued "She Sure Can Rock Me" b/w "Crawdad Hole" and "Flip, Flop, and Fly" b/w "Rock Bop." At this time, he began receiving fan letters from Europe. In the 1980s, Earls was contacted by Stomper Time Records' owner Dave Travis to perform overseas. However, it wasn't until 1996 that Travis finally convinced him to make the trip: "I didn't even think about going to Europe until then. I just didn't want to fly." Earls played Hemsby with an English band, the Crawdads, as backing: "I really couldn't believe what was going on. I thought Elvis Presley would come alive because they treated me like that." In 1998, Enviken Records in Sweden released *Game of Love*, which included songs "Game of Love" and "Coming Back Home" that Earls wrote in the 1950s but never recorded. Also included was a song about his good friend and favorite singer Carl Perkins: "I wrote 'Tribute to Carl Perkins' down in the basement right after Carl died." He always features a medley of Perkins' songs as well as Charlie Feathers' "Wedding Gown of White" and "Tongue Tied Jill," Warren Smith's "Rock 'n' Roll Ruby," and Eddie Bond's "Rockin' Daddy" in his set list. Earls added, "The fans overseas know all my songs, and I better do the words right."

Two

Louisiana Hayride Stars

Wanda Jackson

In the mid-1950s when rockabilly was hitting its stride, the critics deemed it inappropriate. It was considered taboo for a male to sing those songs, laden with so-called teenage rebellion and sexual innuendo, let alone a female. An example by a male artist would be "Oh Baby Babe" by the Rock and Roll Trio. There were very few females who took the chance to sing rockabilly back then, but one female's songs in particular shook up the world. That gal was Wanda Jackson, and she would become known as the Queen of Rockabilly.

Jackson was born on October 20, 1937, in Maud, Oklahoma. She was an only child. Her father was in a dance band before he settled down to marry, but the Depression shattered his dream of becoming famous. Her mother worked for the government and stayed home. She would later become Jackson's seamstress.

Jackson began singing at the tender age of six. By fourteen, she was singing professionally with her own radio show. Her musical influences included Jimmie Rodgers, Hank Williams, and Hank Thompson, her mentor: "I learned so much from him."[1] Thompson heard her radio show and invited her to sing with his band. He also helped Jackson to get her first recording contract with Decca Records in 1954. Her first offering was with Thompson's singer, Billy Gray. It was called "You Can't Have My Love" and rose to the top five on the country charts. "You Can't Have My Love" was a song in which Jackson sang, and Gray answered her with spoken lines.

Her father taught her how to play the guitar. When she graduated from high school in 1955, it was decided that her father would be her manager and go on the road with her: "I wanted my reputation to stay intact; that was very important in those days. I think it still is."

One of the first tours she participated in involved a young singer who was dubbed "The Hillbilly Cat." She didn't know who Elvis Presley was at the time because they weren't playing his records in Oklahoma City. However, her cousins in West Texas had heard all about him, and they were thrilled to learn that she would be working with him.

Jackson's first impression of Presley was that he was "tall, dark, and handsome." As the tour progressed, they spent more time together, and a romance blossomed: "He gave me his ring, and I wore it around my neck for a year or so. Of course, I lived in Oklahoma City, and he lived in Memphis, so when we weren't on tour we couldn't actually date."

Wanda Jackson looking lovely onstage in 1956 (courtesy Wanda Jackson).

"The first time I worked with Elvis was in 1955, I worked quite a few long tours with him there within a couple of years, and he was the one that encouraged me to at least try rockabilly. We didn't have a name for it then, but he said this style of music that I'm doing and by then Carl [Perkins] and Jerry Lee [Lewis]. I remember telling him, 'Well, I don't think that I can because I'm really just a country singer.' He said, 'Yeah, but you have the voice, and you like the music, and you got a feel for it.' He even took me to his home in Memphis. We went in his bedroom, and we played records, and he picked up a guitar and sang. He really helped me a lot."

She caught on fast and soon realized what all the fuss was about: "I began to realize pretty shortly the rhythm that this guy had. I had never seen anything like that, girls going crazy over a singer. That was a shock and was very interesting. He was just such a likable guy. He loved life and laughed all the time."

Prior to Presley's advice, Jackson was strictly a country singer, but she saw firsthand the impression he and others were making on the youth, and soon she jumped on the bandwagon too. In 1956, she signed with Capitol Records. Her first release was "I Gotta Know," which combined both her singing styles of rockabilly and country into one song. There weren't any rockabilly songs written for women, so she started writing her own, with a few exceptions including Betty Hutton's "Hot Dog, That Made Him Mad" and Annisteen Allen's "Fujiyama Mama."

Jackson went on to write "Mean Mean Man, whose inspiration came from her father; he told her to write a song about a guy who treats you bad, "Cool Love," which was written on her way home from school one day with Vicki Countryman: "I think it's one of my better rock and roll songs." The inspiration for "Rock Your Baby" came from her passion for dancing: "I love to dance. Anytime, I could find a guy who could dance, I would date him." "You Bug Me Bad" was a new catch phrase that she had heard about guys and their temperamental feelings.

Her biggest hit in the United States was "Let's Have a Party," which was originally recorded by Presley and featured in his movie, *Loving You*. However, it was The Collins Kids' version that Jackson was most familiar with. When she heard it, she commented: "I'd like to sing that song. I learned it from their record." She would open all her shows with that song, and the fans really dug it. She originally recorded it for her first Capitol album, *Wanda Jackson*, in 1958, but it wasn't released until 1960 as a single. It hit number thirty-seven on the Billboard charts, and in 1989 it was featured in the Robin Williams' blockbuster movie *Dead Poets Society*.

Capitol maintained a hectic recording schedule with three albums and four singles released a year. Some of these singles that became signature tunes were "Funnel of Love," "Riot in Cell Block #9," and "I Gotta Know." Her session musicians included Joe Maphis, Buck Owens, Ralph Mooney, and Merrill

Moore. Even though it has been noted in various places, Jackson never recorded with Gene Vincent's group, The Blue Caps: "I guess it sounded like them on one of my records, and they wrote it down as such."

By 1958, she was introduced to Bobby Poe and The Poe Kats. Before long, The Poe Kats' Vernon Sandusky and Big Al Downing became regular members of Jackson's touring band. Downing had a rough time of it since he was a black man. Clubs wouldn't allow him to use the restrooms; he couldn't eat in the restaurants, and he couldn't check into the hotels. On one particular occasion, a club manager approached the band and said, "Hold everything, no blacks are allowed in this club, so the piano player will have to go." Downing got up to leave, but Jackson stopped him, and said to the owner: "He's a member of my band, and if he goes, we'll all go then, to get you off the hook." He knew an audience was waiting, so he let Downing play with the band. Jackson felt awful about the injustices that Downing had to deal with on an almost daily basis: "Al was such a charismatic person." She asked him once how he could stand the treatment; and his reply was "It's just the music."

Besides problems with the venues, she struggled to get airplay. Capitol Records tried to ensure airplay by infusing a country song with a rockabilly one on each single that was released, but to no avail. She still received little or no airplay. The only way she received any kind of recognition for her music was through live appearances, so she soon realized that television was the best venue for her to pursue. She made numerous appearances on *Ranch Party*, where she became friends with fellow rockabilly Lorrie Collins: "Lorrie was one of my favorite people. I just really loved her. I always thought she was very, very good." Jackson also made appearances on the *Ozark Jubilee*.

Jackson's voice and style fit the realm of rockabilly perfectly, but her fashion sense was still too country: "I got tired of wearing cowboy boots and hats. I wanted to add a little glamour and sex appeal [to my wardrobe]." She began designing her own dresses. Her mother was a professional seamstress, so she made them for her: "They were the perfect fit; they fit me like a glove." Her dresses included a lot of sequins and fringe. Rose Maddox influenced both her musical and fashion senses: "She was feisty and dressed in rhinestones and flashy clothes. I was quite young, but I remember seeing her and thinking that's what I want to do. I want to be a singer like her."[2]

It seemed her sense of style got her into as much trouble as the songs she was singing. When she appeared on the *Grand Ole Opry* in 1956, she received quite a bit of flack: "We made a special dress [for the *Opry*]. It was white with red silk fringe around the skirt and a sweetheart neck with rhinestone spaghetti straps. Ernest Tubb told me that I was on next. I told him, 'Yes, I know, I'm ready.' I had my guitar on. He said, 'Well, you can't go on the stage of the *Grand Ole Opry* like that.' I said, 'What do you mean?' He said, 'You can't show your bare shoulders and arms.' I told him, 'Well, this is all I brought.' His reply was 'Get a jacket or something and cover it up, or I can't call you on.' She put on her white leather fringe jacket, sang her song, and told her daddy 'Let's get out of here. I'm never doing this again.' I was so upset. They didn't tell me the rules, had they, then I would have dressed accordingly." Presley had a bad experience on the *Opry* as well, but both were successful on the more accepting *Louisiana Hayride*.

Jackson revealed that she was a big hit in Japan, spending seven weeks over there on tour in 1959, and one of her last rockabilly efforts, "Fujiyama Mama," produced a number one song for six months. In 2005, it was included in the Johnny Cash biopic, *Walk the Line*.

In 1961, Jackson hit the top ten in the country charts with her self-penned "Right or Wrong," which she originally wrote for Brenda Lee. That same year, she had a country hit with "In the Middle of a Heartache." Both are torch songs. 1965 brought her even more success when her German recording of "Santa Domingo" rose to the top of the charts in six different German speaking countries.

In the late '60s, she gave up singing rockabilly and concentrated primarily on country music and playing various venues in Vegas. In 1971, she and her manager/husband, Wendell became devout born-again Christians. They had a ministry for ten years: "It was very important to us and rewarding in that time of our life."

She returned to rockabilly in 1985, and her first venture was to record a new album and tour in Scandinavia: "There were all those fans. We had sold-out crowds and standing room only everywhere. I was really shocked. It's been very nice to have the revival of rockabilly music."[3] A few years later, she ran into Rosie Flores when they did a rockabilly special together. Flores helped to rejuvenate Jackson's career here in America: "Rosie has been very important to me." In 1996, Flores wanted Jackson to sing a few songs with her on her upcoming CD, *Rockabilly Filly*. She recorded part of it out in Hollywood, and then brought it to Jackson's house where they laid down the vocals: "I told Rosie I would be happy to help her publicize her album any way I could." She got the word out and soon they had more gigs than they could handle. They had to hire a special booking agency to deal with all the gigs that were being offered to them. Flores and Jackson ended up doing a five week tour across America.

Jackson managed to balance a musical career with a marriage and two children, a boy and a girl. When she did have a spare moment, she took up oil painting. She really got involved in it and painted several canvases. However, the bookings became too frequent, and she had to give it up because it proved too difficult to carry the necessary materials on tour with her.

Whether it is in the country, rockabilly, or gospel vein, Jackson loves performing them all. She tours year round: "Rockabilly festivals are so much fun. I just really enjoy them, makes me feel like a teenager again. It's been terrific. I'm having the time of my life."

Some of her favorite artists include Martí Brom and The Barnshakers,

Tanya Tucker, Ray Charles, Big Sandy, Rosie Flores, and Ronnie Dawson. She still listens to Presley, Perkins, and Lewis since they were her friends.

She is especially close to Brom and Flores: "I think Martí and Rosie are the best of the newer artists." Brom and Jackson are "soul buddies," and every year in Brom's hometown of Austin, Texas, they throw Jackson a birthday bash. Also, annually in Jackson's hometown of Maud, Oklahoma, they hold a parade and celebration in honor of Wanda Jackson day. The former Main Street in town has been named after her. Her accolades don't end there since she has earned two Grammy nominations for best performance by a female singer as well as induction into the Oklahoma Country Music Hall of Fame, the Rockabilly Hall of Fame, and the Gospel Music Hall of Fame. Elvis Costello's lobbying finally paid off when Jackson was inducted into the Rock and Roll Hall of Fame in April 2009.

Jackson's fans mean a lot to her, and it amazes her how much they know about her music. "Fans nowadays are very knowledgeable. I am very impressed that they know this body of work so well." "Let's Have a Party," "Mean Mean Man," and "Fujiyama Mama" are the most popular. Fans were treated to two critically acclaimed albums in recent years: 2003's CMH Records' release *Heart Trouble* and her tribute to Elvis, 2006's Cleopatra Records' release *I Remember Elvis*.

Jackson is the consummate rockabilly artist, and Sam Phillips said it best when he presented her with a Sun Records Award: "She never recorded for Sun, but she should have."

Bob Luman

The *Louisiana Hayride*, which held thirty-eight hundred people at the Municipal Auditorium in Shreveport, Louisiana, was a breeding ground for talent between 1947 and 1959. Hank Williams, Slim Whitman, Webb Pierce, Faron Young, Elvis Presley, Johnny Cash, Bob Luman, and countless others started their careers on the *Hayride*. Each artist on the show performed at least two songs on the weekly Saturday night program from eight to eleven. Engineer Bob Sullivan stood just behind the curtain, in a plywood booth with a glass window, about ten feet away from the announcer and used a RCA broadcast amplifier and four microphones to record the live show. The announcer had a microphone and the other three were added to the piano, the electric guitar, and the bass. The drums were played loud enough to leak into the other microphones. There weren't any stage monitors since none of the bands played loud enough to need them. Two microphones were attached to the ceiling in the middle of the auditorium to pick up applause and audience reaction. Luman was a hit on the *Hayride*, and Sullivan remembered "When Elvis was on the show, he would turn his shirt collar or coat collar up round his neck. After he got some reaction, artists began to realize wait a minute this kid's drawing the crowds in here, then everybody on the show began to turn their coat collar up including Bob Luman. Bob always said he went to see Elvis and decided right then that's what he wanted to be. I hated when he left the *Hayride*."[4] Luman never found much success with rockabilly music and is most well known for his pop hit "Let's Think About Living" and his country song "Lonely Women Make Good Lovers."

Robert Glynn Luman was born on April 15, 1937, in Nacogdoches, Texas. He grew up dirt poor, and he couldn't concentrate in school because he was so full of energy. At thirteen years of age, he received his first guitar. His father, who played fiddle, guitar, and harmonica in amateur bands, showed him the basic chords. In high school, Luman played baseball and even tried out for the Pittsburgh Pirates. His musical dreams came to fruition when he formed his first band, a hillbilly ensemble, and imitated the singers he heard on the radio, such as Webb Pierce and Lefty Frizzell. He also listened to rhythm and blues and blues on WLAC out of Nashville. In August 1955, after seeing Elvis Presley play nine one-nighters in a row in the Kilgore, Texas, area, he changed his style from country to rockabilly. He then won a Future Farmers of America talent contest in Houston, which led to a guest spot on the *Louisiana Hayride*.

A short time later, Luman recorded seven demos with fellow Texas rockabilly Mac Curtis' band. The songs included "Hello Baby," "In the Deep Dark Jungle," "Let Her Go," "Stranger Than Fiction," "That's Alright," "Let It Happen," and "You're the Cause of It All." Also that year, Luman worked with a group from Weatherford, Texas, that he called the Shadows. Bassist James Kirkland explained, "They all had families and didn't want to tour. They decided to leave Bob, but he wanted to keep the name. Somebody notified Bob that he couldn't use the name because another band already had a copyright on it. He would have to get their permission, but he just quit using it instead of going to all that trouble. Butch White, the drummer, had played with Bob and the Shadows, and he hadn't quit when the other guys did, so the drum head kept the name painted on it. I know we are referred to as the Shadows because of *Carnival Rock*, but we were never really known as that."[5]

In the summer of 1956, eighteen year old Luman appeared as a member of the doo wop quartet, the Four Diamonds, on the *Hayride*. He went solo since the *Hayride* was strictly interested in hiring Luman. *Hayride* emcee Horace Logan explained, "I had enough sense to know that nobody could really replace Elvis, but what we needed was a fresh young talent with a cute enough face and a strong enough voice to take the girls' minds off of Elvis for awhile."[6] Kirkland recalled, "When Elvis [Presley] left, Bob came in. He kind of took up where Elvis left off. He was doing the same stuff that Elvis was doing [rockabilly and rock and roll]. He would sing 'Maybellene,' 'Mystery Train,' 'Blue Moon of Kentucky,' but we did them differently. Bob did a lot of Elvis' and Carl Perkins' stuff." Luman first teamed up with guitarist James Burton. Burton

Bob Luman and the Shadows rehearsing in James Kirkland's cousin Bennie Sturman's living room in September 1957. From left: Kirkland, Luman, James Burton, and Butch White (courtesy James Kirkland).

remembered, "I was part of the *Hayride* staff band, and Horace Logan called me to ask whether I was interested in meeting Bob and doing some playing with him. We put this little rockabilly thing together with me, Bob, and James Kirkland."[7] Kirkland was working with David Houston and guitarist Sonny Jones on the *Hayride* when he was recruited to play in Luman's band. Kirkland explained, "Horace Logan came to me and asked if I'd like to go out on the road and work three days with Bob. That's what they hired me for. We were just a group that clicked."

The trio only played one club date, at Bear's Paradise in Gladewater, Texas. Luman performed every Saturday night on the KWKH broadcasted show, the *Louisiana Hayride*. Kirkland and Burton were already house band members and received $12.65 for salary, while Luman earned a few dollars more since he was the star. In 1957, drummer Butch White rejoined Luman's band on the *Hayride*.

Money was tight, so Luman and Kirkland roomed together. Kirkland recalled, "We could eat Vienna sausages and crackers, and we could make it. We had a pawn shop half a block from where Bob and I stayed. My bass stayed in that pawn shop part of the time. I got to be friends with those guys. If we got a job, and I didn't have the bass I'd go down and say lookee here I got a problem I got a job to make some money, but I gotta have that bass. They'd loan me my bass; we'd go play, come back, and I'd go in there to pay them. On Bob's Lincoln, I had to build a rack on top. I took a 4x8 sheet of one inch thick outdoor plywood, and I put racks on the bottom of it, and it had suction cups that stuck to the top of the car. I built sides on it where we could put a canvas tarp on it to keep it dry." Their suitcases, Kirkland's bass, White's set of drums, Burton's amplifier, and Luman's guitar were all kept up there. Maintenance on the car was also a struggle. Kirkland said, "We didn't have the money to put a muffler on, so we drove without one. You could hear us coming for three miles."

Luman was well received at the *Hayride* because his stage act was wild and exciting. Kirkland revealed, "Bob had a lot of talent. He was a good entertainer; it was all excitement. When he hit the stage, he didn't just stand there and sing. He did a lot of moving around, although no dance steps like Elvis. He interacted with us musicians. He was exciting to watch because he was so energetic and never stopped. He enjoyed himself, which is what you're supposed to do."[8] Sullivan remembered, "Bob was a happy go lucky guy but hyper. Elvis would let down when he wasn't onstage. You could catch Elvis at a time when he was just worn out or tired. I never saw Bob Luman that way. He was always pickin' at ya or saying something funny. Bob had a personality about him that everybody liked."

The girls went crazy over Luman just like they had for Presley. Logan conveyed, "He was handsome, muscular, athletic, and very personable, what I think girls nowadays might call a real hunk."[9] Kirkland added, "His personality and stage presence were so alive. When Bob walked into a restaurant, people with their backs to the door would turn around and look. Elvis and Bob had the same magnetic personality. Bob was a nice looking young man, and the girls liked him pretty good. When he'd leave the *Hayride* and walk out that stage door, he'd have his shirt torn right off."

Also in 1956, Luman recorded with Kirkland and Burton at KWKH, which was located on the second floor of the Commercial National Bank building in downtown Shreveport. Its actual studio was 35 × 40 square feet with a high ceiling, according to engineer Bob Sullivan, "conducive to good sound." Sullivan added, "I didn't have any echo or equalization." During recording, he took out part of the tape and fed it back into the recorder to create slap back. For equipment, all he had was two turntables, a Magnacord tape recorder, and five microphones. The session occurred between one and five in the morning and produced "Red Cadillac and Black Mustache" and "Blue Days, Black Nights." Sullivan recalled, "Bob was always easy to work with. He projected well. A lot of singers the higher the note the louder they get, but Bob was the type of guy that could sing high or low, and you didn't have to worry about him shouting and breaking the needle on the meter. He just had great control of his voice." The 45 rpm was used as a demo and sent to Lew Chudd at Imperial. Kirkland noted, "Bob Sullivan can get more sound with less equipment than anybody I have ever seen. I'm pretty sure Horace probably sent those to Lew Chudd. Lew liked what he heard and signed Bob to a contract." "Red Cadillac and Black Mustache" was rerecorded prior to its release on Imperial.

In February and March of 1957, Luman with Kirkland, White, and Burton in tow made their first recordings for Imperial Records at Sellers Company in Dallas, Texas. The songs "All Night Long," "Amarillo Blues," "Blue Days, Black Nights," "Red Cadillac and Black Mustache," and "Wild Eyed Woman" were cut at this time.

Prior to their trip to California to film the B movie *Carnival Rock*, which also starred David Houston and The Platters, the quartet performed on a *Louisiana Hayride* package show with five or six other acts in Corpus Christi, Texas, on May 31, 1957. After film production, the band returned to Shreveport to honor Luman's contract with the *Hayride*. However, drummer White went to work with Al and Sonny Jones.

In September, Logan decided to quit the *Hayride* and move his family to California to pursue his interests in the entertainment business. He figured he could break into the movies. His client Luman also made the move. Kirkland disclosed, "I tried to get Bob not to go to California. I talked to him, and I told him Bob you're just now getting started real well, and you're getting to be real popular on the *Hayride*. No one knows you in California. I think you're making a mistake by going right now. If it was me, I'd give it another six months. Of course, he listened to Horace, and we went to California."

Prior to the day they left for California; they played a show with Jerry Lee Lewis at Harvey Hall in Tyler, Texas. Kirkland recalled, "Bob opened the show, and Jerry Lee closed it. Jerry Lee was wild back then. He could annihilate a piano. [However] any time you ever saw Bob onstage I don't care who was on the show with him, I can promise you one thing before the show was over, Bob stole the show. All the other artists on the show came out and watched him from the wings."

The only money they had for their trip to California was the $250 pay from the Tyler, Texas, show. Kirkland acknowledged, "That would have been plenty of money, but the brake booster went out on that 1954 cream and green Lincoln of Bob's. I drove all the way from Sweetwater, Texas, to El Paso, Texas, with no brakes. The next morning when the Ford and Lincoln place opened up in El Paso, we were sitting in the door. They fixed the brakes, but that took most of our money. We then ran out of gas in front of the Knickerbocker Hotel in

Hollywood. We stayed there when we did the movie, so Earl Watson, the doorman, remembered us and let us double park in front until we could call Horace. We called him, and he said 'where you all at?' We said we're at the Knickerbocker hotel. We told him we couldn't come over. He said 'why,' and we said we're out of gas. He said 'go get ya some gas,' and we said we're out of money. Horace came and got us five gallons of gas. We followed him then to Santa Monica. We talked to the elderly couple that managed the apartment complex and explained our situation. We told them we're just moving from Texas out here, and we record for Imperial Records, and we're going to go in and get an advance from Lew Chudd with Imperial. They let us move into an apartment with no money. The next day we met with Lew, and he gave us an advance on record sales. We then went back and paid the people for our apartment rent. We all roomed together."

Luman made several appearances on *Town Hall Party*, a weekly television show that aired out of Compton, California. The cast, especially Joe and Rose Lee Maphis and Tex Ritter, really helped the boys out when they first arrived. Kirkland confirmed, "They took to us and helped us so much. They kind of took us under their wing. We'd have starved to death if it hadn't been for them. We owe a big thanks to them." To make extra money, Kirkland rehearsed artists for record label owner Fabor Robinson, and he along with Burton did session work, including Bobby Lee Trammell's single "Shirley Lee" b/w "I Sure Do Love You Baby."

In October at their second Imperial session, Ricky Nelson overheard the trio rehearsing "Red Hot," and "decided almost immediately that the raw energy conveyed by Burton and Kirkland was precisely what he had in mind in his quest to be a Sun sounding recording artist."[10] Nelson was truly captivated by Burton's chicken picking technique and Kirkland's triple slap bass playing: "While on the *Hayride* with Bob, I had cut the bridge down [on my lavender bass], lowered the bridge and the strings to where they were closer to the neck. That was one way that I changed my sound, and I got a better click out of the slap than everybody else was doing. I was getting the click without getting the real loud boom."

Kirkland wasn't approached right away, but Burton had already spoken to Nelson's father, Ozzie about a contract. Kirkland commented, "Unbeknownst to me and Bob, Burton had already talked to Rick and Ozzie. When we went home for Christmas, we had a tour to work going back, leaving on the 26th of December. We wound up the tour New Year's Eve in Denver with Ray Price, Sonny James, Buddy Knox and Jimmy Bowen and the Rhythm Orchids. As we got into the city limits of Shreveport, Burton told Bob he was quitting and wasn't going back out with him." With more dates to play, Luman had to find a replacement quickly. Fred Carter, who worked on the *Hayride*, filled in on guitar. Kirkland remembered, "He could play the 'Suzie Q' lick, and he could do the string stretching just like Burton. Fred fit in real good." However, soon

Carter decided he wanted to sing. He cut a record and then quit Luman. Kirkland added, "By that time, Burton had already gone to work and signed a contract with Rick. Then in January 1958 we went back out to California [since Horace was Bob's manager, and he still lived out there]. Ozzie called and asked me to come in and talk to him." With the offer of a contract, Kirkland didn't know what to do, so he called his stepfather for advice: "I don't know what to do. I've been offered a contract with Rick Nelson, and I get a pretty good amount of money whether I work or not. My step dad told me, 'let me tell you something you don't figure out what's best for Bob, and you don't figure out what's best for Rick, you sit down and you figure out what's best for you, and you do it.' I had played for nothing and starved so long that this sounded like the world to me. We weren't making any money playing with Bob that amounted to anything, so that's why we quit. I had even taken out of my pocket to help Bob pay his expenses. Bob understood and actually expected it. He said that he didn't blame me. That was one of the hardest things I had to do in my life because I thought a lot of Bob. Bob ended up hiring Joe Osborn to play bass, and Roy Buchanan to play guitar. Roy was one of the finest guitar players ever. He could play anything." Surprisingly, according to Kirkland, "Rick and Bob were friends. There were never any hard feelings; [in fact] they got along great."

With a new band in tow, Luman ended his relationship with Imperial in March 1958 after only three releases: "Red Cadillac and Black Mustache" b/w "All Night Long," "Red Hot" b/w "Whenever You're Ready," and "Make Up Your Mind Baby" b/w "Your Love." Incidentally, according to Kirkland, "Disk jockeys wouldn't play 'Red Hot;' they said it was suggestive." In May 1958, Luman signed with Capitol Records. Unfortunately, only two singles were issued: "Try Me" b/w "I Know My Baby Cares" and "Svengali" b/w "Precious." Capitol requested that Luman change his name, instead of obliging, a year later, he joined forces with Warner Bros.

In the summer of 1960, Burton and Kirkland quit working with Nelson and returned to work for Luman. They were scheduled to play the Showboat Hotel in Las Vegas. As part of his show, Luman impersonated other legendary stars, including Johnny Cash, Tex Ritter, Elvis Presley, and actor Walter Brennan: "Luman toured regularly and was popular in Vegas, where his ability at impressions came in handy."[11] Before the engagement was finished, Burton retreated back to the security of Nelson's band.

The United States Army then drafted Luman, at the same time his single "Let's Think About Living" was beginning to chart, so he didn't have a proper opportunity to promote it. Although, it did reach #7 on the pop charts. In 1961, he was briefly discharged, but just as his newest single "The Great Snowman" was beginning to show signs of life, he was drafted again. During this time, *Billboard* voted him Most Promising Male Artist. Thankfully a year later, he was officially discharged from the Army. In 1964, he got married to Barbara Tisman. By 1965, he was a member of the *Grand Ole Opry*. A year later, his only child, a daughter named Melissa was born. Throughout the 1960s and 1970s, he was constantly on the road. He also continued to play show dates in Las Vegas, where he included both country and rockabilly into his sets. In 1968, he signed with Epic Records where he had some of his biggest country successes: "When You Say Love" peaked at #6, "Lonely Women Make Good Lovers" was a #4 hit, and "Still Loving You" charted at #7.

Twelve days after a *Grand Ole Opry* appearance, Luman died of pneumonia and liver failure on December 27, 1978, in Nashville, Tennessee. He has been inducted into both the Rockabilly Hall of Fame and the Texas Country Music Hall of Fame. Even though he had the most success with country music, his true passion laid in rockabilly. In fact, he was planning on recording a rockabilly album in early 1979 with Mac Curtis as producer. Today, rockabilly fans treasure his Imperial singles and unforgettable rockin' performances of "All Night Long," "This is the Night" and "The Creep" with James Burton, James Kirkland, and Butch White in *Carnival Rock*.

Maddox Brothers and Rose

Maddox Brothers and Rose were hailed as "The Most Colorful Western and Hillbilly Band in America." Their tailor made suits, slapstick comedy, and rockin' hillbilly tunes made them the most popular act on the West Coast in the 1940s and 1950s. The Maddoxes blended feisty barn dance country with elements of small combo boogie woogie and western swing. In the process, they may have invented the whole rockabilly genre.[12] Rockabilly songstresses Lorrie Collins, Janis Martin, and Wanda Jackson all cite Rose Maddox as an influence.

Maddox Brothers and Rose consisted of Cal (John Calvin) born on November 3, 1915; Fred (Fred Roscoe) born on July 3, 1919; Don (Kenneth Chalmer) born on December 7, 1922; Rose (Roselea Arbana) born on August 15, 1925; and Henry (Henry Ford) born on March 19, 1930. There was one other brother, Cliff, who was born a few years earlier than the rest and who was not part of the legendary troupe. Their mother Lula, who sang and played mandolin albeit not professionally, was the patriarch of the band.

Originally from Boaz, Alabama, in the spring of 1933, the family relocated to California, in the hopes of a better life. They walked and hitchhiked from Gadsden to Birmingham, Alabama, sleeping in the woods or staying with relatives, before catching a freight train in Meridian, Mississippi. They first arrived in Oakland, California, before settling in Modesto. There they worked on farms, harvesting crops, such as peaches and oranges. Don Maddox, the only surviving member of his family's band commented, "It's the hardest work there is and has the lowest wages."[13]

To entertain themselves and the workers around them, they taught them-

Maddox Brothers and Rose were the most colorful band in hillbilly music. From left Roy Nichols, Fred Maddox, Don Maddox, Henry Maddox, Cal Maddox, and Rose Maddox (courtesy Glenn Mueller).

selves how to sing and play instruments. Don noted, "Cliff played guitar ever since he was a teenager. Then Cal started playing when he was about fifteen. Rose sang a little bit, but she didn't sing in public. When Fred was eighteen, he was going to the country dances, and he liked the way they played the bass fiddle."[14]

Fred didn't enjoy the intensive labor or cheap pay of migrant work, so he joined the staff at the Rice Furniture Company in Modesto. In 1939, he and his mother convinced the company to sponsor the trio of Fred, Cal, and Rose, known as the Alabama Outlaws, on a country music radio show on KTRB. They agreed under one condition that there be a female singer. Rose remembered, "Fred told 'em 'We've got the greatest girl singer that's ever been.'"[15] She was only eleven years old at the time, and she hardly knew any songs: "I just started learnin' songs as hard as I could. We all did."[16] Don recalled, "I think the first song Rose learned to sing was 'Cowboy's Sweetheart' by Patsy Montana. Patsy Montana influenced her right from the start, but she didn't copy her or anything. All she did was sing that 'Cowboy's Sweetheart' and then she developed her own style." Besides playing on the radio, the Alabama Outlaws also frequented honky tonks. KTRB in Modesto became their home base. They toured with rodeos around the country and played for tips at surrounding clubs.

Two years later, Sacramento's KFBK held a talent contest in which the trio secured first place. As their prize, they received a syndicated radio program. Unfortunately, World War II drafted Cal and Fred into the Army, leaving Rose alone. She auditioned unsuccessfully for Bob Wills and His Texas Playboys.

After the war, Don on fiddle and Henry on mandolin joined the band as well as Bud Duncan on steel guitar and Jimmy Winkle on lead guitar. The band was rechristened Maddox Brothers and Rose. Don remembered, "I didn't really want to be a musician, but they needed a fiddler. They brought a fiddle to me and said 'here learn how to play that.' I learned how to play it good enough to get by, but I never was real good at it. When I first started with the band, I was about eighteen. I was shy and introverted, and the first song I learned to sing was 'Don Juan, the Gentleman from Mexico.' It was recorded by the Sons of the Pioneers, and I learned it off their record. I was afraid of girls. I wouldn't approach them, and they wouldn't approach me. I thought if the girls think I'm a Don Juan then they'll approach me. I took Don Juan for my stage name, and then I became a comedian." With their new lineup, the Maddoxes honed their stage act and for the first time received pay for their lively performances at dance halls. Roy Acuff and the *Grand Ole Opry* had influenced the band. Don recalled, "We listened to the *Grand Ole Opry* all the time."

In 1947, they signed a four year contract with Four Star Records. Maddox Brothers and Rose made several recordings for Four Star, including "George's Playhouse Boogie," "Oakie Boogie," "Navajo Maiden," "Shimmy Shakin' Daddy," and "Mean and Wicked Boogie." Roy Nichols, who later played with Merle Haggard, joined the band during this time, playing rhythm guitar.

In March of 1949, Maddox Brothers and Rose guest starred on the *Grand Ole Opry*. By 1951, the group moved on from Four Star to Columbia Records. Don explained, "We started out with Four Star Records. That was a small label, and they did really good for us, but we thought we could do better on Columbia because that was a bigger record label. We got out of our contract with Four Star and went with Columbia. Looking back, I think that was a mistake because Four Star did more for us than Columbia."

In 1953, they became regulars on the *Louisiana Hayride*, alternating six months in Louisiana and six months in California. Don commented, "When we first were on the *Hayride*, Jim Reeves was a disk jockey at KWKH. We had a morning program. We went down there one morning, and Jim was announcing. We were recording our programs because we toured during the week and then came back on Saturday night. We let Jim Reeves do a number on our show, just to have another act. He was just getting started, so we gave him a break to let him sing with us." KWKH and *Hayride* engineer Bob Sullivan added, "Maddox Brothers and Rose were a great bunch to work with. They had a fifteen minute radio program on the station, but they were never there on a Sunday afternoon. They'd come in and do the *Hayride* Saturday night, then they would come in on Sunday morning, and we would record five fifteen minute radio programs to play Monday through Friday when they weren't there. They were on the road all the time."[17] As their popularity grew from *Hayride* network exposure, the Maddox Brothers and Rose became one of the most popular groups for one-nighters in the business."[18]

Maddox Brothers and Rose were most popular from the late 1940s through mid–1950s. Besides recording over 200 records and regular appearances on the *Louisiana Hayride*, they packed dance halls and honky tonks up and down the West Coast. When the quintet hit the stage, the audience was entertained from the moment they played their first note to their last song. "Whoa Sailor" was a favorite amongst audiences and a staple of their sets, along with "Philadelphia Lawyer" and "Navajo Maiden." Don stated, "'Whoa Sailor' was one of the first tunes that we recorded, and it really made it big, especially on the West Coast. When we'd start to perform it, we'd get an ovation like these rock stars do now. [In fact] that's the only song we ever got an ovation for. When we recorded 'Philadelphia Lawyer,' Woody Guthrie wrote us a handwritten letter complimenting us on how great we were. The record company without our knowledge put on the label that the song was written by us. When Woody Guthrie saw that we were claiming authorship of it, which we weren't, he wrote us a nasty letter, telling us how terrible we were." The band were true show people, by combining slapstick humor, sound effects, and lavish clothing, they kept the venues they played packed to standing room only. Don disclosed, "After we gained self confidence, we relaxed, and we just acted natural. We cut up onstage and told jokes. Everything was spontaneous. Most tunes we played them faster than other people, like 'Oakie Boogie.' We played a lot of dances, so we had to play them at dance speed." Even though Rose was the main vocalist with songs like "Sally Let Your Bangs Hang Down," Don would sing "Step it Up and Go" or Fred might lend his vocals to "Honky-Tonk Man." Don would then tell a joke, and Fred would be the straight man. According to Don, "After I delivered the punch line, he would always slap me."[19] Teenaged fan Glenn Mueller played lead guitar for the group during the summers of 1953, 1954, and 1955. He also provided vocals on "Sending Daffydills."

Their outlandish stage antics kept the audience in stitches, but their Nathan Turk tailored uniforms really made them stand out. Don disclosed, "We had them made by Nathan Turk in North Hollywood. He was making uniforms for the Sons of the Pioneers, Roy Rogers, and Gene Autry. Later on, Nudie came to the forefront and took over." The shirts, jackets, and bell bottomed trousers were decked out with embroidered flowers, rhinestones, and/or bright colors. Their fabulously gaudy flower encrusted cowboy/Mexican outfits of the 1940s defined the country music look for a generation to come.[20] After the Maddoxes popularized the look and Porter Wagoner brought his Nudie suits back to Nashville, all the country stars jumped on the Turk/Nudie bandwagon, including Faron Young, Webb Pierce, Ray Price, George Jones, the Collins Kids, and Joe Maphis.

Even Elvis Presley was impressed with the band's costuming. Don conveyed, "We played the Big D Jamboree with Elvis, Sonny James, and Slim Whitman down in Beaumont, Texas. We had on our fancy outfits with the bell bottoms, and it was kinda hot down there, so we had our jackets off and hung them in the dressing room. We went back there, and Elvis had on one of our jackets, parading around in that. Mama made him take it off. Elvis said one of these days 'I'm gonna get me a fancy outfit like this' and sure enough he did except he got them a lot fancier than anything we ever had."

Presley had been an opening act for the Maddoxes early in his career. In fact, Bill Black, Presley's upright bassist, loved Fred Maddox and patterned his own bass playing technique and stage antics after him. Don acknowledged, "Fred had the true rockabilly feel. He liked that kind of stuff." Don however was unimpressed by Presley, "I didn't care much for Elvis. I just didn't like that kind of music. He didn't appeal to me." Don wasn't the only one, since their mother didn't like Presley either. According to Don, "When Elvis first started getting hot, we were playing at Cook's Hoedown in Houston, Texas. We were gonna be there on Monday night, and he was gonna be there on Sunday night. Mr. Cook said 'you oughta come down and hear this boy he's really good. He's going places.' Mama, she was the boss of our band, said she didn't like Elvis, and she didn't want to hear him. We went down there anyhow. It was just Elvis and the two guys who started with him, and they only had about a hundred people in the place. We sat there and listened at them for about an hour. Mama said 'I can't take this anymore; I'm leaving.' She got up and started to walk out, and of course all of us had to get up and go with her. We walked right by the stage where Elvis was performing, and he watched us from when we got up from our table to all the way until we got outside. I guess we were the only people who ever walked out on Elvis." Later, once Presley got established, Don recorded a parody of Presley's "I Got a Woman" into a song called "The Death of Rock and Roll": "I did that onstage, just making a spoof out of it, and it went over real big. I recorded it on Columbia, but I changed the name of it to the 'Death of Rock and Roll' because it was a parody. The way I did it, I thought it would kill rock and roll."

The Maddoxes enjoyed themselves onstage, but offstage they rarely interacted with or spoke to one another. Even though their mother ruled with an iron fist, they all felt she was the glue who held the family band together. Don recalled, "We were a family, and mama was the patriarch. If we had any complaints, we didn't go to each other to complain, we complained to mama, and mama took care of it. She wouldn't stand for anything. None of us drank or smoked or used drugs. If she wouldn't have been there, we would have been as wild as the rest of them." Lula was the proverbial stage mother, as tough, outspoken, and ambitious as they come.[21]

Hayride engineer Sullivan recollected, "We took the whole *Hayride* to Texarkana, Texas, one time. The venue was a two story [building]. I was coming down the stairs getting ready to sign the station on, and Fred was under the stairs crouched down on his knees, sipping out of a bottle of peach brandy. He was hiding it. I said what are you hiding for? He said 'I don't want Mama to catch me. Don't tell Mama.' Here was this guy 40 some years old afraid his mama was gonna catch him taking a drink. She would be in the studio when we were cutting these things on Sunday [for their radio program], and if one of them made a mistake or said something out of the way, she'd walk up and slap them upside the face, just like they were two years old." The group made extra money by selling 8 × 10 glossy photos of themselves. The pictures cost eleven cents to make and were sold for a dollar a piece.

In 1955, the band broke up into two different incarnations: Rose and Cal in one version with the rest in another lineup with Henry's wife Loretta taking Rose's spot (Maddox Brothers and Retta). Their mother moved Rose to Nashville to make frequent appearances on the *Grand Ole Opry* in the summer of 1956. The *Grand Ole Opry* wasn't interested in the whole band, just Rose. According to Don, "Rose thought she could do better by herself than she could with us because we had reached a plateau. After Rose and Cal left, it ruined the whole thing because people liked the Maddox Brothers and Rose. They didn't want her by herself, and they didn't want us by ourselves, so that ruined it for both of us." As a band, they made their final recording for Columbia in the summer of 1957. At this time, rockabilly legend Glen Glenn joined the band filling in for Cal. Also, Rose signed with Capitol Records, where Cal and Henry appeared with her. Three or four times, both bands had to work together since promoters still wanted Maddox Brothers and Rose. After Glenn was drafted into the Army in 1958, Don bought a ranch in Ashland, Oregon, where he raised purebred Angus cattle: "I made and saved enough money from what Maddox Brothers and Rose were doing to invest in a ranch here in Ashland, and that's what I really always wanted to do, to be a cowboy." As for Fred, he had his own nightclub, Fred Maddox's Playhouse, for awhile.

Throughout the 1960s, Rose toured with Henry and Cal. In the early 1960s, she teamed up with country superstar Buck Owens, who sang harmony on her #4 song "Loose Talk" and #8 hit "Mental Cruelty," as well as four other Top 20 country chart toppers. In 1963, Cash Box named her Top Country Female Artist. Europe beckoned her arrival in 1969. Although, the Maddoxes constituted a highly talented unit, Rose's lead and solo vocals were a major contribution to their appeal and commercial success.[22]

Eventually, all the Maddoxes retired from music except for Rose, who continued to perform her rockabilly classics "Hey Little Dreamboat" and "Wild Wild Young Men" to enthusiastic crowds overseas. She also played at all the major folk and bluegrass festivals. In 1996, her album, *$35 and a Dream*, for Arhoolie Records was nominated for Best Bluegrass Album by the Grammys. On April 15, 1998, Rose died of kidney failure. She was preceded in death by her brothers Cliff, who died in 1949; Cal, who died in 1968; Henry, who died in 1972; and Fred, who died in 1992.

The Maddoxes' influence was noted by the co-founder of Microsoft Paul Allen and the Experience Music Project in Seattle, Washington, when they called Don and Fred's widow Kitty to see if they had any mementos to donate to their exhibit. Don conveyed, "They wanted to know if I had any uniforms. Well I didn't know who was doing that, and I thought it was a two bit outfit. I told them I didn't have any." It was true that he didn't own any of his uniforms any longer since he had given them to his sister Rose when she was in need of financial help to pay her medical bills. Rose sold many of the family's outfits to country star Marty Stuart for his collection. After the call from the museum, Don received numerous others, this time from collectors hoping to buy memorabilia cheap from him and then sell it for a much higher price to the museum. Fred's widow, Kitty, sold the museum some uniforms she had of Fred's for $20,000. For five years, the Maddoxes' career was front and center at the museum for fans to enjoy, but they were replaced by Bob Dylan. Don Maddox is surprised that people remember his family's band and is thankful for their legendary status. Although, he admitted, "I didn't think we were any good."

Elvis Presley

On July 5, 1954, Elvis Presley, Scotty Moore, and Bill Black forever changed musical history. With their Sun recordings, most notably, "That's All Right," "Baby, Let's Play House," "Good Rockin' Tonight," and "Mystery Train," they fused black rhythm and blues with white honky-tonk country. In doing this, they created the fiery rockabilly sound, the very template of rock and roll as we know it.[23] Presley not only influenced legions of singers to follow in his rockabilly footsteps, but he inspired the way they dressed. In his twenty-three year career, he had eighteen #1 hits in the United States and starred in thirty-three movies. In 1982, his home, Graceland, was opened to the public and continues to be the second biggest tourist attraction in America, second only to the White House. There are thousands of Elvis tribute artists, but there is only one true King of Rock and Roll.

Elvis Aron Presley was born on January 8, 1935, in Tupelo, Mississippi. He was born a twin, but his brother Jesse Garon died at birth. Elvis was named after his father Vernon Elvis Presley. Presley's mother, Gladys, became very protective of her only child, and they shared a very close knit bond. Presley grew up dirt poor. He and his parents moved constantly for fear of eviction. His love for music came at an early age and helped him deal with hard times. Presley regularly sang in the Assembly of God church that he and his parents attended. The Statesmen Quartet and the Blackwood Brothers were his favorite gospel groups. According to his friend and former band mate Ronnie Smith, "Elvis really wanted to sing gospel and play piano."[24] In fact, Smith recollected that years later Presley tried out for the Blackwood Brothers at the Assembly of God church in Memphis but was turned away. J.D. Sumner told Elvis after his audition: "Singing just ain't your bag."[25] In 1943, Presley participated several times on WELO's *Saturday Jamboree*, which was an amateur hour, in Tupelo. "Old Shep" was one of the songs he sang. Two years later, ten year old Presley placed fifth with his rendition of "Old Shep" in a youth talent contest held at the Mississippi–Alabama Fair and Dairy Show. For his eleventh birthday, his mother bought him his first guitar.

In 1948, the Presleys moved to Memphis, Tennessee. Soon, Lauderdale Courts became their residence, the same housing complex where fellow musicians Lee and Jimmy Denson, Johnny and Dorsey Burnette, and Johnny Black (Bill's brother) all lived. The boys would get together for rehearsals in both the basement and on the front lawn. At this time, Presley was shy and unsure of his singing capabilities even though he participated. In high school, he was bullied and ridiculed by his peers for his outlandish appearance of bright colored cat clothes and ducktail hairstyle with long sideburns. Most of the other boys wore crew cuts and blue jeans. Several times, classmate Red West had to save him from getting beaten up in the boys' restroom. A few months before graduation, he performed Teresa Brewer's "Till I Waltz Again with You" at his high school's, Humes' Annual Minstrel Show. With that performance, he gained acceptance.

On July 18, 1953, he cut a demo of "My Happiness" and "That's When Your Heartaches Begin" at Memphis Recording Studio (later Sun) for his mother's birthday. This was the first time Presley entered the studio, but unfortunately owner Sam Phillips was not there. Phillips' secretary Marion Keisker, "who was truly the heart of Phillips' early operation," assisted with the recording that day but chatted with the youngster beforehand.[26] When she asked him who he sounded like, he replied "I don't sound like nobody."[27] Marion Keisker commented "that the one thing that made Elvis stand out to me was that he had soul."[28] In January 1954, Presley returned to cut another acetate: "It Wouldn't Be the Same Without You" and "I'll Never Stand in Your Way." This time, Phillips engineered the session and took down Presley's address and phone number. While waiting for a phone call from Phillips, Presley took a job at Crown Electric as an electrician's apprentice. Electrician Paul Burlison, guitarist for the Rock and Roll Trio, remembered Presley transporting supplies to him on the job.

Local guitarist Scotty Moore, who was then playing with country band the Starlight Wranglers, along with bassist Bill Black, was impressed with Keisker's interest in Presley's talent, so he continually asked Phillips for the young singer's phone number. It was the guitarist's hunger to earn a steady position with Phillips, which would allow him to quit his day job and pick guitar for a living, that inspired him to pester Phillips about Presley.[29] After quite a bit of persistence, Phillips finally relinquished Presley's phone number, and Moore called him to set up a meeting. Bassist Black, who lived three doors down from Moore, sat in, and the three of them ran through various country and rhythm and blues tunes for several hours. Presley's musical influences included Dean Martin, Hank Snow, Eddy Arnold, Little Richard, the Statesmen Quartet, the Blackwood

Elvis Presley performing at the G. Rolle White Coliseum in College Station, Texas, on March 19, 1955 (courtesy Steve Bonner Collection).

Brothers, and Roy Hamilton, while Moore admired guitarists Chet Atkins and Merle Travis, and Black patterned his style after Fred Maddox of Maddox Brothers and Rose. Both Black and Moore thought Presley could sing but found nothing extraordinary about his talent.

The next day, on July 5, they traveled to Sun and first recorded "Harbor Lights" and "I Love You Because." It wasn't until they took a break that magic happened. Presley recalled Arthur "Big Boy" Crudup's "That's All Right": "This song popped into my mind that I had heard years ago, and I started kidding around with [it]."[30] Moore and Black then chimed in. Phillips couldn't believe his ears; it was raw, different, and full of emotion. The trio had stumbled upon a new sound; rockabilly was born.

Three days later, WHBQ's disk jockey Dewey Phillips played "That's All Right" on his *Red, Hot, and Blue* radio program. Listeners loved the new single and requests poured in for numerous replays. Presley's parents signed a three year contract with Sun for their underage son. While the song was hot, the band reentered the studio looking for a B side. Bassist Black was the one who thought of Bill Monroe's "Blue Moon of Kentucky." The trio transformed the bluegrass version into a pop song. On July 30, 1954, they shared a bill with Slim Whitman at the Overton Park Shell in Memphis. In August, Sun issued the 45 rpm single, "That's All Right" b/w "Blue Moon of Kentucky."

Between airplay and local appearances at the Bon Air Club and the Eagles' Nest, Presley and his band, the Blue Moon Boys, were making quite a sensation. Presley was naïve when it came to the music business, and he was being inundated with management offers. Upon Sam Phillips' suggestion, Presley contracted with guitarist Scotty Moore to act as his manager. Presley's mother asked that Moore look after her son, which he dutifully did. However, his managerial duties did not last long since he couldn't focus his energy on being both a worthy guitarist and handling financial matters when it came to bookings. Bob Neal soon replaced Moore as manager. Both Moore and Black were extremely helpful in guiding Presley in his early career. They helped him refine his stage act by providing advice on how to hold his guitar and how to stand behind the microphone, and Black was the savior when Presley's audience lost interest. He had a comedic side that helped Presley in a jam. Black would ride and slap the bass, holler and scream, really cut loose. If the audience lost interest in Presley's singing, then Black would take over and have the fans back on their side in no time. *Louisiana Hayride* bassist Tillman Franks noted, "I want to emphasize the fact that Bill Black was such a big part of Elvis making it. The way he hit his bass fiddle, he sounded like a band all by himself. Elvis sang the way Bill played bass."[31]

On October 2, 1954, when the trio got booked on the *Grand Ole Opry*, they figured they had hit the big time. Jim Denny, Opry manager, wondered where the rest of the band was since the record sounded like there was at least four pieces. He was surprised that three guys could make that much music. They performed on Hank Snow's portion. Scotty Moore recalled, "They wouldn't let us do but one song, and that had to be 'Blue Moon of Kentucky' because it was a country song."[32] Applause was mediocre, and Denny commented to Presley that he should go back to driving a truck. Discouraged, they returned to Memphis with a heavy heart.

Thankfully the Opry's rival, the *Louisiana Hayride*, came beckoning. *Hayride* engineer Bob Sullivan disclosed that Tillman Franks got Elvis on the *Hayride*: "Tillman was a bass player and tried to book acts out for extra money. He'd take acts and book them in school houses. Well, he had an act he was managing called Jimmy and Johnny (Jimmy Lee Fautheree and Johnny Mathis). At that time, they were one of the hottest groups on the *Hayride*. The kids were eating 'em up. Tillman told [announcer] Horace [Logan] 'I'm gonna take these kids to New Mexico on Saturday night.' [Fautheree had a homecoming show that would pay $800.] Horace replied, 'No, we can't do without 'em. We've got to keep them here at the show because they are the hottest act we've got going.' Tillman said, 'What if I can find somebody to take their place?' Horace said, 'Well, okay, see what you can do.' Tillman ran down to Stan's Record Shop and bought 'That's All Right' by Elvis. He brought it in the control room and put it on. Tillman told Horace 'What about getting this kid for the *Hayride* to replace Jimmy and Johnny?' Horace listened to it, and he said, 'Well, Tillman, I don't know, is that kid black or white? Find out if he's black, if he is we can't use him. If he's white, we'll talk to him.' They went back to Horace's office, and they phoned Sam Phillips. Sam said, 'Now he's a good looking kid. He's a white kid.' Horace said, 'Well do you think he'd be interested in being on the *Hayride*?' Sam replied, 'Well, sure, he would, I'll have him call ya. He's out driving his truck right now, but he always comes by the studio in the afternoon to see how his record's doing.' About five o'clock, Elvis phoned Horace. He proceeded to ask him if he'd like to appear on the *Hayride*. Elvis about fell over and said, 'Oh yeah, I've got my own band, Scotty and Bill. We'll be there.' The Saturday night they were scheduled to be on they came by the station. I was at the station, and they looked pretty bedraggled from driving all the way from Memphis. They told me who they were and said, 'Where's the *Louisiana Hayride*?' I told them how to get there. When I got there, they were backstage. Elvis was nervous as he could be. When he came out and started doing 'That's All Right,' shaking his legs and jumping around, all the acts on the show really made fun of him. They said, 'What is this, and when is this guy gonna get out of here?' I don't know of a soul that ever thought that he would go any further than the *Louisiana Hayride*. Of course after the fact, everybody said, 'Oh, I knew he was gonna make it.'"[33]

Presley and his band were a hit with audiences on the *Hayride*, and they signed a contract to appear on the program every Saturday night for the next year. With a regular booking, they all quit their day jobs. At the time, Sullivan owned a 1954 black Volkswagen, as he called it the "ugliest thing you ever saw in your life": "I drove it to the auditorium and parked it where I could go upstairs and do my show. One night Elvis came by and asked Horace, 'What is that thing down there?' Horace said, 'Well that's Sullivan's car.' He immediately came over to the booth where I had set up to do my broadcast and said, 'Tell me about your car.' I knew he wanted to drive it." Sullivan handed over the keys. Between his two songs, Presley had an hour off, so "He'd grab my car and drive around. Only problem was when I'd get in it to go home, it would reek of perfume. He had picked up girls in it. I told him one time man you quit hauling them girls around in this thing. I have to roll the windows down going home, let all that perfume out before my wife Judy gets in it to go to church Sunday morning. He told me, 'Man, you can really pick up girls in that thing.' I said, Well, it doesn't work for me." Another time Sullivan recollected that Presley needed a break from the continuous one-nighters: "One Sunday morning when I was signing the station on, Elvis came by. He had been on the show Saturday night [fourth month in a row] and had come by to get his mail. He was sitting down opening his mail and reading it, and he was telling me, 'You know I am absolutely beat.' He had been playing in Arkansas all that week and had to be in Oklahoma City Monday night. He said, 'I don't have a day off for two weeks, and I'm just worn out.' I said, 'Well, man why don't you tell 'em to quit booking you so much?' He said, 'Man, I can't cause a year from now ain't nobody gonna know who Elvis Presley is. I gotta make it while I can.'"

Besides breakneck bookings, Presley and the Blue Moon Boys managed to record five influential rockabilly records for Sun. After the release of "That's All Right" b/w "Blue Moon of Kentucky," "Good Rockin' Tonight" b/w "I Don't Care If the Sun Don't Shine" was issued. 1955 saw the release of three other singles, two songs of which charted. In January, "Milkcow Blues Boogie" b/w "You're a Heartbreaker" hit the streets. "Baby, Let's Play House" b/w "I'm Left, You're Right, She's Gone" showcased the band's development and ease with one another. Presley opened in an ascending, hiccoughing stutter that knocked everybody out with its utterly unpredictable, uninhibited, and gloriously playful ridiculousness.[34] On July 16, it soared to #5 on the Billboard country and western charts. In August, his final single for Sun, "Mystery Train" b/w "I Forgot to Remember to Forget," was issued. The Charlie Feathers/Stan Kesler composition, "I Forgot to Remember to Forget" launched Presley's career as a national country singing sensation. It spent thirty-nine weeks on the country charts at #1. In November, he signed with RCA Victor to the unheard tune of $40,000.

During Presley's stint on the *Louisiana Hayride*, he made the acquaintance of Colonel Tom Parker, who once managed Hank Snow, Eddy Arnold, and Tommy Sands. Parker took the reigns as manager, notifying Presley that he had the talent to make a million dollars, and he was going to help him do precisely that. As manager, he got Presley television bookings and marketed him like a sideshow at a carnival. In 1956, he partnered with Hank Saperstein to market seventy-two licensed products that bore Presley's image and likeness including lipstick, jewelry, and bubblegum trading cards. In fact, Parker is the one who bought Presley out of his contract at the *Louisiana Hayride*. Sullivan conveyed, "He bought out Elvis' contract for $10,000. We had him for another year. It was in his contract that when he left, he would come back for one show. [It occurred at the Hirsch Youth Center on the Louisiana Fairgrounds on December 15, 1956.] We didn't get to see Elvis. He showed up in Shreveport with his entourage, flew in on a private plane, and rented a whole floor at the Shreve hotel. They escorted him through the back door. He ran out onstage, did his thing and left. Nobody even got to talk to him." Parker was also instrumental in slowly phasing Moore and Black out of the picture. The trio's original salary arrangements were Presley at 50 percent, and the other half being split between Moore and Black. Those conditions no longer existed once Parker entered the picture, and D.J. Fontana, who had played with the trio on the *Hayride*, was now a member of the band as drummer.

Nineteen fifty-six was a banner year in Presley's career. With his new label RCA, in January, he entered the studio with the backup vocal group the Jordanaires in tow and recorded his first #1 song "Heartbreak Hotel." Two million copies were sold. In fact, RCA had to facilitate other record labels' pressing plants to fulfill the demand. Presley integrated audiences when he sang Little Richard's "Tutti Frutti" on *The Dorsey Brothers Stage Show*. The flashy cat clothes he wore, that he purchased at Lansky's in Memphis, the rhythm and blues tunes he sang, and the ducktail that he wore really made him stand out on conservative 1950s television. Many celebrities, most notably Jackie Gleason, Frank Sinatra, and Garry Moore along with Carol Burnett, felt he was simply a flash in the pan and would never last, while ministers chastised him for being a contributing factor to juvenile delinquency. In fact, his June 5 performance on the *Milton Berle Show*, where he sang Willie Mae "Big Mama" Thornton's "Hound Dog" caused such a sensation amongst its forty million viewers that Berle received hundreds of letters of pan mail. Presley was classified as a no talent performer but he was simply gyrating like he normally did on his stage show: "Rock and roll music, if you like it and if you feel it, you can't help but move to it. That's what happens to me. I have to move around, I can't stand still. I've tried it, and I can't do it."[35] Incidentally, his single "Hound Dog" b/w "Don't Be Cruel" remained at the top of the charts for twenty-three weeks. Once the commotion from the Berle show settled down, Presley made appearances on the *Steve Allen Show* and the *Ed Sullivan Show*.

Presley always wanted to be an actor, and in 1956, he screen tested for a role in the movie *The Rainmaker* starring Katherine Hepburn and Burt Lancaster. Hal Wallis was so impressed that he signed Presley to a seven year contract with Paramount Pictures. He was leased out to 20th Century–Fox to star in the Civil War epic, *Love Me Tender*. It was a dream of his since he was fifteen years old and an usher at Lowe's State Theater in Memphis. He hoped he would become a serious actor like his favorites Marlon Brando and James Dean. Presley watched Dean's *Rebel Without a Cause* no less than twelve times. Unfortunately, as box office sales warranted, Presley's movie career was lengthy, producing thirty-one films and two documentaries, but unsuccessful as far as award winning. In 1958, his fourth film, *King Creole*, was his only truly dramatic role, perhaps because it was originally written for James Dean, who had been tragically killed three years before.

Presley spent a two year stint in the United States Army. While stationed in Germany, he met his future wife Priscilla Beaulieu. Upon his return to America, he concentrated on movies and recordings with Moore and Fontana with additional backing from Grady Martin, Hank Garland, Buddy Harman and Bob Moore. Black had quit before Presley entered the Army and was successful with his own instrumental combo. In 1957, Presley retired from touring since the crowds became uncontrollable.

On May 1, 1967, Presley married his sweetheart Beaulieu, and nine months to the day their only child Lisa Marie was born. They amicably divorced in 1973. December 3, 1968, marked Presley's triumphant return to performing live with the '68 Comeback Special. This would mark the last time Moore and Fontana would play with him. In 1969, he signed a contract for a lengthy engagement at the International Hotel in Las Vegas. These performances provided the audience with new sounds, an orchestra and a band—the TCB band, which featured lead guitarist James Burton, and new sights, Presley decked out in elaborate bejeweled jumpsuits designed by Bill Belew. The last time he played Vegas was in 1956, and even though he was billed as the "Atomic Powered Singer" at the New Frontier Hotel, he flopped. From 1969 to 1977, he toured non-stop around the country. In 1973, one and a half billion viewers worldwide tuned in via satellite to watch his concert extravaganza *Aloha from Hawaii*.

Presley was a generous soul who gave money to numerous charities as well as cars, houses, and any other material object one could think of to all his family and friends, even strangers. He aimed to please his fans and felt awful if he couldn't perform at his best. Unfortunately, the combination of constantly traveling to a different city every night and an addiction to prescription pills did him in, and he died on August 16, 1977. *Hayride* engineer Sullivan disclosed an experience that announcer Horace Logan had with Presley shortly before he died: "Elvis played the coliseum in Monroe, Louisiana, and Horace went to the show. He said 'Elvis was so glad to see me.' He ran everybody out of the dressing room, told them, 'Y'all get out, we're gonna visit.' They reminisced about the *Hayride*. Elvis told him, 'You know Mr. Logan that was the happiest time of my life. We were all family. I don't have a family anymore. All I've got are these hanger-ons, and they're not family. I wish I could go back and have that family again.' Horace asked him if he had to do it over, would he do it again? Elvis said, 'Oh, heck no, I wouldn't do it the same way. There'd be some changes made.'"

Three

Arkansas Rockabillies

Larry Donn

Fellow Arkansas rockers Sonny Burgess and Billy Lee Riley made quite an impression on teenager Larry Donn. In 1955, Burgess and his band, the Pacers played the Bono High School gymnasium: "I just got so turned on [from watching them that] I was jumping all over the place. The Pacers had a wild stage act with a lot of jumping around and screaming. They really got me sold on rock and roll. That was the spark that made me want to play."[1] Two years later, Donn made the finals at the Craighead County Fair in Jonesboro, Arkansas. He sang Johnny Cash's "Home of the Blues" and "Give My Love to Rose." He didn't win, but his life forever changed after he saw Riley and his band, the Little Green Men perform. Once the show was over, Donn introduced himself to Riley: "Hi, I'm Larry Gillihan. I was in the talent contest. I'd like to get a band together and start playing music. Can you tell me how to go about doing that?" Riley seriously replied with, "The best advice I can give you is if you're not already in the music business, stay out of it." However good Riley's intentions were, Donn had no intention of listening to him: "[Even though] he was my hero, [being a singer] was what I wanted, and I was going to do it." In recent years, he has played piano for Riley, joining drummer J.M. Van Eaton as a Little Green Man. Donn became a bona fide rock and roller in February 1959 with the Vaden Records release "That's What I Call a Ball" b/w "Honey Bun." According to the *Guide to Rare Rockabilly and Rock and Roll 45 rpms* by Tom Lincoln and Dick Blackburn, the Vaden single is a rare collector's item and can fetch in excess of $2500.[2]

Larry Don Gillihan was born on June 7, 1941, in Bono, Arkansas; he was three years old when he first sang in the local cotton patches. Fellow cotton pickers yelled out requests for such songs as "Turkey in the Straw" and "Little Brown Jug," and the youngster sang them. "One time when I was about three, we went to church. Everybody stood up to sing a song, and mother looked down at me, and she said, 'Sing Larry,' so I yelled out just as loud as I could [the first line to 'Little Brown Jug']. She slapped her hand over my mouth and told me to be quiet. I said, 'But you told me to sing.' She said, 'Yeah, but sing what we're singing.' I said, 'I don't know what you're singing. I gotta sing something I know.' As I grew up, I just liked to sing. I enjoyed it. I guess it's the Irish in me because most of my family were musicians." One of Gillihan's uncles played with Bob Wills and His Texas Playboys in the 1940s.

Most of the music Gillihan heard was country and hillbilly, and he considered it too whiney: "Country singers seemed like they sang through their noses." As the 1950s approached, he gravitated toward artists such as mainstream pop singers Doris Day and Dean Martin. Even though Gillihan enjoyed pop music, it didn't move him. By 1955, Bill Haley and the Comets were on the scene: "I began to hear Bill Haley and the Comets, and I liked this. It had rhythm to it. Then I heard Elvis [Presley], and I didn't like him at all. I couldn't understand the words. It was probably six months after I first heard Elvis that I laid in the front seat of my daddy's new '55 Ford and listened to Randy's Record Shop [out of] Nashville, and they played [Presley's] 'Good Rockin' Tonight.' About halfway through that song, something clicked in my head. I just instantly thought man this guy has got something. This is good stuff. It made chills go up and down my back. From then on, I was a rock and roller, and I loved Elvis."

The formation of Gillihan's first rock and roll band occurred in 1957 when he met guitarist Benny Kuykendall at a local talent contest. Kuykendall's brother Scotty played upright bass, and Eddie Reeves played drums. Coincidentally, their cousins were the father-daughter team of Royce and Jeannie Kuykendall, who recorded the country mega hit "Heaven's Just a Sin Away" as the Kendalls.

The band's lineup soon changed. On Saturday, August 13, 1958, the newly formed band was at guitarist Jimmie Coleman's house to rehearse for a session at Sun Studio. It would be produced by Billy Lee Riley, whom they had previously backed at a local show. Within three hours of rehearsal, they needed to have at least two songs written for the session. After Gillihan's proposed songs were quickly dismissed by the band, pianist Richard Manning wrote "That's What I Call a Ball" in fifteen minutes. He also wrote "Molly-O" for the session, but they all agreed it wasn't very good. Riley told them to go back home, write a new song, and then a record would be released. A week or so later, the band broke up. The songs were never released.

Subsequently, Gillihan concentrated all his efforts on recording and performing since his commitment to the rockabilly style had caused conflict between him and the local school administrators. On the second day of his senior year, he was reprimanded for wearing his shirt with the first two buttons unbuttoned and the collar upturned. All the boys were wearing their shirts that way. "I had been wearing the top two buttons open and the collar up on my shirts since 1956, and nobody had ever complained before."

The administration admitted to Gillihan that they were singling him out. The would-be rocker told them he would comply "only if it applied to all male students." By this time, the superintendent was involved and told him, 'We're not concerned with the others. We want you to do what we tell you to do.' Gillihan refused to follow the "new" rules, so the principal told him 'go home and don't come back. I'll see that you never graduate from any school in Arkansas.' According to Gillihan, this new set of rules was set into motion in the summer of 1957 by the new administration, who vowed to clean up the school. Prior to the change, Gillihan was a model student, who won many medals and got good grades. His attitude changed, and his grades dropped once the harassment began. After his suspension, he took a correspondence course and earned his diploma three years later. A scholarship was awarded to him to attend any college he wished, but he turned it down to pursue his dream of becoming a rock and roll singer.

In 1959, members of Teddy Riedel, Bobby Brown, and Donn's bands recorded "That's What I Call a Ball" and "Honey Bun." For the session, Kuykendall wrote "Honey Bun." It was cut three times, but the first cut was released. "That's What I Call a Ball" was rerecorded with the new band. "Everyone thought 'That's What I Call a Ball' was going to be the hit." By contrast, "Honey Bun" only contained six notes and was actually just a "simple rock and roll song," but it turned out to be Gillihan's signature tune.

Prior to its February 1959 release, label owner Arlen Vaden approached Gillihan about changing his name to Don Gill. Gillihan refused, but realized, "if I don't come up with something that I can live with he's going to tack some name on me that I'll hate the rest of my life." Larry Donn is the name he decided upon.

When "Honey Bun" first came out, the group went back to KCLN in Blytheville, Arkansas, where the song was first recorded. Jimmy Haggett spun the new single on his afternoon show and interviewed Donn. That evening, Donn traveled to Paragould, Arkansas, and played a show at the 25 Club with Carl Perkins: "Carl treated me like an equal. It was

Larry Donn rebelling against authority with his upturned shirt collar (courtesy Larry Donn).

fun. If he was standing around talking to important people, and I was there, he always included me in the conversation. He made me feel important."

Arlen Vaden told Donn that to promote "Honey Bun" he had to play many shows without pay. Vaden told him years later that he wasn't trying for a hit but just wanted to book his band into some local clubs to make a little money. "I've always believed that if he had pushed 'Honey Bun' [that] it would have been a national hit."

In 1960, Donn teamed up with Sonny Burgess and Sammy Creason and formed a band. Incidentally, Creason was a famous drummer who played with many artists, including eighteen years with Kris Kristofferson. For two years, they played regularly. Donn's second record "The Girl Next Door" was released on Ad-Bur in 1961, which was previously recorded by Elvis Presley for an album. Burgess released "Today" on side B of Donn's single. In November 1962, Donn went to work as a disk jockey at KNEA in Jonesboro, Arkansas. Alley Records released "Surf Twist" b/w "Sahara" and "One Broken Heart" b/w "I'll Never Forget You." "Surf Twist" was an instrumental and given a good review by *Billboard*, and Top Pop Tunes in Memphis said it was the new record to watch.

In April 1963, when Donn switched stations to KLCN in Blytheville, Arkansas, he decided there was too much traveling involved and quit playing with Burgess.

Throughout the 1970s, Donn continued to record. He ventured into a new endeavor when in 1982 he opened a recording studio/advertising agency with his friend Charles Miller. During the late 1980s, Donn freelanced as a plumber, electrician, and construction worker. He performed all the tasks needed to build a home.

In high school, his English teacher told him that he should cultivate his talent for writing. Little did his instructor know that the written word would pave the way for his international re-emergence. British rockabilly fanzine *Now Dig This* featured Donn's article that promoted his first show in England, in its April 1989 issue. Editor Trevor Cajaio liked Donn's writing so much that he offered him the opportunity to write a monthly column. The job lasted from December 1990 until December 2007. Everyone from Jerry Lee Lewis to Duane Eddy to Bill Haley's Comets read the column. "I literally didn't think it [would] last longer than just a year or so."

Donn ran into another one of his faithful readers, Carl Perkins during Elvis Week 1992 at a tribute to Elvis, which was held at the Ellis Auditorium in Memphis. Perkins was onstage tuning his guitar standing next to guitar virtuoso James Burton. Donn grabbed Perkins by the arm and asked, 'How are you doing, Mr. Shoes?' Perkins replied, 'Larry Donn, it's got to be a hundred years. Man, you sure do write some good stories.' Donn remembered his friend fondly: "There was no better person than Carl Perkins as far as I'm concerned."

As a performer, Donn played the Hemsby rockabilly weekender in England three different times. Like many of his rockabilly contemporaries, he was stunned at the wild crowd reaction. At one of the appearances, a young lady tried to pull him off the stage: "I was walking along in front of the stage while I was singing, just reaching down shaking hands [with the fans], and this girl grabbed my hand and wouldn't let loose." The security guards broke it up by telling her to quit. After the show, he went to sign autographs: "I had to go way to the other end of the room to sign autographs, and she was right at the front door." He signed a piece of paper for her with the following inscription: with all my love forever and ever, thousands of hugs and kisses, Larry Donn. She was so taken by the autograph that she started crying: "It really shook me up to think somebody would be that serious about an autograph from me. If they're fans, and they like me well enough to ask for my autograph, I'll give them anything they want."

Another time in London at the Clay Pigeon, a male fan asked him to sign his arm. Donn noticed that some of the signatures were those of artists who had already passed away. As it turned out, they were tattoos. The fan told him, 'The next time I see you, yours will be too.' A few years later, Donn saw him again. He showed him his arm and said, 'Do you remember that?' Donn replied, 'Son, I'll never forget that as long as I live.'

Twenty-five years in the making, Donn's latest effort *Burning!* showcases the kind of music he grew up listening to, hard-driving rock and roll. Donn believes there is too much billy and not enough rock in rockabilly nowadays. Donn revealed, "I like wild, hard driving, raw, screaming, boogie woogie rock and roll. The wilder [the music is] the better."

Pat Cupp

In May 1956, Pat Cupp recorded "Do Me No Wrong," "Baby Come Back," "I Guess It's Meant That Way," "She's My Little Baby (an early version of "That Girl of Mine"), "I Won't Remember to Cry," and "Long Gone Daddy" (the rockabilly version) at radio station KWKH in Shreveport, Louisiana: "This recording session took about ten hours."[3] RPM Records released "Do Me No Wrong" b/w "Baby Come Back" right after the session while "Long Gone Daddy" b/w "To Be the One" was issued in September. Cupp had to quickly come up with a name for his band: "After about ten hours of recording, Mr. Behari asked me if my band had a name that could be on the record label. I had been trying to come up with a name for several months. I was kidding when I first told Mr. Behari [RPM's owner] that we were called the Flying Saucers, but after I said it, he thought it would get radio people to take a second look and give it a play just to hear the band if nothing else. So, the name stuck with us."

However, a few months prior to his recording session for RPM Records, Cupp tried his luck by auditioning for Sun Records: "A couple of months before I did the *Louisiana Hayride*, my manager had me and my band do a tape at the radio station KOSY where he worked. I had just written some of my songs, and he wanted to send them to Sam Phillips at Sun. We sent them to Sam, but we never heard back from him. I didn't go to Sun Records and see Sam and was never offered a contract. The songs I sent him were the same ones I recorded for RPM. They were just in the raw and had not been really worked out as they were when we recorded them for RPM." His dream of recording at Sun never materialized, and by March 1957, he had become so frustrated with the music business that he traded in his blue suede shoes for combat boots by joining the U.S. Air Force.

Pat Cupp was born on January 21, 1938, in Nashville, Arkansas. In 1953, his family relocated to Texarkana. He was raised in a musical family. Both his parents played instruments as well as his two brothers and one sister. In fact, his mother Ruth played piano in Cupp's band, the Flying Saucers. Cupp disclosed, "Growing up, I was into pop music of the time. I liked Frank Sinatra, Bing Crosby, Vic Damone, and the Ink Spots. I didn't know anything about country music. My family liked the big band stuff, and I was not exposed to anything else until I was a teenager and heard Elvis for the first time. I then became a fan of his and Johnny Cash and all the others."

Cupp recalled, "I have been singing since before I started school. I always loved singing. I got my first guitar at about age eleven after I won a stage show in Dierks, Arkansas. I made five dollars. My dad gave me six more, and I bought a guitar for eleven. It was a white Stella. I had the guitar when I graduated from high school. However, I did buy a new one when I started my band." His father originally taught Cupp how to play guitar. He showed him some chords on a tenor guitar, which had only four strings.

Cupp took his guitar and starting playing with his friend, Chessie Nelson. Nelson introduced him to Elvis Presley's music. The first song he ever heard was Presley's "That's All Right." Cupp remembered, "Chessie had the reputation of being able to sing and sound like the country music stars of the 50s. He could not play the guitar, so he found me and asked me to play for him while he did Elvis' stuff. I learned the Scotty Moore parts, and we became a pair of young guys who gained in popularity with the local teenagers."

Cupp added, "Elvis came to Texarkana one weekend, and Chessie and I went to see him. He was a different type of performer and was well received by the young people. Some of the teenagers had seen us before they saw Elvis. We had performed for both high schools at special assembly programs. Elvis had car trouble outside of Texarkana and could not get to the auditorium in time for the show. The people who were promoting the show knew about Chessie and me and sent someone to find us, so we could keep the audience happy until Elvis and his band could get to the auditorium. Chessie and I performed all of Elvis' songs and were onstage when Elvis got there. Of course, he took over the show, and Chessie and I stayed backstage and watched. At intermission, Elvis asked us to go to his dressing room to visit. Elvis thought it was funny that we did such a good job of performing his songs and just wanted to meet us. We spent all of the break time with him and found him to be just an ordinary guy trying to get his name known in the music field."

Besides singing and playing guitar, Cupp wrote songs, which he began when he was fifteen years old: "None of the first ones I wrote ever got recorded. I wrote the ones I recorded when I was seventeen and eighteen years old." Of the ones that were recorded, his favorite was "Do Me No Wrong": "I thought it was different from anything I had heard at that time. I really thought it would catch on and do something with the teenagers of the day. All my friends liked it." Cupp originally wrote three of his songs about his girlfriend: "'That Girl of Mine' was the first song I ever wrote, and it was about my girlfriend. I married that same girl, and she is still my wife." In 2008, they celebrated fifty years of marriage. Cupp revealed, "I still write music about her."

After Cupp began writing some songs, he took part in stage shows in Texarkana with Carl Perkins and Johnny Cash. His first show was opening for Perkins and Cash. Cupp remembered, "I decided that I wanted to be a part of the new music instead of just playing guitar for Chessie. I began performing as a singer. I was going out onstage by myself and singing the songs I had written. One night, I was to perform; Carl [Perkins] asked me if I minded if he backed me up with his guitar. Since I was doing my own songs, I didn't know if it would work or not but told him if he thought he could follow, it was okay with me. He then asked Johnny Cash's bass man [Marshall Grant] if he would join us. I went onstage and did my songs, and Carl and the bass man followed as if they had practiced it with me. I was very happy with how it turned out."

Pat Cupp was one of the artists who recorded at KWKH in Shreveport, Louisiana (courtesy Pat Cupp).

Cupp formed a band in mid- to late 1955 and after his initial appearance with Cash and Perkins; he did other shows with them as well as with Roy Orbison in Texarkana. He continued on to do his own tour and played stage shows and dances in Arkansas, Texas, and Louisiana. In April 1956, he appeared on the *Louisiana Hayride*, and a week later he signed a two year contract with Joe Behari of RPM Records. Cupp continued doing various shows, where the most requested song was "I Guess It's Meant That Way": "I guess it was a song most teenagers related to. However, I wanted to do whatever the crowd wanted to hear. I always played for the crowd and not for myself. If I played music that I personally liked to play, then I would have been a jazz musician."

In March 1957, Cupp's rockabilly career came to an end when he enlisted in the United States Air Force, due to his unhappiness with both his manager Jim Lefan and his record label. One of the problems was his manager wanted to change his style from rockabilly to rhythm and blues because he thought it would be more commercial. After the release of "Do Me No Wrong," Lefan sent Cupp to New Orleans where he recorded two songs: "Long Gone Daddy" and "To Be the One" with Little Richard's band. This alteration to his style didn't sit too well with him, and he decided he had had enough of the music business for awhile. Even though, he did play in a few different bands while he was enlisted: "We played the Officers' Clubs and the NCO clubs at bases where I was stationed. I was stationed for a year at Goose Bay Labrador. I played in a band there six nights a week. I had a day job and was able to play at night. I was then sent to Barksdale Air Base in Shreveport, Louisiana. I was playing in a band made up of Air Force guys, called the Knockabouts. We played on the air base and in clubs around Shreveport. I played lead guitar and did most of the vocals." It was during this time that he met *Hayride* alum, guitarist James Burton: "I met James while he was playing at Al's Parie. Our band would go to Al's and sit in for James and the bands he was playing with at the time. James Kirkland was playing bass. It was a year or so before both of them went out to California to play for Ricky Nelson."

In 1961, Cupp was discharged from the Air Force and went back home to his family. About a year later, he was asked to join a group of guys, the Variables, who played mostly jazz music: "I was into jazz, so I welcomed the opportunity to play that kind of music. Well, it wasn't long until some of my fans of the 50s found out and wanted to hear some of the rock music I used to do. Since we were playing for private parties, and they were paying the bill; I played some of my old stuff, and the band followed me. We all got a kick out of it and had fun. Popular demand had us doing some of the old stuff, but we did them with more of a jazz flavor than a rock sound. We became very popular within the circle we played for. We did a year of six nights a week at local supper clubs and opened several dance halls in and around Texarkana." The Variables even did a few recordings. In 1967, they issued "After All" and "New World" on their own label Chance.

In 1976, the singer was chosen to take part as an extra in the movie *The Town That Dreaded Sundown*, in which he played the role of a police officer with one spoken line. Cupp remembered, "I happened into this movie by chance. I was watching the filming and was asked if I would put on a police uniform and be part of a scene."[4] Unfortunately, his name doesn't appear in the credits nor did he receive any pay: "It was fun to do, but it also made me realize that a lot of hard work goes into acting. I now have more respect for actors than I had before."

Cupp worked with the Variables through 1995, while maintaining a day job at the Lone Star Army ammunition plant. He retired from the plant in 1998. Shortly after his retirement, he burned his right leg in a lawnmower accident: "It was burned very badly and took four years and five operations to fix it up. At first, I was told that they would have to take the leg off, but the doctor wanted to try and save it. Luck was with me, and he did a great job. I do have some effects from it but not as much as you would think if you had seen the leg right after I had burned it."

Besides that unfortunate mishap, Cupp has had hearing problems since 1987: "It just gradually kept going, and I began to really have trouble around 1995." He did participate at Hemsby in October of that year to rave reviews. In recent years, he has made a comeback with the help of new digital hearing aids. Cupp was able to perform at the Green Bay Rockin' 50s Fest II and the Rockabilly Rebel Weekender in Indianapolis, both in 2005; a return to Hemsby in 2006; and the Crazy Legs Party in France in 2008. Cupp joined forces with rockabilly fans and Wild Hare Records' owners Dave and Kiersten Moore to release a CD of new material entitled *Pat Cupp*. Thanks to the Moores, he also has his own international fan club, which fans can join as a lifetime member for only $25 in America and $30 elsewhere through his MySpace page at www.myspace.com/daddycupp. Members receive a t-shirt with Cupp's photo, an autographed "I'm a Pat Cupp fan" fan, a letter from Cupp, a welcome letter from the fan club, a membership card, and a 25 percent discount sheet for merchandise. Afterward, bi-annual newsletters from Cupp are mailed out to members.

It appears that Cupp's final performance was at the Crazy Legs Party since the doctors told him if he continues to play live he will completely lose his hearing. However, Cupp conveyed, "I do wish I could be enjoying some of the fruits of rockabilly with the old guys that are still around. It would be fun. However, it is a time that has passed by, and I am just grateful to have my name mentioned in the same breath as some of these guys. I will always enjoy talking to fans and will always take the time to acknowledge them if they get in touch."

Bobby Lee Trammell

In the 1950s, Elvis Presley was accused of being too suggestive, but he was tame in comparison to Bobby Lee Trammell. In fact, Trammell was so controversial that he was banned by promoters across the country. Record labels didn't know how to direct him either, so he never had a hit record. His crazy antics

Backstage at the *County Barn Dance* in Baldwin Park, California, in 1957. From left: Bobby Lee Trammell, Johnny Cash, Wynn Stewart, and Glen Glenn (courtesy Glen Glenn).

often got him into trouble and when he broke his wrist at a 1984 festival in Holland, he decided to call it quits and devote his life to political office. Arkansas gave birth to many rockabilly musicians, but none wilder than Trammell.

Bobby Lee Trammell was born on January 31, 1934, in Jonesboro, Arkansas. Raised on a cotton plantation with musically inclined parents, Trammell took interest in music at an early age. Listening to the *Grand Ole Opry* and sneakily to visit his local black Pentecostal church both made impressions on the youngster. However, guitarist Steve Handford acknowledged, "I never heard Bobby Lee say he was influenced by anybody."[5] Trammell loved Hank Williams, memorizing the words to every new Williams' record that was released. Unfortunately, his religious parents didn't approve of his desire to be a singing star. Trammell admitted, "I was much wilder than Jerry Lee Lewis or Little Richard. My family always said to me that I'm ruining the family name by singing rock and roll. If I had sung religious music, my mother would have listened to me all day long."[6] Handford commented "His parents didn't care much for rock and roll. Bobby Lee was real close to his mother. She never really did say anything negative to him, but she let him know she didn't approve of it."

At age fourteen, Trammell sang country music and dreamt of one day performing on the *Grand Ole Opry*. In 1956, Carl Perkins and Johnny Cash played a show at Nettleton High School in Jonesboro, Arkansas, where Trammell was seated in the front row. Perkins called him onstage to sing with his band and suggested he make a visit to Sam Phillips and Sun Records. Trammell heeded his advice and took a demo tape to Sun, unfortunately, too many acts already signed on Sun and more coming in the door to audition left Phillips with his hands full. In two or three weeks, after more rehearsal, Trammell was slated to return, but he couldn't wait and instead moved to California. Trammell confirmed, "If I'd had a little bit more patience, I probably would have been on Sun Records. I didn't have time to wait for Sun which was very stupid of me."[7] In California, he got a job at the Ford Motor Assembly Plant in Long Beach.

Country promoter Fabor Robinson saw Trammell's stage act at the Jubilee Ballroom in Baldwin Park, California, where he first began as an opening act for country legend Lefty Frizzell. Robinson was so impressed that he brought Trammell to his studio in Hollywood to record "Shirley Lee" and "I Sure Do Love You Baby." Both songs were penned by Trammell and released on the Fabor record label in January 1958. These recordings feature guitarist James Burton and upright bassist James Kirkland, on loan from Bob Luman. That same month, "Shirley Lee" was leased out to ABC Paramount since Robinson didn't have the money to distribute or promote it properly. The single reportedly sold 250,000 copies.[8]

In June 1958, Ricky Nelson recorded "Shirley Lee" for both an extended play 45 rpm and his second album, *Ricky Nelson*, released on Imperial. Since Burton and Kirkland were now a part of Nelson's band, they played on his recording as well. Trammell auditioned for the *Adventures of Ozzie and Harriet*, but he was turned down. However, Nelson's father Ozzie requested that he write more songs for Ricky. Trammell refused since he claimed he was too busy with his own career: "I was having too much fun, but now I look back and wonder how much money I could have made by writing some more songs for Ricky Nelson."[9]

In March 1958, he recorded his second single for Robinson: "You Mostest Girl" b/w "Uh Oh," which were complimented by a doo-wop group sounding like a black version of the Jordanaires. "You Mostest Girl" pays homage to Elvis Presley's "(You're So Square) Baby I Don't Care." The session was so demanding and difficult since he wasn't used to all the instrumentation and formality that he nearly quit his contract over it.[10] In September, he recorded "My Susie J, My Susie Jane" b/w "Should I Make Amends" with Joe Maphis on guitar. Unfortunately, his records didn't sell, and his live performances were getting out of hand to the point of inciting riots. Even though he was hired to play on the *Louisiana Hayride*, the bookings never materialized since *Hayride* regular Tillman Franks "described Trammell as downright vulgar—ten times worse than Elvis Presley."[11]

Too many fiascos led Robinson to retire and sell Trammell's contract. In 1959, Warrior Records released "Open up Your Heart" b/w "Woe is Me." All of Trammell's early recordings were rockin' enough, but his antics kept him from having hit records. Promoters and club owners just didn't want to take a chance on hiring him for fear he might do damage to their venues. Without live appearances, it was hard for him to market a new recording. Handford stated "the biggest mistake Bobby made was he never had a manager. He booked his own jobs and managed his own money. Any publicity that he got he created."

Back home in Arkansas, Trammell named himself the first American Beatle and continued to record throughout the 1960s and 1970s. 1962 provided him with his signature song "Arkansas Twist." Joe Lee, engineer and record producer of Alley Records, recalled the making of "Arkansas Twist" and its flip side "It's All Your Fault": "Bobby Lee had heard I was setting up my studio. He came in and said that he had these two special songs he wanted to do. He kept bugging me, and I said well Bobby I'm not really set up to record anything. He said, 'well, can we just put something down? I'll bring a band in.' It was in the winter when we cut those songs. I had a home tape recorder at home that I used all the time, and so I brought it up there [since the AMPEX recorder he ordered hadn't arrived yet]. I started hanging things around the studio like blankets around the drummer. I had coats hanging on this coat tree, and the microphone in the middle of that coat tree. We cut it about five or six times [to ensure] a pretty good cut. We didn't cut both tunes the same night."[12] They recorded "It's All Your Fault" during the day. Lee recalled, "We got about half way through it, and I told Bobby this is not going to sell. I can understand every word you're saying. He said, 'well, what am I supposed to do?' I said well, I want you to go over next door to the restaurant and buy about five packages of chewing gum. When he came back, I said now open them and put them all in your mouth and chew them up and sing with that gum in your mouth. He did it, and I said now that's a hit. Everybody thought he was drinking but I never saw Bobby take a drink in his life. Everybody was just having a good time. It wasn't a party; it was a serious cut. The only time he got his kicks was onstage. That was when he got his highs. Otherwise, he was pretty serious all the time. He did most of the things I would suggest." Lee cut his master acetate for "Arkansas Twist" and "It's All Your Fault" at Phillips International. Lee explained, "I took the tape to Scotty [Moore] and had him cut the master. On 'It's all Your Fault,' we actually added a little more echo because I didn't have my echo chamber working in my studio. I took that master acetate out to a pressing plant on Chelsea Avenue in Memphis, and I told them I only wanted three hundred pressed. I said it's a pretty bad record. I don't think it's going to do any good." Two dubs were cut from the master that day and brought back home with Lee to Jonesboro. He took the records over to a friend of his, who owned jukeboxes, to see what he thought. His friend put the records on one of the jukeboxes. Lee recalled, "He listened to both sides for about forty-five minutes to an hour. He said, 'That's a good record. I'll take the three hundred.' He then suggested that I bring the dubs to a meeting that the jukebox operators of Northern Arkansas and Southern Missouri was having. I was wondering how I was going to pay for the pressing. I ended up selling 4,600 records that night. We sold close to 8,000 records before it was ever played on the radio station." Sam Phillips told Lee "that 'It's All Your Fault' is the hit, man. You're pushing the wrong side.'" Fortunately, Lee didn't heed his advice.

During the early 1960s, Trammell had Steve Handford on guitar and Jimmy Payne as part-time bass player. In fact, it was Trammell's brother Dale, a dead ringer for James Dean, who fronted the band and played piano. Handford recalled, "We were playing with Dale, and then first thing I knew Bobby Lee said 'boy you guys got one heck of a band. I'm gonna start using you as my band.'" Payne remembered, "He was one of the greatest showmen I know of. We did four forty-five minute sets a night. He always opened the show with 'Arkansas Twist' and did it at least once each other set. He'd do some of Billy Lee Riley's old songs."[13] "You Mostest Girl" and "Shirley Lee" were also staples of his set list. Often times, he would just call out songs on the spot, which made it stressful and frustrating for the musicians who backed him.

Trammell and the band played a seventeen week engagement in Tupelo, Mississippi, playing every weekend. Most of the club dates that they worked, Trammell made $1800 to $2000 while the band only received $15 or $20 a piece. Handford conveyed, "Bobby Lee was tight with his money." Trammell would sell 45 rpm singles out of the trunk of his car. However, he did give quite a few away. At the shows, he'd toss them into the audience like Frisbees. In Oklahoma, a young man got injured when a flying disc hit him in the mouth.

Handford remembered Trammell's wild stage antics like it was yesterday: "He'd jump up onstage and start taking his clothes off. One night he set a piano on fire. He told them what he was going to do. They got an old piano up there, and he shot lighter fluid all over the piano. It ran down his sleeves. He didn't know it and set the piano on fire, and it nearly burned him up too. He shook that coat real quick. Everybody just thought that was part of the show." Trammell was always breaking microphones because he would jump up and down and jerk the cords past their limitations. Handford ended up repairing the broken microphones. Bassist Payne recalled, "Bobby would do anything to get attention." At another show, Trammell was twisting to his song "Arkansas Twist" on top of a jukebox when the bubble gave way, and he landed his feet on the turntable.

He even dyed his hair green just to be different besides wearing outlandish green and orange outfits. Handford revealed, "He had these big old high collars like Elvis wore, but he had them cut to where his ears would stick out. Sometimes it was embarrassing when he came out there like that." One of his suits was crafted from the material of his grandmother's vintage satin gold drapes. He liked how the fabric shined.

In 1972, Trammell scored on the country charts with "Love Isn't Love" on the Souncot record label. Five years later, he recorded a bluesy version of "It's All Your Fault" for the Sun International label. At this time, Trammell took a break from performing.

In 1984, Trammell participated in the rockabilly revival with a solo appearance at the Rockhouse Festival in Eindhoven, Holland. As usual, he put on a wild and frantic show even though he was not completely up to par. The show ended abruptly in disaster when Trammell tried to jump on the piano. He landed awkwardly on top of the piano; wobbled, lost his balance and fell, breaking his wrist in the process.[14] The Holland performance would be Trammell's last. He gave up his musical career and entered politics. Handford added, "Bobby was pretty smart, and he was always curious about politics." In 1997, he was elected to the Arkansas House of Representatives where he served until 2002. He also held a position in the Quorum Court until he died.

Trammell died on February 20, 2008. The dream that fans had hoped would come true, Trammell someday returning to the stage, was no longer possible. All that was left was the musical legacy he left behind; those unforgettable performances and the raw uninhibited singles that he recorded.

Ronnie Hawkins

Ronnie Hawkins, "Mr. Dynamo," popularized the club circuit in Canada. He formed his first band, The Hawks, in 1958, and they went onto superstar status as the Band. The Band were successful on their own as well as providing the electrified sound for Bob Dylan in the mid–1960s. Throughout the 1960s and 1970s, Hawkins continued to record and perform. In 1992, he played at the inaugural party for former president Bill Clinton, who is one of Hawkins' biggest fans. Hawkins and the Hawks have been praised as the best rock and roll band to ever play the Toronto music scene.

Ronnie Hawkins' Hawks famously became known as the Band and helped to electrify Bob Dylan's sound (courtesy Ronnie Hawkins).

Ronnie Hawkins was born on January 10, 1935, in Huntsville, Arkansas. All of his relatives were musicians, including his first cousin Dale Hawkins, who scored a hit with "Susie Q" in 1957. At three years of age, Hawkins began singing: "I just wanted to be a showoff. All my relatives on the Hawkins' side were amateur musicians, even my dad. Dale's father was an unbelievably talented musician. Everybody sang songs for something to do. My mother's parents had a Victrola with all these old sad songs on it, and I used to listen to them."[15] That's where he first heard Jimmie Rodgers: "He was the first one who just knocked me out with everything he did. Hank Williams was another one. Hank had such good stories. That's what I went by, the story of a song."

In the summer of his junior and senior year in high school, Hawkins hung around on Beale Street checking out the local blues acts: "B.B. King wasn't even eighteen yet and was still playing outside the clubs. All the artists that I met down there were recording for Sun Records. That's when I first heard of Mr. Sam Phillips. When I discovered blues, I started listening to Muddy Waters, Howlin' Wolf, Bobby "Blue" Bland, and all these old blacks that recorded down there at Sun. That's the stuff we were trying to copy. Rockabilly was a bunch of country boys, like me, that all of a sudden really liked the blues, and we tried to copy it." Hawkins volunteered and briefly joined the Army, where he played in special service: "I could go in for six months active duty, and that was the quickest way of getting out. I wanted to get out and get into music."

Hawkins formed his first band, the Hawks, while attending the University of Arkansas, where he studied physical education. In 1958, he unsuccessfully auditioned for Sun: "I did a bunch of demo stuff." He recorded at Sun without a band, sang along with a prearranged song. They gained a following throughout the south by playing clubs and dances. Hawkins disclosed, "I never did play the guitar very much. I learned a few chords at first, but I couldn't keep up with the other musicians that were learning in leaps and bounds. I was trying to learn the words and get us booked by begging someone to let us play. I couldn't keep up with them, so I just turned into one of those monkey acts, where I jumped around and danced." At the time, he owned the Rockwood club in Fayetteville, Arkansas, where he booked Carl Perkins, Jerry Lee Lewis, Conway Twitty, and Roy Orbison. The following year, Hawkins performed a few shows in Canada and was signed to a five year contract with Roulette Records. Roulette issued "Forty Days" b/w "One of These Days" in May, while in August, his biggest hit "Mary Lou" b/w "Need Your Lovin'" soared to #26 on the Billboard charts. Hawkins revealed, "'Mary Lou' was the song that sold the most internationally. Although, I had several songs that hit the Top Ten and even became #1 or #2 in Canada."

In the early 1960s, Hawkins moved to Canada permanently: "I came up here first just as an adventure. Nobody heard rock and roll up here much. We started it. It was a brand new music that worked." The only original member of the Hawks who made the trip with him was Levon Helm. Hawkins conveyed,

"I came out first with all Arkansas boys, but as they got tired of Canada and wanted to go home to their girlfriends, I started finding Canadian musicians that I thought would be able to do the job in a short period of time. I brought Robbie Robertson in as a roadie and then I put him on bass. Roy [Buchanan] was in the group for a short time and taught Robbie a lot. Roy was somethin' else. He was mysterious, but he had a gift beyond belief. Robbie was trained to eventually play guitar. Rick Danko was a butcher in London, Ontario, and he had a little polka type band. He was a good looking kid who had a good voice. I brought Garth Hudson into the band because of his knowledge of music, to teach everybody. [Hudson had aspirations of being a music teacher.] They had lessons everyday. I hired Richard Manuel because he could really sing soul music well." Hawkins wanted to prepare his musicians to issue their own records. By 1963, the Hawks left Hawkins. Robbie Robertson said, "Eventually, Ronnie built us up to the point where we outgrew his music and had to leave."[16]

The Hawks became known as the Band and went to work for Bob Dylan in 1965. They toured with him for a year and were his backing on *The Basement Tapes*. Hawkins continued to perform and record, including a few tours to Europe. In 1984, he won a Juno, equivalent to a Grammy, for Best Country Male Vocalist for his hit "Making It Again." In 1989, he got the chance of a lifetime when he reunited with the Band for the destruction of the Berlin Wall. Six years later, the Band was inducted into the Rock and Roll Hall of Fame. In recent years, Hawkins had a bout with pancreatic cancer. He was acknowledged by Canada when he was inducted into the Canadian Music Industry Hall of Fame in 2004.

Four

Texas Rockabillies

Buddy Holly and the Crickets

Buddy Holly and the Crickets are troubadours of rock and roll. Holly is considered the king of western bop and the father of Tex-Mex, which according to Cricket Jerry Allison is "a mix between Gene Autry and Clyde McPhatter."[1] Scoring top ten hits, captivating audiences at Alan Freed shows, and permeating the airwaves helped them gain worldwide appeal. Not fade away seemed to be Holly's mainstay, until February 3, 1959, when he was tragically killed in an airplane crash. However, the music still lives on today thanks to the Crickets—Sonny Curtis, Jerry Allison, and Joe B. Mauldin, who continue to tour.

Charles Hardin Holley (more famously known as Buddy Holly) was born on September 7, 1936, in Lubbock, Texas. He had three siblings, a sister and two brothers. His brothers Larry and Travis played an integral part in his love of music. His brother Travis explained, "Buddy got most of his musical talent from mother's side of the family. Our father loved music, but he couldn't carry a tune in a bag, but he would insist on us playing. Most of the songs that we sang of course were Baptist songs."[2] Holly joined his brothers in an amateur contest after their parents convinced them that Buddy was too cute to be left behind. Being a kid, he won over the crowd with his vocals on "Have You Ever Gone Sailing (Down the River of Memories?)." He also played violin on the show, but that didn't last long since Holly didn't like playing the instrument. When his parents later bought him a steel guitar, he complained, "I don't want a guitar like that; I want one like Travis' got," so he borrowed his brother's guitar.[3]

When Holly was twelve years old, he teamed up with classmate Bob Montgomery. They were a country duo, who harmonized like the father of bluegrass Bill Monroe. At that time, Holly played a four string banjo. Holly's father was a carpenter, and the young boys worked as his apprentices to pay for studio sessions. In 1954, they recorded a demo of "Flower of My Heart." Buddy and Bob, as they were known, were Lubbock's most popular act.

Sonny Curtis soon joined the group: "I had a friend from Meadow, Texas, where I grew up, [who had] moved to Lubbock, and went to school with Buddy [Holly] and Bob Montgomery. He kept coming back home to Meadow saying 'Man, you got to meet these two guys who play bluegrass.' I was a big bluegrass fan. One day, he took me over to meet them. After school, we all got together at Buddy's house, and we sort of skipped all the small talk and went straight into picking music. That was about 1954.... We were doing songs like 'Flower of My Heart,' which Buddy and Bob wrote and a whole bunch of contemporary country and bluegrass stuff. I [also] remember playing 'Changing All Those Changes' really early on."[4]

Curtis learned how to play guitar at a very early age: "I had a lovely aunt who taught me how to play 'Little Brown Jug.' I was so small at the time that I couldn't reach all the way across the neck. I had to play on the top four strings." As he grew older, he taught himself more guitar techniques but did take a few lessons from local jazz hero Clyde Hankins.

A few years later, Holly formed The Three Tunes with Curtis and bassist Don Guess. Curtis recalled, "We got a contract for Decca Records through a road manager for Marty Robbins. [Robbins was a friend of theirs]. We traveled to Nashville three or four times to record [at Bradley's Barn]. The very first sides we cut were 'Blue Days-Black Nights' b/w 'Love Me.'" After those initial recordings, they played nightclubs and hung out at radio stations hoping to catch a break.

Their early rock and roll sound was heavily influenced by Elvis Presley. Curtis revealed, "Buddy was a huge fan of Elvis' music. We didn't really tour with Elvis, but we were on some of the same shows. As a matter of fact, Elvis and Buddy got to be pretty good friends." The trio switched from performing country music to rock and roll right after seeing and opening for Presley at the Fair Park Auditorium in Lubbock. Their reaction was: "Wow, this is great! This is what we ought to be doing." Curtis explained, "We had the very same makeup as Elvis. Don Guess played the upright bass, I played the electric guitar, and Buddy sang the songs. We did all of Elvis' tunes like 'Good Rockin' Tonight' 'Baby, Let's Play House,' and 'That's All Right.'" Curtis played the guitar riffs exactly like Scotty Moore. They both loved Chet Atkins, their musical influence. Curtis added, "We were Elvis clones, too bad we didn't look like him."

Those early Decca records, such as "Ting-A-Ling," "Rock Around with Ollie Vee," which Curtis wrote, and "I'm Gonna Set My Foot Down" pay homage to Presley's early rockabilly style. Presley was a major influence, but listening to the radio program *Stan's Record Rack* out of Shreveport helped Curtis and Holly incorporate blues artists, such as Lonnie Johnson and Lead Belly, into their music as well. Even though Curtis appeared on those Decca rockabilly recordings and an early country version of "That'll Be the Day," by the time The Crickets were formed, he had left to tour with country superstar Slim Whitman.

Buddy Holly and the Crickets in a 1958 promotional photo for Brunswick Records. From top: Jerry Allison, Buddy Holly, and Joe B. Mauldin (courtesy Steve Bonner Collection).

Jerry Ivan "J.I." Allison originally met Holly when he was in the seventh grade, and Holly was in the eighth at J.T. Hutchinson junior high school in Lubbock: "He was just another student. I don't even remember where I met him. I think it was on the playground. I didn't become friends with him until high school. After seeing Buddy and Bob play, I was very impressed." The first song Allison remembered playing with Holly was Bill Haley's "Forty Cups of Coffee," a blues type song. Allison started playing drums in the school band in fifth grade. He eventually took lessons in junior high school. His musical influences included singers Little Richard and Bill Monroe and Little Richard's drummer Charles Connor.

The band practiced almost every night, trying to achieve a hit song. One night just Allison and Holly were rehearsing at Allison's mom's house when they thought of a song. Allison commented, "Buddy had a tune in his head and said, 'Hey, let's write a song.' I said that'll be the day. He said, 'That's a good idea,' so we wrote it in about thirty minutes."[5] The title for "That'll Be the Day" was taken from a line spoken by John Wayne in the western movie *The Searchers*.

Songwriter Sonny West remembered, "In 1956, Buddy was going to Nashville and recording his rockabilly songs. He even recorded 'That'll Be the Day' in Nashville. It was a terrible recording because he was singing way out of his range."[6] Decca and Nashville didn't seem to have a clue, so Holly and Decca parted ways after only a year.

Joe B. Mauldin was still in high school when he began playing upright bass for the Crickets. Mauldin acknowledged, "I knew of Buddy. I had seen J.I., Sonny, and Buddy doing jobs around Lubbock. I was playing with another band. I didn't really know him until thanks to J.I.; they needed a bass player for a job they were going to do over in New Mexico, and J.I. suggested they talk to me about it. From then on, I was just kind of a permanent part of the Crickets."[7] Mauldin was influenced by Elvis Presley's bassist Bill Black and Fats Domino's bassist Irving Charles.

Allison also recruited guitarist Niki Sullivan for the Crickets. Sullivan first met Buddy Holly at a jam session in Lubbock, Texas. Holly was impressed by his guitar playing, so Sullivan then joined the group.[8]

Allison and Holly came up with the Crickets for the group's name. According to Mauldin, "there was a group called The Spiders out at the time who had a record called 'Witchcraft,' and we all really dug that record. That's what made J.I. think 'Hmmm, The Spiders are hot, so maybe [another] insect type group, so he came up with the Crickets."

Soon, Bob Thiele signed the group to Coral/Brunswick Records in New York. However, all dealings with them went through manager Norman Petty. In June 1957, "That'll Be the Day" b/w "I'm Lookin' For Someone to Love" were the first songs released by Coral's subsidiary Brunswick. West recollected, "Buddy's name was not on the record for 'That'll Be the Day' as artist. It was under a group name, the Crickets. Originally this was done to hide the fact that Holly was on the record as he was still under contract to Decca Records and was not supposed to be recording that song for five years because he had recorded it in Nashville for Decca. As it turned out, the Crickets' recording of that song was put out on Brunswick, a company that belonged to Decca, so they could not actually sue their own company."

A disk jockey in Cincinnati, Ohio, liked "That'll Be the Day" so much that he played it continuously throughout his hour long radio show. By August, the song hit #1 on the Billboard charts. Allison and Mauldin both were ecstatic to hear that it had topped the charts. Mauldin added, "Oh yeah, I was tickled to death because that was my first time ever being a professional musician, so to speak, because I was very young. I was really happy, just made me want to get back in the studio and cut some more things to see if we could get another one." Allison remembered it as if it was yesterday: "I was as happy as I could possibly be. It was pretty unbelievable."

After "That'll Be the Day," Holly and the Crickets were non-stop hit makers. Holly's guitar playing on his Fender Stratocaster was unique and made his songs stand apart from others because he played on all of the strings in an always downward motion. According to Sonny Curtis, "he was a rhythm lead guitarist."[9] Coral next released "Peggy Sue" b/w "Everyday." "Peggy Sue" was written about Allison's first wife and was originally titled "Cindy Lou" with a slow Latin rumba beat. The #3 song was the first rockabilly hit to feature that style of drumming. While trying to record "Peggy Sue" after many dissatisfying takes, Niki Sullivan flipped a switch on Holly's guitar, allowing him to break into the now famous guitar solo.[10]

At this time, there were records released as Buddy Holly and also as the Crickets simultaneously. Allison retold the story behind this experimentation: "We had a thing where we could cut a whole bunch of records. We started out 'Peggy Sue' without any background vocals, so we put ones out that we wanted background vocals on as the Crickets. That way we could put two records out at once. It was crazy to think you could release two records and expect them to get played, but it worked for three [of them]: 'Peggy Sue,' 'Words of Love,' and 'That'll Be the Day.' We cut 'Oh Boy' and 'Peggy Sue' at the same time." "Peggy Sue" was credited to Buddy Holly while "Oh Boy" was credited to the Crickets. Allison added, "People didn't realize what people looked like or who was in the band [back then]," so they did not know that they were essentially buying the same record.

Sonny West, who met Holly at a radio station in 1956, wrote Holly's 1958 #10 hit "Oh Boy" while its flip side "Not Fade Away" was co-written by guitarist Niki Sullivan. In regard to "Oh Boy," West affirmed, "Whenever Buddy went to Clovis to rerecord 'That'll Be the Day' that's when I had written 'Oh Boy.' He heard it from a demo I had made in Clovis in February 1957. You'd have to be living under a rock not to know 'Oh Boy.' Some people thought it was a little suggestive. Ed Sullivan didn't like it. He didn't want Buddy to sing it." However, on the Crickets' January 26, 1958 *Ed Sullivan Show* appearance, they were slated to perform two songs, but when Sullivan found out that Holly was going to sing "Oh Boy" whether he liked it or not, all of a sudden they ran out of time. Therefore, they only sang their first choice, "Oh Boy." Sullivan invited the group back for a third appearance, but he was turned down.

February 1958 saw releases of "I'm Gonna Love You Too" b/w "Listen to Me" and "Maybe Baby" b/w "Tell Me How." If one listens closely right after the last note of "I'm Gonna Love You Too," you can hear a cricket chirping. Mauldin remembered, "When we would get up in the echo chamber, he would hide. We would go back down to the studio, and he would start chirping again, so we just played over him." According to Sonny West, "Norman's echo chamber was in the loft of a building next door that was lined with tile. He would send the signal to a speaker in the loft, pick up the sound from one of the microphones, and return the sound back to his console. Microphones were placed at different distances from the speaker. This way he could choose how much delay he was looking for on any particular session. This was usually done late in the night so as to not get any traffic noise from the street."

"Maybe Baby" was another song with an interesting story behind it. Allison recollected that rockabilly legend Dale Hawkins was the one who convinced them to keep it with a swing beat: "We were playing it for Dale up in New York at the Brooklyn Paramount. We got to be friends with him. He said 'Man, you ought to cut it like "Lucille," like Little Richard does it,' so we went back and rerecorded it because of him." "Maybe Baby" peaked at #17 on the Billboard charts.

Sonny West composed another song for Holly, "Rave On," which was released by Coral in April 1958 with its flip side "Take Your Time." West was thrilled that Holly chose another of his songs to record: "Buddy was the kind of artist who could turn a song that didn't really sound all that exciting and make it exciting. You could do 'Rave On' pretty dully if you wanted to but when it comes on your ears kind of perk up because of the way he did it. I recorded 'Rave On' before he did, but his record was much better than mine. Most of the recordings that were released as solo recordings by Buddy did not have backing vocals. One exception was 'Rave On.' Buddy loved the song. Norman thought it was a bit country sounding. I think Norman helped arrange the backing vocals for the session, which took place in January 1958 at Bell Sound Studios in New York. Norman is playing piano. Also, there were two professional guitarists on it since Buddy did not play guitar on the song. Union session vocalists were also used. I would say both Norman and Buddy could see that it needed the vocalists to fit the market at the time. I guess they were right." Holly had a #37 record with "Rave On."

Numerous record releases kept the group in high demand. Alan Freed booked Holly and the Crickets on several successful tours with other stars of the day, including the Everly Brothers, Chuck Berry, Eddie Cochran, LaVern Baker, Paul Anka, and Bo Diddley. Promoters thought the Crickets sounded black, so they were booked to play usually all-black venues, including the Apollo Theatre in New York City, the Royal Theatre in Baltimore, and the Howard Theatre in Washington, D.C. Allison remarked, "That was our kind of music. We were big fans of theirs [artists like Little Richard]. We were trying to sound black." In 1958, they played a three week tour in England and Australia. Allison recalled, "We acted as crazy as possible, rock and rolled it. Buddy always jumped around a lot and acted silly. Joe B. would lie on his back to play bass, and Buddy would get down and sing into his bass mike."[11]

Most of Holly's signature songs (from 1957 and 1958) were recorded at Norman Petty's Recording Studios in Clovis, New Mexico, with the exception of "Maybe Baby" and "Rave On." Besides engineering, Petty was the group's manager and applied his name to many of the songs as co-songwriter. Sonny West revealed, "Norman was quite good at writing songs, although not especially adept at rock and roll type material. The way he got his name on most of Buddy's songs, my songs, and lots of others is that he just took the liberty. Since he had the power to either help us or not, most of us reluctantly agreed. On most of the songs he actually had little or nothing to do with as far as writing." Although Holly's musical genius and Petty's engineering was an ideal combination. According to Sonny Curtis, "Norman Petty was a great engineer. He was able to just capture the raw talent that was being presented to him." West recalled, "Norman really had an ear for recording songs and for getting the most out of the artists. He knew music."

The year 1958 had its share of highs and lows for the Crickets. Niki Sullivan left the group. Jerry Allison released a solo effort, "Real Wild Child," with accompaniment by Holly on guitar. Holly married Maria Elena Santiago in August 1958. The group then disbanded in October. Allison and Mauldin were going to move to New York City to be with Holly, but Norman Petty quickly talked them out of their decision.

With Holly's move to New York City, he became a producer and incorporated string arrangements into his songs. In the next few years, Coral released "It Doesn't Matter Anymore," "Peggy Sue Got Married," and "True Love Ways." Settling into married life, Holly wasn't going to go on tour for awhile; unfortunately financial issues changed all of that. Holly, the Big Bopper, Ritchie Valens, Dion and the Belmonts, and Frankie Sardo all went on a tour of the Midwest, more famously known as the Winter Dance Party tour. It was the middle of winter, and the towns they stopped in like Green Bay, Milwaukee, and Kenosha, Wisconsin, were all frozen tundra. When the buses' heaters didn't work properly, Holly chartered a three seated plane after their last show in Clear Lake, Iowa, to get them to the next town. He and his two bandmates Waylon Jennings and Tommy Allsup were supposed to be the passengers, but Jennings and Allsup switched places with the Big Bopper and Valens at the last minute. The plane crashed shortly after takeoff and took the lives of all those on board. Holly perished on February 3, 1959 at only twenty-two years of age. It is known as the day the music died and referred to as such in the 1971 #1 song "American Pie" by Don McLean.

Contrary to popular belief, the Crickets were not going to see Holly in the next town to tell him how they wished to reunite. They had a phone call to him waiting for him to return it, but he never got their message. They were "devastated" when they heard the news of Holly's untimely passing.

Even after Holly's death, the Crickets remained busy. Sonny Curtis became a successful songwriter penning such hits as The Everly Brothers' "Walk Right Back," Bobby Fuller Four's "I Fought the Law," which completely embodies Holly's sound with the Crickets, and *The Mary Tyler Moore Show* theme song "Love Is All Around." He and Jerry Allison also played on Eddie Cochran's final recordings: "Cut Across Shorty," "Three Steps To Heaven," and "Cherished Memories." Niki Sullivan retired from the recording business altogether and took a job at Sony Records. In 1978, he reunited with the Crickets for one night only at a Buddy Holly Festival. He passed away in 2004.[12] With one time Cricket Jerry Naylor, they had a few minor charted hits. They recorded an album with pop singer Bobby Vee, and in the late 1980s Paul McCartney played on and produced a single for them, "T-Shirt." The Crickets also continue to tour, spreading the magic of Holly's music to the masses. Today, Curtis, Allison, and Mauldin are sometimes joined by Glen D. Hardin on the road. Hardin arranged "An American Trilogy" for Elvis Presley. He was with Presley for eight years, from 1969 to 1977. Curtis added, "We all grew up together. Glen D. and I went to school together when we were kids." Hardin was not a member of The Crickets while Holly was still living.

Even after fifty years of his passing, Holly's influence has not diminished. When the British Invasion hit American shores, the first song recorded by The Beatles was "That'll Be the Day," and The Rolling Stones paid homage to Holly by recording "Not Fade Away." Pop songstress Linda Ronstadt recorded "It's So Easy," "It Doesn't Matter Anymore," and "That'll Be the Day" while country superstar Tanya Tucker sang "Not Fade Away." Musicians and fans alike appreciate that Holly was able to go from a nobody to a somebody without compromising himself: "The appeal is following the hero's journey, a story of a self-confident and determined young man joined by trusty companions: a mentor, a muse, and a true love only to meet the incomprehensible: death in his prime."[13]

Sonny West

Norman Petty engineered most of Buddy Holly's sessions, including his number #1 hit "That'll Be the Day," at his studio in Clovis, New Mexico. Prior to Holly's arrival, Petty briefly managed and recorded another native of Lubbock, Texas, rockabilly Sonny West. In September 1956, Petty's label Nor-Va-Jak released "Rock-Ola Ruby" b/w "Sweet Rockin' Baby." Unfortunately, the record did not sell well due to lack of promotion and distribution. However, today it is a rare collector's item, fetching in excess of $1500, amongst rockabilly enthusiasts.[14]

Sonny West was born on July 30, 1937, in Lubbock, Texas. He is the youngest of the family, which includes one brother and two sisters. His father was a sharecropper, and the family was constantly on the move looking for work. West acknowledged, "Not only was I a loner by choice but also because nobody ever knew me. I was left to my own designs when I was young."[15]

Music provided an outlet for his solitude. He originally played mandolin then switched to guitar in 1952. At fifteen, he began taking music seriously by singing country blues with classmates at school programs. West's early musical influences included his grandfather and country legends Hank Williams and Jimmie Rodgers. Willie Nelson's "Maiden's Prayer" was one of the first songs he sang. West recalled, "I didn't hear a lot of the blues players until I was in my early teens."

In 1956, West put together a four piece band to do some recording. By this time, Elvis Presley and Carl Perkins had been successful with rockabilly, so West decided to try his hand at it: "Rockabilly was a natural way for me to go because I didn't hear what I really wanted to hear on the radio. When I started to hear some things I liked, I said that's it. One of the songs I always loved was Ray Charles' 'I Got a Woman.' I just loved the overall sound of it. One of my favorite rockabilly artists was Carl Perkins because he seemed to nail it. He just had it. Elvis' records from '54 and '55, I loved all of those. I also liked Bo Diddley's early stuff. I knew I couldn't do country, and I didn't like to do ballads, so where else was I gonna go? I've always loved rockabilly, and I always will."

Around this time, he received a new Martin acoustic guitar: "I had my name painted on it. I don't know how it came about if I had instructed the guy or he did it as a lark [but it came out as Sonnee West]." His name also appeared as Sonnee on his first record. For recording, West wanted to duplicate the slap back echo that Sam Phillips had at Sun Studio, so in May 1956 he went to Memphis to audition for Phillips. West remembered, "I went to see Sam Phillips to see if I could work something out with him. I took off and went over there just on a whim. I had to wait around a long time to talk to him. I said I'm not gonna leave until I do. I was just sure that he would want to hear me." With his self composed "Rock-Ola Ruby" in tow, he was thoroughly disappointed when Phillips didn't have the time to listen to him: "He told me he had too many artists to deal with."

After Memphis, West recalled, "I found out from a disk jockey that Norman Petty had the only studio around that could really record. The slap back echo was the only way Elvis Presley's songs would have gotten as much attention as they did because Sam had a perfect delay in the tape. Norman would never use a tape delay. He thought tape delay was rigged. He didn't have his echo chamber built yet, so instead we recorded at the Lyceum Theatre [which was built in 1920 and had cathedral sound]. I recorded 'Rock-Ola Ruby' and 'Sweet Rockin' Baby' there live on reel to reel tape. Norman had the best there was at the time, an AMPEX recorder, and it happened to be portable enough that he put in on the back of the truck and took it down to the theatre. It worked

Sonny West singing his signature tune "Rock-Ola Ruby" onstage in Lubbock, Texas, in 1956 with upright bassist Jim Metze (courtesy Sonny West).

out real good. After the show, we cut those two records and put them out on his label, Nor-Va-Jak."

Only seven hundred copies were produced, two hundred 78 rpms and five hundred 45 rpms. West acknowledged, "They didn't sell that's why they're such big collector's items today. According to the *Guide to Rare Rockabilly and Rock and Roll 45 rpms* by Tom Lincoln and Dick Blackburn, "Next to Elvis' Sun rockabilly pieces, this may be the next most sought after rockabilly record by collectors who may not specialize in rockabilly."[16] West continued, "We went around to radio stations. In those days, you could go to the station, talk to the disk jockey, and he'd put the record on and play it. Without any distribution, except locally, you just can't get anywhere."

He and his band continued to play locally although there wasn't really any money in playing: "We played a lot, sometimes for $10 or $15 a piece and sometimes for free. I had to work a lot of other jobs to help pay for my sessions." An unsupportive family didn't help matters either, but he refused to let these factors deter him: "My dad thought music was foolishness. He told me, 'There's a few guys in the music business that have it all sewn up, just forget it.' My dad wouldn't have spent a dime on my music. He figured it was going to take me straight to you know where. It makes you stronger if you can live through it. I'm quite sure that actually helped me."

By 1957, West began to concentrate his efforts on songwriting. He decided it was time to write love songs: "I was looking over some of the old show tunes that they had in the '30s in a book that I had, and something kind of clicked." He then wound up at Norman Petty's Recording Studios in Clovis, New Mexico, whose size was equivalent to Sun Studio and provided him with acetate copies of his recordings. In February, he recorded a demo of "Oh Boy." "Oh Boy" was a #10 hit for Buddy Holly and the Crickets in 1957.

Close to the end of 1957, Petty took over as manager and got West a recording contract with Atlantic Records: "When Atlantic came along, I thought maybe I'm going to get into the big time, but it just didn't happen." West then wrote "Rave On," which was really hard to write: "I wrote it four or five different ways at four or five different times. I took it over to Clovis, and I started to record it, and Norman just turned the recorder off and walked out of the control room. I said what's wrong? I figured if I'm paying for the recording then he'll record anything I want. He said, 'Aww, that'll never work.' He never did tell me what was wrong with it. I can imagine it must have been pretty bad if he couldn't stand to listen to it. I went back and worked on it some more." In December, he recorded "Rave On" for Atlantic. Even though he was signed to a two year contract with at least four releases, Atlantic released only one single "Rave On" b/w "Call on Cupid" in February 1958. "Rave On" turned out to be the bigger success for Buddy Holly and the Crickets, peaking at #37 on the Billboard charts.

Petty failed at being West's manager: "In late 1958, I recorded a song there and spent my last dollar, paying for the musicians and the session. I had worked really hard at manual labor to save the money. Following the session, I went into the control room, and he had the contracts all made out listing him as an equal writer. This was the last straw for me. I refused to give him writer credits. He immediately grabbed the contracts and ripped them in half, mumbling something inaudible and his face red with anger. I took the ripped contracts and my tapes and left. I never went back there to record." He wasn't actively involved in West's career anyway since he was busy with Holly. West acknowledged, "Norman really didn't have time for me."

When West's recording career didn't pan out like he had anticipated, he made the choice not to move to Nashville like some of his contemporaries: "I was a little stubborn about going to Nashville, and I shouldn't have been. I should've gone and hooked up with some people. I could have really gone somewhere."

In 1961, he started a family and became involved in the jukebox business, which lasted for seven years: "First of all, I went to work for a company that had some jukeboxes, and I learned how to work on them. I sort of had a knack for it." Then he started his own company and operated it for awhile before moving to a bigger company in Albuquerque where he ordered records for jukebox placement in restaurants and bars. West chose the records from a flyer that Dallas' One Stop distributor had and because he belonged to the Music Operators of America he was given free samples: "If you were a member, the big record companies would send you samples of their latest records." At one time, he even owned a 1960 Rock-Ola jukebox.

West returned to playing in the mid–1970s. Since then he has made a successful return to rockabilly with appearances at the Hemsby Weekender in England, Green Bay Wisconsin's Rockin' 50s Fest, the Clovis Music Fest, and the Viva Las Vegas Weekender. His set usually includes Hank Williams' "Move It On Over": That's one I like to do in my shows. It kind of identifies what rockabilly came to be." In 2002, England's Rollercoaster Records released *Sweet Rockin' Rock-Ola Ruby*, which included his best known songs along with new recordings. Lance Records out of Albuquerque released *West Texas Wind* in 2005. Besides recording and performing, West also takes guitars and customizes them.

Even though West had a couple of rockabilly releases, "Oh Boy" and "Rave On" are his claims to fame. "Oh Boy" has been featured in the television programs *Quantum Leap* and *Happy Days*. In 2006, *American Idol* contestant Bucky Covington sang "Oh Boy" on the hit reality show. It was West's favorite song to write: "I can't write a song that's better than 'Oh Boy.' I'll probably never outdo it." As for "Rave On," in the December 9, 2004 issue of *Rolling Stone* magazine, they listed it as one of the 500 greatest songs of all-time, ranking at #154. The song was also featured in the 1998 movie *Pleasantville* starring Reese Witherspoon and the 1988 mega hit *Cocktail* starring Tom Cruise. Although folk rocker John Mellencamp sang the song for the soundtrack, not Buddy Holly: "It took Buddy Holly thirty years to sell what they sold in a few months."

Gene Summers

Many musicians have influenced Gene Summers, including Hank Ballard and the Midnighters, Carl Perkins, Hank Williams, Lefty Frizzell, Carl Smith, and Tommy Sands, but his biggest musical influence is Elvis Presley. He never got a chance to meet Presley, but Summers' wife, Dea wrote a song entitled "Goodbye Priscilla" that pays homage to the singer. In 1977, the song was released as a one sided single; its reverse side was blank. The record label was interested in pushing only the one song; unfortunately it didn't catch on with the buying public and was pulled from the shelf. Summers' entire career was held back due to lack of promotion by various record labels. He was a big hit in Europe and wasn't even aware until the rockabilly revival in the late 1970s. In 1958, Summers began his recording career with "School of Rock and Roll," and fifty years later released a new album *Reminisce Café*, which contains new material that sounds like recordings from the 1950s. The CD was released on February 1, 2008, exactly fifty years to the day that his first single was issued.

Gene Summers showcasing his rebellious side in a 1958 publicity photo for Jan Records (courtesy Gene Summers).

David Eugene Summers was born on January 3, 1939, in Dallas, Texas. Summers is an only child and attended school in Duncanville, Texas. His whole family was very supportive of his musical endeavors. The Moore Brothers, which consisted of his uncles and singing aunt, made regular radio appearances and played shows in the Dallas/Fort Worth area. At age six, Summers entered local talent contests. In sixth grade, he took guitar lessons from Trick Brothers National Guitar Institute, where he learned the basic guitar chords. By 1954, Summers had formed his own vocal group, the Four Star Quartet. They sang doo wop and gospel music all throughout high school. When he graduated in 1957, the quartet received a music scholarship to the Howard Payne College in Brownsville, Texas. However, around that same time Summers had begun work with his new band The Rebels and decided not to accept the invitation to attend college. The Rebels consisted of James McClung on guitar and Gary Moon on drums, who were both classmates of Summers. The bassist, Benny Williams, played in a lounge music combo before signing on for rock and roll with The Rebels. After helping to promote the band, Bill Brown occasionally played piano for them.

Jed Tarver, who would later write Summers' songs "Twixteen" and "Nervous," saw Summers and The Rebels on local TV and made them an offer. Tarver, who wrote under his wife's name Mary Tarver, told them if they recorded his song "Straight Skirt" that he would get them a recording contract with Jan Records. He came through on the deal, and on February 1, 1958, "School of Rock and Roll" b/w "Straight Skirt" hit the market. According to Summers, "Straight Skirt" just missed making Billboard's Top 100. He had patterned his phrasing in that song as a tribute to Tommy Sands. Shortly after the release of "Straight Skirt," Mercury Records wanted to lease the Jan masters for release. However, a deal was never finalized, and Mercury's hottest group The Diamonds recorded their version of "Straight Skirt," also released in 1958.

In June 1958, Jan Records released "Nervous" b/w "Gotta Lotta That" and later that same year "Twixteen" b/w "I'll Never Be Lonely" was issued, this time on the Jane label. An alternate take of "Gotta Lotta That" was recorded at the time but not released because of its suggestive lyrics.

Baltimore was one of the biggest areas for record sales, so Summers and The Rebels toured extensively and appeared several times on the *Buddy Deane Show* and the *Milt Grant Show* to help promote the records. The publicity agent even had Summers stay with him and his wife while promoting "Nervous" and "Straight Skirt."

By 1961, The Rebels had called it quits. Summers had a new band The Tom Toms and toured the West Coast with Chuck Berry, Bobby Hendricks, and the original Drifters. Summers remembered Berry as being very prolific in country music. While touring on the bus, "Chuck would play guitar, and we would all sing along on songs like Roy Acuff's 'Wabash Cannonball.'" [17] There were several times in 1961–1962 when Dea and Gene would have after hour parties at their home with Bill Pinkey's Drifters in attendance. In 1963, Summers had his biggest selling single with "Big Blue Diamonds," which would also become his signature song throughout the 1960s and 1970s.

One of Summers' friends was fellow Texas rockabilly, Johnny Carroll. They had met in 1957 after Carroll wrapped filming for the B movie *Rock Baby, Rock It*. In the late 1960s, Carroll bought a nightclub in Dallas. One night while Summers was listening to the radio, he heard that Carroll had been fatally shot at the club. Shortly before Carroll died, Summers told him he was the one who had started the rumor of him being dead. Carroll said, "So you're the one. Man, I always wondered who did that!" He had been shot and in critical condition but luckily pulled through.

Besides music, Summers has worked on other projects. Real estate became a passion for him in 1968. Using his birth name, he bought investment properties for future resale. From 1970 until 1975, Summers owned his own nightclub in Dallas called the Bandit. In 1984, he gave acting a try when he played a preacher in the movie *No Safe Haven*, starring Wings Hauser and released by Forum Home Video in 1987.

One of his hobbies includes collecting 45 rpm records. One of his most prized records is Presley's "That's All Right" on Sun, for which he only paid thirty-five cents from a local jukebox dealer in the early 1960s.

In 1961, Summers married his high school sweetheart, Deanna. They have three sons: Steve, Shawn, and Dusty. Shawn is also a singer/musician and has joined Summers onstage both in the U.S. and abroad. Steve is heavily involved in real estate and has attended most all of his dad's U.S. and European concerts. Dusty was a member of the U.S. Armed Forces and is now involved in sales and insurance adjustments. Summers made his rockabilly comeback with an appearance in Lille, France, on February 16, 1980. It was his first ever European appearance. Shortly after that he headlined the first Scandinavian Rock & Roll Meeting held in Liessel, Holland. Also in 1981, Summers co-headlined the first International Rockabilly Festival in France. He also appeared on the national French television program *Le Grande Echiquier* with Jacques Dutronc that drew an estimated viewing audience of 20 million. Since then, he has played many of the major rockabilly festivals including Viva Las Vegas, Hemsby, and Green Bay's Rockin' 50s Fest.

The highlight of Summers' shows is when he treats the fans to his favorite song "School of Rock and Roll." Incidentally, in 2006, "School of Rock and Roll" was selected by Bob Solly and Record Collector Magazine as one of the 100 Greatest Rock 'n' Roll Records. Solly wrote: "It's one of the most perfect rock 'n' roll records that never became a hit. Everything about it is just right. If you are only allowed one rock 'n' roll record on your desert island, this is the one to take."[18] The rockin' single has also been featured by Bob Dylan on his satellite radio program *Theme Time Radio Hour*, and it was also presented in the British television series *You've Been Framed*.

Lew Williams

Cat music began in 1953, was a precursor to rock and roll, and evolved into a sound that was similar to rockabilly in its instrumentation and feel. Lew Williams is the artist most often associated with this genre: "It was created, pioneered, and enhanced in Texas by young white artists who had previously been country singers, and it was directed to the white teenage audience."[19] His June 1954 recordings of "Cat Talk" and "Teenagers Talkin' on the Telephone" are prime examples of early cat music. Cat music was absorbed into rock and roll in 1956. In January 1959, Williams stopped performing but reemerged on the scene in 2000 to reclaim his title: the Cab Calloway of rockabilly music.

Lew Williams was born on January 12, 1934, in Chillicothe, Texas, the youngest of three children. At an early age, his mother entered him in amateur contests and he won, according to him, "more than I should have." Williams added, "They used to say that I could sing before I could talk." By nine years old, he had grown tired of the contests and decided to quit: "A lot of the contestants on the amateur shows were girls, so I thought it was kind of sissy. I think it was more important to my mom. She really got a kick out of that. I did at first, but if your friends aren't doing it, and they think you are not one of them well then it's only human nature that you would want to see things like your friends." When he was eleven years old, his family moved to Dallas.

In 1949, he received his first guitar, a used Silvertone acoustic: "I really didn't know how to play it. I didn't know very many chords." A year later, when both were seniors at W.H. Adamson High School in Dallas, his friend Alex Keller began to teach him: "He was taking guitar lessons, so he taught me some more chords and let me have some of his old books." Keller and Williams soon started playing some school parties together. Then on Senior Day (May 30, 1951), just before graduation, they put a novelty band of other senior students together called The Things. It was a real primitive lineup with a washtub bass, washboard, lead guitar, and rhythm guitar. Williams recalled, "I think we were supposed to do one song, but we did more than that. I used to be a yodeler back in those days [including songs from Jimmie Rodgers' songbook]. We did a couple of songs together and then I sang Hank Williams' 'Long Gone Lonesome Blues' and put in a chorus of traditional yodeling as the ending. When finished, I was shocked as the auditorium went wild. It was applause like people dream about. That was a big turning point in influencing me to see if I could do anything with my music."

During his senior year, Williams began songwriting, thanks in part to an article he had read about Hank Thompson in the *Dallas Times Herald* newspaper that said Thompson began writing songs in high school. All of the songs Williams recorded for Imperial he wrote himself.

In the fall of 1952, Williams enrolled at Midwestern University in Wichita Falls, Texas. He assembled a country band of college students, the Texas Drifters, and soon had a twice weekly radio program on KTAT that broadcasted out of Frederick, Oklahoma, north of Wichita Falls. When he was home on weekends or holidays, Williams began spending as much time as possible at Jim Beck's Studio in Dallas, which was well known as a major recording studio for country music.

He had recorded some demos earlier, but his first real session was at Beck's in June 1953 where he recorded four country songs. The following spring, Flair Records of Abilene, Texas, released "I've Been Doin' Some Slippin' Too" b/w "Please Don't Tell a Lie About Me."

At that time, Williams was strictly performing country music. In fact, during the spring and summer of 1954, he appeared every Saturday night at the WFAA Saturday Night Shindig in Dallas, a three hour live country music show from the Texas State Fairgrounds. However, offstage, he was continuing to listen to race music and honing his cat music song writing and singing style in preparation for his next recording session. Williams acknowledged, "I remember as a senior in high school, when listening to race music, I'd sing along with the vocalists and go with the feeling. I couldn't keep still listening to the beat. I loved it, but I couldn't follow the music on my guitar. I didn't know all the chords and couldn't find the ones I did know fast enough, so I'd fake the chords or sing along without playing. When I was first writing and singing this new adaptation of country/race music, I didn't know what to call it; there was no name for it. It was only after I got to know Jim Beck better in 1953 that I heard the term cat music. Jim was the first person I ever heard use the term, and it's likely that he named [the genre] cat music."

Williams' first early cat music recording session took place in June 1954 at Beck's studio. He scraped his savings together in order to pay for the songs he wished to record, which included "Cat Talk" and "Teenagers Talkin' on the Telephone." At this session, he used steel guitar, lead guitar, rhythm guitar, bass, piano, drums, and two saxophones, combining the instrumentation of both country and race music: "Jim was like a mentor. He gave me a lot of suggestions on my style and delivery. It was his idea to use two saxes instead of one on the first session."

His songs "Cat Talk" and "Teenagers Talkin' on the Telephone" were based on the local region's teenage slang of the day: "I wanted the songs to have words that teenagers would understand, something they would relate to."

Lew Williams is the artist most often associated with "cat music" (courtesy Lew Williams).

Beck played the recordings for the A&R men of numerous major labels, but none responded favorably: "The sound, with the mix of country and race music instrumentation, was controversial or just too different from what they were used to releasing. One even asked Jim, 'What the heck is that?'" Williams added, "Jim was serious about making cat music a new form of music, targeting the teenage market. He continually urged me, and I'm sure other young country artists to begin leaning toward the beat and feel of race music. I had listened to race music since high school, so it wasn't new to me." The Dominoes' "Sixty Minute Man," blues artists Clarence "Gatemouth" Brown and Leadbelly, country stars Jimmie Davis, Gene Autry, Hank Thompson, and Ernest Tubb, the big bands of World War II, and negro gospel music all played major impacts on his style.

Unfortunately, Williams' family didn't approve of his newfound devotion to cat music: "My mother could not understand why I was spending my money to record that kind of stuff. To her, you didn't sing black people's music. It got bad when it looked like I really had wasted my money when as enthusiastic as Jim was he was not able to get any record companies at all interested in the music."

Even though the first session in June 1954 went nowhere, Williams still believed cat music offered more potential for him than traditional country music. In early September, just before going back to college for the fall semester, he recorded another cat music session with four new songs at Beck's studio. Due to the fact that the cuts from the first session were considered so radical and controversial, the saxes and steel guitar were eliminated for the second session. Williams kept the race music feel and beat and instead used lead guitar, rhythm guitar, bass, piano, and drums, which were the instruments commonly used later in rockabilly.

Beck arranged for several more A&R men from larger labels to hear the recordings, but still none were interested enough to offer a recording contract: "Jim urged me to let him place the material with a smaller label, but I had been on a small label and was willing to bite the bullet and hold out for a large label with strong national distribution. At college, from then on, the only music I sang was cat music. I was totally dedicated to the sound. I continued to write more songs, refine my style, and submit more demos."

Finally in July 1955, Williams secured a recording and writing contract with Imperial Records. Williams explained, "The ironic part is that Imperial was one of the large independent record labels that had passed on my early first phase cat music recordings, and here they were, a year later, ready to record cat music." In 1956, Imperial released three Williams' singles, "I'll Play Your Game" b/w "Don't Mention My Name," "Cat Talk" b/w "Gone Ape Man," and "Bop Bop Ba Doo Bop" b/w "Something I Said."

Although his recordings have a jazz element to them, it wasn't intentional on his part: "I never thought about jazz much, at least not as my musical style.

Some of the recordings such as 'Bop Bop Ba Doo Bop,' 'Something I Said,' 'Centipede,' and 'Abra Cadabra' [which were recorded in September 1956 in Hollywood], were backed by jazz musicians Barney Kessel, who was probably the greatest guitarist of that day, and Ernie Freeman, a famous jazz pianist. I was just blown away. It's a wonder I wasn't intimidated when I went into the studio because Barney Kessel was kind of my hero. He was so good, and I felt so honored to have him play guitar on that session." Jimmie Haskell produced the session. Williams added, "I was the first artist that he ever produced at Imperial. Up to that time, he had been the band leader." Williams quickly learned that Haskell was a perfectionist: "I was his for the day at the rehearsal studio. He would have me sing the songs because I had no lead sheets. He had me go over them and over them because he was writing what he wanted each instrument to play during the recording. I had never experienced anything like that."

Billboard Magazine spotlighted different records that they thought were the best releases at the time. Williams' "Centipede" was one of the singles featured in their April 6, 1957 issue. Williams explained, "The spotlight prompted radio play, but not enough sales resulted to make any of the major city charts."

In the following months, Williams wrote some songs with established Nashville writer Mae Boren Axton, and he rearranged and recorded a demo of her song "Sea Sand," which was used to get Ferlin Husky to record the song. Williams' song "Your Love" was recorded by Porter Wagoner.

In August 1957, Williams graduated from Midwestern University with a degree in speech and education. As a member of the Texas National Guard, he fulfilled a required six month active duty assignment in the U.S. Army, returning to civilian status in May 1958. He then made another run to establish himself as a recording artist. His music publisher at the time, Buddy Killen at Tree Music in Nashville, introduced him to Mac Wiseman, A&R man at Dot Records. Wiseman signed him to a contract and recorded him in Nashville in September 1958. For the Dot session, he used the same Vik Wayne, and in November of that year, "The Girl I Saw on Bandstand" and "I Saw You Crying in the Show" were released on Dot's subsidiary label, Hamilton.

Local shows and television appearances followed. Then an apparent booking on *American Bandstand* seemed to be the way to the top. Unfortunately, the episode was cancelled at the last minute because the producers felt that Williams' song "The Girl I Saw on Bandstand" was capitalizing on the show's name.

He realized that being a performer was not going to pay the bills, so in January 1959 he stopped trying to make a living as a recording artist and concentrated his efforts on songwriting and managing talent: "It did not seem feasible to me to continue as a performer with an unsure income when I had a family to support. I knew I was a good songwriter, and I knew quite a bit about managing talent, which came pretty naturally to me."

From 1959 through 1962, with partner Adrene Bailey, he operated Le-Drene Productions, in Dallas. They managed, booked and recorded artists, and produced rock and roll stage shows primarily for their radio station clients. A second studio, Sonic Productions for mostly black musicians, was established with Phil York when the Le-Drene Productions' partnership was dissolved.

No longer active in the music business, Williams became a marketing consultant and special events producer in 1964. He founded and produced the Miss Tan America Pageant, the country's first national black pageant, from 1964 to 1967. In the mid–1960s he became involved in the mail order business and later moved into the publishing field. Other business ventures included producing seminars and professional sports management. Since 1985, he and his wife/partner Anita have been direct response marketing consultants and publishers.

Williams didn't fully discover how popular his music was until November 1998 when record collector Richard Parker told Williams' wife that he was listed on the Internet. Around that same time, Bear Family released a compilation of Imperial recording artists as part of their *That'll Flat Git It* series. However, Williams wanted nothing of it even though his wife wished to purchase the new release: "I had been very dissatisfied with the results I had gotten with my music." Unbeknownst to him, fate would soon alter his decision. Without his knowledge, Anita decided to ask around and see how much people knew about Williams and his 50s recordings. Soon she was inundated with emails, including invitations for appearances and induction into the Rockabilly Hall of Fame. However, he politely declined and said he was not interested. Williams acknowledged, "I could not fathom that the recordings that were not really big in the United States in the 50s could be big in Europe now."

Writer Kevin Coffey from Scotland located Williams in November 1998 and notified Bear Family Records in Germany. In early 1999, Richard Weize of Bear Family contacted Williams and arrangements were made to reissue all of his 50s recordings. In October, the label released a CD, *Cat Talk* and an LP, *Teenagers Talkin' on the Phone*.

After much encouragement, Williams decided to step back onstage at the 2000 Viva Las Vegas Weekender: "I had expected the audience to be my age. I had no idea that so many young kids would be there. I was really shocked." In 2001, he made his first trip to Europe to play the Rockabilly Rave in England. Williams conveyed, "The crowd was singing all my songs so loud we could not hear the monitors onstage. That was the greatest compliment anyone could get. Everyone knows 'Cat Talk.'" In the United Kingdom and Europe, "Cat Talk" is credited with being one of the primary records that sparked the rockabilly revival in the late '70s. Three record albums, a band, a music publishing firm, and two music magazines have all been named after the song. Also, some devotees have cat talk tattoos.

Since he rediscovered his love for the music, he has made several trips to Europe and performs at one festival per year. However, the backing band has to be spot on. Williams explained, "When I left music, it was in the '50s, so my music thinking is still in the '50s. I was away from music for forty-one years and if the band backing me doesn't play exactly like the records it really throws me off." Williams has no regrets. He and his wife love meeting the other performers and legions of fans worldwide: "We have such fun with the music."

Huelyn Duvall

While Lew Williams had a jazz element to his rockabilly singles, Huelyn Duvall had a pop feel to his. Duvall enjoyed a few years of success and five releases on Challenge Records before going on hiatus in the early 1960s. In 1985, he performed at the Rockhouse 25th Annual Rock and Roll Festival in Eindoven, Holland with Eddie Bond and Janis Martin. Today, Duvall continues to perform for enthusiastic fans. Robert Plant of Led Zeppelin once said: "Jimmy Page and I used to ride around England listening to Huelyn Duvall songs, getting inspiration for our music. The songs had lots of energy and were innocent and sincere."[20]

Huelyn Duvall was born on August 18, 1939, in Garner, Texas. He was the third of five children, which included three sisters and one brother: "One of my sisters played the piano, and my dad played a little guitar but nothing professionally. At fourteen, I started listening to country music [to artists such as Hank Snow] and my dad got me a Gibson J50 acoustic guitar."[21] A year later, he was "trying to sing."

While in high school, in 1956, Duvall befriended Lonnie Thompson, who played lead guitar. On the weekend, they cut songs at a local radio station. Then, every day during the week a different song aired. Thompson's boss at the dairy, where he milked cows, told the duo they should add a bass player. Thompson discovered upright bassist Ralph Clark, and he soon joined the lineup, rounding out the Troublesome Three as they were called. Johnny Thompson, Lonnie's twin brother, provided backup vocals, played rhythm guitar, and sometimes sang lead. James Mathison occasionally played drums for the ensemble.

Between 1956 and 1957, the Troublesome Three frequently performed at local high schools, colleges, radio stations, theaters, and sock hops. The Majestic Theater and the Cowtown Hoedown, both located in Fort Worth, were regular bookings. The Cowtown Hoedown was strictly a country venue. Duvall altered that rule when he told the band one night that they were going to rock the house and see what happens. Several encores later, rock and roll was there to stay.[22] The trio played rockabilly from late 1956 through the fall of 1957: "We were doing [songs by] Johnny Cash, Johnny Horton, Elvis [Presley] and Carl Perkins." Incidentally, Duvall cited Horton, Perkins, Presley, and Marty Robbins as musical influences. During this time, Duvall also performed a few times on the Big D Jamboree in Dallas. It was an unusual venue since they also held wrestling matches there. At Duvall's first appearance, his guitarist Thompson wanted to use the house band's amplifier, but its guitarist replied, "heck no you're not gonna blow up my amplifier." Duvall and his band mates found that to be pretty amusing since they were playing rockabilly, not heavy metal.

In the summer of 1957, Thompson united Duvall with songwriter Danny Wolfe. In fact, Wolfe wrote the majority of Duvall's recorded material, including "Comin' or Goin'," "Hum-Dinger," "Three Months to Kill" "Friday Night on a Dollar Bill," "Pucker Paint," and "It's No Wonder," which he co-wrote with Duvall. Duvall explained, "He liked the novelty in a song." Wolfe also acted as Duvall's manager and secured him a recording contract with Gene Autry's label, Challenge Records. His first session took place on September 27, 1957, at Owen Bradley's Studio in Nashville where he was accompanied by Grady Martin on guitar, Floyd Cramer on piano, and Buddy Harman on drums. The Jordanaires were brought in to sing backup. Duvall was extremely disappointed that his friends and band members were not used: "I didn't really know how to argue with them about it. Challenge sent me to the studio in Nashville to do the session. They were paying for it. We didn't even have a full band. They did it to try to get the best musicians they could get." Unfortunately, that was the end of the Troublesome Three as they soon disbanded. Duvall recalled, "During recording, Owen Bradley would turn the lights down, trying to get me in the right mood to sing." At this first session, "Teen Queen," "Comin' or Goin," "Boom Boom Baby," and "Pucker Paint" were recorded. In December, "Comin' or Goin" b/w "Teen Queen" was released on a 45 rpm single.

On January 27, 1958, Duvall traveled to Hollywood, California, to record at the famed Gold Star Recording Studios. There he cut "Friday Night on a Dollar Bill," "You Knock Me Out," "Hum-Dinger," and "Fools Hall of Fame." Duvall was hired to play lead guitar on the Champs' #1 song "Tequila," but "I didn't feel like I could, so I turned it down. I went to the session to do the harmony, ooh's and aah's, for Side A, 'Train to Nowhere.'" He also participated in the yelling of tequila at the end of the instrumental classic. Duvall had a six week stint lined up in Las Vegas Dave Burgess, the Champs' rhythm guitarist and singer in his own right, but a disk jockey in Cleveland, Ohio, became enthralled with "Tequila," and the gig was cancelled.

On May 25, 1958, Duvall returned to Nashville for his final Challenge recording session. Only three songs were recorded: "Juliet," "Three Months to Kill," and "Little Boy Blue." Challenge issued three singles in 1958: "Hum-Dinger" b/w "You Knock Me Out," "Three Months to Kill," b/w "Little Boy Blue," and "Juliet" b/w "Friday Night on a Dollar Bill." After the release of "Little Boy Blue," Duvall played a show at the Memorial Auditorium in New Orleans with Jimmy Clanton, Bobby Darin, and Dale Hawkins: "I enjoyed the show. It was fun. Dale's one of my favorite artists." At a gig in Fort Worth, Duvall performed on the same bill with Eddie Cochran: "We met before the

Huelyn Duvall gearing up for his debut on Gene Autry's label, Challenge (courtesy Huelyn Duvall).

show, and I remember him coming into the dressing room. I had never met him, and he had never met me, but he pointed his finger and said 'Little Boy Blue.' [Cochran told Duvall it was one of his favorite songs.] It was a big song out in California at that time. I wasn't touring a whole lot, and he thought I should've been. He was a cool guy and a nice guy. Eddie loved ballads, which I liked a lot too." "Little Boy Blue" peaked at #88 on the Billboard charts, but was in the Top Ten on the West Coast, in Dallas, and in New Orleans.

Republic Pictures inked a seven year contract with Duvall to star in a movie a year, but nothing ever transpired. To add insult to injury, his bookings were diminishing as well. Duvall continued to record demos for Wolfe, hoping to score a hit. Duvall remembered, "I actually recorded 'Life Begins at Four O'clock' in the studio. Danny sent it to Imperial, intended for Rick Nelson to do." Wolfe didn't notify Duvall until a few years later that Lew Chudd wanted to sign him to a contract: "I was under contract to Challenge and my manager Danny Wolfe. They wouldn't even tell me about it, but that would have been a break in my career." Duvall also made demo recordings of "Double Talkin' Baby," which Capitol Records released on an extended play single by Gene Vincent, and "Modern Romance," which Dot Records issued on a single by Sanford Clark.

In 1959, Starfire released the single "It's No Wonder" b/w "Across the Aisle," which was recorded at Wolfe's studio in 1958 with rock and roll singer Tooter Boatman's band. In 2003, Boatman's drummer Clayton Glover worked with Duvall again: "It was a joy to have him on that tour." Throughout 1959 and 1960, Duvall and his new band the Arrows enjoyed a regular Friday and Saturday night booking at Andy's in Strawn, Texas. Challenge Records released Duvall's final single for the label, "Pucker Paint" b/w "Boom Boom Baby," in 1960. A year earlier, Billy "Crash" Craddock scored a #1 hit with "Boom Boom Baby" in Australia.

In 1961, Duvall got married and moved to Houston. He quit the music industry and instead wrote and developed online banking software for the next thirty-four years. Duvall explained, "I love the music, but I don't like the downsides of it. It ceased to be fun when there wasn't enough money in it." He played a few private clubs in the 1970s and 1980s. Then, in 1985, Duvall received a call from Collectors Records' owner Cees Klop to go to Europe. The Rockhouse 25th Annual Rock and Roll Festival in Eindoven, Holland with Eddie Bond and Janis Martin was Duvall's reemergence onto the rockabilly scene. "Pucker Paint" remains a fan favorite: "I don't hardly get through a show over there that somebody's not hollering for 'Pucker Paint.'"

Thanks to entertainer and fan Johnny Vallis, Duvall returned to the forefront in 2000. He played the Hemsby Weekender in England where Sweden's Wildfire Willie and the Ramblers served as his backing band. Duvall disclosed, "They came to Dallas and called me on the phone and said they wanted to meet me. Well, I said sure, if I can. I almost didn't go, and I would have regretted that. I found them to be the coolest group of guys. It reminded me of my band back in the 1950s. I went over to the little show they did, and they sounded so authentic. Then I got invited to do a show at Hemsby in England. I said I will come on one condition, and that is if the backing band is Wildfire Willie and the Ramblers. The promoter said 'no problem; we think they're one of the top bands in Europe.' I got there, and it was just so cool. They knew all my songs. I've been with them a lot. It's great fun to work with those guys. They are #1 in my book. I get to relive those songs better than I did 'em when I was singing 'em. Nobody plays with backup vocalists anymore. I love it, makes us a different deal. It really brings my songs to life. They're just not the same without it. Songs like 'Boom Boom Baby' and 'Hum-Dinger' that I never hardly do simply because I hardly ever have had a backup vocal group." Today, Duvall continues to record new material, including 2008's Goofin' Records release *Get Carried Away* with Wildfire Willie and the Ramblers, and do the occasional tour overseas: "I'm very fortunate to have the opportunity to do it again."

Five

California Rockabillies

Ricky Nelson

Ricky Nelson got his start in show business at the age of eight when he and his twelve year old brother David appeared for the first time on their parents' radio program, *The Adventures of Ozzie and Harriet*, in a skit entitled "Invitation to Dinner," which aired on February 20, 1949. On October 3, 1952, its viewing audience expanded when the Nelsons moved from radio to network television. Nelson became a singing sensation after he sang Fats Domino's "I'm Walkin'" on the April 10, 1957, episode. Within a month, record sales exceeded 500,000 copies, and it eventually peaked at number four on the Billboard charts. After his initial success, he was featured on the cover of numerous magazines and with his top notch rockabilly band; he had a score of hits. Throughout his career, Nelson made a series of musical comebacks. Unfortunately, a tragic airplane accident ended Nelson's and his entire band's lives on December 31, 1985. In 1986, he was posthumously inducted into the Rock and Roll Hall of Fame. Fellow musicians affectionately called him the Hollywood Hillbilly, and his legacy lives on today with numerous releases by Capitol Records and Shout Factory of both his music and episodes of *The Adventures of Ozzie and Harriet*.

Born on May 8, 1940, in Teaneck, New Jersey, his birth certificate read Eric Hilliard Nelson, but he was called Ricky from the very start. His parents Ozzie Nelson and Harriet Hilliard were show business veterans. In the 1930s, Ozzie conducted his own big band while Harriet was the featured vocalist. She also appeared in a few movies, including *Follow That Fleet* with Hollywood heavyweights Ginger Rogers and Fred Astaire.

The movie *Here Comes the Nelsons*, which also starred Rock Hudson, served as a pilot episode for the television version of *The Adventures of Ozzie and Harriet*. Once the comedy sitcom moved to television and NBC, Ozzie took a hands-on approach serving as producer, director, cameraman, film editor, actor, drama coach, sound technician, and head writer. It was innovative for its time. It was the first sitcom that showed a married couple sleeping in the same bed, and it showcased the first music video, Ricky Nelson's "Travelin'

Man."[1] From 1952 to 1966, four hundred and thirty-five episodes aired that included aspects of their real lives, including birthdays, holidays, and anniversaries.

As soon as Ricky Nelson became a regular on his family's show, he transfixed the audience with his uncanny way of making people laugh. Introduced as "irrepressible Ricky," his brother David served as straight man to his witty persona. Nelson's trademark, "I don't mess around boy," was created by his uncle Don Nelson.[2]

Beginning in 1957, *The Adventures of Ozzie and Harriet* showcased Nelson's latest song releases. Originally, Nelson wanted to record a song strictly to impress a girl he was dating at Hollywood High School. However, his father soon got him a contract with the jazz based label, Verve Records. They released two singles "I'm Walkin'" b/w "A Teenager's Romance" and "You're My One and Only Love" b/w "Honey Rock, which was actually an instrumental that showcased jazz guitarist Barney Kessel. Kessel had played guitar for Ozzie Nelson when he had his big band. An album, *Teen Time*, which featured other Verve acts, and an extended play 45 rpm were also released.

Rehearsing "My Bucket's Got a Hole in It" before an appearance on the *Adventures of Ozzie and Harriet,* from left, James Kirkland, Richie Frost, Ricky Nelson, and James Burton (courtesy James Kirkland).

"High school friends recall young Nelson making frequent forays to Hollywood's biggest record store, Wallich's Music City, in quest of the latest vinyl singles with the bright yellow Sun label."[3] Nelson's biggest musical inspiration was Sun Records' Carl Perkins. The first rock and roll record he ever bought was Perkins' "Blue Suede Shoes." According to Nelson, "I wanted to sound like him as much as I could."[4] If Perkins inspired his sound, then Elvis Presley certainly inspired the way he looked. At seventeen, Nelson had his naturally dark brown hair dyed black to look more like Presley. In the episode "Hairstyle for Harriet," Nelson dressed up as Presley for a costume party. Unlike Presley, Nelson didn't have to move and interact with the crowd for the girls to scream. Nelson's bassist James Kirkland responded, "The teenage girls went crazy over Rick."[5] Nelson usually just stood there with his eyes closed, a technique he used claiming it made him hear himself better.[6] Guitarist James Burton disclosed, "You know Rick used to like to close his eyes a lot when he was singing and getting into the feel of the song. I guess that was one of his trademarks. And I'd be over there and get to cuttin' up, and Ozzie would say, 'Hey, you're going to have to cool it.' He wanted us to have a good time but not to overdo it."[7]

Presley was considered overtly sexual in both his appearance and movements and chastised by critics and parents alike, while Nelson was the boy next door and overall accepted. Thanks to the estimated eighteen million weekly viewers, Nelson's musical appearances on the wholesome family show helped to improve relations between rock and roll and the grown-up crowd.[8] According to Kirkland, "Rick could have been as big as Elvis, but Ozzie wouldn't let him. Every show with the exception of one was a sell out. He drew a different fan than Elvis. He was a little more of the All American boy next door type." Bodyguard Jack Ellena confirmed that status, "Ozzie always made sure that Rick was straitlaced, not the hippie type. He always dressed nice, never drank or swore. He was clean cut, just a really good kid. That was Rick's persona."[9]

Kirkland added, "Rick liked Elvis better than Carl Perkins. We went to see Elvis when he was in L.A. [at the Pan Pacific Auditorium on October 29, 1957]." Kirkland, James Burton, Bob Luman, and Nelson all watched the show from backstage. Kirkland elaborated, "That was at the time that they were going to lock Elvis up if he wiggled one bit. He took his hands and made a little halo over his head, just stood there and never moved a muscle. Police had told him [before the show] 'We'll walk out there and cuff you and take you off that stage.'"[10]

Incidentally, Nelson and his bodyguards beat Presley and his entourage playing football at a park in North Hollywood on two different occasions. Of course, Nelson had an advantage; former Los Angeles Rams' Jack Ellena and Charley Britt were both on his team. Ellena recollected, "I think Elvis and Rick became pretty good friends. I know Elvis always had really nice things to say about Rick."

In 1957, Nelson signed with Lew Chudd and Imperial Records. His first single released on Imperial was "Be Bop Baby" b/w "Have I Told You Lately That I Love You." At Hamilton High, he made a special guest appearance at a Four Preps' show, which was his first professional gig. Bruce Belland of The Four Preps remembered, "We sang four or five songs and then brought Ricky on. He turned absolutely white — he was very shy, and I definitely remember having to physically drag him onstage, he was so intimidated."[10] Nelson sang three songs: "I'm Walkin'," "A Teenager's Romance," and Presley's "Blue Moon of Kentucky." The girls screamed and rushed the stage and Nelson realized "from that moment on, I knew that making records and singing before a live audience was the beginning of a new world for me. I'd been in show business nine years, but I'd never felt like that before."[11]

After his initial appearance with The Four Preps, he did a short tour of Florida. It was a mob scene. Once he returned home, his father made a phone call to former Los Angeles Rams' linebacker Jack Ellena, who had already been working on *The Adventures of Ozzie and Harriet* as a stuntman and extra. He quickly hired Ellena to be Ricky's bodyguard. Ellena remembered, "Rick had started singing and took his first road trip to Florida. He became a big hit overnight. Gals grabbed his tie when he was getting into the car and darn near choked him to death. He was completely unprepared [for the mob scene]. Rick said, 'I got to get somebody to go with me and take care of me,' so that's when I got the call from Ozzie. At the time, I was working on my master's degree at UCLA, but Ozzie assured me that taking the job would not interfere with my studies."

Nelson was a hit with the ladies both onstage and off. He and fellow rockabilly Lorrie Collins had a year long relationship. In fact, he wrote the song "Don't Leave Me This Way" about their romance.[12] Former teen actor Steve Stevens remembered how he became friends with Nelson: "People who were not around at the time have no idea how big a star Ricky was. I was dating a country star, Lorrie Collins, of the top country act The Collins Kids. Lorrie was invited to a party at the Nelsons' mansion in the Hollywood Hills and asked me to go with her. She had never met Ricky but was told he was a fan. After introductions, we settled in along with the rest of the young Hollywood crowd. We knew many of the group and felt at home. During the party, I thought Ricky was flirting with Lorrie, and she was flirting back. I had a few drinks and the jerk that I was, called Ricky out. How stupid, there I was all of five foot seven and a hundred and thirty five pounds, acting like a tough guy. Ricky was a big guy. Nothing happened, but Lorrie being embarrassed by my actions, demanded we leave. The next morning, I realized what I did and how stupid and childish I was. I went back to Ricky's and apologized. He invited me in and wanted to talk about how it was to work with Annette [Funicello]. That day started a friendship, and I got to know the whole Nelson clan and found them to be very special, caring down home folks."[13]

On October 8, 1957, Bob Luman and his band, which included guitarist James Burton and bassist James Kirkland, ran through some songs at Imperial. Nelson came into the office that day and overheard them recording "Red Hot." According to Nelson, "I was in Lew Chudd's office, and I heard this band, particularly an unbelievable guitar player. The bass player played slapped bass, which I really liked. That was rock and roll as far as I was concerned."[14] At the time, Kirkland had his lavender bass and after Ricky left, "Jimmie Haskell eased over to me and asked 'if he wanted to hire you, would you paint that bass red?' I said 'if he wanted to hire me, he could name the color.' I didn't realize that we were going to work for him." Nelson had found the perfect rockabilly band to create the sound he had been looking for. He had used Joe Maphis and studio musicians on his first album, *Ricky*. Reaching number one, the album gave Nelson credentials equal only to Elvis Presley.

According to Kirkland, "On November 18, 1957, we did the first recording session, 'Stood Up' and 'Waitin' in School.' Burton and I did the background singing on 'Stood Up.' Joe Maphis was not on the session. What Burton played was what was selling. Joe Maphis was a fantastic musician, but he didn't play the string stretching, chicken pickin' type blues guitar that Burton played. I got to give Burton credit, at what he does—he's the best there is." "Stood Up" reached number two on the Billboard charts while "Waitin' In School" hit number eighteen.

A few days later, Kirkland remembered, "Rick asked us if we would work a couple of shows with him before we went home for the holidays. We played the first show with Rick before Thanksgiving in 1957 at the Long Beach Municipal Auditorium in Long Beach, California. We then ate Thanksgiving dinner with Rick and his family at their house. The next night we did a show with Rick in San Diego." These two shows would be the only time that Kirkland would play his upright live with Nelson. From then on, he always used his electric bass since it was easier to transport.

Without Luman or Kirkland being aware, Burton had already signed on with Nelson. It wouldn't be until January 1958 that bassist Kirkland would be contacted and asked to sign a contract. Drummer Richie Frost had already been recruited and appeared on the "Stood Up" session. Frost remembered, "I had a friend who lived nearby that was a real estate broker. My wife worked for him. He was also a trumpet player, who had played in Ozzie Nelson's dance band. He contracted the musicians who recorded the theme music for *The Adventures of Ozzie and Harriet*. Ozzie called our friend, telling him that Rick wanted to sing and asking him to recruit a drummer for his band. I got the call and met Rick, James [Burton], and James [Kirkland] all for the first time at the bungalow for rehearsal. Rick wanted to have his own band. However, I was not under contract with Rick; I freelanced. They never offered me a contract, and I never asked for one."[15]

"Nelson's affection for rockabilly was genuine. His band was a rock and roll powerhouse that could outplay even Elvis Presley's fabled trio of Scotty Moore, Bill Black, and D.J. Fontana."[16] Once the holidays were over, the band went back to work. They next recorded "Believe What You Say" and "My Bucket's Got a Hole In It." Kirkland said, "I know that 'Believe What You Say' was a different style. That was the most solid sounding rockabilly that was ever recorded. It was more solid than anything that Elvis had ever done. 'Believe What You Say' was Rick's sound. When I went to Nashville four years later, steel guitarist Jimmy Day told me that every musician up there had pulled their hair out trying to duplicate that sound, and nobody could get it. We heard something that no one else could hear. Burton and I were just able to tune into the particular sound and feel that fit Rick the best." Rockabillies Johnny and Dorsey Burnette's composition "Believe What You Say" peaked at number four on the Billboard charts, while its flip side "My Bucket's Got a Hole In It" charted at number twelve. In addition, the Burnettes wrote nineteen other songs for Nelson, including some of his biggest hits, "Waitin' In School," "Just a Little Too Much," and "It's Late."

According to Kirkland, "Rick recorded at Masters Studio. We had a small group, so usually it didn't take us long to get a song together. There was a bungalow at the TV studio, so after Rick got done rehearsing for the latest episode, we would go over there and run through new material. Our arrangements for the songs would all be done ahead of time. It was the slapping stuff on my standup and what Richie Frost was doing on drums that helped give Rick the sound that he had." Nelson's sound was a co-op effort, not one musician in particular standing alone. Guitarist James Burton added, "That's how you make hit records—teamwork. No one guy in the group is making it happen, it's team playing."[17] While recording, Nelson played on one track, Burton on another and the rhythm section of Kirkland, Frost, and Gene Garth (piano) on the third. Jimmie Haskell produced the sessions. The background vocals were added later when Imperial sent the tapes to Nashville for the Jordanaires to overdub. Kirkland added, "That way if Burton or Rick did something they didn't like, then they could change just their part. We had no headphones. Burton had a mike in front of his amp. The piano was miked through the board. The drums just had a mike. I didn't amplify my bass. Instead, I used two microphones, one at the top and another at the bottom. A song was usually recorded in just three or four takes, and a session usually took three hours. However, I remember once it took us four hours to get one song. We were just about to call it quits and work on it another day when I made a joke. Everyone laughed, and it made us relax. The next take we had it. The engineers behind the board were so good at what they did that they could split a word or put two takes together, and no one would notice. That was way before anyone else, including Nashville, was doing that."[18]

While recording with his rockabilly band at Imperial, Nelson had a tendency to experiment with different sounds. However, A&R man Jimmie Haskell had strict control over which songs Nelson actually recorded. As bassist Kirkland stated, "Jimmie told us what to play and how to play it. That takes away from the feel. Rick would go over the songs with us, but Jimmie would change them. Rick wouldn't go against what Jimmie said."

When Burton and Kirkland first joined Nelson's band, they didn't realize that they would also be making television appearances as part of the musical sequences on *The Adventures of Ozzie and Harriet*. The band was playing live, but the viewer never heard them. Nelson lip synched and the band played to pre recorded version(s) of the week's song(s). Kirkland commented, "Rick got it spot on, never missed a word. Each time he sang a song, it was exactly like the record. Rick was the best at lip synching than anyone I ever saw."

April 4, 1958, was a turning point in Nelson's career. He topped the Billboard charts with the melancholy teen anthem, "Poor Little Fool." Nelson originally hated the song. The original version was up tempo, similar to that of Presley's "Good Rockin' Tonight." Sharon Sheeley wrote the song about her ill-fated romance with married Don Everly of the Everly Brothers. Nelson's bassist Kirkland retold the story, "She brought Rick 'Poor Little Fool,' and it was an up tempo rock song. He told her, 'I can't use it.' She came to his house and cried big tears. He [then] pitched that tape to me and [James] Burton, and he said, 'See what y'all can do with that.' We slowed it down to what it is and changed the chord progression on it. Then Rick recorded it. He liked it, and it was the biggest [song] he had. She never ever said thank you. We would have done some more stuff with her if she had acted like she had appreciated it. Rick never did record anything else for her. The original version wasn't any good." Sheeley was none too pleased that Nelson changed the song without her knowledge. At a Hollywood coffee shop, Nelson's brother, David spotted her and congratulated her on the success of the song. She replied, 'You can tell your brother thanks a lot! He ruined my song.'"[19]

Also in April, his show at the Hirsch Youth Center on the Louisiana State Fair Grounds caused the girls to go into hysterics. As Pericles Alexander reported for *The Shreveport Times*, "Nelson shook his left shoulder then his right hip and leg. Every twitch of the body was an occasion for wild and frantic screaming."[20] Ellena remembered, "Rick and the band could really stir up the gals. Ozzie put a stop to that. He didn't want Rick to be another Elvis. He didn't like the swiveling hips. He wanted Rick to stand up there and sing and be a little more sedate." Ellena made sure Rick didn't move around too much.

Nelson's live performances were the variety type with other acts on the bill. Nelson was the headliner. 1958's Miss Oklahoma Anita Bryant and *Louisiana Hayride* alums, The Browns were the opening acts on a few of the dates. In fact, The Browns participated in the late night jam sessions with Nelson in Oklahoma. Ellena remembered, "Rick always went to bed late. He couldn't get to sleep, so he stayed up and sang."

According to drummer Richie Frost, "We had a set routine, and we did it pretty much without any variation from place to place. There was just one long scream for forty-five minutes, so you couldn't hear anything. I could hear James [Burton]. He would clue me in sometimes if I needed it. The girls didn't really come to hear Rick; they came to see him, to be with him. They had all of his recorded work, that's where they could listen to him." Nelson sang his hit songs, and sometimes he threw in a couple that he never recorded. Bassist Kirkland commented, "When Rick did 'What'd I Say,' he really rocked it. Rick used to break a lot of strings [when we played live], so he used my 1951 Gibson [acoustic] as a spare. [In fact] that same Gibson was played by [James] Burton on 'Lonesome Town.'"

On the Sunday before Labor Day 1958, Nelson and his band broke attendance records at the Steel Pier in Atlantic City. Kirkland recalled, "At the time, Frank Sinatra held the attendance record [with 41,000], and we broke it [with 44,221]." According to Frost, the venue was a pier that jetted out into the water, and at the end of it was a big ballroom. "There weren't any seats in the ballroom, strictly standing room only. That was a wild scene because they packed the kids in like sardines." He remembered that there were podiums set up in various places on the dance floor with Steel Pier security standing above all the screaming kids. Nelson's own security stood onstage to protect him. According to bodyguard Ellena, "I had to actually stand on the stage and keep pushing the gals down that were trying to climb onto the stage." The humidity outside, the ballroom with no air conditioning, and the mere fact that the girls were in Nelson's presence, caused several of them to faint. They were passed over the crowd and into the arms of the stagehands, who took them outside to get some fresh air. Frost commented, "We were up there playing behind Rick, and here they're carrying girls in a dead faint out on either side of you all throughout the concert."

Sometimes, Nelson's shows turned into spectacles because of fanatical females. Frost explained, "They mobbed Rick, and the only time we, as a band, were bothered was when the gals thought they could get to Rick through us. I can remember [at a show date] in Texas they had the backstage completely locked up, so that nobody could get in. I was standing out by the gate talking to one of the guards when a young teenage girl beckoned me. I went over and said 'yeah what can I do for you?' I don't remember her words exactly, but she offered to go to bed with me if I would get her in to see Rick. Of course, I declined. I was married with two kids and quite a bit older than the other guys. I was quite shocked."

After a show in Indianapolis, Indiana, the governor, his wife, and his daughter visited Nelson in his hotel room. Kirkland recollected, "They weren't letting anybody get on the elevator, unless you were a guest in the hotel. They had the stairs blocked because of the teenagers. Former L.A. Ram and Nelson bodyguard Paul Cameron and I had talked to two young ladies. They called us, and we were going down to get them. The minute that we opened the door, two different girls hit the door and nearly knocked me and Paul down. One of the gals scratched me and tore my favorite red shirt off trying to get into where Rick was. The other bodyguard Jack Ellena came, and we threw them out in the hall. Security then came up and got them. The girls had climbed the fire escape and came through a window. From then on, the security was outside the door."

At a show in Vancouver, British Columbia, according to Frost, "we pulled up in a stretch limousine. The girls were around front, but apparently somebody saw us coming around the back. Rick, James [Burton], James [Kirkland], manager Maury Foladare, and the two bodyguards all got out. I was the last one out of the car. As I was getting out, I saw the girls coming around the side of the building on a dead run. I didn't know quite what to do, but I decided I wasn't going to endure it. I got back in the car and closed the door. By that time, the mob was upon them, and they got some souvenirs. They all got roughed up a little bit, except me." No matter how uncontrolled and zealous the fans could get, he loved them. Kirkland recalled, "Rick signed autographs until everyone got one or until we had to leave."

At that same show in Vancouver, the band had to deal with the brightness of the stage lights. Kirkland explained, "I missed [seeing] Rick and Burton, so I kind of backed up and shaded my eyes, so I could see. They were lying down on the floor. Rick had the mike stand with his feet sticking up in the air, and he was singing. Burton had his guitar behind his head, propped up on his elbow playing. Me, I wasn't going to be outdone, so I just flopped down there, laid on my back and played too." The next day, a photo of the guys made the front page of the *Los Angeles Examiner*. "Ozzie didn't say a word until we got ready to leave the next time. He said, 'I'd appreciate it if you guys didn't lay down on the job anymore.' We knew what he meant and that there wouldn't be any more of it."[21]

After 1960, Nelson's sound changed with the replacement of upright bassist James Kirkland. Kirkland said, "I quit Rick in the early summer of 1960. We only worked during the summer on tours and then in the studio or on the show. Half the time we spent back in Texas and Louisiana, so we got stale as musicians. We couldn't work with anyone else while we were under contract with Rick, so Burton and I quit."

He and Burton went back to work for Bob Luman at the Showboat in Vegas. The Showboat hired them for six weeks and then rehired them for another six weeks. However, the second time around after rehearsals and only two days before they were to open, Burton decided to go back to work for Nelson. Kirkland stayed on and played with Luman for nearly six months before Luman got drafted into the Army. Kirkland then worked with Jim Reeves, who was reluctant since he had played for Nelson. He remembered Reeves' comment, "I don't want no damn rock and roller."

With the addition of Joe Osborn on electric bass, "Travelin' Man" topped the Billboard charts. When he turned twenty-one years old, Nelson decided to drop the "y" on his name in hopes of ridding himself of the teenage image. He no longer wanted to be a teen idol but be regarded as a serious musician. In 1963, he left Imperial Records and signed a twenty year contract with Decca/MCA, which was unprecedented at the time. However, the hits started to fall by the wayside when America was hit by the British Invasion. On April 20, 1963, when Nelson married actress Kristin Harmon teenage girls around the globe were heart broken. They had four children together, actress Tracy born October 25, 1963; musician twins Matthew and Gunnar born September 20, 1967 (who have performed their father's songs as a tribute to his legacy in recent years); and musician Sam born August 29, 1974.

In the 1970s, Nelson helped create country rock with The Stone Canyon Band, whose various incarnations existed from 1969 through 1985. Nelson made a musical comeback with his self penned "Garden Party." He wrote the song after a bad experience at the October 15, 1971, Madison Square Garden Rock and Roll Revival Concert. "Garden Party" was a number one hit on the Adult Contemporary charts, and it peaked at number six on the pop charts. In 1981, Nelson recaptured his early rockabilly sound both on record and onstage.

Nelson made a brief rockabilly comeback and was slated to do tours with both Carl Perkins and fellow California rockabilly Glen Glenn. Unfortunately, the tours never transpired as he, his band, his girlfriend, his sound technician, and his road manager were all killed when his small airplane crashed in a field near DeKalb, Texas, on New Years' Eve 1985.

To those who felt that Nelson's music was strictly for the teenagers or that he wasn't really a rockabilly artist, then they should take heed from Creedence Clearwater Revival's former front man John Fogerty when he said, "I've always considered Rick equal to the Sun Records' artists. Maybe he came from Hollywood, but the sound was strictly Memphis."[22]

The Collins Kids

The Collins Kids, which teamed siblings Larry and Lorrie Collins, were one of the biggest musical acts in the 1950s, but because of their regular appearances on Tex Ritter's *Town Hall Party* and their talent not being taken seriously by their label, Columbia Records, their record sales suffered.

Lawrencine (Lorrie) was born on May 7, 1942, in Tahlequah, Oklahoma, and Lawrence (Larry) was born on October 4, 1944, in Tulsa, Oklahoma. They both started performing at a very young age because they came from a musical family. Their mother and her sisters were all musicians. According to Lorrie, "We all played an instrument and sang in church."[23] In fact, their mother was one of their biggest influences and helped them write songs, including "Hot Rod."

Besides Larry and Lorrie, there were two other sisters. The oldest sister was bossy, but Lorrie never was bossy with Larry even though she was a little older. Lorrie revealed, "We were so close and on the same wavelength."

Lorrie first began her musical career in 1950, at the time her brother Larry was not part of the act. She won a talent contest hosted by western swing bandleader Leon McAuliffe in a Tulsa, Oklahoma, ballroom. McAuliffe told Hazel Collins, her mother, that Lorrie was good and that California was where they needed to be. By 1952, Hazel took Lorrie to California to audition. Upon their return, Lorrie played a guest spot on the *Louisiana Hayride* alongside Hank Williams and Johnny Horton.[24] A year later, the whole family decided to make a permanent move to the "golden state." Lorrie commented, "California was a big opportunity for us." Larry and Lorrie originally sang as solo acts and won amateur contests. Larry would rehearse in one room and Lorrie in another, and they would drive their parents nuts. Finally, their father came up with the idea for them to become a duo, and they soon joined forces.

In 1954, Larry and Lorrie began work on a weekly television program called *Town Hall Party*, or as it was syndicated *Ranch Party*. Amateur night was every Friday night on the show, so when they performed and won, they were hired to appear on the show every Saturday night for the next fifteen years. Tex Ritter gave them their very own segment and introduced them as "something for the youngsters."[25] It was here that Larry met his mentor and friend Joe Maphis: "Joe inspired me by playing with me and doing duets. I watched him."[26] Besides appearing with Larry on *Town Hall Party*, Maphis also played guitar on The Collins Kids' recordings from 1955 until 1957. Maphis played a double-necked Mos-Rite guitar with his name inscribed on the necks. Larry saw that guitar and wanted one just like it because he thought it was so cool. He got his wish; however, it took him awhile to get used to playing it. Merle Travis, another *Town Hall Party* regular, was also an influence on Larry's guitar playing.

From the age of eight, Larry practiced his guitar constantly for seven or eight hours a day. In regard to Travis and Maphis, Larry commented, "Neither one of them sat down and taught me anything. It was up to me to do my part. I learned a lot from watching and playing with them. My mom taught me a few chords and from there I just picked it up on my own. It was just a gift."

Lorrie's musical influences included Kay Starr: "I loved her powerfulness," Jo Stafford, Teresa Brewer, and Maddox Brothers and Rose.

On July 25, 1955, they signed a recording contract with Columbia Records, and their first release was "Beetle-Bug-Bop" b/w "Hush Money." "Hush Money" was a cutesy kid's song, in which Larry pesters his sister into giving him money in exchange for keeping quiet about her newfound romance. Larry and Lorrie sang about subjects that were familiar to teens and pre-teens. Columbia considered them to be a novelty act, so they were none too thrilled when Larry and Lorrie wanted to cut ties with the cutesy kids' songs and do more rebellious rockabilly tunes. As Larry explained, "Don Law was our producer for Columbia

The Collins Kids as a brother and sister rockabilly act early in their careers (courtesy Larry and Lorrie Collins).

Records. They chose most of the material back then. He chose 'Party.'"²⁷ Mitch Miller, head of A&R, was adamant in the press about his distaste for rockabilly and rock and roll, so it was no wonder that The Collins Kids were not given a fair shot.

While at Columbia from 1955 until 1959, The Collins Kids wrote most of their own songs, including "Mercy," "I'm In My Teens," "Hop, Skip, and Jump," and "Whistle Bait" and did all of their own arrangements. It was at this early age that Larry began his songwriting career. In 1973, he co-wrote "Delta Dawn" with Alex Harvey, which turned into a hit at the same time for three different artists in three different fields: Tanya Tucker in country, Helen Reddy in pop, and Bette Midler in R&B. "Delta Dawn" was also nominated for a Grammy. Larry co-wrote "You're the Reason God Made Oklahoma" with Sandy Pinker. The song was a hit for country singers David Frizzell and Shelly West. In 1981, it won the Academy of Country Music's Song of the Year as well as being named Song of the Year by the National Songwriters Association. That same year, Clint Eastwood added the song to his film *Any Which Way You Can*.

In 1957, Larry and Lorrie did package shows with Carl Perkins and Johnny Cash. They weren't treated like kids even though they were. Larry and Lorrie toured quite a bit with them, and they both commented, "You could not have met nicer or more talented people than those two." Larry added, "Carl was one of our dearest friends. Clayton [Carl's brother and bass player] was crazy. Of course, so was I, everyone was back then."

Once, while on tour in Canada, Larry's voice changed on stage right in the middle of a song: "It was embarrassing. I was rocking out on "Whistle Bait," and all of a sudden my voice cracked, went from real high to real low."

Besides touring extensively, The Collins Kids appeared on many television programs, including *The Steve Allen Show*, *The Ed Sullivan Show*, *American Bandstand*, *Ozark Jubilee*, the *Grand Ole Opry*, and the pilot episode of *Shindig*, which was originally a country show.

When Larry and Lorrie were not touring or making records, they attended Hollywood Professional School because it allowed you time off in case you needed to tour. Some of the most famous youngsters of the day also attended the school, including Annette Funicello, Tuesday Weld, Ryan O'Neal, Jimmy Boyd, Molly Bee, and Brenda Lee. Larry and his date double dated to the prom with Lee and her date.

In 1957, Lorrie began dating another up and coming star, Ricky Nelson. Nelson was a big fan of The Collins Kids and often came down to watch them appear on *Town Hall Party*. Lorrie even appeared on a few episodes of his family's show, *The Adventures of Ozzie and Harriet*. Lorrie remembered singing "Just Because" with him on the show: "Just Because" was fun to sing with Ricky."

Nelson was smitten with the raven-haired beauty, and the feeling was mutual. However, he was too shy to call and ask her for a date, so he had Glen Larson of The Four Preps call and set it up instead. It was the beginning of a beautiful relationship that lasted over a year. Lorrie acknowledged, "We had a lot in common. We really loved each other a lot."[28]

Larry occasionally acted as chaperone. Often more times than not, he would stay at home, and Nelson and Lorrie would arrive to find him waiting up for them. Nelson and Larry would then sit and play guitar and write songs until two or three in the morning. Lorrie even co-wrote a song with Nelson. It was entitled "My Gal," but unfortunately it was never recorded.[29]

Nelson and Lorrie were engaged to be married, but their parents disapproved of marrying at such a young age. Nelson had given her his ring, one that was gold with comedy and tragedy masks on it. When they broke up, she gave it back to him. Today, his original bassist James Kirkland has that ring in his possession.

In 1959, Larry and Lorrie again toured with Johnny Cash. Cash's manager, Stewart Carnall convinced Lorrie to elope with him. Even though, Carnall was several years her senior, the marriage lasted twenty years. The next day the elopement was all over the newspapers. Nelson was crushed when he read the headlines. He had lost his true love forever. Years later when Lorrie ran into

Nelson in Lake Tahoe, she had this to say about the experience: "I saw Rick at Lake Tahoe when I went there with my two daughters. When I was in his dressing room, he said to me 'Why?' and walked out of the room. It was sad."[30] Biographer Joel Selvin referred to Lorrie as Nelson's "first real love in his life."[31]

Lorrie remembered her romance with Nelson like it was yesterday: "Ricky was good inside and outside, a wonderful guy and real talented. He was real fun to be around. He truly loved what he was doing. Music was his life. He was another one who made some awfully good records."

Both she and Larry were devastated when they heard the news that Nelson was tragically killed in a plane crash in 1985. Larry commented that "Ricky, Elvis, and guys like that were special people. They really made an impression on your life."

Elvis Presley was also a big fan of The Collins Kids. According to Larry, "He used to come down to *Town Hall Party* and ask us to do certain songs when he was in town. He was a hell of a guy. He was the man." Lorrie added, "There will never be another one."

After Lorrie ran off and got married, it put a strain on the whole family. Larry noted, "It put a damper on the act. We had movie deals lined up, and things were going well."[31] The year 1961 was the last time that Larry and Lorrie recorded together as The Collins Kids with only occasional appearances until they resurfaced in 1970 at the casino lounges in Reno, Las Vegas, and Lake Tahoe, Nevada. In 1993, they reformed as The Collins Kids as part of the rockabilly revival.

They do not tour as much anymore, only two or three shows a year. They tour now for pure enjoyment and not to make a living. Larry explained, "We are actually here because of the fans, for the way they look and for the way they act, and for the music. We are very fortunate in our lives we can do this now because we enjoy it." When they were young, Larry and Lorrie never had any other jobs besides singing. Music was their first love and remains that way. Larry and Lorrie love singing the songs that made them famous amongst rockabilly enthusiasts.

Since they have reemerged on the scene, The Collins Kids have been voted Europe's Best Rockabilly Act. "Whistle Bait" is a huge hit over there, the standard rock and roll record. "Hot Rod" is another one of their biggest records. Their most requested songs at shows are "Whistle Bait," "Hot Rod" and "Hoy Hoy"; however, their favorites to perform are "Rockin' Gypsy," which is an instrumental, and "Mercy." "'Mercy' is a great song and a fun one to sing," added Lorrie.

When they play shows or festivals, Deke Dickerson and his band The Ecco-Fonics is usually their backing band. As Larry and Lorrie were preparing for their first European tour, Dickerson auditioned for them at their homes in Reno, Nevada. Dickerson knew all the songs they ever recorded, and he wanted every song to sound exactly like the original. If they performed the songs differently, he was the first to correct them.

Even though The Collins Kids were underappreciated in rockabilly's heyday, their records and *Town Hall Party* appearances stand the test of time. To this day, they continue to wow audiences with their high octane performances. Once they set foot onstage, it is like stepping back in time for both the fans and performers alike.

Glen Glenn

Rockabilly music started in the South and most importantly with that pivotal moment on July 5, 1954, when Elvis Presley recorded "That's All Right" at Sun Studio in Memphis, Tennessee. Others may have been singing the new form of music earlier, but he is the one who jumpstarted the revolution and kicked the door down for legions of rockabilly singers to follow. "Mr. Everybody's Movin'" Glen Glenn's main musical influence was Presley: "He's the guy who started it all. Without Elvis, nobody would have made it. We all wanted to be Elvis. He influenced everybody that sang rockabilly, and there was no rockabilly before Elvis."[32] Glenn started his career singing country music, but once Presley hit the scene he switched to rockabilly. He may have only had three releases on ERA records, but his impact is profound. His signature tune "Everybody's Movin'" has been recorded by the Stray Cats and the Cramps and sung live in concert by Bob Dylan, Bruce Springsteen, Tom Petty, and Neil Young. The recordings Glen Glenn and guitarist Gary Lambert made for the ERA label during the late 1950s are regarded as the pinnacle of West Coast rockabilly.[33]

Orin Glenn Troutman was born on October 24, 1934, in Joplin, Missouri. Glenn remembered, "They should have named me Glen Orin because they always called me Glen."[34] He is the oldest of five children, has four sisters. Both parents loved country music. His dad liked to sing and play guitar around the house. While in grammar school, Glenn sometimes came home during his lunch hour to listen to Bob Wills and His Texas Playboys' hour long radio program on KVOO in Tulsa, Oklahoma. Every Saturday evening, he tuned into the *Grand Ole Opry* on his static ridden radio. As a youngster, he sang songs around the house by listening to records and songs from the radio. Glenn revealed, "Ever since I was a kid, my whole life has been nothing but music."[35]

At age thirteen, the family moved to California: "My dad was a house painter. He worked well in the summertime, but winters were cold and sometimes painters didn't get a lot of work. We moved to California, and he thought he was in heaven because it was warm all the time." The relocation allowed him to work all year round.

Glenn first played a Gibson guitar but then switched to a Martin D28: "Gary [Lambert] helped me a lot because I knew nothing about a guitar. Gary was a natural. He helped me learn how to get the different chords. It's a lot easier to sing than play guitar."

He met Lambert in the ninth grade. About a year later, they discovered that they shared a love of country music: "He found out I sang, and I found out he played guitar, so we started practicing together. We did a few square dances, but those didn't pay anything." Chet Atkins and Merle Travis were Lambert's musical influences, while Glenn cited Hank Williams, Hank Snow, Webb Pierce, and Lefty Frizzell.

As a junior in high school, Glenn quit to pursue his interest in music. Glenn conveyed, "They didn't treat me well in school. I joined the Glee Club, and Mrs. Peck kicked me out. She said 'You sing too loudly. You're not a singer.' It broke my heart." After he received some local exposure thanks to the television program, *County Barn Dance*, Mrs. Peck called him: "She said 'Glen is there any chance you could come down to the high school and do an assembly?' I said no, I will not do that. She said 'why not?' I said you told me I couldn't sing and kicked me out of the Glee Club. I was mad she asked." Also, while he was in school, Glenn found it difficult to get a date since all the girls he wished to date really wanted to date the jocks: "The girls thought those guys were really something else. They frowned on me." Well, as soon as some success came his way, suddenly those same girls found Glenn to be quite desirable. However, to their dismay Glenn then wasn't interested.

In 1952, Glenn and Lambert got advice from country star Joe Maphis, whom they saw play every Sunday night at the Riverside Rancho in Los Angeles. They were too young to actually attend the show, so they stood outside and watched. Maphis told them they should audition for KXLA's disk jockey Squeakin' Deacon's amateur talent contest, which was held at the Riverside Rancho. They entered the contest one Sunday afternoon, and Glenn sang Maphis' original "Dim Lights, Thick Smoke, and Loud Loud Music." They won a wristwatch: "That's what made me think I could be a singer because it was hard to win that competition." After they won, Glenn christened the duo the Missouri Mountain Boys even though Glenn was the only one who was born in Missouri.

Starting in 1953, the *County Barn Dance* became their television home for two and a half years. It aired every Saturday night, and children could attend the show. The bands played a big dance afterward until midnight or one in the morning, and no drinking was allowed in the dance hall. Roland and Clarence White were on the show, and they became known as the Byrds. The Three Little Country Girls: Jean, Glenda, and Caroline Smith also appeared on the *County Barn Dance*. Incidentally, Jean and Glenda along with Wynn Stewart's sister Beverly sang the backup vocals on Glenn's recordings of "Kathleen," "Laurie Ann," and "I'll Never Stop Loving You." Maddox Brothers and Rose appeared often as guest stars. According to Glenn, "They could even outdraw the big guys in Nashville, like Ray Price, who were having all the hits. When they walked onstage, they sparkled [because of their tailor made Nudie suits]. They all dressed alike. They entertained you from the minute they started until they got done."[36]

In late 1954, he started listening to disk jockey Dick "Huggy Boy" Hugg on a local blues radio station, where he heard blues, rhythm and blues, and doo wop. Also in 1954, Glenn began experimenting with recording songs on Lambert's AMPEX home recorder. By January 1955, Glenn began incorporating rhythm and blues into his act. He recorded Gene O'Quin's version of "That's All Right" live at KXLA in Pasadena, California. Shortly after this recording, Glenn became familiar with Elvis Presley's version. In fact, KXLA refused to play rockabilly records, so Glenn took the records home with him; therefore, becoming familiar with otherwise obscure acts.

In 1956, Glenn's cousin through marriage Porter Wagoner invited him on a tour of the Midwest and East Coast as well as appearances in Missouri. There he performed on package shows with many of the major country stars of the day such as Marty Robbins, Ferlin Husky, Slim Whitman, and Ray Price. Also during this time, Glenn made regular appearances on *Ozark Jubilee*, which aired nationwide on ABC-TV. There he sang "Shake, Rattle, and Roll," much to Wagoner's chagrin. Wagoner advised him that he should continue singing country music and forget about that new kid Presley. After a few months of working with Wagoner, Glenn became homesick and returned to California.

Maddox Brothers and Rose were a regular act on the *Louisiana Hayride* in Shreveport as was Presley. Glenn disclosed, "They would be in Shreveport for six months and then they'd come out to California for six months. Every time they came out here, they told me about this young guy at the *Hayride* named Elvis Presley. I said Elvis Presley? Nobody can have a name like Elvis Presley and do anything. He ought to change his name. I was singing country music then. They told me 'Elvis comes onstage, and he goes wild. This kid's different. We've never seen anybody like him. You got to get on this kid's style, Glen.' I told Fred [Maddox, bassist for the group] I don't think I'd like him."[37]

Glen Glenn wearing his famous Turk cactus shirt (courtesy Glen Glenn).

Glenn had already heard Presley's first release, "That's All Right," and he decided to order all five Sun records. Unfortunately, they weren't sold in record stores in California, so they had to be ordered. It took three weeks for Glenn to receive them: "They didn't play very good. You played them a few times, and they really got scratchy, so I threw them all away when he came out on RCA Victor [since RCA had re-released the five singles]. I said well he sounds pretty good, but he doesn't sound country." Glenn wasn't impressed until he saw Presley's television appearances on *Stage Show*, hosted by Tommy and Jimmy Dorsey.

On April 4, 1956, only a day after his first appearance on the *Milton Berle Show*, Presley played the San Diego Arena. This concert would alter Glenn's life forever: "Gary and I went down to see him [along with Gary's date Jean Smith and her sister Caroline]. I remember on the way down, I said, 'Well, he won't pack that place.' I had been to the arena before because I used to go down there a lot to see some of the big country guys [like Marty Robbins, Carl Smith, and Ray Price]. That place held about 10,000 people, and sometimes they wouldn't pack it. Gary and I got there, and that place was so packed with mostly girls. I said to Gary, how are we gonna get to see Elvis? They're not gonna let us backstage. Well Fred Maddox went too [without us knowing]. Gary and I got our tickets, and we were seated way in the back. We looked down and saw Fred standing next to a guard by the backstage entrance. I said that's Fred Maddox, let's go down there and talk to Fred. Maybe he'll get us backstage because he knows Elvis. We went and saw Fred, and he said, 'Well, c'mon backstage.' I said I don't want to go backstage now I want to see Elvis onstage and then I want to go back after his show. The guard said, 'Well, I'll remember you boys. After the show's over you come on back to see me, and I'll get you backstage.'" Glenn and Lambert returned to their seats and watched the show: "They had a comedian come on first, and he was good. The crowd just booed him, get off of here we want Elvis. He wasn't on for long as he had to leave. Well, when Elvis came on, that really got me because he just went crazy. It was the best show I ever saw. Scotty [Moore, his guitarist] and Bill [Black, his bassist] stopped playing, and D.J. [Fontana, his drummer] just played. All Elvis did was shake, shake, shake for about three or four minutes. His legs were going wild, and he was all over that stage. You could hardly hear him, the girls were screaming so loud. I told Gary man we've got to start doing something like him. After he sung his last song, we said okay let's try to get down there and see Elvis. Well because of all the girls we could hardly get back down there. It took us a long time to scoot through. They had the building surrounded." Finally, they got to the guard, and he remembered them since there were very few guys in the audience. They then spent two or three hours with Presley because he couldn't leave. After that incident, they started making the announcement "Elvis has left the building." Glenn added, "I had plenty of time with him, and I took picture after picture. We talked about some of the people that I knew that he had been playing with." The Navy's Shore Patrol finally escorted Presley safely out of the building.

In September 1956, Glenn and Lambert entered Garrison Studio in Long

Beach, California, and paid for their recording of "It Rains Rain." They were hoping to get a record label interested in signing them, but country music was no longer cool.

A year later, Glenn received the opportunity to tour with Maddox Brothers and Rose when Cal and Rose quit the group. Glenn conveyed, "Rose moved back to Nashville and joined the *Grand Ole Opry*."[38] At the time, she had three separate recording contracts with Columbia Records: as a solo artist, with the family band, and with her sister-in-law Rhetta. Rose Maddox was the first girl singer and influenced rockabilly songstresses Lorrie Collins, Wanda Jackson, and Janis Martin. Fred Maddox had taken a liking to Glenn because he included a lot of uptempo songs in his act: "I was doing rockabilly before the word rockabilly was invented, but I called it hillbilly. They liked what I did because they did a lot of uptempo songs. They wanted someone who could sing rockabilly and do the Elvis type songs. They got out there and really tore the house down. Fred was the first guy that I ever saw slap a bass. Bill Black's main influence was Fred Maddox. Maddox Brothers and Rose fought all the time. They needed someone to take Cal's place because he played rhythm guitar. Fred called Kitty his wife and asked her to call me to see if I would join. I was so excited that I couldn't sleep for two days. They were big time, and I was really just a little kid on television [who was then known as Glen Trout]. Fred hired me, and they had me to finish their tour."[39] Fred Maddox gave Glenn six different Nathan Turk tailored suits. Glenn continued to work with the band and then with Fred Maddox at his club until Glenn was drafted into the Army. Bill Black occasionally filled in on bass for the local shows. During this time, Lambert did a solo venture and even though he didn't play with the band, he also received a few Turk suits.

That same year, Lambert and Glenn joined the television cast of *Cal's Corral*. Eddie Cochran's upright bassist Connie "Guybo" Smith had gotten married and didn't want to go on the road with Cochran, so he instead became a member of Glenn's band. He performed with them on *Cal's Corral* and local shows and played bass on all of Glenn's ERA recordings. Joe O'Dell rounded out the trio on drums. While on Cal's Corral, Glenn performed an Elvis Presley song every Sunday afternoon. Presley tuned in, and he was impressed by Glenn's renditions of "I Got a Woman," "Treat Me Nice," and "Jailhouse Rock": "He told me he appreciated that."

In regard to his live shows, Glenn added impersonations of Presley, Johnny Cash, and Lefty Frizzell. He also incorporated Presley movements into his set: "I knew you couldn't just stand there. You had to entertain the people. Plus, I loved the girls screaming."

Country singer Wynn Stewart convinced Glenn to record some rockabilly demos. On October 7, 1957, Glenn cut Stewart's song "One Cup of Coffee and a Cigarette" and "Kathleen." He took the acetates to independent record labels Liberty, Dot, Challenge, and Imperial: "I couldn't get anybody to buy 'One Cup of Coffee.' They all loved 'Kathleen.' I took an acetate to Jimmie Haskell at Imperial Records. He wasn't too nuts about 'One Cup of Coffee,' but he really liked 'Kathleen.' I thought he was going to sign me to Imperial. He said 'leave me the acetate, and I'll call you.' Well two or three weeks passed, and I didn't hear from him, so I called, and I said I want my acetate back because it cost me three dollars. He told me 'I lost it, and I'm not looking for that kind of stuff.'"[40] As it turned out, Haskell took Glenn's arrangement to "Kathleen" and transferred it to Ricky Nelson's song "Poor Little Fool": "He told Johnny and Dorsey Burnette to arrange Ricky's song just like mine."

Lou Bidell and Herb Newman owned ERA records, which produced the #1 song "The Wayward Wind" by Gogi Grant. Glenn's failure to secure a recording contract led him to ERA: "I went over to ERA. They wanted 'One Cup of Coffee' because it's rockabilly. They liked 'Kathleen,' but they wanted another rockabilly song for the other side. I never considered myself a great songwriter. I always sang other people's songs, but when I got my recording contract I couldn't do that I had to have my own songs." He returned home and wrote "Everybody's Movin'" and "I'm Glad My Baby's Gone." On January 8, 1958, Glenn cut four songs at Gold Star Recording Studios in Los Angeles: "Everybody's Movin'," "I'm Glad My Baby's Gone," "One Cup of Coffee and a Cigarette," and another Stewart composition "Would Ja." He paid $15 an hour for the session, and he is one of the few rockabilly artists who own the master tapes to all of his songs.

On January 20, he was drafted into the United States Army and deployed for basic training. Since Lambert was only three months younger than Glenn, he realized that he too would soon be drafted, so he volunteered instead to be with Glenn. ERA Records notified Glenn had they known this; they would not have signed him to a contract. They rechristened Glen Trout as Glen Glenn: "They didn't tell me they were changing my name. I was already drafted when my first record came out. ["Everybody's Movin'" b/w "I'm Glad My Baby's Gone" was released as a 45 rpm single on March 3, 1958.] ERA sent me a telegram and said 'We've changed your name to Glen Glenn.' I didn't like it, but I wanted a recording contract, so I wasn't going to say anything."

During a two week leave, in April, Glenn returned to Gold Star to record "Blue Jeans and a Boy's Shirt" and "Laurie Ann." At this time, Glenn realized he needed to change the name that R.C. Allen had painted on his guitar pick guard since it read Glen Trout. When the first single was released, Glenn had taken a piece of black duct tape and placed it over Trout. Once he returned to Hawaii, the pick guard then read Glen Glenn and had a few musical notes added for decoration. On June 23, 1958, "One Cup of Coffee and a Cigarette" b/w "Laurie Ann" was released as a 45 rpm single.

"Laurie Ann" was being played all over the radio. It was number one in Los Angeles and Hawaii, and it was featured on *American Bandstand*. By that time, Glenn was stationed in Honolulu: "Disk jockeys knew I was there in

Hawaii because they kept saying there's a soldier boy out at Schofield Barracks. Special Service was looking for me, but they couldn't find Glen Glenn because my name's not Glen Glenn. I was sitting around singing with my guitar in the service club one night when somebody walked up to me and said, 'You're a singer. We're looking for a guy out in the barracks here that sings this song 'Laurie Ann.' They're playing it on the radio constantly. His name's Glen Glenn and thought you might know him.'" Of course they had found their guy, but it took them a month to do so. I was happy I didn't have to be a regular soldier anymore. My job was to entertain the whole Pacific." Incidentally, he met fellow rockabilly Mac Curtis in Korea because Curtis attended one of his shows. Although Special Service and the Army in general didn't do much for Glenn's musical career: "They wanted me to come back and be on *American Bandstand*, but the Army wouldn't release me to go because it wasn't an Army type show."

In November 1958, ERA still had faith in Glenn as a recording artist, so they released the 45 rpm single "Blue Jeans and a Boy's Shirt" b/w "Would Ja." While stationed in Honolulu, Glenn and Lambert played the Show of Stars at the Civic Auditorium with the Everly Brothers, Bobby Day, Robin Luke, and the Four Preps. During his stint in the Army, Glenn recorded only one song, Glenn Mueller's "Kitty Kat" at Webley Edwards Studio.

In 1960, Glenn and Lambert were discharged from the Army. They returned to *Cal's Corral*, and Glenn played shows with Fred Maddox while Lambert got another band together and played weekends at the Palomino Club in Hollywood. During this time, they also got day jobs. Glenn worked in the parts department at General Dynamics, one of the biggest manufactures of missiles in the country. Today, he receives a pension since he worked there for thirty-three years. In 1961, he married Mary Forrester, and they had two children, Teri, born in 1963, and Russell, born in 1968.

In regard to his recording career, Bidell and Newman split ERA Records into two different labels, ERA and Dore. Dore had hits with Jan and Dean's "Baby Talk" and the Teddy Bears' "To Know Him is to Love Him." Glenn switched and recorded for the Dore label. Hoping to capitalize on the teen idol craze; he recorded "Suzie Green from Abilene" and "Goofin' Around" with the Ernie Freeman band. In 1964, his last 45 rpm single was released, "I Didn't Have the Sense to Go" b/w "I'll Never Stop Loving You."

Throughout the 1960s, he occasionally sat in and sang a couple of country numbers with Lambert at the Palomino: "I can sing country just as good as I can rockabilly." By the 1970s, the Teddy Boys in England had latched onto Glenn's records. In 1977, England's Ace Records released the LP *Hollywood Rock and Roll*, which included six of Glenn's legendary tunes. In 1982, he recorded his last album, *Everybody's Movin' Again*, with guitarist Lambert and bassist Smith in tow.

In 1987, Glenn made his first visit to Europe with Rose Maddox. Glenn had received many chances to join the rockabilly revival and tour again, but he wasn't fully aware of his popularity and passed: "I didn't know the scene was so big, and I was working and raising a family. I didn't think rockabilly was anything at that time. In 1987, Dave Travis [owner of Stomper Time Records] gave me a proposition that I couldn't turn down. I played four countries, including Sweden, Holland, Belgium, and England. They wanted Fred Maddox really badly because he played the bass, and he was going to go with me, but he had a heart attack and had to back out."[41] Glenn then recommended Rose Maddox, but at first the promoters weren't convinced since they weren't too enthused about hiring a country singer. Glenn assured them she could sing anything: "If Rose comes over there, you won't be disappointed, believe me. She hadn't been doing rockabilly [but instead country and bluegrass]. She started rehearsing all those rockabilly songs [that she once recorded for Columbia]. When the tour was over, the promoters said, 'We want to thank you for bringing Rose over.' She had torn the shows apart."[42] While In London, Glenn met Robert Plant of Led Zeppelin. Plant stood in line for an autographed photo. When Glenn asked what his name was, he couldn't believe it was the same Robert Plant. Plant admitted that he was a big fan and loved rockabilly.

Upon his celebrated return to rockabilly, Glenn began performing once again regularly at clubs in California. He frequented the Palomino Club and Jack's Sugar Shack, both in Hollywood, and the Foothill Club in Long Beach then later regularly appeared at the House of Blues in Hollywood. The Dave and Deke Combo, Whistle Bait, and Big Sandy and the Fly-Rite Trio were all given their first breaks into rockabilly by opening for Glenn.

In 1994, Robert Rodriguez featured "One Cup of Coffee and a Cigarette" in his television movie *Road Racers*, which starred Salma Hayek and David Arquette. On May 19, 1995, Glenn opened for Bob Dylan at the Hollywood Palladium. Two years later, he was one of the first inductees into the Rockabilly Hall of Fame. 2002 at the Rockin' 50s Fest in Green Bay, Wisconsin, marked the last time Glenn and Lambert shared a stage together. After the show, Glenn signed autographs for four hours. The next artist was prepared to take his spot, but Glenn refused to leave: "I'm not leaving until the last fan comes through."

Since his reemergence on the scene, Glenn has embraced the opportunity to perform again. One of his favorite aspects is meeting the fans and autographing items for them, including Bear Family's 2004 CD releases, *Glen Rocks* and *Dim Lights, Thick Smoke, and Loud Loud Music*: "What amazes me most is all the young people who come to the shows. To have people come and see me and like my music at my age just makes me feel so good. Young rockabillies are the greatest people in the world. I love my fans."[43]

Six

Rockabilly Pioneers

The Rock and Roll Trio

The Rock and Roll Trio consisted of Johnny Burnette on lead vocals and rhythm acoustic guitar, his brother Dorsey on backing vocals and upright bass, and Paul Burlison on lead electric guitar. They began playing together in 1951 but did not record until 1953. Their career as a band lasted only six years, but their impact is still being felt today. Robert Plant and Jimmy Page of Led Zeppelin as well as Pete Townsend of The Who are a few of their famous fans. According to Johnny's son Rocky, "The Beatles were huge Rock and Roll Trio fans. Lennon and McCartney had one Rock and Roll Trio album between them, and they kept stealing it from one another."[1] Their signature tune, "The Train Kept A-Rollin'" has been recorded by over two hundred different acts, including Aerosmith. Aerosmith recorded "The Train Kept A-Rollin'" for their 1974 release *Get Your Wings*. The Rock and Roll Trio's sound can be best described as early punk with a hard hitting take no prisoners approach.

Dorsey Burnett (the e was added later) was born on December 28, 1932, in Memphis, Tennessee, and his brother Johnny was born on March 25, 1934, also in Memphis. Paul Burlison was born on February 4, 1929, in Brownsville, Tennessee. Johnny and Dorsey worked on the riverboats since they were thirteen years old, loading and unloading fruit onto the barges along the Mississippi River. Burlison met Dorsey because they both were prize winning boxers, and then met Johnny through Dorsey. Prior to working with the Burnettes, Burlison played with the legendary blues artist, Howlin' Wolf on both radio and in nightclubs: "It was an unusual experience, but he was a nice guy."[2] The trio's first recorded song was "You're Undecided" b/w "Go Mule Go" for the small independent label Von.

Dorsey and Burlison both worked at Crown Electric with Elvis Presley. Presley served as an apprentice to the electricians. However, he never received his license as an electrician because his musical career took off.

Burlison recalled that Presley used to have his guitar at work and play it on breaks: "He used to keep an old guitar in the back of the shop and play around on it every now and then. His mom would come into the shop and tell him 'lay that guitar down boy and get back to work.'" Burlison also remembered when Presley bought the now famous pink Cadillac, which was a gift for his mother, Gladys: "When he bought his pink Cadillac, his mom was there at work [checking up on him to make sure he was not goofing off on the job], he parked out front and peeked his head in the door and told his mom to 'come look what that old guitar bought me.'"

Presley knew of the trio even before he recorded "That's All Right" because he had seen a few of their shows. In fact, Presley tried his hand at being in a band with the Burnette brothers and Lauderdale Courts' neighbor Lee Denson at the tender age of fourteen, but Dorsey had a jealous streak and soon he and Presley fought too much to continue in a band together. Presley attracted all the girls, which made Dorsey upset. All the guys in Memphis were jealous of Presley because he was too pretty to be a guy. Rocky explained, "One day while they were playing down in the basement, Elvis came down and said 'Okay, I'm here. We can get started now.' They had been practicing Hank Williams' songs, my dad's favorite singer. Dorsey chased after Elvis and scared him. Mrs. Presley came out and made sure Lee Denson promised that nobody would hurt Elvis."[3] That was the last time they played together as a band. They did appear on a bill together once Presley became popular. The trio along with Charlie Feathers shared the back of a flatbed truck, which served as the stage, in front of Katz Drugstore in Memphis. The trio also witnessed Presley's first show at the Overton Park Shell in Memphis. Burlison remembered that before the show Presley was so nervous that he constantly paced back and forth, shrugged his shoulders, and fixed his collar. He added, "The audience kept calling Elvis back, and he couldn't understand what was happening."

Presley's band consisted of Scotty Moore on electric guitar and Bill Black on doghouse bass, but for a while he played with Bill's younger brother Johnny at the Girls' Club near Lauderdale Courts. Burlison knew Moore and Black from the trio playing shows with them on the radio program KWM in West Memphis, Arkansas. When Presley recorded "That's All Right," Burlison was surprised as he had heard him sing but did not think he was anything special: "In fact I did not even know he was that good until he recorded 'That's All Right.' I said that's the boy from the shop. That was the best sound I had heard — just Elvis, Scotty, and Bill. I was going to work one morning, and I heard that song and said wow what a sound." Rocky added, "Elvis was unique. He had his own style. He was the king, and my dad and Dorsey would have eventually admitted to that. Elvis was always really nice to my dad, Dorsey, and my grandmother."[4]

While still in Memphis, the trio frequently played Hernando's Hideaway and the Cotton Club, which were both located on the outskirts of town. From 1954 until February 1956, they were members of Doc MacQueen's swing band, who played every Friday and Saturday night at the Hideaway.[5] One night at the

Cotton Club, Scotty Moore and Bill Black played with Johnny and Dorsey. Moore filled in for Burlison, who was out of town at the time. After the show, a fight ensued. Black and Moore escaped unscathed out the back, but Johnny and Dorsey, the boxers that they were, went out the front door. Before reaching the outside, a farmer stabbed Dorsey in the butt.

Johnny Cash was just starting out in the music business as well, so he and Johnny became salesmen in hopes of helping to make ends meet. Rocky remembered, "Johnny Cash and my dad sold televisions to their moms, but that was about all they could sell." Then they both were salesmen for Melmac and thought they would sell more if they teamed up: "Johnny Cash would knock on the door, and he'd say 'ma'am how would you like one of these unbreakable dishes,' and my dad would drop the dish. Well the first door they went to, they dropped the dish, and it broke into a hundred pieces. If you hit them just the right way, they can break. It was a no sale, but they had fun. They joked about that for years."[6]

The trio branched out of Memphis by winning three weeks in a row on the nationally syndicated TV program, *Ted Mack's Amateur Hour*, which led to a recording contract with Coral Records. In July 1956, they recorded at Owen Bradley's Barn in Nashville. Although not given credit, Grady Martin played lead on those Nashville sessions, including the songs, "The Train Kept A-Rollin'," "Honey Hush," and "Lonesome Train (On a Lonesome Track)." Bob Moore played standup bass on "Rock Billy Boogie" and "Rock Therapy," taking the place of Dorsey, while Buddy Harman filled out the band's orchestration on drums. Burlison's signature fuzztone can be heard on "Tear It Up" and "Oh Baby Babe," from the New York session.

At ten years old, Burlison learned how to play the guitar from his grandmother: "She taught me my first chords. I was left handed in everything I do except playing guitar, so it was really hard on me because I had to reverse my whole thinking. She would put the guitar in my lap and reach her hands around my shoulder to show me how to make chords." He used his uncle's guitar until he could afford to buy his own. He picked up on the different chords by listening to and watching others. He never studied music and did not read it. His musical influences were rooted in gospel, country, and blues.

At twelve, he admired a boy down the street's electric guitar. The boy was an only child, so for Christmas, his parents bought him an electric guitar and a small amplifier. Burlison played the boy's guitar a few times and liked the sound it created. He then electrified his own by putting a telephone mouthpiece on the end of the acoustic. The mouthpiece acted as a pickup, so when he plugged his guitar into the amp it would become electrified.

He originally played a 1952 Fender Esquire, but then he switched to a Fender Telecaster because it had two pickups and could create more sound. Pulling a tube out of his amplifier created his unique fuzzy sound, which was only created in the studio. It was too difficult for him to duplicate live.

The Rock and Roll Trio preparing to record after three weeks winning on the *Ted Mack Amateur Hour* from left, Paul Burlison, Johnny Burnette, and Dorsey Burnette (courtesy Rocky Burnette).

Unfortunately, the Rock and Roll Trio never had a national hit. "Tear It Up" was a regional hit. It sold well in cities like Boston, Baltimore, and New York, even warranting a sheet music edition.[7] Elvis Presley changed his song lyrics to make them more radio friendly. The trio's "Oh Baby Babe" and Presley's "Baby, Let's Play House" are similar in lyrical content, but in Presley's version, the lyrics are altered a bit so not to offend 1950s conservative America.

They appeared on numerous television programs, including *American Bandstand*, where they sang "Blue Suede Shoes" and "Tear It Up" and *The Tonight Show* with Steve Allen. They also were one of the featured bands in the 1956 movie *Rock, Rock, Rock*. In the movie, the trio performed "Lonesome Train (On a Lonesome Track)." Unfortunately, there had been a rift in the band, so Dorsey does not appear. He was upset that their manager Henry Jerome had decided to change the name of the band to Johnny Burnette and the Rock and Roll Trio. As far as Dorsey and Burlison were concerned, it was strictly the Rock and Roll Trio. As for the movie, Johnny Black, Bill Black's brother, got the last minute phone call to fill in for Dorsey.

In regard to touring, they appeared on some of Alan Freed's package shows and in 1956 performed shows with Gene Vincent and the Blue Caps. A summer tour with Carl Perkins led them to pick up a sixteen year old drummer, Tony Austin, who was a distant cousin of Perkins.' An outdoor show at the Westside Nutclub Fall Festival in Evansville, Indiana, showcased their energetic stage act. Austin recalled, "We were hot. The girls tore off Johnny's shirt and mine too. They weren't trying to hurt us though. They just wanted some souvenirs, and we were glad they didn't get our pants. Johnny was very exciting onstage. He'd dance around all over the stage, and he'd fall on his back, kick his legs in the air, and keep playing. He was a great showman." Johnny could move just like Presley. Austin often encouraged Johnny's antics by standing on the drums: "We tried to make things as exciting as we could." Austin teamed up with Johnny quite a bit: "We worked a lot back in those days because Paul had a family to support and a regular job as an electrician [so we would borrow a guitarist and a bass player]. We worked in Pittsburgh and Boston, around Memphis and in Arkansas. I stayed with Johnny until he moved to California. Austin added, "Johnny Black played with us around Memphis."[8] A little later, Johnny and Austin's cousin Carl Perkins worked together. Rocky related, "I grew up with Carl Perkins. He played guitar for my dad during the late '50s and early '60s. They did a lot of shows together. After Carl's car accident, things sort of dried up for him, so he would give my dad a call: 'Hey man, I need a gig,' so my dad would say 'come on.' Carl was a great guitar player, one of the best rock and roll guitar players of all time. He invented a lot of that stuff."

In 1957, when the trio decided that the music business did not accept them with open arms, they parted ways amicably. Their last recordings were done in Nashville with Johnny alone. By that time, Dorsey and Burlison had quit. Burlison put his guitar away, opened his own electrical company and settled down with his family. Rocky explained, "That was just my dad's way of finishing off the contract and getting out of town."[9] The Burnette brothers returned to Memphis and discovered that it was now a one-man town, an Elvis town, so they packed up their families and moved to California to start a new life as songwriters. Dorsey arrived in California first, working for record owner Fabor Robinson. Then they worked primarily for Ricky Nelson, who recorded twenty of their compositions, including some of his biggest hits, "Believe What You Say," "Waitin' In School," "Just a Little Too Much," and "It's Late." According to Rocky, it was actually Ozzie who got them out of their contracts with Coral Records and Henry Jerome."

Rocky retold the story about how his dad and uncle first approached Nelson about recording some of their songs: "My dad found out where Ricky lived. They were out on his front yard drinking whiskey. Ricky and his brother David drove up, and my dad and Dorsey said 'hey Ricky, we're Johnny and Dorsey Burnette.' Ricky then said 'yeah I saw you guys on television last year.' 'We got some songs we wanted to play ya,' and they played him demos of 'Believe What You Say,' 'It's Late,' and 'Just a Little Too Much.' Nelson's reaction was 'This is just what I have been looking for.'" These demos are available on the album, *Together Again: Johnny and Dorsey Burnette*. Rocky commented, "We owe a lot to the Nelson family. Ricky Nelson was our bread and butter."

Around the same time, Johnny became friends with Eddie Cochran. Rocky remembered, "Eddie Cochran was a good friend of my dad's. When we first met him, my dad was out of town, and he had come over to our house to get some musical charts of my dad's. [Johnny had just returned from touring England, and Cochran was going to reuse his charts since they were expensive to draw up.] It was a dark rainy day, and Eddie Cochran looked like a hoodlum. My mom threatened to hit him in the head with a big iron skillet if he didn't leave. So he left, went down to the corner, and gave her a call saying 'Mrs. Burnette I am a good friend of Johnny's, and I came over to get some charts.' She apologized and told him to come back. She gave him the charts and made him a fried chicken dinner." After dinner, he played catch with Rocky and his brother. Johnny and Cochran even wrote a couple of songs together, including "Love Kept a Rollin'," in which Cochran played guitar on the demo.

Johnny and Dorsey also had successful solo careers. Johnny had top twenty hits with "You're Sixteen" and "Dreamin'." Dorsey hit the charts with "(There Was A) Tall Oak Tree." Rocky recalled, "It is one of Bob Dylan's favorite songs. The song was banned in Japan because it reminded them too much of the atomic bomb. A tall oak tree looks like a mushroom cloud."[10]

On August 14, 1964, Johnny was tragically killed when a cabin cruiser struck his fishing boat. It hit in the back of the boat where Johnny was steering and knocked him unconscious. He drowned at the young age of thirty.

Luckily, the Burnettes' musical talent was passed onto their sons. It all began when Rocky, Johnny's son, and Billy, Dorsey's son used to watch the trio rehearse in their living room and as soon as the trio began to play, they would run to their bedroom, grab their wind up guitars, and shake to the songs. They used bathroom plungers as their microphones. Burlison commented, "Dorsey started to call them my little rockabilly boys." Their song "Rock Billy Boogie" is named after Rocky and Billy's antics. The trio were the first ones to coin the term rockabilly by usage in the song.

Rocky and Billy continue performing and songwriting to this day. Billy writes songs for primarily country acts; one of his biggest to date is Faith Hill. He has also backed Fleetwood Mac, Bob Dylan, and John Fogerty. Rocky has built his own career as a rockabilly artist. In fact, his most recent offering was 2007's El Toro Records' release *Wampus Cat*. In 1980, he scored a top ten hit with "Tired of Toein' the Line." Ricky Nelson had recorded it around the same time, but he knew that Rocky was successful with it in Europe and wanted to give him a chance to chart with it in the States. Nelson's version went unreleased until 2000. For fifteen years, Rocky was road manager and opening act for his uncle, Dorsey. Dorsey passed away on August 17, 1979, after suffering a heart attack. Then for twenty-five years, Rocky toured with Burlison paying tribute to the trio's legendary songs. Their first gig was in 1981 at a rockabilly festival in England.

In 1986, Burlison signed on as a member of the Sun Rhythm Section along with Sonny Burgess and Elvis Presley's drummer D.J. Fontana, among others. They played for nine years touring all over the world. Burlison released a solo album in 1997, *Train' Kept a Rollin'*, on Sweetfish Records. Rocky and Billy both guest starred. Performances kept Burlison active until he died on September 27, 2003, after a long battle with cancer.

Rockabilly musicians were often ridiculed by veteran country performers. On a visit to the *Grand Ole Opry*, Johnny witnessed this first hand. According to Rocky, "My dad was there one afternoon when Hank Snow was rehearsing. During the break, my dad introduced himself, 'Hank, I'm Johnny Burnette; I want to get up there and sing with you on the *Grand Ole Opry*.' He said, 'Son you gotta go around the world a few times before you play with me.' My dad told him where to go and said he didn't like any of his old music anyway."[11] Unbeknownst to Snow, the trio's music has influenced as many people as his music has.

Narvel Felts

Rockabilly music, with some notable exceptions, enjoyed a short life-span on the national charts. After the genre's 1954–1957 heyday, many performers quit music altogether while others eventually found success in country music. Narvel Felts, like Charlie Rich, Bob Luman, and Conway Twitty, proved far more successful in country than rockabilly with forty-two singles and eight albums registering on the charts. During his mid-1970s peak, Narvel Felts scored his biggest hits with his versions of "Drift Away," "Somebody Hold Me (Until She Passes By)," "My Prayer," "Lonely Teardrops," and "Reconsider Me."

Albert Narvel Felts was born on November 11, 1938, near Keiser, Arkansas, to a family of sharecroppers. Although named after his father, he was never called Albert. During pregnancy, his mother Lena saw the name Narvel in a magazine story she had been reading. Felts had only one sibling, a sister eight years older than he.

Felts cites Floyd Tillman's "They Took the Stars Out of Heaven" as the first song he ever sang, at age six. As a shy youngster, he sang on the front porch but ran back into the house if he saw someone coming. At age fourteen, he purchased his first guitar from Sears Roebuck. From the start, his family was very supportive: "I'm very grateful for that because if they hadn't of been that would have been so much harder to get into the business."[12]

Blessed with an incredible memory for detail, Felts remembers the day his professional career began. On December 25, 1955, Harold White had heard that Felts could sing and play guitar and asked the young singer to play a few songs with him at the Highway Café, two miles south of Bernie, Missouri. Felts replied bashfully, "You want me to sing in front of somebody. I couldn't do anything like that." Felts' dad then spoke up, "Well, Narvel how do you expect to ever do anything with this if you don't ever sing in front of anybody? Why don't you go with him?" Felts finally obliged but only if his musician friend J.W. Grubbs also went. It would be his first live show. That night, they sat at the counter and sang songs of the day including "Baby, Let's Play House," "Maybellene," and "Rock Around the Clock." After the brief set, an Air Force sergeant told Felts, "Son, don't you ever pick another boll of cotton because you don't have to."

In early 1956, singing Elvis Presley's "Baby, Let's Play House" and encoring with Carl Perkins' "Blue Suede Shoes," Felts won a talent contest at Bernie High School. According to Felts, "the crowd went wild." In attendance sat Weldon Grimsley, a disk jockey from KDEX in Dexter, Missouri. The next day, the record spinner surprised the young singer with the following announcement: "If Narvel Felts is listening, please contact KDEX immediately." Felts' dad drove him eight miles to the nearest phone where the disk jockey told him to grab his guitar and come up to the station. Felts sang a couple of songs with his friend J.W. Grubbs accompanying him on guitar The station manager, Dean Spidel liked them so well that he gave them a regular Saturday afternoon spot.

A few months later, Felts went to the Four Way Inn in Dudley, Missouri, to see Jerry Mercer and the Roving Cowboys. After intermission, Felts was invited onstage to sing. Soon, Mercer was only offered bookings if Felts was part of the show. The band included Leon Barnett on lead guitar, Bob Taylor on drums, and Jerry Tuttle on saxophone and piano. Felts played upright bass when he wasn't singing. Since he couldn't juggle both music and school, the youngster left his education behind to pursue music full time. After Mercer married and quit the music business, the band was renamed Narvel Felts and the Rockets. Childhood friend J.W. Grubbs replaced Mercer on bass.

Felts as featured singer in Mercer's band played his first package show on top of the concession stand at the Family Drive-In theatre on August 7, 1956, in Dexter, Missouri: "I was seventeen, and we opened the show for Roy Orbison and the Teen Kings and Eddie Bond and the Stompers." Incidentally, Orbison was one of Felts' main influences along with Elvis Presley, Carl Perkins, Slim Whitman, Tony Williams of The Platters, Johnny Ray, Patti Page, and Ernest Tubb. After the show, "without me asking, Roy went back to Memphis and put in a word for me. Within a couple of weeks, I wound up with an audition with Sun." Engineer/producer Jack Clement offered him some advice: "He listened to us [me and the guitarist Leon Barnett], and he said 'Well, I'll tell you what, go home and write some more songs, and bring the whole band back, and we'll see what we can come up with.' He said, 'Do your songs in the highest key you feel comfortable with, and the song will have more feel that way. Don't write me anything about rocking, bopping, or jitterbugging. That's a passing fad, and guitar player, don't play me a boogie. Write some ballads. After all, we sold Presley to RCA with a ballad, 'I Forgot to Remember to Forget,' so go back and write me an 'I Forgot to Remember to Forget.'"

At Felts' first Sun session on January 23, 1957, Roy Orbison was in the control booth with Jack Clement. Johnny Cash was hanging around in the front office, and Jerry Lee Lewis was at Taylor's Café next door. Harold Jenkins, more famously known as Conway Twitty, took a chair and dragged it out by Felts' microphone. With that all-star lineup in attendance, Felts recorded "Did You Tell Me," which was mislabeled by Clement as "You Don't Care." Yet, despite positive response, success at Sun was far from guaranteed. At one point, Orbison called Felts and Jenkins over in the corner of the room and told them: "Guys, if I were you, I would look elsewhere for a label because Sam [Phillips'] not interested in you. He's not interested in me. He's not even interested in [Carl] Perkins. He's only interested in [Johnny] Cash and this new kid Jerry Lee Lewis. When my contract's up, I'm gone." Orbison also told Felts and Jenkins that they might want to search out the new record label Roulette. Rockabilly musicians Buddy Knox and Jimmy Bowen were already recording for Roulette. As it turned out, both Felts and Jenkins signed with Mercury a short time later.

Felts' second Sun session took place on April 5, 1957, in which he recorded the first rockabilly version of the Little Walter rhythm and blues classic, "My Babe." "Of course, I didn't hear any rhythm and blues radio up here where I was from. [Fellow rockabilly performer] Matt Lucas was the one who taught me the song." As it turned out, Felts did not sign a contract nor did he have a record released on Sun. Clement told him, "I think we've got a record here, but it may take about a year to get around in releasing it." "I was eighteen years old, and a year sounded like an eternity at that time." During the 1970s, Sun leased all ten songs that Felts had recorded to the British label, Charly. In 1976, Felts first became aware of this when he received a fan letter from Germany that said he owned a copy of "My Babe."

In 2000, Felts ran into Sam Phillips, whom he hadn't seen since 1957. Phillips admitted, "Narvel, I knew you had it. My problem was I was a one man show and had more than I could handle." "It made me really feel good for him to tell me that after all those years."

Later, in 1957, Felts and his band went to Chicago where they auditioned for Mercury Records. Afterwards Vice President Art Talmadge told them to go to Universal Studio to record twelve original songs, which included their first single "Kiss a Me Baby" b/w "Foolish Thoughts." After its release, Felts was mobbed by teenage girls, which occasionally proved frightening. In Poplar Bluff, Missouri, the theatre was so packed that there was no easy way off the stage except the stairs down into the aisle: "I started off the stage, and they just mobbed me." An old man told him, "Here son, get over against a wall and then they won't knock you down.

Narvel Felts shares his trademark falsetto vocal style with only one other rockabilly artist, Roy Orbison (courtesy Narvel Felts).

Well, first thing I knew he was on the floor, and they were just trampling all over him." By this time, Felts was against the wall, but one of the female fans had a pair of scissors in her hands, trying to cut a lock of his hair. She barely missed his face and eyes. "That was a little scary. I had worn a real nice white jacket, and it was totally gone, just ripped to shreds."

In 1959, Felts added a new dimension to his vocals that eventually became his trademark, a falsetto. "It was always there, but I didn't always use it. The first record that I ever used the falsetto on was a song called 'Genavee.' It really didn't become a trademark until I used it on 'Reconsider Me' in 1975." Record producers then requested he put it in every song after that. After Felts left Mercury, he recorded for the Pink label and released a version of The Drifters' "Honey Love" that hit #90 on the pop charts in 1960.

For a year in 1964, he had the *Narvel Felts Show*, which aired on KAIT-TV in Jonesboro, Arkansas. Such rockabilly icons as Carl Perkins, Travis Wommack, and Bobby Lee Trammell were all guests. Felts and Trammell toured together in the 1960s and 1970s. Trammell predicted "Drift Away" would be a big hit: "This one's gonna do it for you. This is the one you've been looking for." He also told Felts that "Reconsider Me" would be a bigger hit than "Drift Away."

However, if there was going to be a future for Felts, he felt it would be in country music. His transition from rockabilly to country was not an easy one. He recorded a straight country record in 1969 for the Celebrity Circle label, and no one liked it. "I had to find the ingredient that country wanted to play on me. My style was a mixture of rockabilly, rhythm and blues, rock and roll, and country, and it all came out as being Narvel Felts."

A country hit proved elusive, and Felts began to think it would never happen. Then the independent label, Cinnamon finally broke Felts' non-charting streak with a cover of Dobie Gray's pop smash "Drift Away." 1974 was a banner year, in which Felts played both the *Grand Ole Opry* and performed in Europe for the first time. He played the Wembley Festival in London and was filmed for BBC-TV singing "Drift Away." After the Cinnamon label folded, Felts signed with ABC/Dot and in 1975, *Billboard* and *Cash Box* named "Reconsider Me" Record of the Year.

The 1970s were a very successful era for Felts with one country hit after another. Artists who had influenced him were now his opening act, such as Lefty Frizzell, Kitty Wells, Don Gibson, Carl Smith, and Carl Perkins. "It kind of embarrassed me," a fact that he acknowledged to Perkins. Perkins replied, "Son you're the one who's hot now. You're the one who sold the tickets. You go out there and do your thing." During this time, Felts also worked with country legends Faron Young and Marty Robbins. They were both big fans of his. Young commented to him, "You're one of my favorite singers," and Robbins stated, "You sing awfully well."

In 1978, Front Street, where Felts had lived since 1966 was officially renamed Narvel Felts Avenue. No other rockabilly holds that distinction of having a street named after him other than Elvis Presley.

Felts didn't play a rockabilly festival until 1986. The singer planned to sing "Great Balls of Fire," "Blue Suede Shoes," and other songs from the rock and roll era, but the promoter notified him that the fans only wanted to hear the songs he had cut. After the show, his son Bub, formerly a heavy metal devotee came home and started playing drums along with the Gene Vincent, Jerry Lee Lewis, and other rockabilly records that Felts had in his collection. Unfortunately, his beloved son was tragically killed in a 1995 automobile accident. As a tribute, Felts sings his version of the Skyliners' "Since I Don't Have You" at most of his rockabilly concerts.

Felts recorded an album of pure rockabilly with producer Ronny Weiser entitled *At Rollin' Rock: Those Pink and Black Days*. Released on the Goofin' label in 1999, it cemented his reputation with European rockabilly fans.

He has wowed sold-out crowds at every major rockabilly festival both in the States and abroad and played England's huge Americana festival five times. The year 2006 marked Felts' thirty-second trip to Europe. His autograph lines are often four hours long, but Felts tries to accommodate each and every fan: "I appreciate the people coming, and I try to make myself available to meet people regardless [of the size of the crowd]." He always stands to greet his fans:

"If they can stand for me, then I can stand for them. If it wasn't for the fans, we wouldn't be in the business."

Art Adams

Even though Art Adams only had two releases in the 1950s, he is one of the most popular amongst fans. His high-octane shows have promoters inviting him back to their festivals. He made his fourth appearance at England's Hemsby Weekender in 2009, more than any other legendary act. His singles "Dancing Doll" and "Rock Crazy Baby" are regularly played by disk jockeys both on radio programs and at record hops. These 45's are rare and two of the more expensive records on the rockabilly market. According to the *Guide to Rare Rockabilly and Rock 'n' Roll 45 rpms* by Tom Lincoln and Dick Blackburn, "Dancing Doll" is worth $300 while "Rock Crazy Baby" is valued at $125.[13]

Arthur Adams was born on February 12, 1935, in Locust, Kentucky. His brother Al, the only sibling of six who shared an interest in music, played upright bass and sometimes performed along with Adams. Their parents divorced when Adams was only 14, and he opted to live alone. He went to school during the day and flipped hamburgers at White Castle during the evenings. Soon after, Adams began singing in public. Although he commented, "I've been singing all my life. I can't remember when I didn't sing. [In regard to guitar playing], there were a couple of kids I knew who played guitar, and I started picking it up."[14] "When My Blue Moon Turns to Gold Again" was the first song that Adams ever sang, and Hank Williams' "Wedding Bells" was the initial song that he played on his guitar. His musical influences included Williams, Ernest Tubb, Carl Perkins, and Jerry Lee Lewis.

In 1953, Adams formed his country band, the Kentucky Drifters with his brother-in-law Dave Logsdon. Adams recalled, "Dave and I were hanging out one day; he was playing guitar and I was singing, and he said 'why don't we get a band together?' I said okay, so we got an upright bass player [and the Kentucky Drifters was born]." Adams took first place and won war bonds in a television contest with guitarist Logsdon where he sang "If Teardrops Were Pennies." Around this same time, Bobby Mullinix, an aspiring artist from Adams' neighborhood, painted "Art Adams" and some musical notes on the singer's D28 Martin guitar.

With the realization that he would be drafted when he turned eighteen, Adams enlisted in the Army and spent a year and a half in Korea. Upon his return, he reunited some of the original members of the Kentucky Drifters and played company picnics and shows in county parks.

In April and May 1956, Adams changed the band's name to the Rhythm Knights and began performing rockabilly music. Radio station WISH in Indi-

Art Adams at 17 strumming his D28 Martin guitar in front of his 1946 Chevrolet Fleet Master Sports Sedan (courtesy Art Adams).

anapolis had the band perform live on-air frequently. Their popularity zoomed, and Adams started to receive many cards and letters from listeners across Indiana.[15]

Adams and the band had the songs "Down in Tennessee" and "She's from Tennessee" when he made a pilgrimage to Sun Records in Memphis. Adams remembered, "I didn't call anybody. I just decided to go down there. I had heard if you just walked in, Sam would talk to you. I walked in the door, and there was secretary Marion Keisker. I asked her is Sam here?" She said he wasn't there, but she saw Adams had a tape. He ended up seeing Sun engineer Jack Clement instead, and he listened to the demo. Adams revealed, "Jack said, 'Well, I'll tell you something I told Johnny Cash, work on getting a more unique sound and then come back.' Jack said he liked it." Upon their return to Indiana, they began working on other songs like "Dancing Doll" with drums and twin guitars. Logsdon remained with the band even after the name was changed to the Rhythm Knights and a drummer and additional guitarist was added to the lineup. However, Logsdon decided he liked country better than rockabilly and left the band: "Dave liked country a lot better than the stuff I was doing." Adams added, "I loved country too, but I just liked to be wild and play the up tempo songs. I was taking some old country songs and juicing them up."

With Logsdon's departure, the band still had to find a recording label. Adams began asking around. Singer Johnny Hargett suggested his Nashville recording label, Cherry. The Rhythm Knights then sent a demo to Cherry's A&R man Joe Dyson. On July 11, 1959, Adams inked a deal with Cherry Records. The contract specified six releases in three years, but only two singles surfaced — "Rock Crazy Baby" b/w "Indian Joe" in September 1959 and "Dancing Doll" b/w "She Don't Live Here No More" in May 1960. "Rock Crazy Baby" was written by a thirteen-year-old named Bob Jones: "He was messing around with it, but he had some crazy words written about a girl and her washing machine. I took the song, changed the words, and put a melody to it." "Indian Joe" and "She Don't Live Here No More" were co-written with Adams' drummer, K.Y. Curly. While "Dancing Doll" was co-written with Betty Stone: "We played at this place called the Pla-Mor, and Betty would come. We just started calling her dancing doll. She came in one night and said she started writing a song called 'Dancing Doll.' I took it, and we finished it up by putting some music to it. We started playing it. Curly came up with the drum kick off, and the people in the club seemed to like it. Betty then started the Art Adams fan club." Adams' songs "Honey Girl" and the instrumental "Orange Blossom Special" never saw the light of day, which to this day remains a mystery. They used guitars instead of fiddles, which was unusual, on "Orange Blossom Special," and according to Adams, "people in the clubs would go crazy over it since we really had it rockin'."

Two years later, Adams called it quits with the Rhythm Knights and formed his rock and roll band, the Epics. They played seven nights a week. Adams recollected, "I actually quit playing the guitar, and I was just fronting the band. We had the drummer, saxophone player, and the bass player sing background. [At first], Bill Stewart played guitar, but he decided to move to California and stay out there for three or four years. When he came back, Jack Scott had joined the group." [Note: Guitarist Jack Scott is not the rockabilly singer Jack Scott, who had a hit with "What in the World's Come Over You?"] The teen dance that they played was two times a month: "We backed Faron Young, Webb Pierce, Marty Robbins, Jerry Lee Lewis, Gene Simmons, Dee Dee

Sharp, and Carl Smith. We'd open up [the show] and then back them. I sang a lot of Fats Domino's songs. I got to meet a lot of the stars, but we didn't get to spend a lot of time together." The Epics were a band for about six years. They had an opportunity to go on the road but declined since they all had day jobs.

In 1968, Adams hung up his rock and roll shoes and started a successful vending company, which lasted for thirty years. In 1980, Peter Braun of Germany's Bison Bop Records contacted Adams in the hopes that he would still have some of his original 45's and be willing to sell them to him. Adams disclosed, "I got a call from Peter, and he came to my house. I sold him twenty 45's at $20 each. Then the next time, I had any inkling that people might have liked my songs was when the Stray Cats came out with 'Rock This Town.' A fan from Texas got in touch with me, and we went to a record convention. He had a copy of 'Rock Crazy Baby' and played it for the teenagers. They all thought it was the Stray Cats. That's how close it was to the ear." Adams' comeback year was 2003 and with thanks to Canadian fan Steve Kelemen, he was inducted into the Rockabilly Hall of Fame, and Collector Records released the CD *Rock Crazy Baby*, which included never before released songs and a 1959 Indianapolis TV live show and interview. Then the offers poured in for the singer to play Hemsby, the Viva Las Vegas Weekender, and countless other festivals around the world.

When he hit the stage in Vegas, his first show back after thirty-four years of retirement from the music business, he couldn't believe it. Adams conveyed, "All the attention at Las Vegas was unreal. I'd walk in a room, and people would get up and run over to me and say it's him." Every where he went, admirers stopped him for his autograph and/or wanted his/her photo with Adams. The Hemsby Weekender in England was Adams' next stop on the comeback trail: "When I was booked to do Hemsby, Bill Stewart went over with me and played guitar. I sang 'Indian Joe,' and I think everybody in the place was doing the war whoop with me." When he ventured into another room to see rhythm and blues act Eddy Clearwater, a disk jockey was playing "Dancing Doll." Adams reflected, "at least a couple hundred people were in there. They took me down front, and the disk jockey announced I was there. I think about everybody in the place stood up and applauded, and I gotta tell ya, tears were rolling down my eyes." Also at Hemsby, Adams sat and signed autographs for over two hours: "I couldn't believe the lineup." He loves meeting the fans: "I'll sign anything. Whatever they want me to sign, I'll sign it."

When Adams isn't able to travel with his regular band, which includes Tim Gibson, Danny Thompson, and Tom Woodward on lead guitar, Mike Strauss on upright bass, and Mark Cutsinger on standup drums, he is usually paired with top notch European acts such as Sweden's Wildfire Willie and the Ramblers. In fact, at a remote venue in Sweden, they drew the largest audience that the club ever had with 1,011 in attendance. The promoter couldn't believe it, and Adams was shocked to learn he had sold $900 in merchandise.

One of Adams' favorite aspects is meeting the various legendary acts and newcomers to the scene. Many of them have worked with him on shows and have become his friends, such as the Stardevils, Rory Justice, Jerry King and the Rivertown Ramblers, The Buzzards, The Infernos (backed Adams three different times at Hemsby), the Rip Cords, Ruby Ann, Mandy Marie, Sonny Burgess, Glen Glenn, and Janis Martin. Adams revealed, "Janis was my favorite. I loved her."

Adams remains busy with recordings. In 2005, Collector Records released *Rockin' My Way Around*, and in 2006, Flying Saucer Records released *Dancing Doll*. When not on the road, he enjoys bowling. In fact, Adams plays in a league with four other men and averages 185.

His popularity mystifies him, but he loves every minute of it. Adams still hopes to play in Japan and Australia and on the *Grand Ole Opry*: "I can remember being seven or eight years old having a broomstick microphone and pretending I was on the Opry. I'd love to sing 'Rock Crazy Baby' on the *Grand Ole Opry*. It is my dream."

Laura Lee Perkins

Rockabilly singers in the 1950s were predominately male. It was difficult for them to gain society's approval, let alone a female. It was considered taboo for a girl to sing a wild rockin' song. The most well known of the rockabilly gals— Wanda Jackson, Janis Martin, Barbara Pittman, Brenda Lee, Lorrie Collins, and Laura Lee Perkins were all chastised by parents and religious leaders. However, thanks to their determination to sing rockabilly, they left an indelible mark on history and influenced legions of gals who followed in their footsteps. Laura Lee Perkins' six recordings on Imperial Records showcased her ability to rock with the best of them and gave credence to *Billboard Magazine*'s decision to give her the nickname "the female Jerry Lee Lewis."

Laura Lee Perkins was born Alice Faye Perkins on July 20, 1939, in Killarney, West Virginia. Her father was a coal miner, and both her parents were musically inclined: "In West Virginia, everybody plays an instrument or sings. I was an only child, and we each had a guitar. My parents and I used to play and sing harmony together all the time because there wasn't any TV when I was growing up. We had to entertain ourselves."[16] At age three, Perkins taught herself how to play guitar, learning by ear: "I had to stand it up in order to get a hold of the neck." The guitar was too big for the toddler to sit down and play. Her parents showed her a few chords once they recognized her interest: "I was in the living room one day, playing the guitar, and my mother came in to see who it was." Her mother was amazed by her astuteness at such a young age: "She asked, 'how did you find that [chord]?' I said I don't know; it just sounds good. Living in a valley between four mountains, I spent half my time climbing.

I would take my guitar up in the mountains and sing, hearing my voice echo."[17] She added, "I sang in church, and I entertained in school. I was always in all the plays and [programs]. I [even] played trumpet in the school band." In fact, she later learned how to play multiple instruments including organ, ukulele, drums, harmonica, flute, and accordion.

In 1957, Perkins graduated from Stoco High School in Coal City, West Virginia. She was listening to the acts of the day such as Elvis Presley, Jerry Lee Lewis, Pat Boone, The Everly Brothers, The Platters, Fats Domino, and Connie Francis when she began playing the piano. Perkins explained, "A neighbor lady gave me an old piano, and I taught myself [how] to play." Before Sunday church service, she practiced on their piano for two hours. She would usually stop playing her boogie woogie music before all the members arrived. Although, one day the preacher took notice and asked, "What are you playing on my piano? That doesn't sound like church music." However, his comments didn't deter Perkins any as she returned the following week to hone her skills.

Soon after graduation, Perkins left West Virginia to pursue her dreams. She left home on a Greyhound bus destined for Cleveland but instead settled in Elyria, Ohio, where she got a job as a waitress. Perkins remembered, "There was a radio station, WEOL, across the street [from the restaurant]. I went up there with a couple of girlfriends one night because we were driving around listening to the disk jockey on the radio in the car. We went up to see him [Jeff Baxter], and there was a piano. I started playing ['My Babe'], and he came out and said, 'Hey, you're pretty good.' He got out the tape and taped me and made a couple of calls to a very famous disk jockey in Cleveland [by the name of] Bill Randle." They sent her demos of "My Babe," "Hound Dog," "No One Will Ever Know," "Remember Me, I'm the One," and "Oh La Baby" to Sam Phillips at Sun Records and Lew Chudd at Imperial Records. Perkins acknowledged, "I got a letter back and offered a contract from both companies. I had been to Tennessee, but Los Angeles, California, sounded like the moon to me. I just wanted to go to California since I had been very sheltered." She had never traveled outside of the South nor been on an airplane. It didn't hurt that one of her favorite singers, Ricky Nelson, also happened to record for Imperial.

The teenaged songstress took Chudd up on his offer, and Jeff Baxter, the disk jockey who had discovered her hidden talent, and his wife escorted her on her trip to California. Perkins recalled, "One week before we went we found out since I was only eighteen I couldn't sign any legal papers. We drove all night to get to West Virginia and have my daddy sign over legal guardianship to Jeff." Once they arrived at the Knickerbocker Hotel, she phoned the studio: "There's one thing you have to do for me, I have to meet Ricky Nelson. They said, 'Oh, that's no problem. We'll set it up for tomorrow. You can spend the day with him.' They took me to the studio [where the *Adventures of Ozzie and Harriet* was filmed]. There was a piano [set up], and Ricky and I played and sang all day together. I met [his brother] David, [and his parents] Ozzie and Harriet.

Laura Lee Perkins looking glamorous in her evening gown (courtesy Laura Lee Perkins).

I was excited. I loved every minute of it. I have a photo that he autographed to me." Perkins played Ray Charles' "I Got a Woman" because Nelson liked the song: "He kept making me play it over and over. He said he had never heard it [before that day], and I was shocked because I thought everybody had heard that song. We had a wonderful time that day. He was a young kid like me."

As far as her Imperial session, Lew Chudd immediately changed her name to Laura Lee Perkins and assigned Joe Maphis to play guitar on her six legendary sides: "I had never heard of Joe Maphis; it didn't mean anything to me. I was back in the control booth, so I wasn't really with the musicians that much. I spent some time with the piano player, and I believe it was Jimmie Haskell." As it turned out, "Come on Baby" and "Gonna Rock My Baby Tonight" are the only songs she actually played piano on: "To my knowledge, we only did those one time. I don't remember playing those with the band. It was the first time I had ever done 'Come on Baby,' and you can even tell by listening to it. It's terrible, and I hate it. I was trying to read the words because they had just given me the song the night before, and I had never played it on the piano. I listened to the tape in the hotel. I was playing the piano, trying to read the words, and trying to put a little style into it. I think later on they put the band to it."

Originally, they had given her songs to record, but she had other ideas in mind: "When they gave me those other songs to do, I thought I don't like these songs at all. I think I could do better than this, so I told them I'd like to try and write my own songs. I went back to the hotel and wrote 'Don't Wait Up.'" In regard to "I Just Don't Like This Kind of Living" and "Kiss Me Baby," they feature her signature growl: "That's just my style. That's just the way I sing. I only like to do it when I get the feeling to do it. They wanted me to growl after every word. I didn't like that because it didn't feel natural and normal." "Kiss Me Baby" b/w "I Just Don't Like This Kind of Living" were released first on Imperial in February 1958. Five weeks later, they issued "Don't Wait Up" b/w "Oh La Baby." Her other two songs from the session "Come On Baby" and "Gonna Rock My Baby Tonight" were not released at the time.

The two records that were released lay dormant since they never quite caught on with radio station disk jockeys: "In the days of payola, we were having trouble getting disk jockeys to play them."[18] Perkins added, "We would go the studio, and they would look at us and say, 'Well, what else do you have to offer?' when we handed them the record. They couldn't actually come out and say they wanted money. We didn't have any money to give them. It got really bad where we couldn't get anybody to play the record."

After the disappointment of not scoring a hit record, Perkins went back to Elyria: "When I went back to Elyria, I started doing record hops. Most of them were in the Cleveland area and set up by Bill Randle. I did them with the Everly Brothers, Connie Francis, Fabian, Frankie Avalon, and Paul Anka. Avalon and Perkins were scheduled to play a private birthday party for a wealthy teen. They showed up but no band. Perkins explained, "Frankie and I had hardly met, but we entertained all those kids. I played the piano for Frankie. They didn't know the difference. They thought it was great."

By 1959, she moved in with her aunt, who lived outside of Detroit: "She took me downtown to a booking agent, and they signed me up." A year later, she began a three year gig with Tony Thomas and the Tartans. As part of her act, she mimicked Louis Armstrong: "I did a lot of Louis Armstrong. I did the voice of Louis then I'd grab my trumpet and my hanky. I had a lot of fun doing that too. I was very versatile." Her favorite song to sing live was Chuck Berry's "Johnny B. Goode." Perkins sang on the same bill as Frank Sinatra and Bobby Darin in New York City, and Ella Fitzgerald, the Ink Spots, and Liberace in Nevada: "I knew Liberace well, eating dinner with him almost every night. He was the sweetest person."[19] She met her future husband, tool salesman Neal Kitts, while performing at an 8 Mile Road nightclub.

During the 1980s, Perkins found success with writing and recording advertising jingles for radio and television: "I went to Ambience Recording Studio in Farmington Hills, Michigan, one day with my ukulele. I had been making little jingles at home. I had seen an ad for it on TV that Bob Seger had recorded there, so I looked them up in the phone book and found out their address. I just drove over there, walked in and introduced myself and said I write jingles could you use any? He said, 'No we don't do jingles here.' I said, 'Well, you should.' They said, 'Well, let us hear some of your stuff.' I just started playing my ukulele and singing. [She then moved to the piano and started playing it.] He said, 'You know, maybe we will do jingles.' He then got me a couple of jobs." Thanks to those jobs, she was referred and got more. Perkins remembered, "We had a lot of fun doing those jingles. We went everywhere." The studio ended up closing, and she didn't look for work elsewhere. However, she still writes jingles in the hopes that someday she will be able to showcase them.

In 1981, she wrote "DeLorean's Dream" about the famed founder John DeLorean who had developed the car of the same name but later arrested for drug trafficking. Perkins revealed, "I felt terrible for him. I really like 'DeLorean's Dream.' I think I did a good job on that." It was released on a 45 rpm record with "It's Detroit," another song penned by Perkins.

Twenty-two years later, her oldest son, James searched for Tex Ritter's name upon his mom's request, and to their surprise they found her name on a lot of the same websites as Ritter's. Perkins acknowledged, "Seems I was all over the net and didn't know it."[20] At this time, she also found out that she was a part of the Rockabilly Hall of Fame. Today, she and her husband run a successful mail order tool business.

In 2004, Perkins started taking piano lessons: "I wanted to learn how to play the right way. I had this teacher that came to my house every Wednesday. He never knew I was a singer. He thought I was just a housewife who wanted to play the piano." She didn't tell him until she found out how popular she was. Perkins revealed, "He was so excited [to hear that] and said 'well sing something.' He thought she was pretty good. He then called his brother-in-law who was a record collector and within fifteen minutes he told her 'my brother-in-law knows who you are. He's got your records. He saw you sing near Cincinnati and fell in love with you, thought you were as cute as a pin.' Then the piano teacher said 'at the club where I work we have open mike night on Wednesdays, can't you please, please come and sing?' He had me all set up back in August to go, but I got sick and ended up in the hospital that night. All the people that were planning to come to see me sing were so disappointed because I didn't show up." She finally participated in October, where she sang three or four songs each of three sets: "I had a ball. It brought back old memories, and it didn't faze me a bit. It was just like I had been doing it all my life." Her piano teacher then told her the following week, "people are still talking about you." They were commenting on how good she was and asked when she would be returning.

On April 11, 2008, Perkins made a triumphant return to her rockabilly roots by singing her legendary Imperial recordings to a sold out Viva Las Vegas Weekender crowd. Janis Martin and French rockabilly devotee Dominique Imperial Anglares gave her the encouragement she needed to return to the stage. Her enthusiasm for entertaining and her voice was as powerful as they were fifty years ago. Many fans commented that she was the highlight of the whole weekend. Perkins admitted that it was the greatest crowd she had ever worked for.

Big Al Downing

Big Al Downing began his musical career as a member of Bobby Poe and the Poe Kats. A black man working in an all-white band was not easy in the racially charged 1950s. Downing suffered from injustices that today are hard to imagine, but he persevered through it all because he loved the music. He started out in gospel, rockabilly, and rock and roll and later ventured into disco and country. Fats Domino, Bobby "Blue" Bland, and Tom Jones all recorded his songs. Downing enjoyed a career that lasted fifty-two years. His happy-go-lucky persona, like his main musical influence Fats Domino, brought him critical acclaim and legions of fans worldwide.

Alexander Downing was born on January 9, 1940, in Lenapah, Oklahoma, into a family, with eleven siblings. Downing was raised on a farm where he took care of cattle and horses and hauled hay in the summertime. His family was sharecroppers. Picking cotton or chopping wheat was often part of their livelihood. This environment provided inspiration for his first single "Down on the Farm," penned by Downing, guitarist Vernon Sandusky, and singer Bobby Poe. Sandusky disclosed, "His whole family was as poor as church mice. There were twelve kids living in a little shack. They slept on cardboard boxes. Al had visions of making it and becoming a star like Little Richard or Fats Domino. He was as good as they were."[21] As a youngster, Downing took part in his family's gospel quartet. However, country music was his favorite, and he devoted many hours listening to it.

At age ten, Downing started playing the piano. He recalled, "We found an old piano at a junkyard. We were hauling hay and on the way home we found it. We were going to take it home for firewood. About fifty or sixty of the keys worked, so we set the radio on top of it."[22] Downing listened to disk jockey John R. on WLAC out of Nashville where he played Domino and jump blues singer Louis Jordan. Downing added, "Fats Domino would come on, and I'd start trying to find those notes on the piano, and that's how I learned to play."[23] Domino was his main musical influence, but others that impacted him include Ray Charles, Elvis Presley, Jerry Lee Lewis, and Nat King Cole: "I just loved their music and got something from them."

By age fourteen, his parents encouraged him to take piano lessons: "They took me to this old black lady that was a teacher. She said, 'Play something for me,' so I started playing. She said, 'Well, you can just get on out of here now because that's a gift that God gave you, and I'm not touching it.'" Soon, high schools hired him to entertain their students at proms. In 1956, Downing won first prize, which was $25, at KGCF's amateur talent contest in Coffeyville, Kansas, by singing Fats Domino's "Blueberry Hill." Local singer Bobby Poe heard him sing and was so impressed, he hired him on the spot: "I ran over to the theater and signed him up immediately."[24] Downing refused a basketball scholarship to Kansas State University when Poe asked him to join his newly formed band. Poe remembered, "Al was thrilled. He didn't have a car, so I told him I'd pick him up all the time. I was so naïve in them days; it didn't even enter my mind that it was going to be a mixed band.

Big Al Downing possessed the same easy going personality as his hero, Fats Domino (courtesy Beverly Downing).

I was just looking at the talent." Downing acknowledged, "I was glad to get out of that hot sun."

The three piece band included Poe on vocals, Vernon Sandusky on guitar, Downing on piano, and Joe Brawley on drums. They couldn't afford to hire a bass player. The Poe Kats were popular in Kansas and Oklahoma, where they frequently played VFW halls and country beer joints.[25] Sandusky remembered, "We played for white audiences exclusively."

Unfortunately, club owners sometimes gave the band a hard time because Downing was part of the ensemble. Poe explained, "I'd tell the guy hey we're gonna warm up just a little bit here and if you don't want it, [then] we'll send him to the car. That was my way of conning them." Of course, they changed their minds once they heard him. Sandusky recalled, "Once they heard him open his mouth and start to sing, all their reservations that they had about having a black man onstage went away."

The Poe Kats were unique not only for having a mixed band but also for featuring all the hit songs of the day. Poe would sing Buddy Holly, Johnny Cash, Jerry Lee Lewis, and Elvis Presley tunes while Downing imitated Fats Domino, Little Richard, and Larry Williams. Sandusky and drummer Brawley covered the Everly Brothers. Poe commented, "We just killed 'em."

The band's first recordings were for the Fort Worth, Texas, based White Rock record label. Four singles were issues, two credited to Downing "Down on the Farm" b/w "Oh Babe" and "Miss Lucy" b/w "Just Around the Corner," and two credited to Poe "Rock and Roll Boogie" b/w "Rock and Roll Record Girl" and "Piano Nellie" b/w "I Found a New Love." "Down on the Farm" was leased to Gene Autry's Challenge Records for national distribution, but it only scored a regional hit, #1 in the state of Texas. However, due to its release, the foursome secured bookings on the *Dick Clark Caravan of Stars* and captured the attention of Wanda Jackson.

In 1958, Jackson's agent Jim Halsey introduced her to Bobby Poe and the Poe Kats. They were hired as her backing band for both recordings and tours. In April, the band traveled to California to record with Jackson on Capitol. Even though Jackson had the final word, Capitol Records' producer Ken Nelson wasn't altogether sure Sandusky, Downing, and Brawley were suitable enough to back her. Poe didn't appear on the recordings since he didn't play an instrument. Sandusky conveyed, "We went up to Ken Nelson's house. They were picking tunes at that time [for inclusion on the album]. He wanted to meet us and see if we were going to be of the right caliber to back one of his artists on Capitol Records. He went along with her judgment. She told him that we were the right quality to record with her."

As enthusiasts know, the Poe Kats appeared on her first album, *Wanda Jackson*, which featured her best known song "Let's Have a Party." Downing played piano on the uptempo songs while Merrill Moore appeared on the ballads. Sandusky and Downing also provided the background vocals for the album. To round out the band, Nelson recruited Skeets McDonald on upright bass and then unknown Buck Owens to play rhythm guitar. Sandusky and Downing also appeared on Jackson's "Mean Mean Man" and "Rock Your Baby." They never had a contract with Jackson and were paid union scale from Capitol.

In regard to bookings with Jackson, they toured with her throughout 1958 and into 1959 before taking their act to the East Coast. Sandusky recalled, "I just can't explain how nervous I was [before we did our first show with Wanda]. I was going to college at the time [only eighteen years old], and I sat down in my room with my guitar and a little record player. I worked on those songs 'Cool Love,' 'Hot Dog, That Made Him Mad,' 'Fujiyama Mama,' learning all those licks. [At this time, Sandusky was playing a 1957 Fender Stratocaster with a Fender amplifier.] The pressure was on to learn all those guitar parts. When you're working professionally, they expect you to play like a professional. Wanda was great to work with. We always opened the shows for her. [I have to admit] there were a lot of times she had trouble following Big Al Downing. That's how good he was. He was a phenomenal entertainer. Al let his music do the talking. When he did Fats Domino, Little Richard, or Larry Williams, it went over great." Poe added, "All the kids leaned on the stage to watch Al. He was one of the greatest piano players in the world. He was every bit as good as Jerry Lee Lewis."

On the road, Downing faced many racial injustices. Cat calls and name calling were the norm. Texas and Oklahoma were the worst. He also wasn't allowed to step off the stage to use the restroom and had to be snuck into hotel rooms by the other band members. Sandusky stated, "We all stayed in the same room." Downing recalled, "Wanda always stood up for me and so did Bobby Poe. That encouraged me to stay and play and continue on." Jackson threatened many times to leave and not play the booking if Downing couldn't play. Downing recalled, "She did that on several occasions. She was really good that way. She was the best, the most fascinating lady that I ever toured with."

The Poe Kats usually traveled in a 1954 Chevrolet Bel-Air while Jackson rode with her manager father in a Cadillac. Sandusky added, "We were very crowded." Even though most of the band carried their instruments in the car, Downing had to use the house piano, which was usually not tuned and unkempt. According to Sandusky, "Al ran into that all the time. Back then, you just took what you got, and you went along with it. We got by. I would always tune my guitar to the piano. For a long time, we carried a little bitty PA system and one microphone, which Wanda also used."

The band enjoyed working with Jackson. They received decent exposure but not much money, so they quit her and left Oklahoma for Boston where they worked seven days a week, including two jam sessions on Saturday and Sunday, for twelve hours a day.[26] Sandusky revealed, "We didn't make a lot of money. Back then, it was never enough because we all had families we were trying to support. We had visions of stardom on our own." Sandusky worked with Downing until 1964 when he then went to work for country star Roy Clark, which lasted twenty years.

In 1962, Downing recorded Marty Robbins' "The Story of My Life," released first on Kansoma then on Chess Records for mass distribution. A year later, Columbia Records with producer Clyde Otis, who was successful at recording Brook Benton with Dinah Washington, had plans to team Downing with Aretha Franklin. This idea was never realized. Poe explained, "Before Clyde could get it done, he got crossways with Columbia and left." Instead, Lenox Records issued "You'll Never Miss the Water (Till the Well Runs Dry)," a duet with Little Esther Phillips, which hit the pop charts.

Also during 1963, Downing met his inspiration Fats Domino for the first time. While working at Raud's Rock and Roll Club in Washington, D.C., Domino came to the venue to watch the Poe Kats. The weather was bad, so it wasn't a full house. For those who were lucky enough to attend, they received a rare musical treat — Downing and Domino onstage together. Since the band already knew Domino's songs, no rehearsal was needed. Downing and Domino traded verses and swapped playing the piano. Sandusky admitted, "It was one of the greatest times we had." Downing remembered, "Fats walked in with his whole entourage. We were onstage when he walked in. He set me up $20 and wanted me to play 'Last Date.' I made $60 off of him that night because he wanted me to play it three times. I'll never forget that."

As it turned out, Domino recorded four of Downing's songs: "Mary, Oh Mary," "Heartbreak Hill," "Land of Make Believe," and "Met the Girl I'm Gonna Marry." Poe negotiated the deal where Downing would write for Domino: "Al sounded just like Fats Domino if he wanted to. I had him make a demo of four songs we had written for Fats. We used to write as a team: Downing, Poe, and Sandusky. Fats was appearing at the Howard Theater in Washington, D.C. I took the demos over there and when Fats was coming out the back of the theater I just handed them to him. Truthfully, I figured he'd probably just throw them away. The next day he called and asked me to come see him. First thing he said was 'Who's this guy that sound like Fat Domino?' [According to Poe, Fats never called himself Fats but instead Fat]. Al sounded so much like Fats that he could hear himself singing the song. I couldn't believe it. I was thrilled, and Al was especially thrilled."

Poe added, "The deal with Fats Domino was he wanted half of the publishing and half of the writing. At that time, I had a publishing company so I took half of the publishing [and shared it with Vernon Sandusky]. We made the writing Domino and Downing since Al had written those songs personally." ABC Paramount released "Heartbreak Hill" and "Mary, Oh Mary" as singles. "Land of Make Believe" and "Met the Girl I'm Gonna Marry" appeared on the album *Fats on Fire*.

Downing and Domino remained friends for over thirty years. Downing commented, "Fats is a super guy." There was discussion that Downing would record a tribute album to Domino, but it never transpired. Incidentally, Downing's favorite Domino song was "Hello Josephine." On Downing's 1959 release, "When My Blue Moon Turns to Gold Again" b/w "It Must Be Love," Domino's band was used as backing.

In 1964, the band, known as Big Al Downing and the Rhythm Rockers since 1959, broke up. By then, Mitch Corday had replaced Brawley on drums, Poe took on managing duties, and a bassist Johnny Dubas and saxophone player Eddie Kopa were added. Downing fired Poe because he was mad that the rest of the band was taken into the recording studio by Poe to record "She's the One," which became a hit for them as the Chartbusters. Downing vowed he would get a new band.

That same year, "Georgia Slop" originally sung by rhythm and blues artist Jimmy McCracklin, became one of Downing's signature tunes. Downing stated, 'Georgia Slop' was one of my favorites of all-time to record. It had such a groove and such a craziness to it." He commented that his version was "more rockabilly tinged" that McCracklin's original. Downing loved rockabilly: "Nothing finer than rockabilly." In fact, one of his favorite songs, in which he appeared, was Jackson's rockabilly signature song "Let's Have a Party": "I love that song."

In the mid-1960s, his singles were not commercially successful, so he stopped recording for a bit and instead concentrated on touring all over the world and opening for Johnny Mathis, Dottie West, Lou Rawls, and Marty Robbins.

By 1975, Downing scored a disco hit with "I'll Be Holdin' On." The single soared all the way to number one on the Hot Dance Music/Club Play Chart. It was during this time that Downing made his transition to country music. Warner Brothers was instrumental in guiding his country career. In the first two years (1978 and 1979), he had chart success with "Mr. Jones" and "Touch Me (I'll Be Your Fool Once More)," both landing in the Top 20. Also in 1979, he was honored with *Billboard*'s New Artist of the Year. Sandusky explained, "Al Downing had some great records; he really did. [However] until he got over into country music, he just could not get a hit record. Evidently, Al did not get the airplay that he needed to push those songs across, or the labels didn't have enough clout with the radio stations."

The country television programs *Hee Haw* and *Nashville Now* invited Downing to be a guest on their shows numerous times. He was a frequent entertainer on the *Grand Ole Opry* and was inducted into the Rockabilly Hall of Fame, the Oklahoma Music Hall of Fame, and the Kansas Music Hall of Fame.

The year 2002 was the last time Downing performed with Sandusky and Jackson. Sandusky explained, "They had a birthday party for Wanda in Oklahoma City at the Will Rogers' Theater. They called Al and booked him, brought him in from Massachusetts, and then they called me. They had a couple of local guys they put with us to make a group. We backed Wanda for her show, and I played with Al when he performed. It was just fun to go back and play the old tunes that he and I did." Downing revealed, "We [Wanda and I] hadn't seen each other in forty years."

In 2003, Downing released his first new album in more than a decade, *One of a Kind*, to rave reviews. Besides singing and playing piano, he was also successful at producing. He worked with several European musicians, including the album *Straight Beat* for Italian bluesman Edo 'Ndoss. He kept active touring as well.

Downing died on July 4, 2005, from leukemia. Fortunately for his fans, he had built a five decade career around his powerful singing voice and his hard driving rockabilly style piano, which left behind a legacy of music and unforgettable live appearances.[27] Downing always kept his faith in the music: "The music always came first. I enjoyed the music, and I wasn't going to let somebody take that away from me just because of what they believed. I love the fans for letting me do my music the way I wanted to do it, whether it was country, or R&B, or rockabilly. They've always supported me down through the years, and I really, really appreciated it."

Charlie Gracie

In the 1950s, most rockabilly singers were only popular regionally. A handful had national success, including Elvis Presley, Ricky Nelson, Buddy Holly, and Charlie Gracie. In 1957, Gracie scored a number one hit with "Butterfly," which held the top position for fourteen weeks. He had seven Top 20 hits in England, and three in the United States. His tours of England in 1957 and 1958 provided inspiration to future stars Paul McCartney, Graham Nash, and Van Morrison. He appeared on *American Bandstand*, the *Ed Sullivan Show*, and Alan Freed's package shows at the Brooklyn Paramount. 2009 marked his fifty-eighth year in the music business, and he continues to "exceed expectations and win converts among the rockabilly community."[28]

Charles Anthony Graci (the "e" was added later) was born on May 14, 1936, in Philadelphia, Pennsylvania. Gracie, the oldest of three boys, developed a love for music at an early age thanks to his parents: "There was always music playing in my house. My father liked swing and [Frank] Sinatra, [while] my mother liked country: Hank Williams, Hank Snow, and Eddy Arnold. I listened to black music [rhythm and blues and jump blues] on local Philly stations WDAS and WHAT with disk jockeys Douglas 'Jocko' Henderson and Georgie Woods."[29] When Gracie started school, he was bilingual. His grandfather, who had immigrated from Sicily to America, taught him the Sicilian language. Gracie acknowledged, "I was a pretty academically bright kid."

In 1946, he received his first guitar: "My father and I walked down South Street, which had pawn shops and haberdasheries. He had $15 in his pocket to buy me a suit. [However] my dad told me 'to heck with the suit, pick an instrument out and make something of yourself.' My father always loved show business and wanted to be in it, but as a kid he had to work to help out his parents. Originally, Gracie chose a trumpet, but his father said, 'Naw, you don't want that, get a guitar, you'll be a one man band.'" His father taught him two or three basic chords, and then he learned a few more from a family friend: "It came easy to me, even though it had a badly bowed guitar neck. My dad told me 'I'm gonna get you a teacher. You're gonna learn the right way.' I bought my first Gibson in 1950 and studied the guitar for six years. I was a little bashful to sing. I never took a singing lesson. I used to play the kazoo. My father told me, 'Take that thing out of your mouth and start singing.'" He cited guitarists Barney Kessel, Danny Cedrone, and Les Paul, and singers Louis Prima, Big Joe Turner, and Louis Jordan as his musical influences.

When Gracie saw Bill Haley in concert, he knew he was destined to be a rock and roller: "In late 1951/early 1952, my mother and father took me to Quarry Town, Pennsylvania, and they took me to a place called Sleepy Hollow Ranch. Bill Haley and the Saddlemen were appearing there. I'm hearing 'Crazy Man Crazy,' and I said, Oh that's what I really want to do, man. When I saw that, I really got excited."

About the same time, he received his first recording contract: "I was on a show called the *Paul Whiteman Show*. Paul Whiteman was a very famous orchestra leader in the '30s and '40s. Bing Crosby got his start with him. While I'm on this show, Graham Prince, who had a record company called Cadillac Records in New York, heard me." He signed a contract with Prince, and Cadillac Records issued three singles: "Boogie Woogie Blues" b/w "I'm Gonna Sit Right Down and Write Myself a Letter," "Rockin' and Rollin'" b/w "All Over Town," and "T'aint No Sin in Rhythm" b/w "Say What You Mean." In 1953, he switched to 20th Century Records, which yielded two releases: "My Baby Loves Me" b/w "Head Home Honey" and "Honey Honey" b/w "Wildwood Boogie."

The early years of Gracie's career were challenging: "I had been recording from 1951 to 1956 with no great deal of success, just building a reputation and so forth." In 1956, Gracie inked a deal with Cameo Records in Philadelphia. Owner Bernie Lowe, who had played piano for Paul Whiteman on his show, was looking for an Elvis Presley type singer, when he came to Gracie's home and signed him to a recording contract. Gracie noted Presley's talent: "Nobody will ever beat that kid. Elvis was the best of the best. He had everything going for him, and he had a great heart." In December, Gracie went into the recording studio and cut "Butterfly" and "Ninety-Nine Ways." Gracie explained, "By March of 1957, I had a number one hit [with 'Butterfly']. My agent got a call from abroad where my record was doing very well. I never thought I'd be going to Europe to perform. I was thrilled to death. I was a solo act; I didn't have a rock and roll band behind me. I was up there all by myself, and it was kind of scary. Most of those pit orchestras really couldn't play rock and roll, so it was pretty tough. Being a guitarist, I was prepared musically to perform. Thank God I took the nation by storm, just a wonderful miracle of my life."

Gracie toured England in both 1957 and 1958, playing the London Palladium and the Hippodrome: "Back in 1958, Joan and I married, and of course we went on tour together. She came to the Grenada Theatre in London with me in a limousine. I tried to get out where there were the least people. I said to the driver make sure my wife gets into the car because somebody might accidentally hurt her. I make a beeline to the car, and somebody starts grabbing me. We all wore neckties in those days, fully dressed. [To this day, he wears a suit: "I always work in a suit. You should look differently than the people you're performing for. You're a performer, look like a performer."] Somebody pulls on my necktie, but they're pulling on the wrong part, [the part] that tightens it. My lips are turning blue; I couldn't breathe. I knew they didn't mean to hurt me. The driver pulls me away, throws me in the car, slams the door, and we take off. I loosen the tie and catch my breath. My wife says to me, 'What time is it?' I look at my wrist, and my watch is gone. It had fallen off. She had bought me that watch as an engagement gift. It was a twenty-one jewel Benrus with a stretch band. It meant more because she gave it to me. Well the next day we put an ad in the newspaper. You know, I got that watch back. We were going to give the guy a one hundred pound reward, but he wouldn't take it."

Charlie Gracie hit the big time when his version of "Butterfly" went to the top of the charts (courtesy Charlie Gracie).

Gracie was close friends with Eddie Cochran: "He used to come to my house all the time. My mother made him red sauce with meatballs and sausage and lasagna. This kid was even better looking than Elvis. Eddie was beautiful inwardly too, a humble talent." In the late 1950s, Gracie performed on Alan Freed's all-star shows at the Brooklyn Paramount with Cochran, the Everly Brothers, Jerry Lee Lewis, Chuck Berry, and Bo Diddley: "Alan Freed was a great rock and roll aficionado. He used to tell me 'Charlie get your guitar and come in my office.' I'd go into his office, and he'd say 'sit and play for me.' That's how much he loved the music. I remember Eddie Cochran and the Everly Brothers backstage at the Brooklyn Paramount, and we're sitting there talking and playing our guitars. I said what are you gonna do when this thing ends, and they said 'we'll probably go pump gas.' We never thought we were gonna last more than six months or a year. We had more fun backstage than we did on. My dressing room was so full of people I had to get changed in the men's room. I never said no to anybody. When I used to come out of the theaters at night, there'd be thousands of kids there. You had to escape through different exits because they would rip your clothes off. [However] our fame was very small compared to the guys that came later like the Beatles and the Rolling Stones. We never made that kind of money. At our peak, if we made $1000 a night, that was a lot."

Gracie sang "Cool Baby" in the 1957 movie *Jamboree*: "I never thought I'd even be in the movie. That was my claim to fame. When Otis Blackwell wrote 'Cool Baby' for me, I was really thrilled. The picture itself stunk, but there were some great artists in that film: Buddy Knox, Jimmy Bowen, Carl Perkins, Jerry Lee Lewis, Frankie Avalon, Slim Whitman, Count Basie and his Orchestra, and Fats Domino."

That same year, he traveled to Chicago to appear on the *Howard Miller Show*, along with Eddie Cochran, the Everly Brothers, Tommy Sands, Screamin' Jay Hawkins, Chuck Berry, and Tab Hunter: "Howard Miller was a big disk jockey in the Midwest, the Dick Clark of his area." Brenda Lee was also on the show, and her vocals captivated Gracie: "All of a sudden from the wings I hear this little girl singing. I said who is that? What a tremendous voice. She knocked my socks off, never heard anything like that in my life. I said to myself this girl's gonna be a big star."

Gracie had a successful run with Cameo, hitting #1 with "Butterfly" and #16 with "Fabulous." Between 1957 and 1958, Cameo released several singles, including "Butterfly" b/w "Ninety-Nine Ways," "Fabulous" b/w "Just Lookin'," "I Love You So Much it Hurts" b/w "Wanderin' Eyes," and "Cool Baby" b/w "You've Got a Heart Like a Rock." However, his dealings with the label soon came to an end. "Butterfly" had sold over three million copies, but he only got royalties for 600,000 copies. He sued the label for lost wages. The financial success of Gracie's hits bankrolled the Cameo label, which became a dominant force in the music industry for several years.[30] Unfortunately, Dick Clark owned part of the record label, so Gracie no longer received offers to appear on *American Bandstand* and the most powerful disk jockeys across the country refused to play his records. Incidentally, even though he appeared twenty times on *American Bandstand*, he was never once paid the $375 salary. He was required to sign a release form, transferring his pay back to host Clark.

From 1959 throughout the 1960s, he had releases on some of the biggest record labels in America, including Coral and Roulette, to no avail. Even though his recordings didn't receive much airplay, he continued to tour. In 1972, Narvel Felts recorded "Butterfly" for the Hi Record label: "He cut a great country version of it. He's a real nice person and a great performer."

In 1979, his popularity was renewed in Europe when a Canadian fan Richard Growes released Gracie's Cadillac Records and 20th Century recordings on the LP *Charlie Gracie's Early Hits*, first in America then distributed overseas. Since then, Gracie has returned every year to enthusiastic crowds.

In the last ten years or so, Gracie has discovered that superstars Joe Cocker, Cliff Richard, Paul McCartney, Graham Nash, and Van Morrison are all big fans. He couldn't believe any of these guys wanted to meet him: "It's been a great thrill for me to have these guys asking me to perform with them and to meet them. You don't realize the impression you make upon these people. Paul McCartney told me 'Fabulous' has been haunting me for the past forty-five years. I finally put it on my album, *Run Devil Run*.'" Gracie attended the CD's release party in London. In 1999, Gracie met Graham Nash at a Crosby, Stills, and Nash concert: "They invited me backstage and wanted to meet me. Graham told me, 'Charlie I came to see you in Manchester, England, in 1957. I tried to get your autograph, but there were so many people. I saw you, but I couldn't reach you outside of the theatre. [Nash found out where he was staying and chatted with him in the hotel lobby.] You threw a Camel cigarette butt out.' He opened up his wallet, and there's that cigarette butt I threw out." While backstage, Nash requested that he record one song with him, which turned out to be "A Little Too Soon to Tell," released on Gracie's CD *I'm All Right*. Gracie added, "Graham has become a good friend over the years." In 2000, Van Morrison invited Gracie to be his opening act: "I had met him before [because] he came to quite a few of my concerts in Britain. I was getting ready to cut a new CD [*I'm All Right*] here at home, so I told the guys in my band take the month off; I'm just going to use studio guys. All of a sudden the phone rings one day, and I hear this Irish accent on the other end. Van's calling me from his home in Bath, England. He said, 'Well, I'm going out to the coast in about ten days.' I said really, break a leg. I don't know what the guy is going to ask me. He said 'I was just wondering would you like to open for me?' I said sure, I'd love to, tell me where and when." Gracie suggested he do just a couple of songs and use Morrison's band, but Morrison wouldn't hear of it: "When you go up there do a strong half hour, bring your own band. You'll burn my band out." Since Gracie's band was on vacation, he used the studio musicians: "They were all excited because they were big fans of his." Gracie opened for Morrison at the Hilton Hotel in Reno, the House of Blues and the Hard Rock Café in Las Vegas, and the Wiltern Theater in Los Angeles: "It was absolutely amazing. We got standing ovations. I never thought that was going to happen because I figured they're not into my kind of music."

In 2006, Abkco Records released *The Best of Charlie Gracie 1956–1958*, and a year later a documentary on his career aptly named *Fabulous* was issued. Gracie continues to record and tour and feels blessed to have had such a long career: "I've always been fortunate enough for whatever talent God gave me to make a good living all these years.

At least I had a taste of success; there are guys that are a thousand times more talented than me that never even had that opportunity, so I feel blessed to have gotten a gold record and to have had a #1 hit."

Performing has been a highlight of Gracie's life: "It's just amazing that people still pay to come to see me. I can't wait to get onstage whether I'm playing for six, sixty, or sixty thousand. I'm so happy that young people are getting involved [in the scene]. When we're gone, they're going to keep it alive. To me, to entertain an audience is a joy."

Seven

Rockabilly Revivalists

Martí Brom

Queen of rockabilly Wanda Jackson has become both a mentor and a good friend to Martí Brom. Jackson paved the way for several of today's gals on the rockin' scene. Brom remembered how she met Jackson: "I was first on a bill with Wanda Jackson and Rosie Flores [fellow contemporary rockabilly songstress] in San Antonio, Texas, in 1994. We all owe Rosie for helping bring Wanda back. Since then I've been a part of Wanda's annual birthday bashes at the Continental Club in Austin, Texas. We've never sung a duet, but I did play finger cymbals onstage with her and Rosie on 'Funnel of Love.' She also called me up from the audience once to my surprise to sing 'Mean Mean Man' with her band while she stood next to me. I have since developed a very nice friendship with her and her husband, Wendell."[1] Brom has made her mark on the scene with critically acclaimed albums and successful tours. Her first music award came in 1993 when *Music City Texas* magazine named her Best New Act, and in 2000, Freeform American Roots' disk jockeys named her Best Female Vocalist.[2]

Martí (Evans) Brom was born on June 18, 1961, in St. Louis, Missouri. She is the youngest of three girls. In grade school, she gave up recess for glee club: "I always loved to sing." When Brom was young, she spent a lot of time singing along to her record collection. She was a big fan of musicals, especially *West Side Story*. Doris Day, Billie Holiday, and Patsy Cline were all major influences. In fact, she memorized both Holiday and Cline's song catalogs.

Brom spent summers with her grandparents in New Orleans. Her father, Emory, attended Tulane University and introduced her to New Orleans jazz: "He had quite the collection of jazz records. It definitely had an influence on me when I was a kid." When she was thirteen, the family moved to Italy for a year. She soon became acquainted with the jukebox at the corner bar: "In Italy, every street has a corner bar. The street I lived on in Florence was no exception. There wasn't a drinking age, so teenagers would hang out there, play pool and play the jukebox. I had never heard a girl singing rock and roll before. I mostly heard what my older sister Mignon listened to, female folk singers like Judy Collins, Joan Baez, and Carly Simon." In fact, Brom has two older sisters, Mignon and Michelle. Mignon served a very short stint as a folk style coffeehouse singer in the mid-seventies, and Michelle plays saxophone as a hobby as well as sometimes photographing Martí for publicity shots.

Brom added, "The first song I selected on the jukebox was 'Devil Gate Drive' by Suzi Quatro because I was intrigued by the title. Well, I was blown away. I must have played that rocker a million times. The other kids knew 'that American girl' was in the bar when that song was playing. When I returned to St. Louis the next year, I went to a record store and bought her records. Much to my delight when I saw her picture on the cover for the first time, she was no bigger than me and clad in a leather jumpsuit. Oh my, I knew then that I wanted to be a rock 'n' roll singer." Quatro appeared on *Happy Days* as the Fonz's girlfriend Leather Tuscadero. Briefly, she was very popular with oldies fans who were looking for new music.

From that day forward, punk music became a mainstay with Brom, and she subsequently fell in love with the music of Blondie, The Cramps, The Ramones, and The Pretenders. Her obsession with Chrissie Hynde and the Pretenders resulted in the 20-year-old Brom's move to England, where she wished to start her own band. Her stay was short lived: "Well, I wasn't there long enough to start a band as I never made it off the airport grounds. I spent the night in the quite miserable "beehive" with all the other suspected illegal immigrants from Africa and India. Since I only had a one-way ticket to England, they threatened me with deportation. Fortunately, I had just enough money left to pay my way back to St. Louis. I guess if I had managed to remain, I could have called the band Beehive. It was not a good time, and I was very glad to go back to the U.S.A. I wouldn't change a thing because nothing in my life would be as it is if I had stayed there."

Punk music helped develop her love for rockabilly music, and she incorporated the attitude of both into her interpretation of songs. Brom considered forming her own band in high school, but she thought she suffered from stage fright. Years later, her husband Bobby became her biggest fan, and he coaxed her into auditioning for the stage. The Scott Air Force Base Officers' Wives Club held a production of the musical, *The 1940s Radio Hour*, and she made her debut by sashaying onto a big wooden stage in an airplane hangar wearing a slinky slip singing "Blues in the Night," backed by a swinging big band. That experience paid off as she learned that the more the crowd of young servicemen hooted and hollered, the better she liked it. From that moment on, she never again experienced stage fright.

Brom made her rockabilly debut with a Jerry Lee Lewis style rock and roll band, David Lee and the Houserockers, with whom she sat in and eventually recorded a demo in St. Louis before the Air Force reassigned her husband to Bergstrom Air Force Base in Austin, Texas. Once settled in Austin, she met and sat in with acclaimed rockabilly standard bearers High Noon. High Noon then teamed her with fellow musician Todd Wulfmeyer to form Martí Brom and her Jet Tone Boys. Fans commented that her early recordings and performances reminded them of country legend Patsy Cline. Brom agreed that "the register of our voices is similar." On "Blue Tattoo," Brom sounds eerily similar to Cline. Brom's main songwriter Teri Joyce penned the song: "Teri Joyce is my Cindy Walker [who wrote Roy Orbison's "Dream Baby" and Eddy Arnold's "You Don't Know Me"], and I guess that makes me her muse. She wrote 'Blue Tattoo,' which is the favorite of my original songs, and it seems to be everyone's favorite. Teri was one of the first people I met in Austin. She was a guitar strumming clerk at Amelia's, a vintage clothing store."

In 1999, Pete Hakonen, owner of Goofin' Records, was invited by High Noon to catch Brom's live act. He immediately invited her to play some shows in Finland. These shows were the first time she was paired with Goofin' recording artists, The Barnshakers. They recorded an extended play record, *Maybe I Do* while touring in Sweden. Brom commented, "We all just sort of really hit it off musically and personality wise. They make me laugh, which is very important." A few months later, she returned to Finland with Austin based piano player T. Jarrod Bonta to record the full length album, *Snake Ranch*. The Barnshakers double bill with Brom frequently, especially on European dates. The Barnshakers are renown in their own right since they are not only able to accurately capture the sound and feel of many strains of American roots music but to build on it with their own original compositions and powerful songwriting.

Besides her vocal prowess and dynamic personality, Brom adds visual appeal with her vast collection of outfits: "I like vintage stuff, but I like it kind of mixed in with new stuff." Estate sales, garage sales, and thrift stores helped acquire her vintage wardrobe. Her best buys include the 1970s two piece black cotton studded jacket and pant suit that she wore in a promotional photo, and a lace dress that she found in five minutes in a thrift store in her mission to find something in which to grace the cover of her *Feudin' and Fightin'* album. She enjoys sewing and making new outfits with her seventeen year old daughter, Ivy: "The fact that my original outfits are reminiscent of past eras is just a reflection of my taste. I wear what I find or design what appeals to me or helps me express myself onstage. I do consider stage dress an important part of a show. It is also a big part of the fun of being a performer."

Some of Brom's favorite female singers include Brenda Lee, Janis Martin, Connie Francis, Ella Fitzgerald, Etta James, Eartha Kitt, and Wanda Jackson. An album she is especially proud of is 2005's *Heartache Numbers*. She was pleased with both the look and sound of it. Her background in visual merchandising gave her attention to detail. The strictly country selection was a first for her since her prior releases were a combination of rockabilly, country, and rhythm and blues tunes. "Unproclaimed Love," "Eat My Words," and "Whole Lotta Lonesome" were her favorite songs to write. She is equally at ease singing both traditional country and raucous rock and roll: "Janis Martin once or twice told me, 'You sing those country songs real nice, but you need to rock!' I had a very wonderful relationship with Janis these last few years." Brom added, "I'm a rock and roller really at heart and really dig the rocking stuff like 'Black Cadillac.' It is very natural for me to sing a 'make you want to cry' country weeper followed by a 'gonna make you cry' rocker." Reviewers have praised her ability to sing both genres equally well.

Martí Brom striking a seductive pose (courtesy Martí Brom).

Brom has toured the world including Europe, Australia, and Japan. One of the biggest festivals she ever played was in France with country legend Hank Thompson and rockabilly icon Ronnie Dawson. It's always a let down for her to return home after a successful European tour. There are many loyal and enthusiastic European fans. Brom commented, "It's sometimes hard to readjust and come down from some of those tours." She has always included her children in her musical outings and has tended to avoid accepting those few gigs in venues where youngsters are not welcome. Her son, Carson, who is eleven years old, is starting to play the drums and guitar, while Ivy has garnered an impressive record collection of her own. Balancing a home life with a musical career has been an easy one for Brom: "It isn't that hard since I usually only accept very short tours. I also bring my family to the shows, especially local ones. I have never hired a babysitter."

International audiences hold Brom in high regard because her classic tastes tend to keep her true to country and rockabilly roots. Brom's sassy style and sensual vocals pay homage to those who preceded her, including Patsy Cline, Wanda Jackson, and Janis Martin. As those ladies influenced Brom, she is continuing the trend and showing her importance to the scene by issuing quality material; thereby, demonstrating to younger gals such as Miss Lauren Marie and Jessie Lee Miller that being female in rockabilly can be beneficial. Brom explained, "To me, being female has always been an advantage. It takes a lot for a guy rockabilly to stand out because there are so many out there."

Go Cat Go

The rockabilly revival in America took place in the 1970s when England started calling upon 1950s acts to headline various festivals and club dates. From the late 1970s until the early 1990s, Washington, D.C., was making its own mark with local acts: Tex Rubinowitz, Robert Gordon, Billy Hancock, Danny Gatton, and Go Cat Go. Go Cat Go had the shortest career of any of them because its lead singer Darren Spears was tragically killed. However, their legacy lives on. Over in England, "Please Mama Please" has become a modern rock and roll dance floor anthem, peaking at #1 on the Planet Jive Readers' Chart. According to drummer Lance LeBeau, "Darren would have been quite tickled to know how far reaching his song "Please Mama Please" has been. He always felt strongly about this song because it was a reflection of things that were important in his life.[3] In 2004, the remaining members of Go Cat Go reunited for two shows with Eddie Clendening, who lent his vocals to their legendary tunes. Their only CD, *Let's Hear It Once Again for Go Cat Go*, has sold in excess of 9,000 copies.[4]

In 1988, vocalist Darren Spears and drummer Lance LeBeau tried unsuccessfully to form a band. The guitarist wanted to play Led Zeppelin, so it was difficult for them to get through Gene Vincent's "Baby Blue." A year later, Spears recruited family friend Bill Hull to play lead guitar. In fact, he had played in a band with Spears' two older brothers. They had regular jam sessions at the Spears' household, but Darren never came out to sing. Hull explained, "Darren was so shy. His mother would tell me, 'you should hear him sing Elvis.' Darren would only sing in the stairway between the basement and the kitchen. He wanted that echo in the stairwell. I remember listening to him sing 'Love Me Tender.'" Hull was surprised at how good he sounded once he heard him sing: "Darren had a signature sound." Drummer LeBeau, who went to school with Spears, added that "his voice was a gift."[5] The Spears family were originally from Hot Springs, Arkansas, so Darren had a natural southern accent to his voice. Hull commented, "A lot of people thought that he was trying to sound like Carl Perkins or Elvis. That the accent was put on, but that's how they spoke."

Spears' father helped them hone their sound by giving the band old records that he had in his collection. In the 1950s, he used to deliver records to jukeboxes for a small vending company. He told them, "I've got a lot of those records that you all are trying to play." Hull added, "We actually had the Sun records for reference. When I heard those records, I thought man, I got to play this. The energy and sound [of those records] just reached out and grabbed me. We wanted to recreate that authenticity." In order to accomplish that feat, they had to go to yard sales and vintage music shops to buy the actual musical equipment from the 1950s. In 1989, the instrument companies weren't making reissue models. Hull remembered, "I had to buy three amplifiers to build one good one. Once we had that sound, it was near identical because those were the missing links, old speakers and old tubes. We wanted to have that early Elvis sound, so we went out and found an old Shure Unidyne microphone in Mississippi. We were sounding live like it was recorded in the 1950s." Hull played a 1954 Telecaster on local shows and recordings while bringing a 1952 Fender Relic reissue on the road.

According to Hull, "Darren and I would get together with Lance at Darren's house, out in the garage." At the time of their first rehearsals, Paul Turley was their bass player. Hull acknowledged, "Paul was a great bass player, but he played a Fender electric pea bass, and that didn't have that slap sound." They offered to help Turley pay for an upright bass, but he had never played one before. He tried his best, but they eventually had to let him go and find a replacement. Washington D.C.'s, own Chris Freeman of the Atomics was persuaded to join the band, but he declined and suggested his brother Brian instead. Hull remembered that Freeman told them, "My youngest brother plays upright bass too, but he's only 15 years old. However, he loves rockabilly." Brian Freeman was soon added to the lineup while they still played in the garage. Freeman played upright bass in the school orchestra and provided the band with its last key element. Hull responded, "Brian was the perfect fit. He was something else, essential to rockabilly." Elvis Presley's "That's All Right" was the first song they performed together as Go Cat Go. The band's name was adopted from Hull's license plate.[6] Their rockabilly influences helped to mold the band into one cohesive unit. Hull was influenced by guitarists Scotty Moore, Chet Atkins, James Burton, and Cliff Gallup while Spears took his inspiration from Elvis Presley and Carl Perkins. LeBeau loved drummers D.J. Fontana and Dickie Harrell, and Freeman adapted bassists Bill Black and Ray Campi's style of playing into his own.

One of Go Cat Go's first shows was at the Bayou, a historic club in Washington, D.C., as an opening act for Carl Perkins. Bassist Freeman wasn't even supposed to be in the club because he was underage, but LeBeau advised the other band members if anyone asked, Freeman was eighteen years old. Hull remembered that Perkins gave the band some invaluable advice: "That's good y'all playing that rockabilly music but always remember, take it further than where you left it." The band's shows in the Maryland area were quite the event since the audience got dressed up in authentic 1950s period clothing and drove their vintage cars. In fact, Go Cat Go made sure they always looked sharp as well. Hull disclosed, "Brian and Darren shopped at thrift stores. They always dressed in authentic clothing. The girls went crazy over them and Lance."

Spears wrote most of the band's material, adding in cover songs only as a reference point for fans. Hull explained, "Darren was an avid songwriter." Spears wrote the lyrics, and the rest of the quartet composed the music. Hull added, "I've never been in a band in my entire life that worked so well with four people. Everybody was on the same page all the time." March 1990 marked

Go Cat Go in a publicity shot for their CD *Let's Hear It Once Again for Go Cat Go*. From left: Darren Spears, Lance LeBeau, Brian Freeman, and Bill Hull (courtesy Bill Hull).

the release of a self produced cassette tape entitled *Out of Control* with six Spears' originals: "Who Was That Cat," "Forever's Much Too Long," "Time To Rock," "Please Mama Please," "'Till the Cool Cats Cry," and "Ten Ways to Rock." A year later, Rock-a-Billy Records in Denver, Colorado, issued a LP on purple vinyl, which included six new songs. The premier copies were issued without jackets due to the label's financial constraints.[7] The record turned out to be a huge success. LeBeau commented, "We actually made an attempt to get onto the Hemsby bill in 1992, but no one knew who we were."[8] However, Go Cat Go managed to branch out of the Washington, D.C., area with show dates in Texas.

On their way to Texas, they stopped off in Memphis to tour Sun Studio. All long time fans of the Sun recordings, the band could not leave the studio without recording there.[9] Six songs were recorded during the day including Spears' originals "Please Mama Please," "'Till the Cool Cats Cry," and "Who Was That Cat," Billy Lee Riley's "Flyin' Saucers Rock and Roll," Buddy Holly's "Blue Days-Black Nights," Carl Perkins' "Honey Don't," and Elvis Presley's "That's All Right." Sun recording artist Malcolm Yelvington was in attendance. Hull recollected that James Lott engineered the session and told them, "normally I wouldn't tell you guys this, but I really dig your sound and authenticity.

Are you guys going to be back?" They told him they had to leave to do a show in Dallas. Lott told them about CBS and the television program *48 Hours* filming a special episode at Sun that day, and he wanted Go Cat Go to be there for it. *48 Hours* was there taping a segment entitled "Crazy about Elvis." As it turned out, they filmed Go Cat Go's entire two hour session. Unfortunately, only fifteen seconds appeared on the August 12, 1992, episode.

After their Sun stint, they hit the road again to do shows in and around Austin and Dallas with rockabilly trio High Noon. In July 1993, Go Cat Go toured California. Their first show was Ronnie Mack's Barndance at the Palomino in Hollywood. After Hollywood, they traveled to Anaheim to do a show at Linda's Doll Hut with the hillbilly duo, Dave and Deke Combo. A club date in San Diego with western swing quartet, Big Sandy and the Fly-Rite Boys followed. Rounding out their tour in San Francisco, they played numerous dates again with Big Sandy and the Fly-Rite Boys. At one of these shows, Go Cat Go unveiled a new song, "Kiss Me Baby." "'Kiss Me Baby' defined the Go Cat Go sound and marked their musical direction. Sadly, it was never recorded by the whole band," so it has never been released.[10]

Once their highly successful California tour was finished, Go Cat Go returned home and made plans to record and tour full time. There was even talk of a European tour for the summer of 1994. Unfortunately, none of that was to transpire because on September 14, 1993, 28 year old Spears was shot and killed by three teenagers who had stolen his hunting rifle. Hull added, "His death just stunned everybody."

Spears' death marked the end of Go Cat Go and "deprived the world of one of its most promising contemporary rock and roll acts."[11] Bill Hull continues to play music but hung up his rockabilly guitar licks. Brian Freeman finished his schooling and eventually returned to his jazz roots. He currently plays in various jazz bands. Lance LeBeau collected vintage recording equipment and started his own studio in his home. He continues to run Vinylux Records with his wife Wendy, and they have their own rockabilly band the Fleabops.

Fans thought that would be the end of Go Cat Go, but fate stepped in and allocated two tribute shows to occur. In 2004, LeBeau spotted Eddie Clendening at a show he was doing in the area with Deke Dickerson and the Ecco-Fonics. LeBeau had offers in the past to do shows with Go Cat Go, but now he figured the time was right. After all, it had been eleven years since Spears' passing. He approached Clendening about the possibility of doing a couple of shows with them. Within a few minutes, he knew that Clendening was the perfect candidate to give tribute to Spears and his legendary songs. According to LeBeau, "Eddie is a young exciting new talent that I feel will help us as Go Cat Go capture the spirit of the music we made with Darren."[12] A show at the Viva Las Vegas Weekender and one at the Hemsby Weekender in England were scheduled. Go Cat Go realized that two shows would be just the right ending to their short lived but successful journey into rockabilly. The remaining members knew that the time was right for a tribute, and that Spears would have been supportive of it.

Both shows were filled to capacity; fans came to celebrate their music. Hull commented on the Vegas gig, "We opened with 'Good Rockin' Tonight.' I think we played for an hour and a half straight. We ran out of material, and Eddie told them 'look that's all we know.'" They ended up playing "Please Mama Please" twice. Hull played the same Fender Telecaster that he originally played with Go Cat Go. Spears' death prompted him to give it to LeBeau's brother, Preston. Hull added, "It was just like working with Darren, every bit as good. Eddie has that drive and spark that Darren definitely had. If Eddie was nervous, you couldn't tell. It was bittersweet though. I was thinking I wish Darren was here to see these people packed in this club. Once you've played with Darren Spears, what else is there?"

Josie Kreuzer

Josie Kreuzer has been called the female Hank Williams and has made her rockabilly mark by doing things her way.[13] In 1992, she formed an all girl rockabilly ensemble, Whistle Bait. In early 1996, Whistle Bait disbanded, and Kreuzer went solo. Three releases followed on her SheDevil record label. Kreuzer describes "her sound as rockabilly honky tonk with a switchblade beat."[14] Burned out from constant touring, she has been on hiatus since 2002. However, future plans include releases on her SheDevil record label and appearances at festivals.

Kreuzer's vast musical knowledge is due in part to her mother's record collection: "Some of my earliest memories are of being the host DJ at my mom's parties before I could even read, picking out albums based on the cover artwork alone."[15] Her love for 1950s fashion and music began when she was eleven years old dressing in her mom's cardigan twin sets and writing songs. Kreuzer explained, "I started writing songs, just with my voice and a cheap tape recorder. I couldn't play an instrument, but I would sing these melodies that I wrote."[16]

Performing at an early age was out of the question for Kreuzer since she was a very shy child: "I couldn't even get in front of people without my knees or voice shaking. I was terrified. I would fantasize about performing, and I had this collection of songs I had written." She really wanted to share those songs with the world: "I would slowly start playing songs for people because they knew I wrote songs. They would come over, and they would say 'let me hear a song.'" Eventually, she found the courage to perform in front of larger audiences. The first self-composed song she remembers singing live is "Ball That Jack."

Kreuzer is proudest of her songwriting: "My songs are like my children. When you write a song, and people know the lyrics, and they sing along; it's just a great feeling." Her favorite songs that she has written are "Wild Man" and "Just Passing Through." She considers herself more of a songwriter than either a singer or a performer. Seeing other rockabilly bands prompted her to sing her own songs: "When I am watching a band like High Noon or Big Sandy, it makes me want to get onstage and do what they're doing."

At sixteen years of age, she and her single mother moved to New Orleans. Kreuzer recalled, "We lived in the French Quarter at that time. You can't walk down the streets in the French Quarter without hearing street musicians playing or the music drifting out of the clubs on Bourbon or Decatur Street. You hear music basically everywhere you go: Dixieland jazz, Cajun, Zydeco, blues, and jazz. It's an amazing atmosphere to grow up in. I credit moving to New Orleans with opening my mind up to a lot of different ways of living: different foods, different vernacular, and different music."

Around the same time, she credits Elvis Presley's "Blue Moon" as a turning point: "One of the most pivotal moments for me was the first time I heard Elvis' version of 'Blue Moon.' I became obsessed with the sound of the record, and the way his voice was recorded. 'Blue Moon' haunted me, and it was the first song that actually piqued my interest in how things were recorded and produced." The heavy reverb, delay on the vocals, and minimalism of the recording caught her ear. Kreuzer added, "I wanted to know how to achieve that sound, and I wasn't going to rest until I knew how it was done."

It is no surprise that Presley is a major influence on her overall sound, but she also cites Carl Perkins, The Collins Kids, Janis Martin, Barbara Pittman, Patsy Cline, Sonny Burgess, Faron Young, Charline Arthur, and Wanda Jackson. In fact, she would love to work with Jackson: "I would love to record with Wanda. She still has that spunk and wonderful voice. I'll always love her." In regard to songwriting, Hank Williams and Willie Nelson have influenced her the most.

She attended high school in New Orleans and got a job at Tower Records. She soon became their oldies record buyer. Kreuzer added, "I just grabbed the Rounder,

Josie Kreuzer in a publicity shot for her 1997 CD release *Hot Rod Girl* (courtesy Josie Kreuzer).

Caroline and City Hall catalogues and ordered all of these cool looking records, practically everything on Bear Family [Records].[17] While everyone else in the store was listening to Jane's Addiction, I would play The Collins Kids over the sound system." One of the first albums she purchased at Tower for her own collection was Jack Scott's double album *Grizzly Bear* on Charly Records. New York City's fanzine *Kicks* was also instrumental in purchasing releases for both the store and her own growing collection. Kreuzer acknowledged, "I spent entire paychecks on records."

While working at Tower, Fats Domino and B.B. King would stop in to check out their latest releases. Kreuzer commented, "They came in to see who they needed to sue." Those experiences and other horror stories led her to start her own record label. Before her debut CD, *Hot Rod Girl* was released, she formed SheDevil Records: "I named it SheDevil as a tribute to all of the unsung women of the past, like Charline Arthur, Sparkle Moore, and Barbara Pittman, amongst others, who were great but never got the recognition for what they did."[18] According to Kreuzer, "I grew up very distrustful of record labels and the music industry. It was just ingrained in me. Fats Domino and B.B. King talked about how people would steal their music. I had bad experiences with producers too, where they wanted to change me." SheDevil gave her complete control over all aspects of her recording, including publishing, production, design, promotion, and publicity. Kreuzer explained, "The work doesn't end; however, I don't have one single bit of regret. I think it was worth every ounce of energy and every cent because I was able to do it my own way."

When she was seventeen years old, she received her first guitar and began learning basic chords from a Hank Williams' songbook. She then left New Orleans because she couldn't find like minded individuals who wanted to play rockabilly and honky tonk music. Kreuzer commented, "I was coming from a place where I didn't fit in, even in New Orleans, there really wasn't a rockabilly scene. I didn't think there was anyone else like me in the world. I like 50s stuff. I like to dress in 50s clothes. I was on a little mission, and that's probably why I moved to so many different cities, to find a place where I felt I belonged." She moved to San Francisco and Austin then eventually to Los Angeles. Kreuzer recalled, "When I moved to Los Angeles, the very first rockabilly show I ever went to was a Big Sandy and the Fly-Rite Boys' show. When I walked in the door, I remember thinking I am home. I was in heaven. I would talk about The Collins Kids to people in New Orleans, and they had no clue who they were. I couldn't believe it when I came to Los Angeles and found people who knew who The Collins Kids were. It was refreshing."

Once settled in Los Angeles, she took an ad out in The Recycler, a free local newspaper, to find a band. Incidentally, *The Recycler* aided the punk band X in forming their lineup. After a few months and talking to a lot of really strange people who didn't even know what rockabilly was, Kreuzer began to form the all girl rockabilly band, Whistle Bait, which took its name from The

Collins Kids' 1958 single. First on board was guitarist Teri Tom. According to Kreuzer, "She liked The Blasters and X, so she wasn't into the vintage rockabilly as I was, but we hit it off right away." Tom posted an ad at McCave's Music Store in Los Angeles, and that's how bassist Jennifer Quinn became part of the troupe. Through word of mouth, they recruited their first drummer, Cleo Ramone. Within a year, the lineup would change with the addition of Elaine Ferraro on drums.

Whistle Bait was Kreuzer's first band, and none of the girls knew anything about performing. They got a lot of advice from fellow musicians and saw a lot of rockabilly shows to get an idea of what was needed and required to play in the clubs. Rehearsal one to two times a week led to bookings at Linda's Doll Hut in Anaheim, The Palomino and The Blue Saloon in North Hollywood, and Jack's Sugar Shack in Hollywood. A major performance occurred when they opened for rockabilly legend Glen Glenn at the Palomino on December 10, 1994. Kreuzer recalled, "Our very first show was at The Foothill [in Long Beach, California]. We were all very nervous because we were opening for High Noon. It was great though. If I listen back to any of the old recordings, I hate them because we were all so raw and totally green. We had a lot of fun though. Our shows were very energetic. I always wore high heels, and I would jump around and hop off things, but I never hurt myself. I'm surprised, but I must have had good coordination."

Whistle Bait performed together for three years and even made a few recordings. Unfortunately, none of these have ever been officially released. According to Kreuzer, "We never left California nor had any record releases, but people all over still remember that band. I guess we must've made quite an impression." Supposedly, there is a Whistle Bait poster on display at the Rock and Roll Hall of Fame and Museum in Cleveland, Ohio.[19] Their final show together was at the House of Blues in Los Angeles as part of the annual celebration of Elvis Presley's birthday.[20]

Kreuzer went solo after a failed booking with Whistle Bait for England's weekender, Hemsby. Whistle Bait had been receiving a lot of media attention; however, there was disagreement on where the band was headed musically. Kreuzer wanted to remain true to her traditional rockabilly roots while the other members wanted a more modern almost psychobilly edge. Kreuzer remembered, "We couldn't come to terms with how we wanted things to go, so we decided to go our separate ways. Unfortunately, we had already booked a show at Hemsby. I really wanted to play it, and I'm sure they did too, but they decided not to. I called the promoter Willie Jeffrey and said look my band broke up, but I really want to fulfill this show. If you want, I'll come and do it myself." He agreed, and that was her first billed appearance as Josie Kreuzer. Kreuzer recalled, "I had never played with any other musicians onstage except for those girls. I was terrified that the songs would sound horrible [with only one rehearsal]." With backing provided by The Ricardos, the show turned out really well.

In 2005, Whistle Bait reunited briefly. They rehearsed for the taping of a new show, a spinoff to Bravo's makeover hit, *Queer Eye for the Straight Guy*. Guitarist Teri Tom was going to be the featured participant. Unfortunately, the spinoff never got aired, so the reunion was short lived.

Kreuzer's debut solo CD, *Hot Rod Girl*, was released in 1997 with members of Hot Rod Lincoln as her band: "We're old friends. I've always admired their musicianship. Buzz [Campbell] is amazing, one of the best guitarists I've worked with aside from Teri Tom. He's always looking to learn new things, which is what I think makes a great guitarist."[21] She didn't tour with that lineup, and the band she formed had no drummer. It was a more traditional backing, stripped down to only three pieces. *Hot Rod Girl* was highly revered, earning rave reviews and was voted one of the Top 10 CDs of 1997 by Stockholm, Sweden's newspaper *Aftonbladet*. In 1998, Kreuzer was named best artist and best female vocalist by Pamona, New Jersey's, WLFR 91.7 FM Roadhouse Fever's annual reader poll. A year later, her second CD *As Is* was released on SheDevil.

Beggin' Me Back in 2002, featured Mark Neill as producer. Neill produced Ricky Nelson's last recording session, unfortunately both unfinished and unreleased. Kreuzer enjoyed her experience with Neill: "Mark Neill is just one of the most amazing people to work with. He was the first producer that I used on my CDs, and I was skeptical going into it because I had a distrust of producers. Mark is a musician's producer. He was so easy to work with." He knew the sound Kreuzer wanted and exactly how to achieve it: "He's an encyclopedia of music and recording knowledge. He just knows how to get what you want. I learned a lot from techniques he would use and his production style." Fellow rockabilly Rip Carson played bass on *Beggin' Me Back*, which was another reason it was a hit. This particular CD seemed to have a fitting title since this would be Kreuzer's last release for awhile.

Throughout the years, Kreuzer graced the stage of several weekenders and festivals, including the Rockabilly Rebel Weekender in Indianapolis, Indiana, the Rockin' 50s Fest in Green Bay, Wisconsin, the High Rockabilly Festival in Spain, and the Greazefest in Australia. The Greazefest was her favorite because she was treated like a rock star: "They treated us really well. We had a man servant and our own mansion. The show was incredible, and it was sold out. There were even girls there who had my name tattooed on their ankles."

She decided to take a break from recording and touring in 2002. Contrary to popular belief, her break wasn't because she decided to get married. Kreuzer noted, "My husband Eric is my biggest supporter. In fact, he wants me to do shows. My last tour was so hard for me. It just left a very bad taste in my mouth, and I didn't want to do it for awhile." Even though, she hasn't been seen; she has continued writing songs: "Nothing has really changed for me, but then again no one can see what I'm doing." She's currently in the process of arranging songs for a new album.

Kreuzer promises that there will be future releases on SheDevil Records, and she will tour again. Kreuzer added, "It's a pleasure to be a part of the rockabilly scene. The greatest thing was the very first time I ever went to a big rockabilly festival; I was in awe, because I could see everybody from all the different cities that I played all in one place." If fans are eager to see Kreuzer in and around the scene, they can always catch her at the Viva Las Vegas Weekender. She attends every year with her husband, and they proudly display their 1932 Hot Rod Ford Coupe.

The Dave and Deke Combo

The Dave and Deke Combo, a hillbilly/rockabilly act with a little comedy mixed in, was formed in 1991 and featured the vocal harmonies of Dave Stuckey and Deke Dickerson. As a band, they released two albums and backed numerous rockabilly legends, including The Collins Kids. After five years together, they decided to go their separate ways. Today, both are successful in their solo careers but have reunited in recent years as the Combo. The Dave and Deke Combo is one of the best loved and best remembered rockabilly bands of the 1990s.[22]

Dave Stuckey was born on October 20, 1959, in Kansas City, Missouri. He began his love affair with music at the age of ten when he picked up the guitar. Two years later, he began singing, and while in high school he taught himself how to play the drums: "Our band practiced at my house. I started messing around on the drums when our drummer wasn't there."[23]

Kansas City was a hot spot for jazz, blues, country, rockabilly; it had it all. Stuckey remembered the city with fondness: "The real formative medium for me was listening to Top 40 radio on WHB. I was pretty well obsessed with the station and would often listen to my little portable [radio] under the covers late into the night."[24] These days he cites western swing legends Hank Penny, Bob Wills and His Texas Playboys, and Tex Williams, and jazz greats Louis Armstrong, Earl Hines, and Django Reinhardt as his musical influences.

Stuckey has always been in bands and is a big record collector: "I got interested in rockabilly through the back door of punk rock in the '70s. When I was in college up in Denver in the late '70s, there was and still is a great record store called Wax Trax. I used to make my pilgrimage to Wax Trax, and I'd buy punk 45's. I remember one day buying something, and the guy behind the counter said 'hey you think that is crazy, you oughta hear this.' He brought out from behind the counter one of the first European rockabilly reissues, which was *Chess Rockabillies*. I brought it back to the dorm, and I flipped. Rockabilly was obviously the punk music of its day. Things were never the same after that. The fever really caught and didn't subside for quite some time."[25]

In 1987, Deke Dickerson and bassist Steve Mace formed the surf garage lineup, the Untamed Youth. After they opened a few times for groups such as the Paladins, Dickerson asked his old friends Billy Miller and Miriam Linna of Norton Records to book them on a tour in New York City. Dickerson acknowledged, "When Billy and Miriam saw us play, they immediately wanted us to sign with Norton Records. They were very encouraging and wanted us to record as soon as possible."[26]

During one of these tours, Dickerson met his future bandmate Dave Stuckey: "I actually met Deke over the phone before he moved to California." Dickerson was on tour with the Untamed Youth and staying with Norton Records' owner Billy Miller. Stuckey conveyed, "Deke was staying with Billy and happened to get on the phone, and we started chatting. I said, 'Oh the Untamed Youth, I got your album. A real teenage surf band? You guys are great.' We just hit it off. That started a long series of phone conversations. At one point, Deke said, 'You know the band is moving out to California and since I'm coming out there why don't we start a rockabilly duets [type band]?' It sounded great to me, and we got together. We started working up some stuff, our favorite vocal harmony rockabilly and country numbers. I'd already been playing with Lloyd 'Lucky' Martin, and Bobby Trimble played drums with us. We had to share Bobby with Big Sandy, but we had fun from day one." In 1991, The Dave and Deke Combo were assembled, but since the whole band from the Untamed Youth decided not to move to California, Dickerson asked Stuckey to fill in on drums. That gig lasted three years.

The late '80s-early '90s rockabilly scene in southern California didn't get started until Lloyd Martin began booking acts every night of the week at the Blue Saloon in North Hollywood. During the week, Martin brought in local acts such as Big Sandy and the Fly-Rite Trio and the Dave and Deke Combo, while on the weekend he brought in legends such as Sleepy LaBeef, Ronnie Dawson, Rudy Tutti Grayzell, Janis Martin, and Rose Maddox. Johnny Powers was one of the first to play California during this revival. Stuckey disclosed, "We used to just love his 'Long Blond Hair,' 'Rock, Rock,' and all his great records. I played rhythm guitar with the Fly-Rite Trio, and we backed him at the Blue Saloon and a couple other venues. That was one of those eye opening moments where you listen to those old records, and you think you'll never see the guy live. It was just mind-boggling to get to play with a guy like that." Stuckey acknowledged, "That club and the local bands built the scene. Suddenly people started coming to the Blue Saloon specifically to see rockabilly. It was really rockin' at that point." Soon the legendary Palomino Club and Ronnie Mack's Barn Dance got on the bandwagon and offered more places for fans to see live rockabilly acts.

The Dave and Deke Combo interspersed comedy into their country music. Stuckey commented, "Deke and I have always loved country comedy acts [such as] Lonzo and Oscar and Homer and Jethro, and [singer] Little Jimmy Dickens. With our records, we tried to get a little bit of them into our music." Dickerson added, "Our shtick was that I was the idiot; Dave was the straight man."[27]

The Dave and Deke Combo in a promotional photo for their 1996 CD release *Hollywood Barn Dance*. From left: Lance Soliday, Shorty Poole, Deke Dickerson, and Dave Stuckey (photograph by Dave Harrison, courtesy Dave Stuckey).

In 1996, the Dave and Deke Combo called it quits. Dickerson wanted to explore his rockin' side while Stuckey wanted to pursue his country roots. Stuckey admitted, "I've always been more of a fan of the 'billy side of rockabilly. It's always been easier for me to play the country side of it. Shoot, I even a played five string banjo for a time when I was a teenager. I was sorry that the band broke up at the time, no question about it. I thought things were really starting to happen for us. At the same token, if it hadn't happened, I wouldn't have gotten to do a bunch of the stuff that I've done since then, which I've had so much fun doing. [That includes] cutting a western swing record in Austin with my outfit the Rhythm Gang, being backed by the Japanese western swing band the Rollin' Rocks in Tokyo, and meeting and playing with Jeremy Wakefield, the Lucky Stars, and Whit Smith from the Hot Club of Cowtown."

During the Combo's reign, they performed at the Hemsby Weekender on three different occasions. They also backed The Collins Kids at one of these appearances. Stuckey explained, "We were the first ones to back The Collins Kids when they came back out of retirement. We were over in England doing the Hemsby Rock and Roll Weekender. We got talking with one of the organizers, and he said 'well, we've talked The Collins Kids into playing again. Would you guys be interested [in backing them]?' Of course, we jumped at the opportunity. We said, we'll go up to Reno and rehearse with them. We can't wait." Stuckey added, "We hit it off with them right away. They really seemed like family. At the rehearsal, they sounded great right off the bat. Then at the festival it was amazing to see the huge crowd of people who were crazed to see them again and to find they were as good as they were [in the '50s]. It was a terrific experience."

The other half of the dynamic hillbilly duo, Derek Dickerson was born on June 3, 1968, in St. Louis, Missouri. Dickerson received his nickname Deke from some friends, and it has become his moniker: "When I was about fourteen or fifteen, my buddies started calling me Deke after we all watched the Elvis movie *Loving You*. I didn't mind since Deke sounded like a shortening of Derek."[28] From the beginning, Dickerson's family was supportive of his career choice and provided inspiration: "My dad is the greatest dad in the world, and I'm so grateful that he supported my musical endeavors so much when I was a kid. [His father's Bill Haley and Elvis Presley records made quite an impression on the youngster.] My grandmother Maude Dickerson, who died in 2003 at the age of ninety-four, played many instruments, including guitar and autoharp, and she would take out her false teeth, so she could play the harmonica."

Dickerson began singing at a young age: "I never had voice lessons. I just remember singing at the top of my lungs since I was a little kid, driving everybody crazy. At thirteen, he obtained his first guitar: "When I saw Chuck Berry [on the television show *Sha Na Na*] duck walking with his guitar, I decided then and there that was what I wanted to do. I took a few lessons, but my hippie teacher told me I wasn't ever going to get any better if I didn't stop listening to Buddy Holly, so I immediately quit his lessons and taught myself by listening to records." Larry Collins of The Collins Kids and country music guitar virtuoso Joe Maphis are his musical influences. Dickerson mentioned, "Joe was truly the king of the strings. I never got to meet him since he died in 1986, but I am good friends with his widow Rose Lee and his son Jody. I play a Mosrite double neck guitar not because I'm trying to imitate Joe Maphis, in fact I play in a completely different style, but I like playing this guitar because it carries on a tradition, a tradition that was very close to being dead."

For Dickerson, music was a constant thought so paying attention in school was challenging: "I was this totally hyperactive kid at school, and the guidance counselor took me to the local community radio station. I hit it off with the program director Bill Wax and freaked him out at my knowledge of early rock and roll. He took a chance on me and gave me my own show, at age thirteen. For a couple of years, I did a show every Friday night at seven P.M., spinning rockabilly, blues, country, surf, and garage. It was a great learning experience. I'm sure I spun a lot of Ronnie Self since he is one of my favorite rockabilly singers."

At this time, Dickerson frequented garage sales and thrift stores obtaining rare rockabilly, country, surf, and garage record gems, thereby expanding his musical vocabulary. Dickerson stated, "I found *Two Guitars: Country Style* by Speedy West and Jimmy Bryant when I was fifteen. That record changed my life. It was unlike anything I had heard up to that point."[29]

At sixteen, Dickerson received the chance of a lifetime, seeing Jerry Lee Lewis live in concert. Dickerson explained, "I was working at a local grocery store, and Pepsi had a contest—if you saved bottle caps, you could get a free plane ticket. For three months, I saved bottle caps and got one thousand of them, which I redeemed for a plane ticket to New York City. When I was out there, Jerry Lee was playing at the Lone Star Café, so I went there with Billy Miller and Miriam Linna from Norton Records. The show was amazing. I was a little sixteen year old geek standing in the front row loving every minute of it. Afterwards, Miriam took me downstairs to try and meet Jerry Lee. We snuck through all these corridors and right as we turned the corner we saw Jerry Lee sitting on a beer keg. As soon as I opened my mouth to say Jerry Lee will you ... this four hundred pound bouncer grabbed both of us and threw us out of the club."

His first show was in Columbia, Missouri, where he grew up. Dickerson admitted, "I had the world's worst rockabilly band, the Rockin' Tailfins. We did an open mike gig at a local club, and I remember that when I went to rock out in the audience, I tripped over my guitar cord and fell flat on my face. Luckily, I recovered without smashing my guitar and lived to rock another day."

Eventually, Dickerson formed his own record label, Ecco-Fonic. Hightone Records signed Dickerson in 1997, thereby launching his solo career. According to Dickerson, his first and biggest selling solo recording, *Number One Hit Record*, has sold over 10,000 copies. While his CD *Deke Dickerson in 3 Dimensions* is his proudest recording moment because "it really does showcase all the different sides of my musical personality."

Besides being active on the road for 225 shows out of the year with the Ecco-Fonics (which include drummer Chris "Sugarballs" Sprague and sometime bassist Jimmy Sutton), Dickerson remains in high demand as a backing artist: "I enjoy doing my own thing the most, that's for sure, but I'm a big fan of the older artists, so it's always a blast to back them up too. I'm grateful to have the chance to play with these guys now because I'm the last generation that will get to perform with these original '50s artists." The Collins Kids, Dale Hawkins, Earl Palmer (original drummer for Little Richard and Fats Domino), and Glen Glenn are all acts that have showcased Dickerson's guitar versatility: "I love Dale. He is such a real original rockabilly. He is a country guy with a deep love for rhythm and blues. When it comes out of him, it's rockabilly, the perfect mixture of the two. Now as for The Collins Kids, they are great and so much fun to play with. I have played with them many, many times from 1992 until the present. Our show at Green Bay in 2002 was such a blast. They are such nice people, and I was always such a fan of their music, so it's a real honor to be able to share the stage with them. Working with Earl Palmer was absolutely one of the greatest thrills of my life. There will never be another drummer like him. He was the greatest rock and roll drummer of all time, and I'm so proud that I got to work with him. When I first moved out to L.A., I played a lot of shows with Glen, and I love playing with him. He's such a great cat. I was happy that Bear Family asked me to do the liner notes [for *Glen Glenn Rocks*] because I wanted to do Glen proud." Dickerson continues to write liner notes for Bear Family CDs and box sets as well as writing a regular column for *Guitar Player* magazine.

Other accolades for Dickerson include Hallmark Guitars launching a Deke Dickerson model guitar, his songs appearing on the movie soundtracks for *Election*, *Sideways*, and *Alien Avengers*, and his hosting of an annual Guitar Geek festival where notables such as The Collins Kids and the Crickets are headliners.

Stuckey keeps busy with his own band, the Rhythm Gang as well as being drummer for the Lucky Stars and the Bonebrake Syncopators. In the mid-90s, the Lucky Stars had one of their first gigs opening for the Dave and Deke Combo at the Doll Hut in Anaheim, California. The Combo liked the band so much that they released the Lucky Stars' first EP on their own Bucket Lid record label. Stuckey revealed, "In the years following the Combo's split, they had lost a drummer, and [singer] Sage [Guyton] called and knew I had played. Although, I was extremely rusty at the time, I hadn't played since the Untamed Youth days [except for backing Ray Condo once], I said well if you'll have me I'll do it. That was 2002. Sage is such a great songwriter, and Russ Blake is a great picker. That's a lot of fun too." The Bonebrake Syncopators is a jazz ensemble that combines traditional jazz, be-bop, and western swing. The Lucky Stars' Jeremy Wakefield also plays in this band as well as Wally Hersom, T.K. Smith, and D.J. Bonebrake.

In addition to music, since 1984, Stuckey has immersed himself into the world of television and movies: "I'm a writer and editor of television promos and movie trailers." He also edited music videos for Los Lobos' "La Bamba" and Dwight Yoakam's "Honky Tonk Man," "Always Late," and "Little Sister."

In 2005, thanks to persistence from festival organizers Tom Ingram and Marc Mencher, the combo reunited on stage. Stuckey revealed, "It's so much fun to play for people who weren't even around back when we played in the '90s." The first reunion show was at the Viva Las Vegas Weekender where they showcased their second bassist Shorty Poole while their second show at the Rockin' '50s Fest II in Green Bay, Wisconsin, featured original bassist Lloyd Martin. Since then they've tried to do all the shows with both bass players. Stuckey disclosed, "We really had a hard time deciding what the set list was going to look like. We had over one hundred songs to pick from, but everyone remembered the songs from the start — like the proverbial getting back on the bike."

At the same time, the Dave and Deke Combo reunited to record a new

CD, *There's Nothing Like an Old Hillbilly: Lost and Found Treasures, 1991–2005* since they wanted something new to sell at the shows. On it, they recorded a parody of Elvis Presley's "In the Ghetto," a song called "In the Meadow." Stuckey wrote it in 1996 for an Elvis Presley tribute show that promoter Art Fein organizes annually: "We always tried to do something different rather than the standard covers you might hear. We used to do songs from Elvis' movies, which we all loved. I wrote a parody of 'In the Ghetto,' Homer and Jethro style, into a song called 'In the Meadow.' After the show, Big Sandy came up to me, and he asked me what Homer and Jethro record that was off of since he didn't have that one. I thought oh great it worked. I was so tickled. I just wanted it to sound as much like a Homer and Jethro song as I could. One of the best things about writing original material has been when you meet somebody that doesn't know what the covers were and which were the originals." After the House of Blues' performance, they never did anything with "In the Meadow" until Dickerson mentioned it when they were recording the new CD. They are pleased with the reception it has been receiving. Stuckey remarked, "It's been going over very well at shows. It's great to hear people laughing in the crowd."

It has been a lot of fun for the Combo to do these reunion shows. In fact, Stuckey commented, "I would go so far as to say that it's almost more fun now than it was then."

High Noon

There were two rockabilly revivals in the United States (excluding the major festivals that have sprung to life in the last fifteen years): the late 1970s/early 1980s with acts such as Robert Gordon and the Stray Cats and the late 1980s/early 1990s that included bands such as the Dave and Deke Combo and High Noon. High Noon was formed in 1988 and is a traditional rockabilly trio that features Shaun Young on vocals and rhythm guitar, Sean Mencher on lead guitar, and Kevin Smith on upright bass. Even though they called it quits in 1997, the band has reemerged several times due to their popularity amongst both fans and festival organizers alike. High Noon is quite probably, in fact, the most respected rockabilly band of their generation.[30]

High Noon's vocalist and rhythm guitarist Shaun Young, was born on January 22, 1968, in Wheatridge, Colorado. Young's entire family is musically inclined: both parents sing, his mother plays the piano, his two younger sisters both sing and play the piano, and his younger brother has a masters' degree in choral arrangement. Therefore, he grew up surrounded by different genres of music. Young explained, "My mom and dad sang Everly Brothers' songs in harmony while we drove around in the car. My dad sang Jack Scott, Buddy Holly, Webb Pierce, all kinds of old country and rock and roll songs. I really had a great childhood and the best parents anyone could have."[31] In fact, one of the first songs Young ever sang was the Everly Brothers' "Wake up Little Susie": "I remember singing that with my dad when I was four or five [years old]." Every Sunday, Young attended church services: "We sang all those great old southern gospel hymns. I also got to see all the southern gospel quartets, [such as] the Statesmen, the Couriers, and the Blackwood Brothers, when they toured through. They were rocking! It was powerful music."

His parents were very encouraging: "They were the most supportive parents in all of rockabilly history. They drove to the first Viva Las Vegas we played, the first two Green Bay festivals, and a lot of old fans of High Noon have met my parents and became friends [with them]. I lost my mom in 2004 and the support I received from High Noon fans around the world was amazing." Even though Young's dad experienced a stroke in 2006, remarkably he is still able to sing his favorite songs.

As a youngster, Young would listen to his dad's Buddy Holly 45's and his mom's Johnny Cash records. He heard "Summertime Blues" by Eddie Cochran and thought it was genius. Young added, "I just didn't know that the kind of old rock and roll I liked was rockabilly. I love all kinds of roots music." One of his all-time favorite singers is Tony Williams from the Platters: "I got to see him sing about five years before he died, and he was amazing. I just love his voice." Young has numerous musical influences, but he cites Buddy Holly, the Everly Brothers, Carl Perkins, Elvis Presley, and Gene Vincent at the top of his list. Young acknowledged, "Ronnie Dawson was the biggest direct musical influence."

At sixteen, he began playing guitar. The teenager had learned a few chords when he was younger but never really applied himself until he was in high school. Young admitted, "It wasn't long after [that] I learned to play 'Lawdy Miss Clawdy' that the school choir director heard me singing and beating on my guitar and told me I had to join his jazz choir. Before I knew it, I was playing Tony in [my school production of] *West Side Story*." Two years later, he formed his first band the Shifters.

With the Shifters, Young met bassist Kevin Smith. Their bassist wasn't showing up for rehearsals, so Smith grabbed his bass and sat in with them. Young recalled, "It was obvious that he was a better bass player than the guy we had, so we fired our bass player and hired Kevin." After a tour through Austin in January 1988, the band moved there in February: "We were floored by the scene, so we moved there right away."

A few months later, they met guitarist Sean Mencher: "Sean was playing with a country band, Chaparral, and they opened for the Shifters. Kevin and I were very impressed by his playing and songwriting. He dug our energy, so we started talking about rockabilly and how we thought a band should sound." Guitarist Sean Mencher remembered, "I was pickin', using my thumb pick. Shaun and Kevin both said 'that guy's a rockabilly picker.'" Young added, "The three of us ended up jamming in Sean's garage in August 1988. Kevin had never even seen anyone slap an upright bass live when he started doing it. We had so much fun playing Elvis' Sun tunes and such, we all decided this was the band we had all dreamed of. [However] it took some time to figure out how to play the music with the sound that we loved because there was no band to go see that sounded like Carl Perkins in 1956." Mencher recalled, "We just played for hours [in the garage], every song we knew. We didn't know that anybody else knew what we knew and loved it as passionately as we did with a commitment to the sound. We worked so hard to discover what made it. I remember our first trip to Nashville; I looked up Scotty Moore in the yellow pages." They visited him at his workplace, IPC Graphics, where they asked him questions such as did Bill Black loosen his E string, or was he slapping? They also asked about Moore's thumb picking technique and his EchoSonic amplifier. Mencher added, "We just wanted to make sure that such a beautiful tradition was never lost. We also wanted to say that you can do it in the same style but make it relevant to right now."

Lead guitarist Sean Mencher was born on March 16, 1961, in Washington, D.C. As a youth, he sang and played guitar a little. However, it wasn't until he was eighteen years old that he began to focus on the instrument. Originally, his younger brother Marc was supposed to take guitar lessons, but he wasn't really interested. Instead, Sean attended: "I went to the guitar lesson, and I just loved the sound of the guitar. From then on, I wanted to play." Incidentally, Marc is a successful booking agent, most well known for booking the talent for the Rockin' 50s Festivals in Green Bay, Wisconsin. Mencher's parents were also supportive of his musical endeavors. His father plays the piano: "He's an excellent pianist, and my mom has great taste in music. They love music."

At the time, Washington, D.C., was a melting pot for music with blues, bluegrass, and rockabilly at the forefront. Mencher saw blues giants' Muddy Waters and B.B. King in concert, and he commented that "the bluegrass scene in D.C. is like no other." In the late 1970s, he discovered rockabilly after attending a Tex Rubinowitz concert in a city park: "It blew me away. I thought he was great. I was aware of Carl Perkins and Buddy Holly. [While Mencher was still in high school, he saw Carl Perkins in concert.] [However] when I saw Tex, I didn't really know what rockabilly was. I was just a kid who skateboarded around D.C. with my buddies listening to Ted Nugent. Tex's show was better than anything I had been exposed to." Combining Rubinowitz with hearing Merle Travis on WAMU and also listening to a local blues band the Nighthawks, those events confirmed Mencher's destiny.

He ranks guitarists Merle Travis, Chet Atkins, Scotty Moore, Les Paul, Cliff Gallup, and singers Carl Perkins and B.B. King at the top of his musical influences.

High Noon's first gig was a fill in for Chaparral. Young explained, "Their drummer couldn't make the show, so Sean asked Kevin and me if we wanted to fill in with the trio. We had just started to mess around in Sean's garage, so we didn't have a name for the band yet. We were literally minutes before the start of our set, when Sean had mentioned that he had watched *High Noon* [with Gary Cooper] the night before. We all agreed it was a great movie and decided to call the trio High Noon."

The trio's first recordings together were demos of five songs. Young thinks they were "I'm Not Blue," "My Tears Keep on Falling," "Flatland," "My Ex Is Why," and "When She's Good." Young remembered, "We made cassette copies and sold them for $5 at gigs. We must have gone through five hundred of those things."

High Noon was in especially high demand in the early days. They played everywhere and kept busy. Mencher remembered, "We sometimes played four gigs a day. If we didn't have a gig, we'd stand on the street. I had a battery powered amp. We just wanted to play." Young conveyed, "Most of our gigs were four forty-five minute sets a night, and the nights we didn't have a gig we rehearsed. We used to play every Saturday morning from 10–2 at the Austin Farmer's Market. We got paid in produce. One gig we always had fun doing was next to the oldest grocery store in Austin, Ave B grocery. We would play Sunday afternoon on the flat bed shrimp trailer after they unloaded the shrimp. Boy, that trailer stunk on hot Texas summer days. We could play any club because we played rockabilly. In Austin, most everyone didn't really care what anyone looked like as long as the music was well played. Old Austin hippies loved High Noon. There wasn't the division you see in a lot of other places." The first time they went to England they couldn't believe the rockabilly scene. Mencher recalled, "Our minds were blown because we were around hundreds of people who loved the same music that we did."

In the early 1990s, the Continental Club in Austin was a frequent booking for High Noon: "Steve Wertheimer at the Continental Club has been one of our greatest supporters through the years. I love to play there. All the gigs there with Ronnie Dawson were pure magic." Lisa Pankratz only played drums with High Noon when they backed Dawson.

Off and on for ten years, they played with Ronnie Dawson. Young conveyed, "Kevin and I were both huge fans of Ronnie's records before we ever met him." In fact, Smith often wore a leather jacket with a painted rocket ship and the words action packed, referring to one of Dawson's signature tunes. Several attempts to initially meet Dawson failed. Young recalled, "We kept leaving notes for each other at clubs we would both play. Finally we got booked on a show together in Santa Barbara, California. When we did meet, it was like old friends meeting. He was a great friend, who I miss everyday, and one of the biggest thrills of my life was when he recorded 'Home Cookin'.' Ronnie was just the greatest showman I have ever known." Mencher commented, "We all had the same spirit and love of the music." In 1994, High Noon with Pankratz were invited to back Dawson at Carnegie Hall in New York City. Mencher conveyed, "Of course, we jumped at the opportunity." At that same time, they all

In the early 1990s, High Noon regularly played the Continental Club in Austin, Texas. From left: Sean Mencher, Shaun Young, and Kevin Smith (courtesy Shaun Young).

performed with Dawson on *Late Night with Conan O'Brien*. Dawson sang one song, "Monkey Beat City," and O'Brien briefly interviewed him. Mencher disclosed, "Conan came up and said to Ronnie, 'What have you done to these people?' Ronnie lit that place up, but we poured gasoline all over the fire. Ronnie was so great. He just rocked."

Besides Dawson, High Noon had the pleasure of backing some of the greatest names in rockabilly and some of their heroes, including Johnny Carroll, Gene Summers, and Ray Campi. Mencher revealed, "I couldn't believe we got to work with any of them."

Rockabilly revivalists Big Sandy and the Fly-Rite Trio, the Dave and Deke Combo, and Go Cat Go were all part of High Noon's extended family. Young admitted, "All of us were forming bands around the same time in different parts of the country without knowing about each other. Then we all started to tour and cross paths and share information about clubs to play and radio stations to send our records to." High Noon was great friends with Go Cat Go. They first met Go Cat Go's drummer Lance LeBeau when High Noon played a club date in Nashville. LeBeau gave them a copy of Go Cat Go's demo tape, which included "Who Was That Cat?" Mencher explained, "That's why High Noon recorded that song, [which appears on their 1997 release, *Live in Texas and Japan*]. Darren Spears [lead singer of Go Cat Go] was a brilliant songwriter and a fantastic singer." Mencher also recorded another Spears' original "Little Baby Doll" for his solo self-titled 2006 CD release.

In 1991, Young began playing the drums. Bobby Trimble, drummer of Big Sandy and the Fly-Rite Boys, used to stay at Young's house when he and the band had bookings in Austin: "I loved the way he played the drums, so he started to show me some things while they were staying at our house. Around that same time, Martí Brom had moved to town and was trying to put a band together. I told her I'll play drums for you, even though I had no idea what I was doing. That band was the original Martí Brom and the Jet Tone Boys, [whose] name came from my house being next to the old airport. We would rehearse and record in the extra bedroom and these big jets would come into land. It got so loud we'd have to stop until they passed." Smith played bass and Todd Wulfmeyer, former member of the Shifters, played guitar.

High Noon went on hiatus in 1996. According to Young, "The decision to take a break came from just pure burn out. We had been on the road for eight years straight and no matter how fun that is when you're still struggling to make a dime, it can get old. Kevin, Sean, and I are all family guys. We like to have a good home life, and that's hard to maintain when you're on the road." Young took a job as a CAD operator and technical service representative for a high purity pumping parts supplier.

The trio's hiatus gave each member a chance to do other projects. Young played drums with a jump blues band the Jive Bombers, recorded *Wiggle Walk* at Fort Horton Studios: "I'm very proud [of that album]," and is currently playing lead guitar with the surf band the Thunderchiefs. Mencher performed with fellow roots musician Wayne "The Train" Hancock and produced newcomers to the scene the Two Timin' Three, the Starline Rhythm Boys, and Jessie Lee Miller: "I've always wanted to produce. I enjoy assisting others, who I like or respect, to realize their music." Besides fronting his own combo, he has backed Young Jessie, Hank Williams III, and Billy Lee Riley. Smith filled in with the Brian Setzer Orchestra and filmed an upright bass instructional video.

High Noon has reunited on occasion since 2000 to enthusiastic fans and thrilled festival organizers. Viva Las Vegas was their first gig back on the scene. Young commented, "We always knew we would play together every chance we got. We have too much fun to stop altogether. I think we had and still have a special thing that happens when we play together. We just click."

In December 2005, Dwight Yoakam called Smith to work with him. After an audition then a performance at Yoakam's annual New Year's Eve gala at Buck Owens' Crystal Palace in Bakersfield, California, Smith was offered a year long deal with Yoakam. He still tours with him today. If bassist Smith is not available, then Jimmy Sutton steps in. 2006's appearance at the Rockabilly Rave in England was the first time Sutton was brought in to play bass. Young revealed, "Jimmy is the man we call when Kevin can't make a gig. We had some festivals already booked when Kevin got the job with Dwight Yoakam, so we asked Jimmy, and I'm glad we did. It was great to play with him, what a talent." Mencher added, "The Rave went brilliantly, and there were some amazing reviews that came from that. Kevin is irreplaceable, and no one could ever touch him, even though Jimmy is no slouch."

Throughout their career, High Noon has kept their popularity alive with numerous show bookings and several recordings including 45's, CDs, and even a 78 rpm. Mencher recalled the songs included on the 78 were "Baby Let's Play House" b/w "Too Much Trouble": "We just wanted to do it for kicks because we thought it was cool." Their CD, *What Are You Waiting For*, which was released in accordance with their appearance at the Rockin' 50s Fest in Green Bay, Wisconsin, received rave reviews from both critics and fans alike. One of High Noon's highest honors was being named Best Rockabilly Band by *The Austin Chronicle* for seven consecutive years.

Tex Rubinowitz

In the 1970s, punk music came to the forefront. New York City was a hot spot with the popular nightclub CBGB for bands such as the Ramones, Blondie, and the Talking Heads. Future rockabilly revivalist Robert Gordon performed punk music with the Tuff Darts. Not surprisingly, punk and rockabilly were quite similar in its simplicity and raw emotion. More often than not, punk fans embraced the rockabilly community. Tex Rubinowitz discovered that fact when he began playing rockabilly in the D.C. area. "Hot Rod Man" is Rubinowitz's signature song, and while he is no longer performing or recording, his legacy is preserved thanks in part to bands such as High Noon who cover his songs.

Arthur Lee Rubinowitz was born on October 10, 1944, in Abilene, Texas. Rubinowitz explained, "Being born in Texas, I picked up the nickname of Tex at eight or nine years old."[33] His mother was musically inclined, played a little of every instrument but mainly guitar and piano while his father was the theater officer at Camp Barkeley in Abilene, Texas, where he and Rubinowitz's mother met. He has one sibling, a brother named Ben, who was born with brain damage.

At age three, he sang his first song "You Are My Sunshine" to his grandmother. Although he doesn't recollect it, he does remember his relatives later praising him for his exemplary performance and referring to him as their little singer.

Since his father was in the military, the family moved quite a bit. Rubinowitz commented, "My earliest influences were '40s and early '50s pop and country music. The first performer I remember knowing was Hank Williams. My father was in the U.S. Army and stationed at Ft. McClellan in Anniston, Alabama, in 1951/1952, and you heard a Hank song at least a few times a day."

They moved to Springfield, Virginia, in 1954. A few years later, AM radio became a highpoint for young Rubinowitz. He tuned into the local stations and heard his first rockabilly records. However, they played various singers and songs, everything from "I'm Movin' On" by Hank Snow and "Please Help Me I'm Fallin'" by Hank Locklin to "Oh Julie" by the Crescendos to "Hound Dog" by Elvis Presley and "Honey Don't" by Carl Perkins. Rubinowitz heard a wide variety of music, but his favorite was rockabilly: "I was a rockabilly wannabe from about the sixth grade in 1956 until about 1962 when I was in the eleventh grade. Now I don't mean a performer or musician but a rockabilly guy, a cool guy like James Dean, Elvis Presley, Gene Vincent, or the fellows who were upper classmen in high school. I loved rockabilly and rock and roll and would sing it all the time, but I didn't know how to be in a band or play an instrument, so it was just for me. I was proud that I knew that Carl Perkins wrote and recorded 'Blue Suede Shoes' before Elvis." Vincent was one of his favorite singers, and Perkins and Presley were also among his early musical influences: "I became an Elvis fan right away."

As a senior, he became friends with fellow student Pete Sellers: "Pete was a very good guitar player, and I encouraged him to play in the senior talent show. He won and was later voted most talented male of our class and in appreciation I guess he decided to teach me a few chords on the guitar." Sellers only gave him two or three lessons, teaching him the basic chord progressions. Rubinowitz remembered easily picking up the C chord but having difficulty with the G7: "I struggled for months and months but then I finally got it." Hank Williams' "Jambalaya (On the Bayou)" was the first song he ever learned to play on the guitar.

During this time, folk music was all the rage. Even though Rubinowitz's heart still laid in rockabilly, he felt he would give folk singing a try: "After I learned to play simple folk songs at get togethers, I would sing a rockabilly song and a lot of folks thought I ruined the hootenanny. [He would sing "Linda Lu" by Ray Sharpe or "Red Cadillac and a Black Moustache" by Bob Luman.] I know what they mean now, rockabilly was not very hip in the folk days, and I was ruining what they were trying to be, but I really loved those rockabilly songs."

Between 1963 and 1970, Rubinowitz kept his musical dreams at bay and took a regular job as a ski mechanic. However, by 1970, there was a pop/folk revival happening with James Taylor, John Prine, Jim Croce, and Kris Kristofferson, and he figured he would get on the folk bandwagon once again. Rubinowitz added, "I especially liked a guy named Jesse Winchester who had a real southern background to his music even though he lived in Canada. I started going to the folk open mikes, and I did mostly Hank Williams and other old country songs. If things went well, I would throw in something like "Red Cadillac and a Black Moustache." There was a very popular local band named the Rosslyn Mountain Boys that did a set of old and modern honky tonk country and rockabilly. I thought it was great what they were doing, and I wanted to be like them. Other bands started doing rockabilly songs in their sets. One of the best was Danny and the Fat Boys with Danny Gatton on guitar and Billy Hancock fronting and playing bass."

After a few years of playing folk music, he decided to assemble a traditional country band, the Casa Loma Cowboys. They performed big band music in a country style: "We played mainly military NCO and Enlisted Men's Clubs. I think we played every base in the D.C. area. We weren't very good, but we were willing to work cheap, so we got a lot of work. Then in 1976, I got a gig at an old run down country spot in Alexandria, Virginia, called the Country Hut. It wasn't much, but it was steady work Friday and Saturday night, five sets a night for $100. I had to learn some of the modern country songs of the day, but I could also do my old country cover songs."

At this same time, Rubinowitz worked with fellow local guitarist Danny Gatton repairing old guitars and making guitar pickups. Rubinowitz acknowledged, "I tried out for a job at a joint called the Annandale Grill, but the person making the decisions didn't think we were good enough. When he found out I worked with Danny, he hired us. [Unfortunately] most of the musicians didn't really want to play the music I wanted to, and their heart wasn't into it."

The last lineup of the Casa Loma Cowboys in 1977 was the most popular since they played mostly rockabilly songs: "Some folks were coming just to see us play our rockabilly set. Robert Gordon's first album, *Robert Gordon and Link Wray*, was out and I was getting a case of rockabilly fever. I started going to record stores to buy copies of the songs I used to hear when I was a young fellow. [The first record he ever purchased was Jerry Lee Lewis' "Great Balls of Fire."] We started adding more and more of those songs to our set. There was one song that wasn't really a rockabilly song, Marty Wilde's 'Bad Boy,' but I really loved it. I had only heard the song a few times and I really wanted to do it."

In the spring of 1978, Hancock and Rubinowitz played a show with the Father of Rockabilly, Charlie Feathers. Rubinowitz recalled, "That helped fire me up and got me more excited about rockabilly." Unfortunately, Rubinowitz's band members decided they didn't need him any longer: "They were trying to steal all of the gigs I had gotten for us and the only thing that saved me was the new drummer, who gave me such a hard time I had to fire him. At that point the whole band left." With a remainder of shows to play, Rubinowitz had no choice but to use pickup bands: "That was very tough going."

Hancock and Rubinowitz decided to team up: "Billy and I were hanging out a lot then and that summer we decided that since we were not doing that well we would do just rockabilly, even if no one else cared. He put the Tennessee Rockets together with me on rhythm guitar and singing half the songs. We started back at the bottom doing military bases and the good old Country Hut. Nothing much happened that summer, but Billy knew Jim Kirkhuff and

Jon Strong, who were trying to start a bluegrass record label, Ripsaw. Billy talked them into thinking about putting out some rockabilly 45's. He recorded his first singles sometime that summer or early fall, and I started writing some of my own songs like 'Ain't It Wrong,' 'Feelin' Right Tonight,' and 'Hot Rod Man.'" Incidentally, Rubinowitz appeared on Hancock's *Shakin' That Rockabilly Fever*, which was released in 1981 on Solid Smoke.

Kirkhuff and Strong told Rubinowitz if he could get a good recording of his songs that they might be willing to release them as 45 rpm singles. Rubinowitz disclosed, "I went into BIAS studio in Falls Church, Virginia, with Billy and the Rockets on a Saturday morning in December 1978. Bob Dawson engineered, and we recorded 'Bad Boy,' 'Ain't It Wrong,' 'Feelin' Right Tonight,' 'Hot Rod Man,' and 'Red Cadillac and a Black Moustache.' I listed my mom as one of the producers because she paid for the recording time." The band featured Hancock and Bob Newscaster on lead guitar, Bryan Smith on upright bass, Jeff Lodsun on drums, and Rubinowitz on rhythm guitar and lead vocals. Ripsaw released two 45 rpm singles: "Bad Boy" b/w "Feelin' Right Tonight" and "Hot Rod Man" b/w "Ain't It Wrong."

In 1980, Rubinowitz formed his own band, the Bad Boys. At that time, rockabilly guitar virtuoso Eddie Angel joined the lineup: "Bryan Smith was the stand up bass player in the Tennessee Rockets and had played in a jug type band called the Star Spangled Washboard Band. Eddie had played with them. Scotty Flowers was the drummer in the band and introduced me to Eddie. Eddie loved rockabilly music and when I played him the tape of my songs he got excited that maybe there would be a rockabilly music scene again and that was the kind of music he wanted to play. We spoke about playing one day." They worked together until Rubinowitz quit the music business in 1987. Angel helped him write "Missy Ann," which was written about one of Rubinowitz's girlfriends and "No Club (Lone Wolf)." Angel and Rubinowitz also wrote "Rock 'n' Roll Ivy" about Poison Ivy Rorschach of the Cramps, whom Rubinowitz met in 1979. During his 1981 tour of France, he wrote "Cavan Likes to Rock/Rockabilly Rules." Rubinowitz conveyed, "It was about Crazy Cavan and the Rhythm Rockers. They were the stars of the tour, and we were the American nouveau rockabillies and were having a tough time at some of the shows. My song about Cavan helped me do a little better with the French Teddy Boys."

Besides recording and touring, Rubinowitz took an interest in building guitars: "I started getting into guitars in the early 1970s when I moved back in with my folks. I had some extra time, and I started dreaming about all kinds of guitars. I was taking lessons from a guitar teacher named David Parker at the Guitar Shop in D.C., and he had a little gig in Springfield, Virginia, where I lived. Many of his students would show up there, including Billy Averett who was a chief in the Navy and wanted to learn to play classical guitar. One night he brought in a guitar he had made, and Dave played it for a set. I asked or should I say begged Billy to help me build one of my own. About this same

Tex Rubinowitz performing at the Wax Museum in Washington, D.C., in 1983 (courtesy Tex Rubinowitz).

time, I bought a new Fender Telecaster from Phil Zavarella's music store. Phil told me that Danny Gatton had a little guitar repair business and could make my new guitar play and sound better. I went over to his place and dropped my Tele off for him to do his magic. We started doing some work together about a year later. I made Charlie Christian guitar pickup frames, and Danny wound the coils; we then installed them in Telecasters. Danny had one in his '53 Tele. It looked and sounded great, so many of the other players wanted one of their own. We did that for a few years but then he had a chance to open a vintage music store, and I was playing more gigs. I'm still working with machinery and making some guitar parts from time to time. I'd like to make the Charlie Christian pickups again."

In 1984, "Hot Rod Man" was featured in the movie *Roadhouse 66* starring actor Willem Defoe and actor/rockabilly singer James Intveld. Rubinowitz remembered, "Jim and Jon of Ripsaw made that deal. I didn't have anything to do with it. I was happy it happened but hoped it would lead to something big, which it did not. I did get some money from BMI when it was first shown on TV, but the movie companies usually don't pay much for music."

By 1987, Rubinowitz had grown tired of continually paying his dues and not getting very far: "I quit playing when my mom got sick and needed me to help take care of her. I felt my chances for anything other than local success were becoming very slim. I wasn't really having any fun playing and with my mom needing my help I thought I'd take a break for awhile. I never got to perform again other than a benefit or something like that. I thought I had some good ideas, but I couldn't get them off the ground." Since then, he has been trying to readjust to normal civilian life. He has found the transition to be challenging. However, he's happy that he sang and recorded rockabilly music and that people seemed to dig it, but he is thankful to be out of the business since he has seen too many of his friends end their lives over not succeeding.

Eight

Today's Sensations

Kim Lenz

It has been difficult for females to gain acceptance in any genre of music, but especially in rockabilly and rock and roll. Wanda Jackson, Janis Martin, and Lorrie Collins are respected and revered today for their songs, but that wasn't the case back in the 1950s. It was considered taboo for them to sing about their explorations into adulthood. Kim Lenz has experienced injustices firsthand. Touring and performing two hundred shows a year for almost four years was no easy task. It was hard for her to find a microphone that would be sufficient to carry a female voice then it was dealing with soundmen who didn't want to alter the mixing board to suit her needs. Many of them accused her of not knowing what she was talking about because she was a woman. Lenz proved the skeptics wrong by becoming one of the most promising female artists on the rockabilly scene today. In fact, in 1997, *The Dallas Observer* voted her Best Female Vocalist of the Year.[1] From emails she has received, she has inspired other young women to start their own band. According to Lenz, her first two albums both exceed 10,000 in sales. With those kinds of sales, she has proven a force to be reckoned with.

Kim Lenz was born November 1, 1966, in San Diego, California. She grew up listening to all types of music. Lenz explained, "Old style country came from my mom, while my dad listened to [disk jockey] Wolfman Jack in the 1950s.[2] He used to always play Roy Orbison, Gene Vincent, and the Beach Boys." When she attended high school, she heard the Stray Cats. In 1988, she moved to Los Angeles and had a job with a management firm that specialized in music publishing. There she listened to radio station KPCC and fell in love with American roots music. However, Lenz acknowledged, "I'm influenced by really all music. Rockabilly speaks to me because [the combination of hillbilly and rhythm and blues] was something amazing that changed the face of music. Rockabilly is all about the passion behind the music."

Lenz began singing in her junior high school choir. She didn't become professional until she was twenty-six years old: "I went back to college to get my undergraduate degree in psychology, anthropology, and sociology at the University of North Texas. It is a big music school, and I met a lot of people in the music program." She used to have jam sessions at her house and then she started a band, which was called Rocket, Rocket. Lenz added, "I just got hooked." Her first gig was at a coffee house to about thirteen people in which she sang Wanda Jackson's "Cool Love" and "Let's Have a Party." Lenz revealed, "I only had to do that once and said I have to do this." Unfortunately, Rocket, Rocket only played a few shows and lasted six months.[3]

After moving to Dallas, Lenz and her husband regularly attended Bar of Soap, a popular nightspot with a laundromat in back, to see rockabilly bands play live. A few doors down, a guy Lenz recalled simply as Ralph had a store that sold various rockabilly items. He and his band volunteered to back Lenz since she showed interest in playing the venue but didn't have a band. She was playing a Fender Jaguar guitar at the time, so Ralph decided to name the band Kim Lenz and her Jaguars. Lenz was not keen on the name since she didn't want to use her real name nor did she care for the jaguars being her band name. Ralph told her not to worry about it since she could always change it later. The makeshift situation didn't last long, although the fiery redhead kept the band's name. She soon recruited different band members, including lead guitarist Mike Lester, upright bassist Jake Erwin, and drummer Robert Hamilton. By 1996, they started doing regular shows at clubs.

Lenz and her Jaguars made their debut on record with an extended play 45 rpm, which contained the following songs: "Shake a Leg," "Up to My Old Tricks Again," "Bop City," and "One Blast Off." Critics said that she couldn't tour with only a 45 EP, but she simply told them "just watch me." After a show in San Francisco, Larry Sloven, owner of Hightone Records contacted her about a recording contract. At the time, Hightone was her dream record label. Without her being aware, record label owner/producer Ronnie Weiser and Big Sandy's former manager Alan Larman had been working on her behalf.

In 1998, her self titled debut album hit the market. The cover was an exact replica of the 1957 album, *Gene Vincent and his Blue Caps*: "I took a Polaroid of Gene's album and gave it to the guy who was doing the design and told him I want it to look like this as much as possible." Later, a friend gave her a copy of that vintage album, and she couldn't believe how similar hers had turned out in comparison. Shortly after the release, her guitarist Mike Lester decided he didn't want to tour. Lenz ended up calling Nick Curran, who had recently played with rockabilly legend Ronnie Dawson. Curran hit it off immediately with the band and learned all of Lenz's songs quickly.

In 1999, for her second album, *One and Only*, she and the Jaguars recorded at Kingsway Studio, which is located in the French Quarter in New Orleans. Big Sandy produced it while Carl Sonny Leyland played piano. They used vintage equipment and completed the album in six days: "We felt so lucky to record there. It was the most fun I've ever had in my life."

Kim Lenz having fun onstage with her guitarist Nick Curran (courtesy Kim Lenz).

Lenz includes songs from Gene Vincent, Janis Martin, Johnny Carroll, Carl Perkins, Barbara Pittman, Wanda Jackson, Ray Smith, Charlie Feathers, and Elvis Presley in her live sets. However, to be taken seriously, she felt the need to write some original material. Lenz remarked, "Songwriting is one of my favorite parts of the whole process. I wrote 'Dancing Me to Death' in response to the whole swing [movement] and how it got so out of hand." People seemed to care more about dancing than the actual music. Ironically, she used to teach others how to swing dance. In 1997, "Saturday Jump" was introduced at her first major rockabilly festival appearance, the Denver Rock 'n' Rhythm-Billy Weekender. She had seen Bill Haley's Comets at the 1996 Denver weekender, and she wrote it as a tribute to them.[4] Her favorite song that she wrote and her favorite to perform is "Thinkin' 'Bout You."

Country star, Faron Young inspires her when she performs live. Lenz had viewed his 1950s *Grand Ole Opry* appearances and noticed that he gave his all when performing. Young would wink at the camera to interact with the audience. Lenz did that too in her early shows. Lenz conveyed, "When you're a performer, you're supposed to be entertaining people. I always try to keep that in mind." It is important for her to connect with her audience.

One of her career highlights came when she sang with Janis Martin onstage at the 1998 Viva Las Vegas weekender. It was one of Martin's first shows back in the States playing at a festival, and she was naturally apprehensive. It was arranged that Lenz would sing onstage with her, and to her recollection the song they sang together was Martin's "Will You Willyum?" Lenz remembered, "Janis was the real deal, a rockabilly rebel." Being the opening act for Carl Perkins at the Hard Rock Café in Dallas was another major highlight of Lenz's career. Perkins was impressed by her performance: "She was a Texas wildcat."[5] Lenz got to meet and talk with him for twenty minutes: "He was such a wonderful sweet person. He gave me some really good advice and a lot of encouragement."

According to Lenz, "I have been so blessed. I haven't met one musician in the rockabilly scene who isn't just amazingly kind, nice, and supportive." She has worked with or at least met many of the rockabilly legends. Some of them include Glen Glenn, Wanda Jackson, Joe Poovey, Ronnie Dawson, and Lew Williams.

In recent years, Lenz limited her number of personal appearances because she decided to have a family. She is married and has a seven year old son. Lenz remarked, "I kind of got burned out on touring." Since 2002, she has had The Nu Niles as her backing band, whom she affectionately refers to as her Spanish Jaguars.

In 2007, she reformed the original Jaguars, which includes Nick Curran on lead guitar, Jake Erwin on standup bass, and Scotty Tecce on drums. They had all been members of Lenz's band previously, but as a unit they had never recorded together. In 2008, she formed her own Riley Records label which pays homage to her Irish ancestry, and recorded a new album with famed engineers

Billy Horton and Ethan Allen. It featured a mix of Lenz originals combined with a few covers. She hopes it will be one of the biggest rockabilly records ever. Recognizing modern marketing needs of the modern age, in addition to its availability on both CD and vinyl LP, the songs will be sold individually through iTunes and Amazon. Since she started, she feels rockabilly has become more submerged into the mainstream's consciousness.

With her newly founded record label perhaps women will finally have an equal voice in rockabilly. It is something that they have struggled to get for fifty years.

The Casey Sisters

In 1999, an amateur talent show took place at the Viva Las Vegas weekender. Two gals dressed exactly identical in blue western cowboy shirts hit the stage. They sang the Miller Sisters' "Real Gone Jive" and The Collins Kids' "They're Still in Love," while being backed by Detroit's Big Barn Combo. It was the first time they had sung together, except for the rehearsal they had received at Ronnie Weiser's pre VLV party. At the talent show, unbeknownst to them, the owner of Tail Records from Sweden was in attendance and was so enthralled with their appearance that he offered them a recording contract. Thanks to some encouragement by Swedish rockabilly Wildfire Willie, Caroline Gnagy and Rachel Fenton took the offer. The Casey Sisters had arrived.

Caroline Gnagy was born on July 29, 1972, in Maryville, Missouri. Her father was a maestro Flamenco guitarist for forty years. He taught Gnagy and her brother music theory and how to sing harmonies. He was very supportive of her musical talent. Unfortunately, he didn't get to see her sing professionally. He died in 1997. Gnagy's grandfather, John influenced Andy Warhol and other painters from 1946 until 1970 with his *Learn to Draw* series.

Gnagy sang from fifth grade on in school choirs. As a teenager, she went to see various live bands, everything from rockabilly to surf to punk. In 1987, she wanted to start her own heavy metal band but could never find enough members willing to participate. Gnagy almost attended college to become an opera singer: "I could see myself burning out on opera, so I decided against going to the conservatory."[6] She had friends, including her high school voice teacher, who attended the conservatory, and she saw how stressed out opera singing had made them. In 1997, when she began singing rockabilly, she had to undo almost everything she had learned classically.

In November 1997, Gnagy formed the Cowtown Playboys. Going to the Indianapolis rockabilly weekender gave her inspiration to start singing rockabilly: "The music was so inspiring, and I met so many great people." Starting the band helped her to deal with her dad's death, which had occurred two months previously. She wishes her dad could be alive to see her perform.

In 1998, Kim Lenz and her Jaguars opened for the Cowtown Playboys in Lawrence, Kansas. Soon after, Gnagy became Lenz's road manager. When Lenz got signed to Hightone Records, Gnagy went on a month long tour from Texas to the West Coast: "Kim Lenz was so wonderful to me." She was so patient and so nice to Gnagy, who had been grieving from the loss of her father. Every night, Lenz either called her onstage to sing a song with her or allowed her to sing a song on her own. It gave Gnagy exposure: "I'll always be very grateful to her for that." During this time, Rachel Fenton finished her work as a Patsy Cline tribute artist and was signed on as new lead singer of the Cowtown Playboys without Gnagy's realization. Once Gnagy returned, she attended a few of the shows where Fenton was the lead singer. They hit it off and decided to put an act together.

Their voices blended perfectly together, and when they hit the stage it was magic. The talent show at the Viva Las Vegas weekender was the first time they had sung together, but it was such a success that they were booked on the bill for the next Viva Las Vegas weekender.

In 1999, Fenton moved to Austin and lived with Gnagy for three years. Even though they are not blood related, they regard one another as sisters. Both gals are equally influenced by the Miller Sisters, The Davis Sisters, Jimmy and Johnny, The Louvin Brothers, Wanda Jackson, and The Collins Kids. Gnagy's

The Casey Sisters, Rachel Fenton, left, and Caroline Gnagy at the Rockin' 50's Fest II in Green Bay, Wisconsin (author's photograph).

individual influences include Wayne Hancock, Rudy Tutti Grayzell, Johnny Paycheck, Faron Young, and Loretta Lynn, while Fenton's influences include Janis Martin, Brenda Lee, Etta James, Little Richard, and Wynona Carr.

They experienced recording and touring together for the first time. When it came to record their first album, *Who's Crying Now*, the recording was postponed for about a year because they couldn't afford to bring over the Big Barn Combo. The owner hired the band that backed The Casey Sisters. Fenton commented, "They were perfect for our sound." After every song, the Tail Records' engineer yelled, "I think that's a killer."[7] All the songs were recorded live on vintage equipment.

A 1937 RCA microphone was used to record their voices. It was double sided, so the girls could sing at the same time. Since Fenton is quite a bit shorter than Gnagy, she had to stand on a gas can in order to reach the microphone. Gnagy wrote most of the songs for the first album, and Fenton just added harmony to her songs. "Jump Jive Party" was written with Kim Lenz in mind. "You Can't Have Him" was written out of friendly competition amongst one another for cute rockabilly boys.

In 2002, the Casey Sisters were booked along with High Noon, Cave Catt Sammy, and Wanda Jackson for the annual Buddy Holly celebration in Lubbock, Texas. It was a highlight of their career. Janis Martin was in attendance when they performed at the Rockin' 50s Fest in Green Bay, Wisconsin. They saw her in the audience smiling and enjoying the show and couldn't believe their luck. Gnagy said, "I don't think they realize how much it means to the younger artist to see them there."

Besides performing, Gnagy is also a writer. She has written articles for various music publications including *Blue Suede News* and is currently working on a book about Texas jukejoints. She would like to produce documentaries as well if she could find adequate funding.

The other half of the Casey Sisters, Rachel Fenton was born on July 20, 1977, in Kansas City, Missouri. Her parents have always been supportive of her career. They have attended many of her shows. Fenton confirmed, "They have been beyond and above supportive, probably more than most parents." Fenton has an older brother, who is also a professional musician. At age nine, she started performing. The first song she sang was "Open Your Heart" by Madonna. Her dad had a country band, so she used to sit in with them. One of the songs she sang with the band was Patsy Cline's "I Fall to Pieces."

It is thanks to Cline that Fenton knows about rockabilly music. When she worked as a Cline tribute artist at her friend's restaurant, one of the waitresses was really into the music and gave her a Wanda Jackson CD. Fenton realized that was the sound she was looking for. She loved it but didn't know it was called rockabilly. Cline is naturally one of her favorite artists along with Little Willie John, Wynona Carr, Roy Orbison, Buddy Holly, Carl Perkins, Jerry Lee Lewis, Johnny Cash, Etta James, Little Richard, and Elvis Presley ("who doesn't love

Elvis?"). Gnagy's favorite singers are Faron Young, Bill Haley, Buddy Holly, The Everly Brothers, and Tommy Duncan, who was one of the singers with Bob Wills and His Texas Playboys.

Fenton's most cherished memory was opening as a solo act for the Green Bay Rockin' 50s Fest II in 2005: "It was major pressure on me. I was the most nervous I've ever been for a show." At the Green Bay Rockin' 50s Fest III in 2007, she went onstage to dance for Little Richard, when he asked for volunteers, during his version of "Bony Maronie."

Fenton and Gnagy took a hiatus from the Casey Sisters. Fenton decided to do a solo rhythm and blues career while Gnagy pursued her 1960 country stylings. In April 2008, the Casey Sisters reunited at the Viva Las Vegas weekender. Gnagy released her solo country CD, *This Broken Crown,* in September 2008 as Caroline Casey and the Stringslingers.

Fenton has recorded two rhythm and blues albums so far *'Cause I Feel Good* and *There's a New Miss Rhythm in Town*. While recording *'Cause I Feel Good*, she sang live with the studio musicians but did not record her parts until they left. By the time, she went to record her voice, she had laryngitis. "Ooh, He's Fine" was written about Nick Curran. Fenton was trying to write a song similar to "The Girl Can't Help It," where every guy wants to be him, and every girl wants to be with him.

At twenty-two years old, she began serious songwriting. She eventually learned how to play the guitar because it was easier to write songs if she knew how to play an instrument. Her favorite song to write was "Too Late to Rock." It was written about the drummer of Cave Catt Sammy, who was her boyfriend at the time. He had a tendency to talk too much. Her favorite album recorded as a Casey Sister was *Crazy Spree* because they had established their direction. Fenton started writing songs by then. She writes songs about how she would like her life to be, not how it is.

Female artists have had struggles since day one in the music industry. Fenton concurred, "Girls not only have to have the talent but the look to go along with it. It's expected of them. It's not just about being a good musician; you really have to look good too. That's just how it is." Fenton's style can best be described as eclectic. She likes many different eras. She wears sparkly, gaudy, and provocative clothing. She even owns over one hundred pairs of shoes. Gnagy has been wearing vintage clothing since she was eighteen years old. Her collections include books on music and records, especially 78 rpm's. The female artists stick together. Contrary to popular belief, there is no behind the scenes fighting. Ruby Ann, Mary Ann, Cari Lee Merritt, Martí Brom, Dawn Shipley, Kim Lenz, Rosie Flores, and The Honeybees are all good friends of theirs.

Fenton commented, "I love country and rhythm and blues equally, so that's why rockabilly is so perfect because it is a combination of the two. I have met so many wonderful people, and it is so much fun to go to these festivals. I have made a lot of really great friends. The music is fun. You can dance to it.

That's what I love about rockabilly is that you have the opportunity to see your idols from time to time. I've met Ruth Brown, Wanda Jackson, and Janis Martin. It doesn't really get better than that." Gnagy feels that rockabilly and country music touches people in such a profound way unlike any other music. She loves the beat of rockabilly, which has "an unstoppable irresistible pull through its lyrics." Gnagy added, "I do all of this, writing and performing, because I love it not because it pays me anything."

Carl Sonny Leyland

Promoters usually set up contemporary rockabilly musicians as backing bands for the 1950s stars since most do not have their own touring band. It's not uncommon to see the same band or members of one band back up several different artists from several different genres. Pianist Carl Sonny Leyland has backed up a who's who in rockabilly, rock and roll, and blues. His versatility and talent to make any artist sound as good as their original records puts him in high demand at festivals: "You do build up a good knowledge base of different styles and then you can draw from that when you need to."[8]

Carl Sonny Leyland was born on January 16, 1965, in Ashford, England. As an only child, Leyland spent quality time with his father, who was an amateur drummer: "When I was growing up, he had a lot of the old rock and roll records—Jerry Lee Lewis, Little Richard, and Bill Haley. He also had old country records, including Hank Williams and Jimmie Rodgers and jazz records. I grew up hearing all that stuff and liking it." Leyland began playing in the English pubs at fifteen years of age, chaperoned by his father. Later, they played on some shows together: "We did quite a few things together. It was cool."

Leyland could play the banjo, trumpet, trombone, accordion, and guitar but chose the piano as his primary instrument: "I can pretty much handle anything that comes along on the piano." Boogie woogie recordings from the 1930s and 1940s inspired him the most: "They were the driving force that got me playing music." Leyland added, "I listened to the records and slowed them down to half speed." Therefore, he was able to improvise early on and add to the records instead of strictly copying the original recordings. Incidentally, Leyland has an extensive record collection, which he plays on his 1961 Rockola Princess jukebox. Working at a piano shop for a year helped him hone his talent, "It was good to learn those skills in restoration and repair because I've had to put them to use a lot of times." His musical influences include singers Jerry Lee Lewis, Carl Perkins, Bill Haley, Little Richard, and Sonny Burgess, and pianists Pete Johnson, Albert Ammons, and Meade "Lux" Lewis. Six months after taking up the piano he decided to provide the vocals on the songs as well. Rhythm and blues shouter Big Joe Turner's "I Ain't Gonna Be Your Low Down Dog No More" has become a staple of Leyland's live shows.

Carl Sonny Leyland testing out a new boogie woogie tune in 1992 (courtesy Carl Sonny Leyland).

A few years later, Leyland played at various venues in Norway and met the band Johnny J and the Hitmen from New Orleans who invited him to come to America: "They were there about three or four days, and I befriended them. The singer said, 'If you ever want to come over and visit I've got an apartment where you can stay.'" Leyland was twenty-three years old when he moved to New Orleans: "I always had it in my mind to come to America if I could get the opportunity. I wanted to see what it was like. It was way different from what I was used to, but I was open to it." Living in New Orleans for ten years, he played the blues circuit. Leyland explained, "There really wasn't a scene for rockabilly. [In 1981, Leyland had become a part of the British rockabilly scene, buying obscure records and dressing the part.] Most of my career, I've made my living from playing blues." After awhile, he formed his own rock and roll trio, playing songs by Jerry Lee Lewis and Fats Domino. Although he was tempted to play his own material, he felt it best to stick with songs the crowds knew. While in New Orleans, Leyland performed at three Jazz and Heritage Festivals.

Since New Orleans didn't provide an outlet for Leyland's rockabilly talents, he moved to California in 1997: "When I listen to rockabilly, it touches something inside of me. It becomes a part of you and the framework of your life." Then a year later he became part of Big Sandy's Fly-Rite Boys. He toured with them for three and a half years, recorded an Extended Play 45 rpm record *Radio Favorites*, and was featured on the CD, *Big Sandy Presents the Fly-Rite Boys*. One of his most memorable experiences occurred at the Denver Rock and Rhythm-Billy Weekender where a band had cancelled, and Leyland was called upon to find a replacement. He joined forces with fellow Fly-Rite Boys Ashley Kingman and Bobby Trimble and bassist Brent Harding from Deke Dickerson and the Ecco-Fonics. Leyland remembered, "It went really well. It was everything that rock and roll could be. Bill Haley's Comets who came on next commented 'We really liked that band' and invited us back onstage to play." While on tour with Big Sandy, he became friends with Kim Lenz and her Jaguars. Leyland played piano on all of Lenz's tracks for her second album, *One and Only*, and wrote "Comin' Back Strong" for its release. Also, at this time, Leyland made guest appearances on all of Deke Dickerson's albums. After his stint with Big Sandy, Leyland became involved with the traditional jazz scene, thereby forming his current trio.

Nowadays besides keeping busy with his trio, Leyland backs numerous rockabilly, rock and roll, and blues acts at festivals worldwide. He has played with a who's who in music: rockabilly acts Billy Lee Riley, Janis Martin, Sonny Burgess, Gene Summers, and Joe Clay, and rhythm and blues greats Lowell Folsom, The Cleftones, Young Jessie, Ruth Brown, and Jimmy McCracklin to name but a few. Leyland acknowledged, "It has been a dream come true. I always tell the artist that it really means a lot to me to have met them and played with them, and that it's an honor." It's surreal for Leyland to think that he is backing the artists whose records he heard when he was just a kid such as Billy Lee Riley, whose recordings of "Red Hot" and "Flyin' Saucer Rock and Roll" Leyland first heard when he was only twelve years old. Leyland explained, "You want to do your best for the guys you're backing up. In a lot of cases, it makes them really feel at ease if they can hear something that sounds pretty similar to their records." Even though Leyland is in high demand, he still considers what he does to be a work in progress and always keeps in mind that "music is the main focus."

Eddie Clendening

Eddie Clendening has made quite a name for himself in only ten years of showcasing his talent. He has backed such notables as Dale Hawkins, Pat Cupp, Billy Lee Riley, and Hayden Thompson besides fronting his own band, the Blue Ribbon Boys. In September 2008, he was recruited to portray Elvis

Presley in the critically acclaimed musical *Million Dollar Quartet*, which is based on the December 1956 Sun Studio impromptu jam session that included Elvis Presley, Jerry Lee Lewis, Carl Perkins, and Johnny Cash. At twenty-five years old, he is a veteran on the rockabilly scene and is highly revered by his peers.

Chris Edward Clendening was born on February 27, 1983, in Denver, Colorado. He changed his name from Chris to Eddie because his father and four uncles are all named Chris. He wanted to have his own identity.

His love for rockabilly came at a young age thanks in part to his grandparents and his own research. At twelve, he was sporting a pompadour and checking out local record stores for rare rockabilly gems. His interest was in listening to the music and didn't consider performing at that time: "The first songs I really remember having an impact on me were the Ritchie Valens' recordings like 'Ooh My Head' and 'Come on, Let's Go.'"[9] He spent the majority of his time playing baseball since he saw himself as a future ball player. Clendening did not realize that there were others who loved the rockabilly scene as much as he did. Kurt Ohlen introduced him to the rockabilly world through the Denver weekenders he used to organize. Clendening's first appearance on the road was as guest singer with Ohlen's band, the Ranch Rhythmaires. Clendening conveyed, "We spent a week on the road. I was pretty young, but I knew then that I am happiest when I'm moving from place to place."[10] Ohlen owns Wormtone Records and once played bass in Clendening's band, the Blue Ribbon Boys.

Clendening began singing in 1998. The first band he was in, no one knew how to sing, so he volunteered: "The band started when I was in ninth grade. I had a friend named Chris Houghton that had been in class with me for a few years, and we buddied around together. I had also known the drummer Sean Wetstine for a few years but didn't know he played drums until he offered to stop by with his kit and play with us. We were all out at a show and ran into Aaron Pope from Sedalia, Colorado. He had been a guitar player, who switched to upright bass. We started out at Chris' mom's garage just for fun but got offered a show, opening up for a touring act at a private party and from there we decided to go with it. That lineup lasted for about three years, now after many changes I'm working with bassist Chris Chew who I had worked with while playing guitar for GT and the Sidewinders. Jeff Yeary is singing a bit and playing rhythm guitar and an El Paso transplant named Mark Millard is on the drums. We were lucky that together we really seem to have a good time, so it's been working out for a few years now in this formation."[11] Clendening picked up the guitar shortly after forming his first band: "I had a guitar, but I never really tried playing it; it just kind of hung on my wall."[12] He taught himself some basic chords and went from there. He owns both a Gibson ES-295, which is a replica of Scotty Moore's, and a Martin acoustic, which has a tooled initialized leather covering, similar to Presley's. Clendening's covering is unique in that the underside is loaded with autographs of rockabilly legends such as James Burton, Scotty Moore, Dale Hawkins, Glen Glenn, and Pat Cupp. In fact, Charles Underwood, the cover's original designer, replicated one for Clendening with his name instead of Presley's.

Clendening's big break came when he played on Hayden Thompson's set at a pre-party for the Viva Las Vegas Weekender at Gilley's Saloon and Dance Hall. Paul Ward and Steve Scott of Cave Catt Sammy bet twenty dollars each that he wouldn't jump onstage and play Thompson's guitar in the middle of his set. According to Clendening, "Hayden was playing the piano, and he had his acoustic sitting on a stand. I jumped up and grabbed it, played a couple of tunes, walked off stage and collected my cash. Afterwards I expected a very

Eddie Clendening, right, meeting with one of his heroes, rockabilly legend Glen Glenn, at the Rockin' 50's Fest II in Green Bay, Wisconsin (courtesy Carole Homer).

upset Hayden Thompson, but he thought it was great and thanked me for my enthusiasm."[13] Another musician he got a kick out of playing with was Jimmy Lee Fautheree of Jimmy and Johnny fame: "He was just such a nice guy and a great musician. He invited us, Deke [Dickerson] and the band, to his house, and his wife made dinner for us." It was also quite an honor for him to share the same stage with Billy Lee Riley: "Billy Lee is a really cool guy. He's not at all what I expected. I never knew that he closes his eyes when he sings because he is so nervous. Different stuff like that is real interesting because he seems like such a wild man."

To prepare for his gigs, Clendening plays the old records. However, sometimes that is not enough because "either they don't remember how the song goes or have changed it through the years."

In 2003, Deke Dickerson gave Clendening a call to play rhythm guitar on thirty-three dates on his tour; one of those stops included the Ponderosa Stomp in New Orleans. Clendening didn't have any idea that he would be playing with such notables as Elvis Presley's sidemen: Scotty Moore, D.J. Fontana, and James Burton.

Clendening received the opportunity to sing Presley's hit, "Hound Dog" with guitarist Moore and drummer Fontana as backing. He was later razzed a bit by Moore for shaking his leg during the performance. Clendening explained to him that he "had to do a little something extra for the Elvis fans out in the audience."

Presley is one of his favorite singers as well as one of his musical influences, along with Bob Luman and The Shadows (which featured guitarist James Burton and upright bassist James Kirkland) and Pat Cupp. Although he admits he likes all the rockabilly guys, as well as crooners Dean Martin and Bobby Darin. Clendening does a birthday tribute to Presley every year in Denver, where he resides, and he enjoys singing "Baby, Let's Play House" at his shows. His favorite aspect of Presley is how he was able to combine "innocence with sex appeal." He was both "unassuming and dangerous" at the same time.

In 2004, rockabilly's beloved band Go Cat Go decided to reunite for two shows, one at the Viva Las Vegas Weekender and the other at Hemsby in England. The band's drummer Lance LeBeau spotted their new vocalist, Clendening, while playing with Deke Dickerson and the Ecco-Fonics: "I got a call from Lance and based on my voice thought I would be a good candidate. Of course, I agreed because I had been a fan of their music for some time. A lot of their songs had been a part of my regular play list. I didn't meet the other guys until the rehearsals before the shows. We had a great response from both shows. Both times we had to spend at least an hour at the autograph table. I won't go as far as to say I had anything to do with that. It's just a credit to the band and the original front man/songwriter Darren Spears. I had a blast with all the songs, but by far the biggest response was for 'Please Mama Please.' They are all great guys, and I think not only did it mean a lot for them to see how much their music means to so many people, but I think it was also a long overdue step in the grieving process for their friend."[14] Clendening added, "I hope that for them, and for the fans, I did what they were looking for."[15]

A year later, Clendening backed up one of his influences, Pat Cupp at the Rockin' 50s Fest II in Green Bay, Wisconsin. He remembered the experience with fondness: "Pat is a great guy and entertainer. I've always loved his recordings, and it's great when you get to meet someone you've admired, and they turn out to be so down to Earth and fun to work with. I know he has struggled with his hearing over the years, but I really hope to see him playing, and I would definitely welcome any opportunity to work with him again."[16]

In 2006, Clendening's long awaited full length CD *Rage of the Teen-Age* was issued by Denver's own Wormtone Records. Clendening featured several top notch rockabilly bands as backing including Deke Dickerson and the Ecco-Fonics, Ike and the Capers, Nick Curran and the Nitelifes, and Cave Catt Sammy. Ten cover versions appear but, "most of the originals were written with my old partner Mike Molnar. He was a member of my live band for some time before he relocated to Austin, Texas. We just tried to get a few tunes that sounded like some of our favorite stuff at the time. I think we had a lot of Joe Clay in mind with the heavy snare drum. We also had a period of trying to make it sound as simple as possible but stay interesting."[17] Several years prior to this release, only an extended play was available with "Hot Liquor," "I Love a Woman," "Messin' Around," and "That Girl of Mine." Clendening disclosed the story behind "I Love a Woman": "It was the first song I ever wrote when I was fourteen. There was a girl I had a crush on, and I was always a bit awkward around her. The day before we had the recording session booked I decided I was gonna try to write her a song for her birthday, so I ended up writing that in about two minutes, and we pushed a cover song we had scheduled to do and worked 'I Love a Woman' in instead. I re-recorded it later the way I had heard it in my head, and it ended up on the *Rage of the Teen-Age* record. As far as the girl, I didn't hear much of anything from her after giving her the song. I guess I came on a bit too strong."[18]

Clendening's rockabilly career continues to soar; even Bruce Springsteen knows who he is. The Boss saw Clendening in concert, on the same bill with the Queen of Rockabilly Wanda Jackson and his future wife Ruby Ann at Asbury Lanes in Asbury Park, New Jersey: "I did see him at the show and actually shared a drink with him. He was a great guy, very nice and encouraging. It was nice to see someone of that level of fame just there to admire someone else. He was a real down to Earth guy. He even paid to get in. I'm not sure how much of my set if any he saw, but he said he enjoyed it."[19] As long as major celebrities like Springsteen are fans, rockabilly will never die.

Ruby Ann

There are quite a few rockin' gals on the American rockabilly scene, including Martí Brom, Little Rachel, Kim Lenz, and Cari Lee Merritt; and they are known worldwide. However, in France, there is a gal by the name of Ruby Ann that has a ton of spunk and a voice to match. She sings in a hillbilly bop style with a growl in her voice equal only to Wanda Jackson's.

Contrary to popular belief, there is no rivalry among the female rockabilly songstresses. They all get along and wish the best for one another. Ruby Ann revealed, "I'm very pleased to see so many girls getting involved [in the scene] and a lot of them I consider friends of mine. With all the festivals popping up everywhere, I hope to meet [even] more. We all have our own special differences [that we bring] to the stage as the music is [becoming] more widely available. Each subtle difference makes for interesting changes, even on often overdone material."[20]

Born in Coimba, Portugal, Ruby Ann started singing in 1998 at age twenty-one when she formed her band, The Boppin' Boozers. Both her parents were musicians. Her father played Fado guitar, which is Portugal's most famous musical genre, and her mother sang in a traditional Portuguese band.

Ruby Ann became interested in the rockabilly scene and its music through her friend Felipe who was constantly traveling. He would bring home rockabilly music from London, introducing Ruby Ann to it. Ruby Ann disclosed, "I used to sing a lot just for fun, but my friend and guitar player from the Boppin' Boozers told me I had a good voice."[21] She heeded his advice and participated in the Hemsby Weekender talent show. Even though she didn't win, the booking agent for the Cruise Inn in Amsterdam was so impressed that he hired her for the venue. However, her first show took place in Porto, Portugal: "I was so nervous. All my friends were there, waiting to see if I was any good."[22]

Her musical influences include Charline Arthur, Faron Young, Dean Martin, Johnny Cash, Lefty Frizzell, and Patsy Cline. Listening to Cline convinced her that she wanted to be a singer: "She was the first female that really impressed me."[23] In fact, she sings many of Cline's rockabilly tinged songs in her live sets including "Seven Lonely Days," "Gotta Lot of Rhythm in My Soul," and "Love Me Honey Do." Ruby Ann acknowledged, "I enjoy the fast numbers for the live shows. However, I personally like singing both the uptempo rockers as well as the ballads."

The Boppin' Boozers recorded their second full length album, *Honky Tonk Mind*, at the legendary Tail Records in Sweden. Tail is the home of Jack Baymoore and the Bandits, Jesse Al Tuscan and the Lumberjacks, Charlie Thompson, and Eva Eastwood. Artists like to record there because the studio has vintage equipment and pays particular detail in replicating the 1950s sound. Ruby Ann added, "We were lucky to have afforded the time to do our record there, and we enjoyed it very much." Although, recapturing the 50s sound isn't as important to her as getting a quality sound: "It's neat to sound like a 50-year-old record, but I'd prefer to do a nice Capitol Records type sound and wait 50 years for it to sound like musical sandpaper."

One of the songs she recorded at Tail was Laura Lee Perkins' "Gonna Rock My Baby Tonight." Ruby Ann isn't too keen on singing covers though, so the Perkins' cover is a rarity: "I prefer to make my own music and let them do the same. I would hate to leave a black mark on anyone's shining career with my nonsense." However, Ruby Ann enjoys meeting the legends: "There is a lot of history living in those people, and it's neat to experience a small part of that."

Ruby Ann embarks on a solo career (courtesy Ruby Ann).

The Boppin' Boozers played the Rockabilly Rave, D-Day, and the High Rockabilly festivals and also made television appearances in Portugal, Spain, and the Netherlands. In April 2005, Ruby Ann performed for the last time with the Boppin' Boozers at the Rockin' 50s Fest II in Green Bay, Wisconsin: "It was our first time in the U.S., and people loved the show. I felt good about it because it was my first gig after a year [off]. When I left the stage, I had that thing in me telling me I couldn't stop."[24]

Since then, she has gone solo and has played with people that know her material and do a nice job with it. Ruby Ann acknowledged, "It's a different experience being without a regular band; however, it's a nice change to have the room I want creatively to make myself happy." In 2007, she recorded a full length album for Wild Records, *Train to Satanville*, which included tracks featuring her husband Eddie Clendening on lead guitar.

Even though she has worked as an architect, she stays committed to singing rockabilly because "there is always new music to discover, not to mention the opportunities to travel and meet new people and see new things. I am not currently working as an architect; however, the pay is better should I decide to return to that. At the moment, I prefer to enjoy life and the music and [therefore put up with] the poverty that goes [along] with it."

Sue Moreno

Europe has never abandoned rockabilly music and its artists. Since day one, the country has embraced the American music form. Rockabilly is immortalized through record collectors, major festivals, and record hops. Even today, songs that were recorded fifty years ago are still climbing the European charts. A fact that is even more surprising is that new bands and artist pop up everyday. Even if English is not their first language, they find a way to break through the language barrier and sing the songs of their rockabilly heroes. Sue Moreno of the Netherlands is one such artist who has embraced the 1950s music.

At the age of six, Moreno started singing. Around the same time, she fell in love with Elvis Presley and his music. Moreno admitted, "Elvis has always been and always will be one of the biggest influences for me. I also fell in love with the style and image of Eddie Cochran."[25] Her other musical influences and favorite artists include Dean Martin, Ann-Margret, Hank Williams, Patsy Cline, and Johnny Burnette. Their influence is evident in both the songs Moreno chooses and the way she presents herself onstage.

Her family has been very supportive of her musical endeavors. Her parents and her brother have all seen her in concert: "It was great when my parents came to see me at the Screamin' Festival in Spain." It was her dad who introduced her to rockabilly: "He has a big music collection including lots of rock and roll. He gave me his old record player and 45 rpm records when I was young. I played the Elvis ones over and over and loved it."

In 1978, when the movie *Grease* came out, she sang "Hopelessly Devoted to You" and walked around her stairs just like Olivia Newton John's character in the movie. Moreno recalled, "I went to music school when I was fourteen years old and started seriously working on my voice, music, and guitar." At fifteen, she formed her first band, Memphis. It was comprised of fellow music students, and they performed their songs for class. In 1991, after Moreno graduated from high school, she moved to America for a year. She lived on the East Coast. During the day she worked as a nanny while at night she sang at various clubs in the area.

As time passed, Moreno honed her stage act. She can sing it all, from country to pop to rockabilly to songs sung in Spanish. Even though her regular backing band is The Flaming Stars, she has shared the stage with both Darrel Higham and The Barnshakers. However, her favorite people to work with were Johnny Burnette's son Rocky and Rock and Roll Trio's guitarist Paul Burlison: "I very much enjoyed singing with Rocky and Paul on their last European tour. It was very special because it was their last tour. With the passing of Paul, it remains a fond memory."

Moreno recently recorded with Italian rockabilly guitar virtuoso Marco DiMaggio: "He's such a talented musician. It is great to record, write, and perform with him." Their collaborated effort *Bye Bye Blues* was released in 2006 on Jungle Records. Moreno wrote half of the songs on the album, including her favorites "Forever" and "Drivin' on the Highway of Love."

In her native land, she has been dubbed the Female Elvis. Moreno remembered, "The first time I read it was when someone put it in the title of a big interview in the national paper here in Holland. Sometimes when I perform at Elvis festivals, people call me on stage as the Female Elvis." Even though she is flattered by the comparison, she feels no one can live up to that image. Since 2004, she has been featured on various Elvis festivals: "It is great to play them being an Elvis fan, and I enjoy playing his very broad [range of songs]. Elvis' fans are very loyal and enthusiastic." She would love to play Elvis week in Memphis, which helps to mark the anniversary of Presley's death. She has had the opportunity to play with Presley's drummer, D.J. Fontana and holds Presley's guitarist Scotty Moore in high regard. Moreno conveyed, "Scotty's one of the coolest guys and greatest guitarists. D.J. is so great. Just the idea that they were there when it all started; it is such a special feeling to be onstage with them."

There are no signs of Moreno slowing down any time soon with her show dates fully booked and a new album release with The Blasters, Danny B. Harvey, and Slim Jim Phantom of the Stray Cats on the horizon.

Besides singing, she has had experience in modeling and acting. Coincidentally, Moreno earned her Master of Arts degree in film and television. She eventually would like to incorporate her backgrounds of music, dance, and per-

Sue Moreno revealing her pin-up side (courtesy Sue Moreno).

formance into all one show. Moreno would enjoy meeting Ann-Margret, whom she feels has accomplished this feat successfully.

Moreno's overall look is very important to her. She enjoys adding accessories such as gloves, hats, and high heels to her 1950s wardrobe. Having a designer who recreates famous outfits doesn't hurt either. Anne Marie of ReproVintageClothing.com is a dear friend of hers, who has reproduced Presley's red and white cowboy outfit from his movie *Loving You* and the red fringed one shoulder dress that Wanda Jackson has worn in publicity photos just for Moreno. The outfits are one of a kind and are handmade. Moreno disclosed, "I like the excitement, the sexiness yet stylish [side] of the 50s pinups and 50s [movie] stars." She incorporates how she looks with the songs she sings. Julie London and Ann-Margret inspire her sound and look through their sultry vocals and overall sex appeal. Moreno has been told that she resembles a mix between actresses Jane Russell and Marilyn Monroe.

Whether touring with her band The Flaming Stars, Marco DiMaggio, or as a solo act, Moreno has been given the chance to tour the globe. Some of the major festivals she has played include the Eddie Cochran weekender in England, the Summer Jamboree in Italy, and the Green Bay Rockin' 50s Fest. She always enjoys coming back to play in America: "I very much enjoy touring in the States. It is the country where it all came from, where people truly understand. I can't wait to go back."

Dawn Shipley

Dawn Shipley began singing professionally in 2001. Her music can best be described as upbeat and fun — a mixture of rockabilly, hillbilly, and rock and roll with elements of traditional rhythm and blues, jazz, and honky tonk.[26] Since then, she has shared the stage with Wanda Jackson, Rosie Flores, James Intveld, and the Paladins. In 2006, the Los Angeles Music Awards' blind judging competition named her Best Americana Female Singer/Songwriter of the Year and Artist of the Year.[27]

Dawn Shipley was born on November 10, 1974, in San Antonio, Texas. At four years old, she sang in the church choir and played her grandmother's piano. Her grandmother gave her instructional books and taught her the major keys. Shipley was a faithful student, practicing whenever she could. Classical compositions were the first songs she tried to replicate. As a youngster, her mother played a lot of country music, but at the time Shipley didn't appreciate the genre: "Country roots my mom instilled in me. She loved Merle Haggard and Conway Twitty. I hated all that stuff. I tried to rebel as much as I could until I was about twenty-four."[28] Shipley instead was a fan of 1980s new wave music, and it wasn't until many years later when she heard Patsy Cline that she realized that she was destined to sing in that style.

Through the club scene in Austin, her love for rockabilly grew: "The music was so much more musical than a lot of the other stuff I was listening to. I experienced hillbilly, honky tonk, and rockabilly, and it just seemed to fit." Some of those roots bands she originally heard were Squirrel Nut Zippers, The Spankers, BR549, Deke Dickerson and the Ecco-Fonics, Big Sandy and the Fly-Rite Boys, and Ronnie Dawson.

Shipley began songwriting at age nine, but she didn't become serious about it until she moved to Texas: "I wasn't 100 percent confident in my abilities, especially as a songwriter. I'd written some of my songs by that point but was very shy about sharing them. I had two practices with a group of guys, Shaan Shirazi on guitar, Buck Johnson on drums, and Beau Sample on bass. The reason why it didn't work was because of the fact that I wasn't sure of what I wanted to do. Those guys were all in demand and very busy and being new and not so confident, I wasn't ready to start booking gigs right away. I realized then that I needed more time to find my exact niche musically prior to trying to get the band together."[29]

While in Austin, she received vital experience by sitting in on the same sets as local acts Martí Brom, Dale Watson, and Roger Wallace at venues such as the Continental Club and Ginny's Little Loghorn, but it wasn't until 2000 when she moved to Los Angeles that she felt ready to go solo. Big Sandy and the Fly-Rite Boys and Deke Dickerson and the Ecco-Fonics made it easier for her "because as soon as I got to L.A. they introduced me to a lot of people."

Her first band was called Dawn Shapely and the Midnight Boys. Her lineup included Shipley on vocals and rhythm guitar, Tom Plante on bass and vocals (he and Shipley shared vocals), Tom Short on guitar then replaced shortly thereafter by Joel Morin, and Tony DeHerrera on drums. Incidentally, Plante still has a band by the name of the Midnight Boys. Shipley explained how the band transformed into the Sharp Shooters, "Tom Plante was away on business, and we had to find a new bass player because we had lots of requests for shows. He had come up with the name the Midnight Boys, so he wanted to keep it. We then changed the name to Dawn Shapely and the Sharp Shooters, and Tony Macias joined the band on bass."[30] The name Shapely actually began as a joke: "In Austin, when I was trying to get a band together, I was hanging out with a couple of my friends, and we were talking about band names. One girl came up with Dawn Shapely and her Dimensions, which we all laughed so much about. I wanted to use it, but I was too much of a weenie to go all out with the Dimensions part (but looking back that would've made much more sense), so I just used the Shapely part. When recording our first CD, *Step It Up*, Mark Neill, who engineered and produced the session, talked me into using my real last name, which I'm very happy about."[31] As far as the Sharp Shooters: "I actually had a little contest amongst a small group of friends. My friend Yvonne Cooprider came up with the name."[32]

She and the Sharp Shooters performed for the first time at a house party on July 4, 2001. That September, they opened for the Paladins at Crazy Jack's

Dawn Shipley and the Sharp Shooters recorded their 2003 release *Step It Up* at Mark Neill's studio. From left: Lance Tamanaha, Dawn Shipley, Randy Stanton, and Marcel Riesco (courtesy Dawn Shipley).

in Burbank, California. 2003 saw the release of their first CD, *Step It Up*, which was recorded at famed producer Mark Neill's studio. Shipley noted, "Mark did a wonderful job of giving the songs a very rare and traditional feel."[33] Fellow contemporary rockabillies Rip Carson and Carl Sonny Leyland guest starred on the album. Carson played rhythm guitar while Leyland played piano. Shipley explained, "I figured I should concentrate on singing."

El Toro Records released their second CD, *Baby If I...*, in 2006. One of its songs "Bear with Me Baby," was also featured on the Bear Family 30th Anniversary CD. While "My Rockin' Baby" was written for a movie: "The movie was called *When Gods Wore Grease*, and it features our music throughout."[34] Shipley added, "I think we've grown tremendously since *Step It Up*, and it shows."[35]

Shipley gives credit to Patsy Cline as her main musical influence: "I love singing her 'Gotta Lot of Rhythm in My Soul.' That's just such a fun song." Although she also loves Janis Martin, Wanda Jackson, Charlene Arthur, Barbara Pittman (she met Pittman at the Viva Las Vegas Weekender in 2002, which was "one of the thrills of my life"), Faron Young, Buddy Holly, Elvis Presley, and Johnny Cash, among many others.

Besides singing, Shipley has a job as a software developer and enjoys the hobby of sewing. Shipley conveyed, "I make my own clothes." She even makes her own patterns.

Various incarnations of the Sharp Shooters have existed, but its current lineup features Shipley's husband Marcel Riesco on guitar (he also leads his own rockabilly band, Truly Lover Trio), Randy Stanton on bass, and Lance Tamanaha on drums. Fans and critics alike have sung their praises in regard to both their recordings and live performances. Appearances at the Viva Las Vegas Weekender, the Rockin' 50s Fest III in Green Bay, Wisconsin, the American Music Festival in Chicago, and two years in a row at the Shake the Shack Rockabilly Ball in Seattle, Washington, have shown audiences that their rockin' honky tonk style is here to stay.

Buddy and Suzy Dughi

Husband and wife team Buddy and Suzy Dughi began playing together in 1990 with the formation of their high octane neo-rockabilly band, Hot Rod Trio, along with drummer Pete Bonny. Numerous CD releases and frequent club and hot rod show dates have made them one of the most popular bands on the Southern California scene today. The Dughi duo have various incarnations of their talents including the traditional rockabilly lineup of Suzy Q and her Be-Bop Boys and the Buddy Dughi Combo as well as the traditional country stylings of the Buddy and Suzy Combo. Besides playing music, in 2008, Buddy Dughi further cemented his rockabilly future by signing with Gretsch who asked him to endorse their legendary electric guitar.

When Buddy Dughi was seventeen years old, he took notice of rockabilly music. Even though his parents were both fans, "My mother saw Gene Vincent and Eddie Cochran live at the Brooklyn Paramount Theater," it wasn't until Dughi purchased the imported "white album" by the Stray Cats that he felt he had discovered something new.[36] Around the same time, he began singing. In fact, the first song he ever sang was Billy Lee Riley's "Flyin' Saucers Rock 'n' Roll." Dughi has based his singing style on "some of the more obscure Sun artists with the real hiccupy-hillbilly wildness" and Gene Vincent, who is his favorite.[37] Playing guitar came earlier, when Dughi was in the fifth grade: "First I tried playing drums along with Beatles' records [in fact, their album *Meet the Beatles* made Dughi realize that he wanted to be a musician], but my parents suggested I take up guitar instead."[38] Dughi added, "My mom and dad had put me in a guitar class where I had to play America's 'A Horse with No Name.'" In regard to his musical influences, Paul Burlison of the Rock 'n' Roll Trio, Cliff Gallup of Gene Vincent's Blue Caps, and country guitar greats Joe Maphis and Merle Travis rank top on his list. Eddie Cochran, Buddy Holly, and Brian Setzer have also influenced his style: "Brian Setzer had a very big impact on me when I was first learning how to play in a rockabilly band."[39]

Dughi had three different bands, the Moonlight Wranglers, the Rockits, and the Round-ups before creating Hot Rod Trio. He conveyed, "Hot Rod Trio was formed when our bass player, Steve Herney, quit to go off to college. We had no bass player and had several shows already booked. Back then, in 1990, there were very few upright bass players, unlike today when everyone seems to play slap bass or try to anyway. My girlfriend Suzy Proche [later Dughi] really loved rockabilly music, so I got her to learn to play upright bass." Suzy Dughi confirmed, "Buddy encouraged me to learn since I knew the songs so well from attending every show for the past three years. After a few weeks of Buddy showing me bass lines on the guitar in the keys of E and A, we got an upright bass. Within about a month, I played my first show, fingers bleeding and all, but I loved it! I think the first song I learned was the rockabilly anthem 'Tear It Up.'"[40] Pete Bonny was already a bandmate with Buddy Dughi: "I met Pete through an ad I placed in the newspaper for a drummer. I had played with him for about six years in the Rockits before forming Hot Rod Trio."

Dughi's wife, Suzy, was born on August 7, 1968, in Augsburg, Germany, while her dad was stationed in the Army. Luckily, her parents always supported

Hot Rod Trio gearing up for a performance at the Mooneyes annual car show. From left, Pete Bonny, Buddy Dughi, and Suzy Dughi (courtesy Buddy and Suzy Dughi).

her love for rockabilly: "They were always happy while I was growing up that I listened to rockabilly and oldies rather than the current [hits of the day] that most kids were listening to." When she was about five or six years old, she discovered her mom's *Beatles for Sale* album: "I would listen to it over and over. My two favorite songs on it were 'Honey Don't' and 'Everybody's Tryin' to Be My Baby.' I loved the guitar sound. It wasn't until I heard the Stray Cats many years later that I recognized that guitar sound and found out who Carl Perkins was and that it was called rockabilly. I then began to dig deeper and discovered more and more cool songs and artists that I really liked, among them Ricky Nelson, Elvis, and everything on Sun [Records]."

While attending Mission Viejo High School in Mission Viejo, California, her love for the music also began to influence the way she dressed. Unfortunately, kids her age didn't understand or appreciate the rockabilly lifestyle as she did: "There weren't any other rockabilly people at my school after my freshman year. People thought I was a real weirdo for wearing 50s clothes like cashmere sweaters, pencil skirts, and spike heels. That look was totally out of style, and the Madonna look was in. They said derogatory things to me, but I learned that I just had to be me and stick up for what I loved and not let them bother me in order to be happy."

As a bassist, she began playing at twenty-two years old. Her biggest influence is legendary bassist James Kirkland. Her dream was realized when they played together on a show in October 2007. Dughi acknowledged, "I always try to watch other players to see what they do differently, so I can add to my playing and become a better bass player. Among the most influential players is Bill Black perhaps because he is the most well known and most heard, but for me there is a special place in my heart for James Kirkland. As most people who know me are aware, I have been a huge Ricky Nelson fan since I was about fifteen years old. I not only love his singing but also his fabulous and talented backing band, including one of my favorite guitarists James Burton and bassist James Kirkland. I always loved the sound of James' slap bass. I think he influenced my playing before I ever knew I [would play bass] because I listened to his playing so much. He continues to be one of my idols and a great inspiration to me and my playing, not to mention he is a super nice guy. I also have to give credit to Lee Rocker of the Stray Cats for bringing the big clumsy instrument back into vogue."

Five years after she began playing bass, Dughi started singing. The first song she sang was The Collins Kids' "Hop, Skip, and Jump." Dughi explained, "I had a hard time at first singing and playing bass smoothly."

Being involved with three different bands and working a full time job, she finds very little time for her hobbies. However, when she does find a spare moment, she loves shopping for vintage clothes, purses, shoes, and records: "I have a collection of about forty Lucite purses and tons of old 45's. My greatest find was when I was sixteen, and I found the December 1958 issue of *Life* magazine with Ricky Nelson on the cover." Her husband's hobbies include fixing up hot rods (he has a picture with Carl Perkins by the first hot rod he ever built) and collecting records and guitars. One of the guitars he had custom made for him, which he also plays often, is a double neck TNM designed by Terry MacArthur.

One of their other bands featuring Suzy on vocals is Suzy Q and her Be-Bop Boys. In October 2005, they played their first live show at the Elks Club in Van Nuys, California, which was a tribute to Gene Vincent and sponsored by the Rockabilly Hall of Fame. There they got to meet their namesake Dickie "Be-Bop" Harrell. Harrell was Vincent's original drummer and provided the frantic screams on Vincent's signature song "Be Bop a Lula." Three years later, her band's full length album, *Cool Baby*, was released. Seven of the songs are originals, penned by Dughi herself.

Dughi feels very fortunate to share her life and love of rockabilly with her husband Buddy. She commented that "he has evolved into an extremely versatile and influential guitar player who continues to expand his style by always trying something new." They both love playing music. Buddy admitted, "When you are picking and singing, you forget about everything and live for that moment. It is very exciting to play live because you never know what will happen next." One of their most memorable gigs was playing at a car show when Brian Setzer sat in with them.

Even though the Dughis have fans all over the world, they haven't played overseas yet. Their first appearance at a festival was with Suzy Q and her Be-Bop Boys at the Viva Las Vegas Weekender on April 11, 2009. Buddy disclosed, "I think Viva Las Vegas will be a lot of fun, and I think Tom Ingram is a great guy who puts on a great show."

Cari Lee Merritt

Cari Lee and the Saddle-ites were a female led rural boogie band, a mix between hillbilly, western swing, and rockabilly. The group's vocalist Cari Lee Merritt described their sound as "more hillbilly and western swing oriented than straight rockabilly."[41] In this genre, women as front people tend to be a little more under the microscope than men, which can be challenging. Merritt explained, "We will more often be criticized by both music critics and the public. There still aren't a lot of women out there singing rockabilly, so I think they're passed off as little Barbie dolls onstage. Although, I think that's changing quickly. I think the expectation is high, but I also think the delivery is high." Merritt has certainly proved her appeal as both a hillbilly singer and a rhythm and blues temptress. In 2005, she was nominated "Best Female Vocalist of the Year" by the Association of Texas Music.

Cari Lee Merritt was born on August 3, 1970, in San Francisco, California.

At ten years old, she began listening to the syndicated radio program, the *Dr. Demento Show* where they played mostly novelty tunes. She enjoyed it because it was different than the pop music of the 1980s, artists such as Madonna and Michael Jackson. Also as a youngster she found a box of 45 rpm records that her mother listened to when she was a teenager: "It was all 50s pop tunes [which included "The Purple People Eater" by Sheb Wooley and "Why Do Fools Fall in Love" by Frankie Lymon and the Teenagers"], but it was cool to hear what my mom was listening to back then."[42] Her mother was constantly playing a wide variety of music, everything from Creedence Clearwater Revival to B.B. King. In junior high, Merritt developed a love for punk rock bands like the Sex Pistols and Blondie.

When she was about nineteen years old, she started collecting records that were Blue Beat and Jamaican Ska. Merritt recalled, "I started drawing parallels between some of the early Jamaican Ska and some of the American doo wop." Then she got interested in rhythm and blues and jump blues, which led to rockabilly, western swing, and jazz. The first time she heard rhythm and blues queen Ruth Brown's "This Little Girl's Gone Rockin'," she immediately became a fan. Merritt listened for days afterward hoping the disk jockey would play it again since she knew the name of the song but not the artist. When the disk jockey played another Brown song "Mama, He Treats Your Daughter Mean," she visited several record stores looking for records by Brown. Merritt revealed, "They all looked at me like I had just come from Mars."[43] She finally found a shop that could order some of her singles. For Merritt, the music leads to research of their lives: who they are and why they didn't have a hit record? Merritt added, "That whole thing is very fascinating to me. I'm always discovering different records and different artists that I've never heard of before or different takes on the same style of music that it really keeps me interested from contemporary musicians who have various takes on original rockabilly to the old time artists."

Merritt's musical influences include veteran singers Kay Starr, Anita O'Day, Ruth Brown, Wynona Carr, Charlie Feathers, Maddox Brothers and Rose, and Hank Thompson and contemporary musicians the Lucky Stars, Big Sandy, and Martí Brom.

She didn't begin her professional singing career until she was twenty-six years old. Prior to that, she was a catalog and runway model and actress: "The entertainment industry in that aspect for me really turned me off because I witnessed things that quite frankly disgusted me. I decided to quit modeling and quit pursuing any kind of film career." She even had a bit part as an extra in the 1987 movie *The Lost Boys*, also starring Corey Haim and Corey Feldman. Merritt continued with her psychology degree and went into substitute teaching.

In 1992, she met her former husband at a Big Sandy and the Fly-Rite Trio show. Their love of music and the fact that they were both big record collectors brought them together. According to Merritt, "It wasn't until Steve asked me to learn how to play guitar [that I took an interest in singing]. Then I started writing songs, and that was a lot of fun. I don't think it was ever supposed to be anything real serious. I never really expected to even release one album."

Her first appearance in the spotlight occurred at a jam session at Club Deluxe in San Francisco in 1997, where she sang Elvis Presley's "That's All Right." Afterward, she was approached by promoters hoping to book her for other venues, even though she didn't have a band. Luckily for her, the guys she played with that night volunteered and became the Saddle-ites. Originally the lineup included Merritt on vocals and rhythm guitar, her former husband Steve Merritt on lead guitar, Billy Wilson on steel guitar, Rick Quisol on drums, and Brendan Gluek on bass.

A year later, at the Hemsby Weekender, she sang backup for rockabilly legend Glen Glenn: "Jean [wife of guitarist Gary Lambert] was supposed to come up and sing because she was the original vocalist along with her sister on Glen's 'Kathleen' and 'Laurie Ann.' She hadn't sung for fifty years, and she was very nervous. She said 'well, I won't do it unless Cari Lee comes up and does it with me.' I was very honored. It was really amazing. They are such good people."

In 2003, Merritt received the chance of a lifetime when she landed the role of Rose Maddox in the local production of the *Maddox Brothers and Rose: A Rockabilly Revue*. The director, Michael Grice, consulted with the last surviving member of the troupe, fiddle player Don Maddox. It all began when Merritt's former husband was offered a chance to audition: "Steve was playing guitar with another guy who played in the Royal Deuces for a stage show called *The Best Little Whorehouse in Texas*, when the producer of the Maddox Brothers and Rose show asked Steve to audition. Steve asked if he was looking for someone to play Rose, and he was. He encouraged me to pursue it. I guess they had been looking for somebody to fill the part of Rose for about two years." To prepare for the role, she consulted with friends and fans that either knew the Maddox family personally or had seen them in concert, most notably Glenn Mueller, and she also listened to live recordings since there wasn't any film footage to watch. Merritt added, "It was a great experience to do that role. It was a showcase show [in Santa Rosa, California], so it ran for only a month [since they couldn't obtain enough funding to travel with the production]. I got to meet Don Maddox, who is now a good pal of ours, Fred Maddox's widow Kitty and their children and grandchildren. We had a special reception after the opening night." At the reception, she heard a lot of great stories and saw a lot of old photos that the family brought. She also sang some of the family's songs with Maddox, including "George's Playhouse Boogie."

They met again when some record collectors in Tacoma, Oregon, invited the Saddle-ites to play a show for their party. Merritt shared, "Don remembered me. He came out, and we played together. We just had a ball. The next year, we did it again with him. We went out to his ranch, where he raises Angus cattle. I got a great opportunity to meet part of the legend of that group. Don is incredibly funny, and is still very active [even participating in fiddle contests]."

Two years later, Cari Lee and the Saddle-ites appeared on the *Grand Ole Opry* for their plaza party. Little Jimmy Dickens was also on the lineup the evening they appeared. Merritt conveyed, "It was fantastic. Nobody had a rock star attitude, and everyone was treated with respect. The promoter's assistant gave us a complete tour. We got to watch the main show from behind the stage. It was pretty exciting for us." On the stage at the Opry, they have incorporated the Ryman circle from the old stage into the new one: "To be able to stand on the circle, thinking about all of the people who had played and stood there before was a pretty powerful moment, very sentimental."

Also in 2005, Merritt experimented with her rhythm and blues side by issuing a few tunes with the Saddle-ites on their album *The Road Less Traveled* and then releasing *Scorched* under Cari Lee and the Contenders. It was released under the Contenders and not the Saddle-ites so as not to confuse fans. They

Cari Lee and the Saddle-ites in a promotional photo for their 2006 CD ***Brought to You Via Saddle-ite.*** From left: Steve Merritt, Cari Lee Merritt, and Danny Santos (courtesy Cari Lee Merritt).

assembled a band based out of Austin, Texas, to participate. Billy Horton produced the album with a hands-on approach, participating in every aspect of production. Merritt commented, "It was a lot of fun to be able to do something completely different from what I normally do."[44]

To complete her look, most of the time Merritt dresses in vintage clothing: "People are fascinated and curious by it. I get a lot of compliments. It's really not a big deal here in the Bay area because everybody is very individualistic and unique in expressing themselves. I make most of my own stage costumes. I started sewing because I'm so tall, since a lot of the vintage clothing doesn't fit me as well as I'd like them to fit. Plus, I just can't afford a Nudie suit or dresses that cost a few hundred dollars. I just don't have the money for that, so it's much easier for me to just make it. It's a lot of fun. I enjoy it a lot. I usually never make the same item twice." Designing her own outfits gives her the freedom to have unique pieces.

Merritt very rarely sews for other people, but she did make the fuchsia and black dress that Martí Brom wears on the cover of her 2005 release *Sings Heartache Numbers*. Merritt explained, "I made that dress for Martí a couple of years ago as a gift. I hadn't even seen her in it until the album came out. I didn't know whether it would fit her or not. I think she looked great in it."

The Saddle-ites had become a three piece combo by the 2006 release of *Brought to You Via Saddle-ite*. Danny Santos was now on bass. It was Merritt's favorite to record because all the band members were contributing songs, and there were duets between Merritt and Santos as well as Santos singing some tracks on his own. Merritt recalled, "When we recorded it, I had pneumonia. It's fun for me to listen to because there's a lot more to it than just me. I generally don't listen to my own albums. I'd much rather hear somebody else's music than my own."

By March 2008, the Saddle-ites had broken up. During their reign, they toured worldwide, opened for Willie Nelson, Emmylou Harris, and Brooks and Dunn, and appeared on local talk shows as well as the national television show, TV 3, in Spain. After the band's demise, Merritt took a break, vowing to never sing again, instead concentrating on her master's degree in clinical social work and spending more time with her fourteen year old daughter, Evie. Merritt explained, "I had no desire to sing again. I was burned out. There was just too much work involved." Even though she had quit, her booking agent convinced her that she needed to sing again. However, this time around it would be for fun and not as a full time gig. At the end of the year, she reentered the rockabilly scene as a solo artist with a performance at the Sacramento Autorama car show. Currently, she is working with either the Hollywood Combo or J.P. and the Rhythm Chasers and singing a lot more jazz, jump blues, and early rock and roll tunes. For now, the Saddle-ites are defunct, but Merritt hopes to record another Contenders album soon.

Cole

It's difficult to make a living as a contemporary rockabilly artist since it involves constant traveling without much pay. Cole's early shows consisted entirely of rockabilly sets, but he learned to make a decent living as a musician he would have to change his style a bit. Cole explained, "My music is more country rock than anything I suppose, a sound that dwells somewhere in between Nashville and Los Angeles. However, you can always hear the rockabilly influence in everything I do. My roots are rockabilly music. That's probably my favorite music to sing. I cut my teeth on it."[45] His musical journey has allowed him the privilege of befriending many of the biggest names in rockabilly and country music, including Carl Perkins and Ronnie McDowell. Today, he sings and records his own music but hasn't forgotten his rockabilly roots.

Larry Joseph Cole was born on July 5, 1973, in Wyandotte, Michigan. His parents divorced when he was a youngster. His father relocated to Georgia, so Cole spent summer vacations visiting him and the rest of the family in Georgia and East Tennessee. Cole's grandfather introduced him to rockabilly, and most importantly, to artists from the Sun roster: "He had a record called *Original Memphis Rock 'n' Roll, Volume 1*. This record first introduced me to Jerry Lee Lewis, Carl Perkins, Roy Orbison, Charlie Rich, Carl Mann, Billy Lee Riley, Carl McVoy, and Warren Smith. I don't think anything inspires me more than the music that came out of Sun. My grandpa, Ralph Cole, was an artist himself, and my fondest memories are watching and listening to him sing and play his guitar. His favorite music was a lot of those Sun records and early country music, so I grew up on those records. [Cole grew up listening to all kinds of music, so some of his favorite singers range from Ricky Nelson, Marty Robbins, Conway Twitty, Elvis Presley, Johnny Cash, and The Statesmen Quartet, right into the more modern sounds of Marty Stuart, Damien Rice, and Jeff Buckley.] My grandpa's the reason I picked up a guitar in the first place. He passed away in July of 1996, and I so very much wish he could have lived to see and meet all the great rockabilly legends I've had the pleasure to work with [because] he would have loved that."

As far back as Cole can remember, he sang. His earliest childhood memory was at three years old going around the house singing Elvis Presley's "(You're the) Devil in Disguise." While in kindergarten, Cole wrote that he wanted to be a famous recording star when he grew up. At eight years old, he received his first acoustic guitar, and much earlier than that, he had a little plastic guitar that he banged around on. As a teenager, he got more serious about playing. At sixteen years of age, he wrote "Your Precious Love," the first song that he completed and thought was worthy of playing in front of others: "About that time, I also became a member of the Nashville Songwriters' Association."

In 1993, a move to Nashville opened new doors of opportunity. His work at Opryland Duplicating and various record labels introduced him to many executives and stars in the music business. Cole added, "I was still living in Nashville and had made some good contacts at TNN/CMT where I held down a day job. It was through that association that I was able to sing one of my songs on that sacred stage [at the *Grand Ole Opry*]. There's a lot of truth behind knowing the right people and being in the right place at the right time."

Two of the stars who gave a boost to Cole's fledgling career were Ronnie McDowell and Carl Perkins. Cole explained, "I was a young guy and a big fan of Ronnie's when I went to see him on November 13, 1992, in Capac, Michigan. I'll never forget it because it was there that Ronnie asked me to join him in song for the first time and unbeknownst to him this was my first time singing in front of such a large audience. The incredible response his audience gave me that night gave me a major push to follow my musical dreams. After that, Ronnie would always have me sing when he saw me at his shows. It was a huge thrill for me, and even though I don't have the pleasure of seeing Ronnie much these days, I will forever be grateful for [the times] when he would let me sing at his concerts."

Cole had this to say about his friend Carl Perkins: "I met Carl a few years before I first shared a stage with him. I had told some promoters when Carl Perkins comes to town, let me know because I would sure love to open for him. Well, one day the opportunity came along. I was a teenager, and I had the pleasure of opening a few of his shows. My very first agent, Joe Rzeppa, was a great help to my career early on, and the one who first booked me with Carl Perkins and Jason D. Williams. Joe also coined my nickname at the time the 'Rockabilly Songbird.' I kept in touch [with Carl] until his untimely passing. Working with Carl was a big highlight for me and kind of a surreal moment. He was always so kind to me and definitely the coolest rockabilly cat that has or will ever walk this Earth. He was extremely pleasant, very informative and helpful to young aspiring artists like me. I miss him to this day."

Perkins and McDowell were cited as Cole's early musical influences along with Conway Twitty, Jerry Lee Lewis, Johnny Cash, and Charlie Rich. However, Elvis Presley ranked at #1: "Elvis changed my life. It got no cooler than Elvis."

Even though Presley's music is often sung in Cole's set, he is strictly a fan and not an impersonator. Cole admitted, "I think a lot of the Elvis influence obviously spilled over into my singing and my style. I used to get told that I looked like Vince Gill or Donny Osmond but sound like Elvis. I've been told a few times that I sound just like Elvis, and while that's always a compliment, I want to sound like myself and for people to know me for my music. It's so important for aspiring talents to follow the paths of those that came before them only long enough to develop as an artist, and then before it's too late, jump off that nicely paved course and blaze their own trail."

Cole has shared the stage with many of his childhood heroes, including James Burton and John Wilkinson from Presley's TCB band, whom he toured with in Sweden in March 2007, The Jordanaires, and W.S. Holland, who originally played drums with Carl Perkins and then Johnny Cash. He has also performed alongside Presley's original guitarist Scotty Moore, drummer D.J. Fontana, and bass singer Ray Walker of the Jordanaires at the Melkweg Theater in Amsterdam, Holland.

Incidentally, The Jordanaires and Millie Kirkham were featured on Cole's first CD, *Lost in Blue Dreams* as well as a Christmas song "Merry Blue Christmas," that he wrote and released: "I have always been a big fan of theirs and very proud to call them friends." On *Lost in Blue Dreams*, they were able to duplicate the 1960s sound, similar to Roy Orbison's recordings for Monument Records: "That's exactly what I was looking to achieve with that project."

Early in his career, Cole opened several shows for Carl Perkins (courtesy Larry Cole).

Today, Cole still incorporates rockabilly into his live shows with songs by Presley, Conway Twitty, Jack Scott, Johnny Cash, and Carl Perkins, but he concentrates on singing his own material. 2009 marked Cole's tenth straight year performing at the rockabilly festival in Jackson with his brother Adam on drums: "We always have a good time in Jackson. It's a very cool event, bringing together many rockabilly legends."

In August 2005 at the Carl Perkins Civic Center, former home of the rockabilly festival in Jackson, Cole got a pleasant surprise when Carl Mann joined him onstage at rehearsal: "I've always been a big fan of Carl Mann's 'Mona Lisa,' in fact it's one of my all-time favorite rockabilly tunes. He walked in, and my band and I started playing 'Mona Lisa.' He stepped onto the stage, and next thing you know he put his guitar around his neck, and he was singing along with us. We ran through a pretty rockin' version, probably one of the best versions I heard him do. It was a big thrill for me. Carl is a good guy, and I'm glad to see him performing again." Cole's name appeared on the billboard with Mann and Narvel Felts: "I'm proud to have been in that grand company."

A year later, Cole became the youngest inductee into the International Rockabilly Hall of Fame, which is located in Jackson, Tennessee: "They presented me with a beautiful plaque that hangs in my music room. I'm very proud of this honor."

Also, in 2006, he released the CD, *Cole* and a video to accompany the single "Rock My Soul."

Cole tours extensively over in Europe and Asia, including Holland, Germany, Denmark, and Sweden. In 2005, he played for a month straight in Taipei, Taiwan. He commented, "I love the overseas shows."

His fans are very important to him. In fact, he regards his fans as family, and he appreciates the fact that they are so loyal by continuing to support him and his musical endeavors: "I truly do have the greatest fans in the world, and I'm very fortunate for that." He has a fan club, ran by RMS Music, that issues online newsletters to keep Cole's fans updated on tour dates and latest releases. Cole added, "My first fan club president was Karen Vanness, and the club was headquartered in Bay City, Michigan. Karen and her husband Ed were very helpful to me early on, and I'll forever be grateful."

Besides being a musician, he is also a fan at heart. Cole has had the opportunity to either work with or meet some of the biggest names in the industry [view his photo gallery at http://www.rockncole.com]. He is good friends with rock and roll legend, Jack Scott: "Jack is a buddy of mine. He's a super warm sweet guy who attends my shows when I play in his area. I do a version of 'The Way I Walk.' It's my favorite song that Jack ever wrote and recorded. He digs my version, or so I hope. I change it up a little bit. I've always wanted to coax him into recording a duet [of it]." At a show in Las Vegas, Chuck Berry once sang "Happy Birthday" to Cole. He also hung out backstage with Berry, and there were several photos taken of Cole with the legendary rhythm and blues singer. Cole disclosed, "That was a big thrill." His experience with seeing Jerry Lee Lewis in concert was also awe-inspiring: "First time I saw Jerry Lee was in 1996 at the Ryman Auditorium in Nashville. He was so incredible that night. He had a gold lame jacket on, and James Burton was up there with him. He tore the house down, did all his songs and was in perfect voice. It was like the greatest rock and roll concert extending back to 1957, a magical experience."

Cole also collects music memorabilia. He has an extensive record collection as well as a few autographs. He has also amassed quite a bit of video footage, mostly of classic country artists, Elvis Presley and Johnny Cash. One of his prized possessions is a Peavey electric guitar, signed by Scotty Moore, Carl Perkins, and James Burton: "I treasure that."

In 2009, Cole laid down tracks for a famous show in Las Vegas called *La Femme*: "Within the show, entertainer Paul Grant does a respectful and fun tribute to Elvis, with a character he created called Elfis, and he hired me to do the Elvis vocals for a track they needed. It's been so long since I've tried to put on my Elvis voice, but it came out eerily dead on and was a lot of fun." He often performs shows in Las Vegas, where he currently resides. With two album releases and fan popularity, Cole continues to achieve his musical aspirations as an upcoming rising star.

Chapter Notes

Chapter One

1. Sonny Burgess, phone interview by Sheree Homer, 2 August 2006. All quotes that follow are from the same interview.
2. Colin Escott, and Martin Hawkins, *Good Rockin' Tonight: Sun Records and the Birth of Rock 'n' Roll* (New York: St. Martin's, 1991), 186.
3. *Ibid.*
4. "Ray Smith," Rockabilly Hall of Fame, http://www.rockabillyhall.com/RaySmith.html, accessed March 10, 2008.
5. Adriaan Sturm, "The Ray Smith Story," *Record Exchanger*, 1982, 10.
6. Stanley Walker, phone interview by Sheree Homer, 21 March 2008. All quotes that follow are from the same interview.
7. Sturm, 11.
8. "Ray Smith."
9. Ken Burke, "Wix Records and the Legendary Ray Smith," *Original Cool*, December 1998/January 1999, 5.
10. Burke, 6.
11. Narvel Felts, phone interview by Sheree Homer, 6 March 2008. All quotes that follow are from the same interview.
12. Burke, 4.
13. Sturm, 12.
14. Howard and Tommie Wix, "Ray Smith," *New Kommotion*, 1978, 12.
15. Hayden Thompson, phone interview by Sheree Homer, 20 November 2007. All quotes that follow are from the same interview, unless otherwise noted.
16. Martin Hawkins, liner notes for Hayden Thompson, *The Sun Years Plus Rock-A-Billy Gal* (Bear Family Records, 2008), 11.
17. Ken Burke, "Hayden Thompson: The Rockabilly Gentleman," *Blue Suede News*, Fall 2007, 17.
18. Hawkins, 19.
19. Burke, 20.
20. *Ibid.*, 18.
21. Hawkins, 35.
22. Ken Burke, "Hayden Thompson: The Rockabilly Gentleman, Pt. 2," *Blue Suede News*, Winter 2007, 20–21.
23. *Ibid.*, 22.
24. Dickey Lee, phone interview by Sheree Homer, 8 August 2006. All quotes that follow are from the same interview.
25. Ed Bruce, phone interview by Sheree Homer, 4 September 2006. All quotes that follow are from the same interview.
26. Colin Escott, liner notes for Carl Mann, *Mona Lisa* (Bear Family Records, 1994), 10.
27. Carl Mann, phone interview by Sheree Homer, 26 August 2006. All quotes that follow are from the same interview, unless otherwise noted.
28. Escott, 2.
29. *Ibid.*, 9.
30. "Revisiting Carl Mann's Rockabilly Roots," HenryCountian.com, http://host1.bondware.com/~henrycountian/news.php?viewStory=271, accessed April 2, 2009.
31. Johnny Powers, phone interview by Sheree Homer, 16 October 2004. All quotes that follow are from the same interview, unless otherwise noted.
32. "Johnny Powers, Long Blond Hair," Blackcat Rockabilly Europe, http://www.rockabilly.nl/artists/jpowers.htm, accessed April 6, 2009.
33. *Ibid.*
34. Liner notes for Johnny Powers, *Long Blond Hair* (Norton, 1993).
35. *Ibid.*
36. *Ibid.*
37. Jack Earls, phone interview by Sheree

Homer, 9 April 2009. All quotes that follow are from the same interview.
38. Bruce Eder, "Jack Earls: Biography," All Music Guide, http://www.allmusic.com/cg/amg.dll?p=amg&sql=11:jiftxqe5ldhe~T1, accessed April 8, 2009.
39. *Ibid.*

Chapter Two

1. Portions of this profile appeared in Sheree Homer, "Let's Have a Party with Wanda Jackson," *Rockabilly Revue*, March 2004. Phone interview by Sheree Homer with Wanda Jackson conducted March 24, 2004. All quotes that follow are from the same interview, unless otherwise noted.
2. Dr. Ken Haskins, *Reminiscing with Music Legends: Radio Interviews, Volume 1*, (Carson City, NV: Rockin' Rev, 2007), 149.
3. *Ibid.*, 151.
4. Bob Sullivan, phone interview by Sheree Homer, 20 November 2006. All quotes that follow are from the same interview.
5. James Kirkland, phone interview by Sheree Homer, 24 July 2006. All quotes that follow are from the same interview, unless otherwise noted.
6. Horace Logan with Bill Sloan, *Elvis, Hank, and Me: Making Musical History on the Louisiana Hayride* (New York: St. Martin's, 1998), 178.
7. Hank Davis, liner notes for Bob Luman, *Let's Think About Living: His Recordings 1955–1967* (Bear Family Records, 2006), 8.
8. Portions of this profile appeared in Sheree Homer, "James Kirkland: The Triple Slap Cat is Back!" *Blue Suede News*, Summer 2008. Phone interview by Sheree Homer with James Kirkland conducted July 24, 2006.
9. Logan, 178.
10. Davis, 30.
11. Craig Morrison, *Go Cat Go! Rockabilly Music and Its Makers* (Urbana and Chicago: University of Illinois Press, 1996), 161.
12. Ken Burke, "The Last of the Maddox Brothers: The Don Maddox Interview," *Roctober*, Winter 2006, 22.
13. *Ibid.*, 24.
14. Don Maddox, phone interview by Sheree Homer, 4 August 2006. All quotes that follow are from the same interview, unless otherwise noted.
15. Mary A. Bufwack and Robert K. Oermann, *Finding Her Voice: The Saga of Women in Country Music* (New York: Crown, 1993), 127.
16. *Ibid.*
17. Bob Sullivan, phone interview by Sheree Homer, 20 November 2006. All quotes that follow are from the same interview.
18. Irwin Stambler and Grelun Landon, *Country Music: The Encyclopedia* (New York: St. Martin's, 2000), 277.
19. Burke, 26.
20. Bufwack, 129.
21. *Ibid.*, 128.
22. Barry McCloud, ed., *Definitive Country: The Ultimate Encyclopedia of Country Music and Its Performers* (New York: Perigeé, 1995), 497.
23. "Cousin Brucie" Morrow with Rich Maloof, *Doo Wop: The Music, the Times, the Era* (New York: Sterling, 2007), 227.
24. Ronnie Smith, phone interview by Sheree Homer, 3 January 2008. All quotes that follow are from the same interview.
25. *Ibid.*
26. Ken Burke and Dan Griffin, *The Blue Moon Boys: The Story of Elvis Presley's Band* (Chicago: Chicago Review, 2006), 12.
27. Peter Guralnick, *Last Train to Memphis: The Rise of Elvis Presley* (Boston: Little Brown, 1994), 63.
28. James Miller, *Flowers in the Dustbin: The Rise of Rock and Roll 1947–1977* (New York: Simon and Schuster, 1999), 72.
29. Burke.
30. Guralnick, 94.
31. Burke, 17.
32. Colin Escott, *The Grand Ole Opry: The Making of an American Icon* (New York: Center Street, 2006), 127.
33. Bob Sullivan, phone interview by Sheree Homer, 20 November 2006. All quotes that follow are from the same interview.
34. Guralnick, 179.
35. *Elvis 56*, prod. and dir. Alan Raymond and Susan Raymond, 61 min., Warner Bros., 1999, DVD.

Chapter Three

1. Larry Donn, phone interview by Sheree Homer, 4 August 2006. All quotes that follow are from the same interview.
2. Tom Lincoln and Dick Blackburn, *Guide to Rare Rockabilly and Rock 'n' Roll 45 RPMs* (self-published, 1998), 20.

3. Portions of this profile appeared in Sheree Homer, "Cupp's a Long Gone Daddy," *Rockabilly Revue*, July 2004. Email interview by Sheree Homer with Pat Cupp conducted on September 23, 2003. All quotes that follow are from the same interview, unless otherwise noted.

4. "Pat Cupp," Rockabilly Hall of Fame, http://www.rockabillyhall.com/patcupp.html, accessed January 15, 2009.

5. Steve Handford, phone interview by Sheree Homer, 29 February 2008. All quotes that follow are from the same interview.

6. Ian Wallis, liner notes for Bobby Lee Trammell, *You Mostest Girl* (Bear Family Records, 1995).

7. Ibid.

8. Dik de Heer, "Bobby Lee Trammell: This is My Story," Black Cat Rockabilly Europe, http://www.rockabilly.nl/references/messages/bobby_lee_trammell.htm, accessed February 6, 2009.

9. Wallis.

10. "Bobby Lee Trammell," Wikipedia, http://en.wikipedia.org/wiki/Bobby_Lee_Trammell, accessed February 6, 2009.

11. De Heer.

12. Joe Lee, phone interview by Sheree Homer, 10 March 2008. All quotes that follow are from the same interview.

13. Jimmy Payne, phone interview by Sheree Homer, 14 December 2008. All quotes that follow are from the same interview.

14. De Heer.

15. Ronnie Hawkins, phone interview by Sheree Homer, 19 April 2004. All quotes that follow are from the same interview.

16. "The Band," Wikipedia, http://en.wikipedia.org/wiki/The_Band, accessed April 13, 2009.

Chapter Four

1. Portions of this profile appeared in Sheree Homer, "Chirping with The Crickets," *Rockabilly Revue*, December 2003. In person interview by Sheree Homer with Jerry Allison conducted July 11, 2002. All quotes that follow are from the same interview, unless otherwise noted.

2. *The Real Buddy Holly Story*, prod. and dir. Paul McCartney, 1 hr. 40 min., BBC, 1984, videocassette.

3. Ibid.

4. Portions of this profile appeared in Sheree Homer, "Chirping with The Crickets," *Rockabilly Revue*, December 2003. In person interview by Sheree Homer with Sonny Curtis conducted July 11, 2002. All quotes that follow are from the same interview, unless otherwise noted.

5. *The Real Buddy Holly Story*.

6. Sonny West, phone interview by Sheree Homer, 9 August 2006. All quotes that follow are from the same interview.

7. Portions of this profile appeared in Sheree Homer, "Chirping with The Crickets," *Rockabilly Revue*, December 2003. In person interview by Sheree Homer with Joe B. Mauldin conducted July 11, 2002. All quotes that follow are from the same interview.

8. "Niki Sullivan," Wikipedia, http://en.wikipedia.org/wiki/Niki_Sullivan, accessed October 18, 2008.

9. *The Real Buddy Holly Story*.

10. "Niki Sullivan."

11. *The Real Buddy Holly Story*.

12. "Niki Sullivan."

13. Craig Morrison, *Go Cat Go! Rockabilly Music and Its Makers* (Urbana and Chicago: University of Illinois Press, 1996), 148–149.

14. Tom Lincoln and Dick Blackburn, *Guide to Rare Rockabilly and Rock 'n' Roll 45 RPMs* (self-published, 1998), 75.

15. Sonny West, phone interview by Sheree Homer, 9 August 2006. All quotes that follow are from the same interview.

16. Tom Lincoln and Dick Blackburn, *Guide to Rare Rockabilly and Rock 'n' Roll 45 RPMs* (self-published, 1998), 75.

17. Gene Summers, phone interview by Sheree Homer, 29 November 2002. All quotes that follow are from the same interview.

18. Bob Solly, *Record Collector 100 Greatest Rock 'n' Roll Records* (London: Diamond, 2005), 142–143.

19. Lew Williams, phone interview by Sheree Homer, 13 December 2007. All quotes that follow are from the same interview.

20. Tony Wilkinson, "Biography of Huelyn Duvall," http://www.huelynduvall.com/biography.htm, accessed April 9, 2009.

21. Huelyn Duvall, phone interview by Sheree Homer, 3 March 2004. All quotes that follow are from the same interview.

22. Johnny Vallis, "Huelyn Duvall," Rockabilly Hall of Fame, http://www.rockabillyhall.com/HuelynDuvall1.html, accessed April 9, 2009.

Chapter Five

1. Phillip Bashe, *Teenage Idol/Travelin' Man: The Complete Biography of Rick Nelson* (New York: Hyperion, 1992), 41.
2. Ibid., 25.
3. James Miller, *Flowers in the Dustbin: The Rise of Rock and Roll 1947–1977* (New York: Simon and Schuster, 1999), 140.
4. Bashe, 64.
5. James Kirkland, phone interview by Sheree Homer, 18 November 2006. All quotes that follow are from the same interview, unless otherwise noted.
6. Bashe, 94.
7. Steve Fishell, "James Burton," *Guitar Player*, June 1984.
8. Craig Morrison, *Go Cat Go! Rockabilly Music and Its Makers* (Urbana and Chicago: University of Illinois Press, 1996), 176.
9. Jack Ellena, phone interview by Sheree Homer, 6 February 2008. All quotes that follow are from the same interview.
10. Todd Everett, liner notes for Ricky Nelson, *The American Dream: The Complete Imperial and Verve Recordings 1957–1962* (Bear Family Records, 2001), 23.
11. Bashe, 75.
12. Joel Selvin, *Idol for a Generation* (Chicago: Contemporary, 1990), 83.
13. Steve Stevens, email interview by Sheree Homer, 18 December 2007. All quotes that follow are from the same interview.
14. Colin Escott, liner notes for Ricky Nelson, *Legacy* (Capitol Records, 2000), 8–9.
15. Richie Frost, phone interview by Sheree Homer, 3 February 2008. All quotes that follow are from the same interview.
16. Miller, 142.
17. Steve Fishell, "James Burton," *Guitar Player*, June 1984.
18. Portions of this profile appeared in Sheree Homer, "James Kirkland: The Triple Slap Cat Is Back!" *Blue Suede News*, Summer 2008. Phone interview by Sheree Homer with James Kirkland conducted July 24, 2006. All quotes that follow are from the same interview, unless otherwise noted.
19. Bashe, 91.
20. Pericles Alexander, "High Water Not Enough to Deter Nelson Fans," *The Shreveport Times*, 27 April 1958.
21. Homer, 15.
22. Bashe, 107.
23. Portions of this profile appeared in Sheree Homer, "Mercy, You Gotta Love the Collins Kids," *Rockabilly Revue*, May 2003. In-person interview by Sheree Homer with Lorrie Collins conducted July 9, 2002. All quotes that follow are from the same interview, unless otherwise noted.
24. Colin Escott, liner notes for The Collins Kids, *The Rockin'est* (Bear Family Records, 1997).
25. Mary A. Bufwack and Robert K. Oermann, *Finding Her Voice: The Saga of Women in Country Music* (New York: Crown, 1993), 229.
26. Portions of this profile appeared in Sheree Homer, "Mercy, You Gotta Love the Collins Kids," *Rockabilly Revue*, May 2003. In-person interview by Sheree Homer with Larry Collins conducted July 9, 2002. All quotes that follow are from the same interview, unless otherwise noted.
27. Dr. Ken Haskins, *Reminiscing with Music Legends: Radio Interviews, Volume 1* (Carson City, NV: Rockin' Rev, 2007), 65.
28. Escott.
29. Bufwack, 230.
30. Haskins, 68.
31. Bufwack, 230.
32. Glen Glenn, phone interview by Sheree Homer, 4 April 2003.
33. Ken Burke, "Mr. Everybody's Movin': The Glen Glenn Interview," *Brutarian Quarterly*, Winter 2008, 23.
34. Glen Glenn, phone interview by Sheree Homer, 12 March 2009. All quotes that follow are from the same interview, unless otherwise noted.
35. Glen Glenn, phone interview by Sheree Homer, 4 April 2003.
36. Glen Glenn, phone interview by Sheree Homer, 20 July 2006.
37. Glen Glenn, phone interview by Sheree Homer, 4 April 2003.
38. Glen Glenn, phone interview by Sheree Homer, 20 July 2006.
39. Ibid.
40. Ibid.
41. Ibid.
42. Ibid.
43. Glen Glenn, phone interview by Sheree Homer, 4 April 2003.

Chapter Six

1. Rocky Burnette, phone interview by Sheree Homer, 28 February 2008.

2. Portions of this profile appeared in Sheree Homer, "Musical Memories with Burlison and Burnette," *Rockabilly Revue*, December 2002. In-person interview by Sheree Homer with Paul Burlison conducted July 11, 2002. All quotes that follow are from the same interview.
3. Burnette.
4. *Ibid.*
5. Craig Morrison, *Go Cat Go! Rockabilly Music and Its Makers* (Urbana and Chicago: University of Illinois Press, 1996), 104.
6. Portions of this profile appeared in Sheree Homer, "Musical Memories with Burlison and Burnette," *Rockabilly Revue*, December 2002. In-person interview by Sheree Homer with Rocky Burnette conducted July 12, 2002. All quotes that follow are from the same interview, unless otherwise noted.
7. Morrison, 106.
8. Tony Austin, phone interview by Sheree Homer, 15 August 2006. All quotes that follow are from the same interview.
9. Rocky Burnette, phone interview by Sheree Homer, 28 February 2008.
10. *Ibid.*
11. *Ibid.*
12. Narvel Felts, phone interview by Sheree Homer, 23 August 2006. All quotes that follow are from the same interview.
13. Tom Lincoln, and Dick Blackburn, *Guide to Rare Rockabilly and Rock 'n' Roll 45 RPMs* (self-published, 1998), 1.
14. Art Adams, phone interview by Sheree Homer, 19 August 2006. All quotes that follow are from the same interview.
15. Larry Goshen with Art Adams, *Rock Crazy Baby: Rockabilly Legend; The Art Adams Story* (Indianapolis: Mentzer, 2006), 13.
16. Laura Lee Perkins, phone interview by Sheree Homer, 14 October 2004. All quotes that follow are from the same interview, unless otherwise noted.
17. Ivan Helfman, "Rockabilly Revival Profile: Laura Lee Perkins Records a New CD," *The Gazette*, 3 August 2006, p. 1.
18. *Ibid.*, 2.
19. *Ibid.*
20. *Ibid.*
21. Vernon Sandusky, phone interview by Sheree Homer, 9 December 2008. All quotes that follow are from the same interview.
22. Big Al Downing, phone interview by Sheree Homer, 29 April 2004. All quotes that follow are from the same interview, unless otherwise noted.
23. Ken Burke, *Country Music Changed My Life: Tales of Tough Times and Triumph from Country's Legends* (Chicago: Chicago Review, 2004), 21.
24. Bobby Poe, phone interview by Sheree Homer, 11 December 2008. All quotes that follow are from the same interview.
25. "Big Al Downing: Biography," Big Al Downing, official homepage, http://www.bigaldowning.com/int/content/view/3/30/, accessed February 16, 2009.
26. *Ibid.*
27. "Al Downing (musician)," Wikipedia, http://en.wikipedia.org/wiki/Al_Downing_(musician), accessed February 16, 2009.
28. Craig Morrison, *Go Cat Go! Rockabilly Music and Its Makers* (Urbana and Chicago: University of Illinois Press, 1996), 221.
29. Charlie Gracie, phone interview by Sheree Homer, 4 April 2003. All quotes that follow are from the same interview.
30. "Charlie Gracie," Wikipedia, http://en.wikipedia.org/wiki/Charlie_Gracie, accessed March 30, 2009.

Chapter Seven

1. Martí Brom, phone interview by Sheree Homer, 24 August 2006. All quotes that follow are from the same interview.
2. Ken Burke, "Martí Brom Biography," Musician Guide, http://www.musicianguide.com/biographies/1608003923/Marti-Brom.html, accessed February 22, 2008.
3. Mark Parcy, "Let's Hear It Once Again for Go Cat Go," Planet Jive News, http://thestreet.freeuk.com/planetjive/news4.html, accessed March 1, 2004.
4. Bill Hull, phone interview by Sheree Homer, 15 April 2004. All quotes that follow are from the same interview.
5. Parcy.
6. Wendy LeBeau, liner notes for Go Cat Go, *Let's Hear It Once Again for Go Cat Go* (Vinylux Records, 1998).
7. *Ibid.*
8. Parcy.
9. LeBeau.
10. *Ibid.*
11. Parcy.
12. Fred "Virgil" Turgis, "Wendy and

Lance LeBeau," Jumpin' from 6 to 6, http://www.jumpingfrom6to6.com/itvvinylux.htm, accessed May 13, 2008.

13. Josie Kreuzer, "Biography," http://www.josiekreuzer.com/bio.html, accessed May 20, 2008.

14. Jenny Meyers, "Josie Kreuzer: Not Your Ordinary Pussycat," *SLAMM: San Diego's Music Magazine*, 27 December 2000.

15. Josie Kreuzer, phone interview by Sheree Homer, 22 May 2008. All quotes that follow are from the same interview, unless otherwise noted.

16. Jeff Miers, "Josie Kreuzer," *Buffalo Beat Magazine*, 18 April 1998.

17. Josie Kreuzer, "Biography."

18. J. Austin Duke, "Jive Talkin' with Josie Kreuzer: The Hot Rod Girl," http://www.jaustinduke.net/interviews/josiekreuzer.pdf, accessed May 13, 2008.

19. Josie Kreuzer, "Biography."

20. Fred "Virgil" Turgis, "Josie Kreuzer," Jumpin' from 6 to 6, http://www.jumpingfrom6to6.com/itvkreuzer.htm, accessed May 13, 2008.

21. Miers.

22. "Dave and Deke Combo: *There's Nothing Like an Old Hillbilly* Review," CD Baby, http://cdbaby.com/cd/davedeke, accessed January 19, 2009.

23. Fred "Virgil" Turgis, "Dave Stuckey," Jumpin' from 6 to 6, http://www.jumpingfrom6to6.com/itvstuck.htm, accessed May 13, 2008.

24. *Ibid.*

25. Dave Stuckey, phone interview by Sheree Homer, 3 August 2006. All quotes that follow are from the same interview, unless otherwise noted.

26. Ken Burke, "Deke Dickerson Biography," Contemporary Musicians, http://www.enotes.com/contemporary-musicians/dickerson-deke-biography, accessed January 19, 2009.

27. *Ibid.*

28. Deke Dickerson, email interview by Sheree Homer, 31 March 2004. All quotes that follow are from the same interview, unless otherwise noted.

29. Ken Burke, "Deke Dickerson Biography."

30. Jon Johnson, "It's High Noon for High Noon," Country Standard Time, http://countrystandardtime.com/d/article.asp?fn=highnoon.asp, accessed February 13, 2009.

31. Shaun Young, email interview by Sheree Homer, 13 February 2009. All quotes that follow are from the same interview.

32. Sean Mencher, phone interview by Sheree Homer, 22 August 2006. All quotes that follow are from the same interview.

33. Tex Rubinowitz, email interview by Sheree Homer, 14 March 2009. All quotes that follow are from the same interview.

Chapter Eight

1. Howard A. DeWitt, "Kim Lenz: The Texas Wildcat," *Blue Suede News*, Summer 1998, 24.

2. Kim Lenz, phone interview by Sheree Homer, 20 January 2008. All quotes that follow are from the same interview, unless otherwise noted.

3. DeWitt, 24.

4. *Ibid.*

5. *Ibid.*, 23.

6. Caroline Gnagy, phone interview by Sheree Homer, 11 November 2007. All quotes that follow are from the same interview.

7. Rachel Fenton, phone interview by Sheree Homer, 14 August 2006. All quotes that follow are from the same interview.

8. Carl Sonny Leyland, phone interview by Sheree Homer, 8 August 2006. All quotes that follow are from the same interview.

9. Eddie Clendening, email interview by Sheree Homer, 13 February 2008.

10. J. Austin Duke, "Jive Talkin' with Eddie Clendening: The Rage of the Teenage," http://www.jaustinduke.net/interviews/eddie.pdf, accessed May 13, 2008.

11. Eddie Clendening, email interview.

12. Portions of this profile appeared in Sheree Homer, "Clendening Leaves Audiences All Shook Up," *Rockabilly Revue*, July 2003. Phone interview by Sheree Homer with Eddie Clendening conducted June 5, 2003. All quotes that follow are from the same interview, unless otherwise noted.

13. Eddie Clendening, email interview.

14. *Ibid.*

15. Duke.

16. Eddie Clendening, email interview.

17. *Ibid.*

18. *Ibid.*

19. *Ibid.*

20. Portions of this profile appeared in Sheree Homer, "Introducing Portuguese Rockabilly Kitten: Miss Ruby Ann," *Blue Suede News*, Fall 2006. Email interview by Sheree Homer with Ruby Ann conducted

September 10, 2006. All quotes that follow are from the same interview, unless otherwise noted.

21. Dave "Long Tall" Phisel and Fred "Virgil" Turgis, "Ruby Ann," Jumpin' from 6 to 6, http://www.jumpingfrom6to6.com/itvrubyann.htm, accessed May 13, 2008.

22. *Ibid.*
23. *Ibid.*
24. *Ibid.*

25. Sue Moreno, email interview by Sheree Homer, 8 October 2006. All quotes that follow are from the same interview.

26. "Dawn Shipley and the Sharp Shooters Biography," http://www.dawnshipley.com/bio.htm, accessed January 20, 2009.

27. "Dawn Shipley and the Sharp Shooters Press," http://www.dawnshipley.com/press.htm, accessed January 20, 2009.

28. Dawn Shipley, phone interview by Sheree Homer, 7 October 2004. All quotes that follow are from the same interview, unless otherwise noted.

29. Dawn Shipley, email interview by Sheree Homer, 18 May 2008.

30. *Ibid.*
31. *Ibid.*
32. *Ibid.*

33. "Dawn Shipley and the Sharp Shooters Biography."

34. Dawn Shipley, email interview.

35. Dave "Long Tall" Phisel and Fred "Virgil" Turgis, "Dawn Shipley," Jumpin' from 6 to 6, http://www.jumpingfrom6to6.com/itvshipley.htm, accessed May, 13, 2008.

36. Buddy Dughi, email interview by Sheree Homer, 10 February 2009. All quotes that follow are from the same interview, unless otherwise noted.

37. Fred "Virgil" Turgis, "Buddy and Suzy Dughi," Jumpin' from 6 to 6, http://www.jumpingfrom6to6.com/itvbuddy_suzy.htm, accessed February 10, 2009.

38. *Ibid.*
39. *Ibid.*

40. Portions of this profile appeared in Sheree Homer, "Rockin' with Suzy Q," *Blue Suede News*, Spring 2007. Email interview by Sheree Homer with Suzy Dughi conducted March 3, 2007. All quotes that follow are from the same interview.

41. Cari Lee Merritt, phone interview by Sheree Homer, 21 February 2009. All quotes that follow are from the same interview, unless otherwise noted.

42. Fred "Virgil" Turgis, "Cari Lee," Jumpin' from 6 to 6, http://www.jumpingfrom6to6.com/itvcarilee.htm, accessed May 13, 2008.

43. *Ibid.*
44. *Ibid.*

45. Larry Cole, phone interview by Sheree Homer, 5 May 2004. All quotes that follow are from the same interview.

Bibliography

Interviews by the Author

Adams, Art. 19 August 2006.
Allison, Jerry. 11 July 2002. Portions published in *Rockabilly Revue*, December 2003, pp. 3–7.
Austin, Tony. 15 August 2006.
Brom, Martí. 24 August 2006.
Bruce, Ed. 4 September 2006.
Burgess, Sonny. 2 August 2006.
Burlison, Paul. 11 July 2002. Portions published in *Rockabilly Revue*, December 2002, pp. 3–10.
Burnette, Rocky. 12 July 2002. Portions published in *Rockabilly Revue*, December 2002, pp. 3–10.
Burnette, Rocky. 28 February 2008.
Clendening, Eddie. 5 June 2003. Portions published in *Rockabilly Revue*, July 2003, pp. 11–13. Also, 13 February 2008.
Cole, Larry. 5 May 2004.
Collins, Larry. 9 July 2002. Portions published in *Rockabilly Revue*, May 2003, pp. 3–7.
Collins, Lorrie. 9 July 2002. Portions published in *Rockabilly Revue*, May 2003, pp. 3–7.
Cupp, Pat. 23 September 2003. Portions published in *Rockabilly Revue*, July 2004, pp. 3–7.
Curtis, Sonny. 11 July 2002. Portions published in *Rockabilly Revue*, December 2003, pp. 3–7.
Dickerson, Deke. 31 March 2004.
Donn, Larry. 4 August 2006.
Downing, Big Al. 29 April 2004.
Dughi, Buddy. 10 February 2009.
Dughi, Suzy. 3 March 2007. Portions published in *Blue Suede News*, Spring 2007, pp. 18–19.
Duvall, Huelyn. 3 March 2004.
Earls, Jack. 9 April 2009.
Ellena, Jack. 6 February 2008.
Felts, Narvel. 23 August 2006 and 6 March 2008.
Fenton, Rachel. 14 August 2006.
Frost, Richie. 3 February 2008.
Glenn, Glen. 4 April 2003, 20 July 2006 and 12 March 2009.
Gnagy, Caroline. 11 November 2007.
Gracie, Charlie. 4 April 2003.
Handford, Steve. 29 February 2008.
Hawkins, Ronnie. 19 April 2004.
Hull, Bill. 15 April 2004.
Jackson, Wanda. 24 March 2004. Portions published in *Rockabilly Revue*, March 2004, pp. 3–7.
Kirkland, James. 24 July 2006. Portions published in *Blue Suede News*, Summer 2008, pp. 14–16. Also, 18 November 2006.
Kreuzer, Josie. 22 May 2008.
Lee, Dickey. 8 August 2006.
Lee, Joe. 10 March 2008.
Lenz, Kim. 20 January 2008.
Leyland, Carl Sonny. 8 August 2006.
Maddox, Don. 4 August 2006.
Mann, Carl. 26 August 2006.
Mauldin, Joe. B. 11 July 2002. Portions published in *Rockabilly Revue*, December 2003, pp. 3–7.
Mencher, Sean. 22 August 2006.
Merritt, Cari Lee. 21 February 2009.
Moreno, Sue. 8 October 2006.
Payne, Jimmy. 14 December 2008.
Perkins, Laura Lee. 14 October 2004.
Poe, Bobby. 11 December 2008.
Powers, Johnny. 16 October 2004.
Rubinowitz, Tex. 14 March 2009.
Ruby Ann. 10 September 2006. Portions published in *Blue Suede News*, Fall 2006, pp. 28–29.
Sandusky, Vernon. 9 December 2008.

Shipley, Dawn. 7 October 2004 and 18 May 2008.
Smith, Ronnie. 3 January 2008.
Stevens, Steve. 18 December 2007.
Stuckey, Dave. 3 August 2006.
Sullivan, Bob. 20 November 2006.
Summers, Gene. 29 November 2002.
Thompson, Hayden. 20 November 2007.
Walker, Stanley. 21 March 2008.
West, Sonny. 9 August 2006.
Williams, Lew. 13 December 2007.
Young, Shaun. 13 February 2009.

Books

Bashe, Phillip. *Teenage Idol/Travelin' Man: The Complete Biography of Rick Nelson.* New York: Hyperion, 1992.
Bufwack, Mary A., and Robert K. Oermann. *Finding Her Voice: The Saga of Women in Country Music.* New York: Crown, 1993.
Burke, Ken. *Country Music Changed My Life: Tales of Tough Times and Triumph from Country Legends.* Chicago: Chicago Review, 2004.
_____ and Dan Griffin. *The Blue Moon Boys: The Story of Elvis Presley's Band.* Chicago: Chicago Review, 2006.
Escott, Colin. *The Grand Ole Opry: The Making of an American Icon.* New York: Center Street, 2006.
_____ and Martin Hawkins. *Good Rockin' Tonight: Sun Records and the Birth of Rock 'n' Roll.* New York: St. Martin's, 1991.
Goshen, Larry, with Art Adams. *Rock Crazy Baby, Rockabilly Legend: The Art Adams Story.* Indianapolis: Mentzer, 2006.
Guralnick, Peter. *Last Train to Memphis: The Rise of Elvis Presley.* Boston: Little Brown, 1994.
Haskins, Dr. Ken. *Reminiscing with Music Legend: Radio Interviews, Volume 1.* Carson City, NV: Rockin' Rev, 2007.
Lincoln, Tom, and Dick Blackburn. *Guide to Rare Rockabilly and Rock 'n' Roll 45 RPMs.* Self-published, 1998.
Logan, Horace, with Bill Sloan. *Elvis, Hank, and Me: Making Musical History on the Louisiana Hayride.* New York: St. Martin's, 1998.
McCloud, Barry, ed. *Definitive Country: The Ultimate Encyclopedia of Country Music and Its Performers.* New York: Perigee, 1995.
Miller, James. *Flowers in the Dustbin: The Rise of Rock and Roll 1947–1977.* New York: Simon and Schuster, 1999.

Morrison, Craig. *Go Cat Go! Rockabilly Music and Its Makers.* Urbana and Chicago: University of Illinois Press, 1996.
Morrow, "Cousin Brucie," with Rich Maloof. *Doo Wop: The Music, the Times, the Era.* New York: Sterling, 2007.
Selvin, Joel. *Idol for a Generation.* Chicago: Contemporary, 1990.
Solly, Bob. *Record Collector 100 Greatest Rock 'n' Roll Records.* London: Diamond, 2005.
Stambler, Irwin, and Grelun Landon. *Country Music: The Encyclopedia.* New York: St. Martin's, 2000.

Liner Notes

Davis, Hank. *Bob Luman, Let's Think About Living: His Recordings 1955–1967.* Bear Family Records, 2006.
Dickerson, Deke. *Glen Glenn, Glen Rocks.* Bear Family Records, 2004.
Escott, Colin. *Carl Mann, Mona Lisa.* Bear Family Records, 1994.
_____. *Collins Kids, The Rockin'est.* Bear Family Records, 1997.
_____. *Ricky Nelson, Legacy.* Capitol Records, 2000.
Everett, Todd. *Ricky Nelson, The American Dream: The Complete Imperial and Verve Recordings 1957–1962.* Bear Family Records, 2001.
Hawkins, Martin. *Hayden Thompson, The Sun Years Plus Rock-A-Billy Gal.* Bear Family Records, 2008.
Johnny Powers, Long Blond Hair. Norton, 1993.
LeBeau, Wendy. *Go Cat Go, Let's Hear It Once Again for Go Cat Go.* Vinylux, 1998.
Wallis, Ian. *Bobby Lee Trammell, You Mostest Girl.* Bear Family Records, 1995.

Film

Elvis 56. Produced and directed by Alan Raymond and Susan Raymond. 61 min. Warner Bros., 1999. DVD.
The Real Buddy Holly Story. Produced and directed by Paul McCartney. 1 hr. 40 min. BBC, 1984. Videocassette.

Periodicals

Alexander, Pericles. "High Water Not Enough to Deter Nelson Fans." *The Shreveport Times,* April 27, 1958.

Burke, Ken. "Hayden Thompson: The Rockabilly Gentleman." *Blue Suede News* (Fall 2007): 16–21.
_____. "Hayden Thompson: The Rockabilly Gentleman, Pt. 2." *Blue Suede News* (Winter 2007): 19–24.
_____. "The Last of the Maddox Brothers: The Don Maddox Interview." *Roctober* (Winter 2006): 22–27.
_____. "'Mr. Everybody's Movin'": The Glen Glenn Interview." *Brutarian Quarterly* (Winter 2008): 23–39.
_____. "Wix Records and the Legendary Ray Smith." *Original Cool* (December 1998/January 1999): 3–10.
DeWitt, Howard A. "Kim Lenz: The Texas Wildcat." *Blue Suede News* (Summer 1998): 23–25.
Fishell, Steve. "James Burton." *Guitar Player* (June 1984).
Helfman, Ivan. "Rockabilly Revival Profile: Laura Lee Perkins Records a New CD." *The Gazette*, August 3, 2006: pp. 1–2.
Meyers, Jenny. "Josie Kreuzer- Not Your Ordinary Pussycat." *SLAMM: San Diego's Music Magazine*, December 27, 2000).
Miers, Jeff. "Josie Kreuzer." *Buffalo Beat Magazine*, April 18, 1998.
Sturm, Adriaan. "The Ray Smith Story." *Record Exchanger* (Issue 30, 1982): 10–14.
Wix, Howard, and Tommie Wix. "Ray Smith." *New Kommotion* (1978): 11–12.

Websites

Big Al Downing Official Homepage, www.bigaldowning.com/int/content/view/3/30/, accessed February 16, 2009.
Black Cat Rockabilly Europe, www.rockabilly.nl/references/messages/bobby_lee_trammell.htm, accessed February 6, 2009. www.rockabilly.nl/artists/jpowers.htm, accessed April 6, 2009.
Bruce Eder, www.allmusic.com/cg/amg.dll?p=amg&sql=11:jiftxqe5ldhe~T1, accessed April 8, 2009.
CD Baby, http://cdbaby.com/cd/davedeke, accessed January 19, 2009.
Contemporary Musicians, http://www.enotes.com/contemporary-musicians/dickerson-deke-biography, accessed January 19, 2009.
Country Standard Time, http://countrystandardtime.com/d/article.asp?fn=highnoon.asp, accessed February 13, 2009.
Dawn Shipley, www.dawnshipley.com/press.htm, accessed January 20, 2009. www.dawnshipley.com/bio.htm, accessed January 20, 2009.
HenryCountian.com, http://host1.bondware.com/~henrycountian/news.php?viewStory=271, accessed April 2, 2009.
J. Austin Duke, www.jaustinduke.net/interviews/eddie.pdf, accessed May 13, 2008. www.jaustinduke.net/interviews/josiekreuzer.pdf, accessed May 13, 2008.
Johnny Vallis, www.rockabillyhall.com/HuelynDuvall1.html, accessed April 9, 2009.
Josie Kreuzer, www.josiekreuzer.com/bio.html, accessed May 20, 2008.
Jumpin' from 6 to 6, www.jumpingfrom6to6.com/itvcarilee.htm, accessed May 13, 2008. www.jumpingfrom6to6.com/itvkreuzer.htm, accessed May 13, 2008. www.jumpingfrom6to6.com/itvrubyann.htm, accessed May 13, 2008. www.jumpingfrom6to6.com/itvshipley.htm, accessed May 13, 2008. www.jumpingfrom6to6.com/itvstuck.htm, accessed May 13, 2008. www.jumpingfrom6to6.com/itvvinylux.htm, accessed May 13, 2008. www.jumpingfrom6to6.com/itvbuddy_suzy.htm, accessed February 10, 2009.
Musician Guide, www.musicianguide.com/biographies/1608003923/Marti-Brom.html, accessed February 22, 2008.
Planet Jive News, http://thestreet.freeuk.com/planetjive/news4.html, accessed March 1, 2004.
Rockabilly Hall of Fame, www.rockabillyhall.com/RaySmith.html, accessed March 10, 2008. www.rockabillyhall.com/patcupp.html, accessed January 15, 2009.
Rockin' Country Style, http://rcs.law.emory.edu/rcs/
Wikipedia—the free encyclopedia, http://en.wikipedia.org/wiki/Niki_Sullivan, accessed October 18, 2008.
_____, http://en.wikipedia.org/wiki/Bobby_Lee_Trammell, accessed February 6, 2009.
_____, http://en.wikipedia.org/wiki/Al_Downing_(musician), accessed February 16, 2009.
_____, http://en.wikipedia.org/wiki/Charlie_Gracie, accessed March 30, 2009.
_____, http://en.wikipedia.org/wiki/The_Band, accessed April 13, 2009.
Tony Wilkinson, www.huelynduvall.com/biography.htm, accessed April 9, 2009.

Index

Numbers in ***bold italics*** indicate pages with photographs.

Adams, Art 153–157, ***154***
The Adventures of Ozzie and Harriet 88, 120–121, 123–124, 126, 132, 158
Aerosmith 142
"Ain't Got a Thing" 15
"All Night Long" 61, 63–64
Allison, Jerry 95, ***97***, 97–102
American Bandstand 20, 113, 132, 139–140, 146, 168, 171
American Idol 106
Angel, Eddie 202
"Arkansas Twist" 89–91
Arnold, Eddy 23, 71, 75, 168, 176
Atkins, Chet 11, 19, 30, 72, 96, 135, 179, 195
Austin, Tony 146

"Baby, Let's Play House" 24, 37, 70, 75, 96, 145, 149, 199, 218
The Band 91, 94
The Barnshakers 56, 176, 222
Bear Family Records 16, 33, 114, 184, 192
The Beatles 102, 142, 171, 227, 229
Beck, Jim 110–112
"Believe What You Say" 125, 147
Berry, Chuck 34, 100, 108, 161, 170–171, 190, 238
The Big Bopper 40, 101
Big Sandy 57, 141, 181, 183–184, 188, 193, 197–198, 206, 215, 225, 231
Black, Bill 26, 32–33, 49–50, 68, 70–74, 76–77, 98, 125, 137–138, 143–144, 146, 179, 195, 229
Black, Johnny 49–50, 71, 143, 146
The Blackwood Brothers 70–71, 194
"Blue Days, Black Nights" 61, 96, 180
"Blue Jeans and a Boy's Shirt" 139–140
Blue Moon Boys (Elvis Presley's band) 12, 73, 75
"Blue Moon of Kentucky" 11, 23, 28, 37, 58, 73, 75, 123
"Blue Suede Shoes" 43, 122, 146, 149, 152, 200

"Boom Boom Baby" 116, 118
"Bop Bop Ba Doo Bop" 112–113
born again Christian 36, 56
Brewer, Teresa 71, 130
Brom, Marti 56–57, 174–177, ***177***, 198, 212, 220, 225, 231, 234
Bruce, Ed 30–36, ***35***
Buchanan, Roy 63, 94
Buddy and Bob 95–97
Burgess, Sonny 11–17, ***13***, 78, 87, 148, 157, 183, 213, 215
Burlison, Paul 17, 71, 142–144, ***145***, 146–148, 222, 227
Burnette, Billy 147–148
Burnette, Dorsey 23, 71, 125, 139, 142–144, ***145***, 146–148
Burnette, Johnny 23, 71, 125, 139, 142, 144, ***145***, 146–148, 222
Burnette, Rocky 142–144, 146–148, 222
Burton, James 58–64, ***59***, 77, 81, 85, 88, ***121***, 122, 124–128, 179, 217–218, 236, 238
Bush, Eddie ***38***, 39, 41, 42
"Butterfly" 168–169, 171–172

Cameo Records 169, 171
Capitol Records 54–55, 63, 69, 164–165
Carnival Rock 58, 61, 64
Carroll, Johnny 108–109, 197, 208
The Casey Sisters 209–213, ***210***
Cash, Johnny 12, 23, 33–34, 50, 57, 63, 78, 83–84, ***87***, 88, 115, 131–132, 138, 144, 150, 155, 164, 194, 211, 216, 220, 226, 235–238
Cat music 109–112
"Cat Talk" 110–112, 114
Cave Catt Sammy 211–212, 217, 219
Challenge Records 115–116, 118, 138, 164
Charles, Ray 57, 103, 160, 163
Charly Records 16, 25–26, 47, 150
Chudd, Lew 61–62, 118, 123–124, 158, 160
Clement, Jack 15, 20, 24–25, 30, 33, 39–40, 45, 50, 150, 155

251

Clendening, Eddie 178, 181, 215–220, *217*, 221
Cline, Patsy 174, 176–177, 183, 210–211, 220, 222, 224, 226
Cochran, Eddie 22, 100, 102, 116, 118, 138, 147, 170–171, 194, 222, 224
Cole, Larry 235–238, *237*
Collins, Larry 129–133, *131*, 190
Collins, Lorrie 33, 55, 64, 123, 129–133, *131*, 138, 157, 205; relationship with Ricky Nelson 132–133
The Collins Kids 33, 54, 67, 123, 129–134, *131*, 183–185, 187, 189–192, 209–210, 229
Columbia Records 33, 66, 68–69, 129–131, 138, 166
Coral Records 98–99, 147, 171
The Crickets 95–96, 98–102, 105, 192
Crown Electric 71, 142
Cupp, Pat 82–86, *84*, 215, 217–219
Curran, Nick 206, *207*, 208, 212, 219
Curtis, Mac 58, 64, 140
Curtis, Sonny 95–96, 98–99, 101–102

"Dancing Doll" 153, 155–156
The Dave and Deke Combo 141, 181, 187–193, *189*, 197
Dawson, Ronnie 57, 177, 188, 194, 196–197, 206, 208, 225
Dean, James 76, 90, 200
"The Death of Rock and Roll" 68
Decca Records 52, 96, 98, 129
"Delta Dawn" 131
Dickerson, Deke 133, 181, 187–192, *189*, 215, 218–219, 225
"Do Me No Wrong" 82, 84–85
Domino, Fats 98, 120, 156, 158, 162–167, 171, 184, 191, 214
Donn, Larry 17, 78–82, *80*
"Don't Wait Up" 160
"Down on the Farm" 162
Downing, Big Al 46, 55, 162–168, *163*
"Drift Away" 148, 151–152
Dughi, Buddy 227–228, *228*, 230
Dughi, Suzy 227–230, *228*
Duvall, Huelyn 115–119, *117*
Dylan, Bob 70, 92, 94, 109, 134, 141, 148

Earls, Jack 47–51, *48*
The Ed Sullivan Show 76, 99, 132, 168
Ellena, Jack 122–123, 126–128
ERA Records 134, 138–140
The Everly Brothers 45, 100, 102, 126, 140, 158, 160, 164, 170–171, 193–194, 212
"Everybody's Movin'" 134, 139

"Fabulous" 171–172
"Fairlane Rock" 24
Feathers, Charlie 50–51, 75, 143, 201, 208, 231
Felts, Narvel 17, 21–22, 26, 148–153, *151*, 172, 237

Fenton, Rachel 209–213, *210*
Ferris Bueller's Day Off 26
Flores, Rosie 17, 56–57, 174, 212, 224
Fogerty, John 129, 148
Fontana, D.J. 76–77, 125, 137, 148, 179, 218, 223, 237
The Four Preps 123, 132, 140
Four Star Records 66
Franks, Tillman 73–74, 89
Freed, Alan 95, 100, 146, 168, 170
Freeman, Brian 179, *180*, 181
Frost, Richie *121*, 124–128
"Fujiyama Mama" 54, 56–57, 165

"Garden Party" 129
Gatton, Danny 178, 201, 204
"George's Playhouse Boogie" 66, 232
Glenn, Glen 22, 69, *87*, 129, 134–141, *136*, 157, 185, 191–192, 208, 217, *217*, 232
Gnagy, Caroline 209–213, *210*
Go Cat Go 178–182, *180*, 197–198, 218
"Gonna Rock and Roll Tonight" 38
"Gonna Rock My Baby Tonight" 160, 221
"Good Rockin' Tonight" 70, 75, 79, 96, 126, 182
Gordon, Robert 178, 193, 199, 201
Gracie, Charlie 168–173, *170*
Grand Ole Opry 11, 12, 37, 47, 50, 63–64, 66, 69, 73, 88, 132, 134, 138, 148, 152, 157, 167, 208, 233, 236
"Great Balls of Fire" 16, 152, 201
"Guess Things Happen That Way" 33

Haggard, Merle 26, 31, 66, 224
Haley, Bill 79, 97, 169, 190, 212–213
Hancock, Billy 178, 201–202
Handford, Steve 88–91
Harman, Buddy 77, 116, 144
Haskell, Jimmie 113, 124–126, 139, 160
Hawkins, Dale 27, 93, 100, 116, 191, 215, 217
Hawkins, Ronnie 21, 39, 46, 50, 91–94, *92*
The Hawks 91–94
Hemsby Weekender 42, 47, 51, 81, 86, 106, 109, 118–119, 153, 156, 181, 185, 189, 220, 232
"Hey Jim" 49
High Noon 176, 181, 183, 185, 193–199, *197*, 211
High Noon (movie) 32, 196
Hightone Records 17, 191, 206, 210
Holland, W.S. 39, 41, 237
Holly, Buddy 22, 40, 45, 95–102, *97*, 105–107, 164, 168, 180, 190, 193–195, 211–212, 226–227
Homer and Jethro 188, 193
"Honey Bun" 78, 80–81
Horton, Johnny 115, 130
"Hot Rod" 129, 133
"Hot Rod Man" 199, 202, 204
Hot Rod Trio 227–228

Index

"Hound Dog" 76, 158, 200, 218
Houston, David 59, 61
Hull, Bill 178–179, *180*, 181–182

"I Forgot to Remember to Forget" 75, 150
"I Love a Woman" 219
"I Sure Do Love You Baby" 62, 88
"I'm Walkin'" 120–121, 123
Imperial Records 61–64, 88, 112–114, 118, 123–125, 129, 138–139, 157–158, 160, 162
"In the Meadow" 193
"It's Late" 125, 147
"It's Only Make Believe" 16

Jackson, Wanda 12, 52–57, *53*, 64, 138, 157, 164, 167, 174, 176–177, 183, 205–206, 208, 210–211, 213, 219–220, 224, 226; bad experience at *Opry* 55–56; relationship with Elvis 52–54
James, Sonny 21, 43, 62, 67
Jennings, Waylon 26, 31, 34, 101
Jimmy and Johnny 74, 210, 218
Jones, George 28, 30, 67
The Jordanaires 76, 89, 116, 125, 237
Joyce, Teri 176
Justis, Bill 20–21, 25, 30

Keisker, Marion 71, 154
Kessel, Barney 113, 121, 169
King, B.B. 50, 93, 184, 195, 231
Kirkland, James 58–64, *59*, 85, 88, *121*, 122, 124–128, 132, 218, 229
Knickerbocker Hotel 61–62, 158
Kreuzer, Josie 182–187, *183*
Kristofferson, Kris 81, 200
KWKH 59–60, 66, 82

LaBeef, Sleepy 22, 26, 188
Lambert, Gary 134–137, 139–141, 232
LeBeau, Lance 178–181, *180*, 197, 218
Led Zeppelin 27, 115, 141–142, 178
Lee, Brenda 31, 56, 132, 157, 171, 176, 211
Lee, Dickey 27–31, *29*
Lee, Joe 89–90
Lenz, Kim 210–212, 215, 220
"Let's Have a Party" 54, 57, 131, 164, 167, 206
Lewis, Jerry Lee 15, 17, 20, 22, 25, 31, 33–34, 37–38, 41, 54, 57, 61, 81, 88, 93, 150, 152–153, 155, 157–158, 163, 170–171, 175, 191, 201, 211, 213–214, 216, 235–236, 238
Leyland, Carl Sonny 206, 213–215, *214*, 226
"Little Brown Jug" 78, 96
Little Green Men 24–25, 41, 78
Little Richard 71, 76, 85, 88, 98, 100, 163–165, 191, 211–213
Logan, Horace 58–59, 61–63, 74, 77
"Long Blond Hair, Red Rose Lips" 42, 44, 46
"Long Gone Daddy" 82, 85
Louisiana Hayride 24, 38, 50, 56–62, 66–69, 73–77, 82, 84–85, 89, 126, 130, 136

"Love My Baby" 23–25
Luman, Bob 57–64, *59*, 88, 122, 124, 128, 148, 200, 218; formation of the Shadows 58–59; Ricky Nelson's involvement 62–63; success on the *Hayride* 57–60
Lyman, Frankie 44, 231

Maddox, Cal 64–65, *65*, 69, 138
Maddox, Cliff 64–65, 69
Maddox, Don 64–70, *65*, 232–233
Maddox, Fred 64–65, *65*, 68–70, 72, 136–138, 140–141, 232
Maddox, Henry 64, *65*, 66, 69
Maddox, Kitty 69–70, 138, 232
Maddox, Loretta 69, 138
Maddox, Lula 64, 68–69
Maddox, Rose 55, 64–65, *65*, 69–70, 138, 140–141, 188, 232
Maddox Brothers and Rose 14, 64–70, *65*, 72, 130, 135–136, 138, 231–232; *Louisiana Hayride* regulars 66, 69
"Mamas Don't Let Your Babies Grow Up to Be Cowboys" 31–32, 34
Mann, Carl 26, 33, 36–42, *38*, 235, 237; recording for Sam Phillips 38–41; working with Eddie Bush 37–41
Maphis, Joe 54, 62, 67, 89, 124, 130, 135, 160, 190, 227
Martin, Dean 11, 21, 71, 79, 218, 220, 222
Martin, Grady 77, 116, 144
Martin, Janis 64, 115, 118, 138, 157, 162, 176–177, 183, 188, 205, 208, 211, 213, 215, 226
Mauldin, Joe B. 95, *97*, 98–102
"Maybe Baby" 99–101
McCartney, Paul 102, 142, 168, 172
McDonald's 36
McDowell, Ronnie 235–236
"Mean Mean Man" 54, 57, 165, 174
Mencher, Sean 193–199, *197*
Mercury Records 150–151
"Mercy" 131, 133
Merritt, Cari Lee 212, 220, 230–235, *233*
"Mona Lisa" 36, 38–42, 237
Monroe, Bill 49, 73, 95, 98
Montana, Patsy 65
Montgomery, Bob 95–96
Moore, Bob 77, 144
Moore, Scotty 11, 32–33, 45, 50, 70–74, 76–77, 83, 90, 96, 137, 143–144, 179, 195, 216, 218, 223, 237–238
Moreno, Sue 222–224, *223*
Morrison, Van 168, 172
Motown Records 43, 45–46
Mueller, Glenn 67, 140, 232
"My Babe" 150, 158
"My Bucket's Got a Hole in It" 15, 125
"Mystery Train" 50, 58, 70, 75

Nash, Graham 168, 172
"Navajo Maiden" 66–67

Index

Neal, Bob 14, 49–50, 73
Nelson, Ozzie 62–63, 89, 120–124, 126, 128, 147, 158
Nelson, Ricky 15, 85, 88–89, 118, 120–129, *121*, 132–133, 139, 146–148, 158, 160, 168, 186, 229–230, 235; recording at Imperial 125–126
Nelson, Willie 26, 34, 103, 183, 234
Now Dig This 15, 81

"Oakie Boogie" 66–67
"Oh Baby Babe" 52, 144–145
"Oh Boy" 99, 105–106
"One Cup of Coffee and a Cigarette" 138–139, 141
Orbison, Roy 14, 17, 25, 31, 34, 50, 84, 93, 149–150, 176, 205, 211, 235, 237
Osborn, Joe 63, 128
Overton Park Shell 37, 73, 143
Owens, Buck 26, 54, 69
Ozark Jubilee 55, 132, 136

The Pacers 11, 14–17, 78
Parker, Colonel Tom 75–76
"Patches" 28, 30
Paul, Les 11, 169, 195
Payne, Jimmy 90–91
"Peggy Sue" 99
Perkins, Carl 18, 24, 31, 34, 37, 39, 41, 43–44, 46, 50–51, 54, 57–58, 80–81, 84, 88, 93, 103, 107, 115, 122, 129, 131–132, 146, 149–153, 171, 178–180, 183, 194–195, 200, 208, 211, 213, 216, 229–230, 235–238
Perkins, Laura Lee 157–162, *159*, 221
Petty, Norman 100–102, 105–106
"Philadelphia Lawyer" 67
Phillips, Dewey 15, 25, 28–29, 49, 73
Phillips, Sam 14, 16, 18, 20, 25, 27, 29–30, 39–40, 43, 45, 47, 49, 57, 71–74, 83, 88, 90, 93, 103, 150, 154, 158
Pittman, Barbara 157, 183–184, 208, 226
Plant, Robert 27, 115, 141–142
The Platters 42, 61, 150, 158, 194
"Please Mama Please" 178, 180, 182, 218
Poe, Bobby 162–167
Poe, Bobby and the Poe Kats 55, 162, 164–166
"Poor Little Fool" 126, 139
Powers, Johnny 42–47, *44*, 188
Presley, Elvis 21, 25–28, 30–34, 40–41, 45, 49–51, 56–57, 60, 63, 67–68, 70–77, *72*, 81, 83, 86, 89, 91, 98, 102–103, 105, 109, 124–126, 133, 136, 138, 142–143, 145–146, 148, 150, 152, 158, 163, 168–170, 185, 190, 193–195, 208, 211–212, 215–218, 222–224, 226–227, 229, 232, 235, 237–238; impact 11–12, 14, 17, 22–24, 29, 37, 43–44, 47, 58, 70, 76, 79, 96, 107, 115, 122, 134, 136–137, 178–181, 183, 200, 236; rockabilly's birth 72–73, 75; stint on *Hayride* 73–76

"Pretend" 40
The Pretenders 175
Price, Ray 14, 17, 23, 62, 67, 135–137
"Pucker Paint" 115, 118

Ranch Party 55, 130
"Raunchy" 20, 25
"Rave On" 100–101, 105–106
RCA Victor 12, 30–31, 75–76, 137, 150
"Reconsider Me" 148, 151–152
"Red Cadillac and Black Mustache" 61, 63, 200, 202
"Red Headed Woman" 11, 14
"Red Hot" 16, 62–63, 124
Reeves, Jim 66, 128
Rhodes, Slim 25
Rich, Charlie 15, 20, 22, 31, 40, 45, 148, 235–236
Riley, Billy Lee 15–17, 24, 30–31, 33, 41, 45, 78–79, 90, 180, 198, 215, 218, 227, 235
Ritter, Tex 18, 32, 62–63, 129–130, 161
Robbins, Marty 14, 17, 21, 24, 31, 48, 96, 115, 136–137, 152, 155, 166–167, 235
Robinson, Fabor 62, 88–89, 146
The Rock and Roll Trio 52, 71, 142–148, *145*, 222, 227
"Rock Billy Boogie" 144, 147
"Rock Boppin' Baby" 31–33
"Rock Crazy Baby" 153, 155, 157
Rock, Rock, Rock 146
Rockabilly Hall of Fame 114, 141, 161, 167, 230
rockabilly revival 16–17, 31, 91, 133, 140, 178
Rockin' 50s Fest 27, 86, 106, 109, 141, 186, 192, 195, 199, 211–212, 219, 221, 224, 227
"Rockin' Little Angel" 18, 21–22
"Rock-Ola Ruby" 102
Rodgers, Jimmie 52, 93, 110, 213
The Rolling Stones 102, 171
Roulette Records 93, 150, 171
Rounder Records 16–17, 184
RPM Records 82, 85
Rubinowitz, Tex 178, 195, 199–204, *203*
Ruby Ann 157, 212, 220–222, *221*

The Saddle-ites 230, 232–234
Sands, Tommy 75, 107–108, 171
Sandusky, Vernon 55, 162, 164–167
"Saturday Jump" 208
"School of Rock and Roll" 107–109
Scott, Jack 31, 43–45, 184, 193, 237–238
Setzer, Brian 47, 198, 227
"She Thinks I Still Care" 28, 30
Sheeley, Sharon 126
Shipley, Dawn 212, 224–227, *226*
"Shirley Lee" 62, 88, 90
Simmons, Gene 26, 50
Sinatra, Frank 76, 83, 127, 161, 168
"Slow Down" 47, 49–50
Smith, Connie "Guybo" 138, 140
Smith, Kevin 193–196, *197*, 198–199

Smith, Ray 18–22, *19*, 208
Smith, Ronnie 70
Smith, Warren 49–51, 235
Snake Ranch 176
Snow, Hank 23, 37, 71, 73, 75, 115, 135, 148, 168, 200
"Something I Said" 112–113
Spears, Darren 178–182, *180*, 198, 218
Springsteen, Bruce 17, 134, 219
The Steve Allen Show 76, 132
Stevens, Steve 123
Stewart, Wynn *87*, 135, 138–139
"Stood Up" 124
"Straight Skirt" 108
Stray Cats 46, 134, 156, 193, 205, 223, 227, 229
Stuart, Marty 70, 235
Stuckey, Dave 187–190, *189*, 192
Sullivan, Bob 57, 60–61, 66, 68, 73–75, 77
Sullivan, Niki 98–99, 101–102
Summers, Gene 107–109, *107*, 155, 197, 215
Sun Records 14–16, 18, 20, 22, 25, 27–34, 36, 38–40, 42–43, 45, 49–50, 57, 71, 73, 75, 82–83, 88, 93, 105, 109, 122, 129, 136, 150, 154–155, 158, 178, 227, 229, 235
Sun Rhythm Section 17, 31, 148
Sun Studio 11, 14, 17, 24, 32, 40, 45, 47, 49, 72, 103, 134, 180–181
Sutton, Jimmy 191, 198–199
"Suzie Q" 27, 62, 93
"Sweet Rockin' Baby" 102
"Sweet Woman" 31, 33

"Tear It Up" 144–146
Ted Mack Amateur Hour 28, 144
"Tequila" 116
"That Girl of Mine" 82, 84
"That'll Be the Day" 96, 98–99, 102
"That's All Right" 11, 17, 23, 28, 37, 47, 70, 72–75, 83, 96, 109, 134, 136, 143, 179–180, 232
"That's What I Call a Ball" 78–80
Thompson, Hank 12, 52, 110, 112, 177, 231
Thompson, Hayden 22–27, *23*, 215, 217–218
"Tired of Toein' the Line" 148
Town Hall Party 62, 129–130, 132–134

"The Train Kept a Rollin'" 142, 144
Trammell, Bobby Lee 62, 86–91, *87*, 151; recording "Arkansas Twist" 89–90
"Travelin' Man" 120–121, 128
Travis, Dave 26, 50–51, 141
Travis, Merle 11, 72, 130, 135, 195, 227
Tubb, Ernest 11, 18, 48, 55, 112, 150, 153
Tucker, Tanya 36, 57, 102
Turk, Nathan 67, 138
Turner, Big Joe 11, 169, 213
Twitty, Conway 15–16, 21, 30, 39–40, 93, 148, 150, 224, 235–237

Untamed Youth 188, 192

Valens, Ritchie 40, 101, 216
Van Eaton, J.M. 17, 24, 41, 45, 78
Vincent, Gene 55, 118, 146, 152, 178, 194, 200, 205–206, 208, 227, 230
Von Records 23, 142

Wagoner, Porter 67, 113, 136
Walker, Stanley 18–22, *19*
Wanda Jackson (album) 54, 164
"We Wanna Boogie" 11, 14
West, Sonny 98–107, *104*
Whistle Bait (band) 141, 182, 184–186
White, Butch 58, *59*, 60–61, 64
Wildfire Willie 118–119, 156, 209
Williams, Hank 12, 18, 21–22, 34, 37, 47–48, 52, 57, 88, 93, 103, 106–107, 110, 130, 135, 143, 153, 168, 182–184, 199–200, 213, 222
Williams, Lew 109–115, *111*, 208
Wills, Bob and His Texas Playboys 11, 65, 79, 134, 187, 212
Winter Dance Party 40, 101
"With Your Love, with Your Kiss" 43, 45
Wolfe, Danny 116, 118
Wray, Link 46, 201

Yoakam, Dwight 192, 198–199
"You Mostest Girl" 89–90
Young, Faron 57, 67, 152, 155, 183, 208, 211–212, 220, 226
Young, Shaun 193–198, *197*

www.ingramcontent.com/pod-product-compliance
Lightning Source LLC
Chambersburg PA
CBHW021347230426
43666CB00006B/439